PEDIATRICS, CHILD AND ADOLESCENT HEALTH

CHILDREN, VIOLENCE AND BULLYING

INTERNATIONAL PERSPECTIVES

PEDIATRICS, CHILD AND ADOLESCENT HEALTH

JOAV MERRICK –SERIES EDITOR –

NATIONAL INSTITUTE OF CHILD HEALTH AND HUMAN DEVELOPMENT,
MINISTRY OF SOCIAL AFFAIRS, JERUSALEM, ISRAEL

PEDIATRICS, CHILD AND ADOLESCENT HEALTH

CHILDREN, VIOLENCE AND BULLYING

INTERNATIONAL PERSPECTIVES

JOAV MERRICK, M.D.,
ISACK KANDEL, PH.D.,
AND
HATIM A. OMAR, M.D.
EDITORS

publishers

New York

NOTICE TO THE READER

Library of Congress Cataloging-in-Publication Data

Children, violence and bullying : international perspectives / editors, Joav Merrick, Isack Kandel and Hatim A. Omar (Division for Intellectual and Developmental Disabilities, Ministry of Social Affairs and Social Services, Jerusalem, Israel and others).
    pages cm
  Includes index.
  ISBN 978-1-62948-342-9 (hardcover)
  1. Youth and violence. 2. Violence in adolescence. 3. Bullying in schools. 4. Violence--Prevention. 5. Youth--Suicidal behavior. I. Merrick, Joav, 1950- II. Kandel, Isack, 1960- III. Omar, Hatim A.
  HQ799.2.V56C46 2013
  303.60835--dc23
                                        2013038300

Published by Nova Science Publishers, Inc. † *New York*

CONTENTS

INTRODUCTION

Adolescent violence is a very visible violence in our modern society, where you just have to open the newspaper or the television and you find yourself right in the middle of it. In order to understand the scope of the problem, we need to look at the epidemiology of global violence. Each year, more than 1.6 million people worldwide lose their lives to violence and for every person who dies as a result of violence, many more are injured and suffer from a range of physical, sexual, reproductive and mental health problems. Violence places a massive burden on national economies in health care, law enforcement and lost productivity. We are talking about a major public health problem. Programs for intervention have been researched and long-term follow-up indicates that early intervention is working and even if such programs would seem to demand a substantial economic investment, they have been proven cost-effective in the long run. In this book, we have gathered presentations on bullying, aggression, violence, suicide and prevention from an international perspective.

In: Children, Violence and Bullying
Editors: J Merrick, I Kandel and H A Omar

Chapter 1

CHILDREN, VIOLENCE AND BULLYING

Joav Merrick, MD, MMedSc, DMSc[*,1,2,3,4]*, Isack Kandel, PhD*[1]
and Hatim A Omar, MD, FAAP[4]

[1]National Institute of Child Health and Human Development, Jerusalem
[2]Office of the Medical Director, Health Services, Division for Intellectual
and Developmental Disabilities, Ministry of Social Affairs
and Social Services, Jerusalem
[3]Division of Pediatrics, Hadassah Hebrew University Medical Center,
Mt Scopus Campus, Jerusalem, Israel and
[4]Division of Adolescent Medicine, Kentucky Children's Hospital,
University of Kentucky, Lexington, Kentucky, US

ABSTRACT

Adolescent violence is a very visible phenomenon in our modern society, where you just have to open the newspaper or the television and you find yourself right in the middle of it. In order to understand the scope of the problem, we need to look at the epidemiology of global violence. Each year, more than 1.6 million people worldwide lose their lives to violence and for every person who dies as a result of violence, many more are injured and suffer from a range of physical, sexual, reproductive and mental health problems. Violence places a massive burden on national economies in health care, law enforcement and lost productivity. We are talking about a major public health problem. Programs for intervention have been researched and long-term follow-up indicates that early intervention is working and even if such programs would seem to demand a substantial economic investment, they have been proven cost-effective in the long run.

* Correspondence: Professor Joav Merrick, MD, MMedSci, DMSc, Medical Director, Health Services, Division for Intellectual and Developmental Disabilities, Ministry of Social Affairs and Social Services, POBox 1260, IL-91012 Jerusalem, Israel. E-mail: jmerrick@zahav.net.il.

INTRODUCTION

Adolescent or youth violence is a very visible violence in our modern society, where you just have to open the newspaper or the television and you find yourself right in the middle of it. In order to understand the scope of the problem, we need to look at the epidemiology of global violence. In 1996 the World Health Assembly declared violence a leading public health issue (1) and as a result of this resolution a comprehensice report was published in 2002 (2).

The World Health Organization (WHO) defined violence as: "The intentional use of physical force or power, threatened or actual, against oneself, another person, or against a group or community, that either results in or has a high likelihood of resulting in injury, death, psychological harm, maldevelopment or deprivation" (3).

The World Health Organization's Global Burden of Disease project for 2000 (2) estimated that 1.6 million people (28.8 per 100,000) worldwide died as a result of self-inflicted, interpersonal or collective violence. In this 2000 project an estimated 199,000 adolescent homicides (9.2 per 100,000) occurred globally or about 565 adolescents died each day due to interpersonal violence with variations around the globe. Homicide rates were 0.9 per 100,000 in countries like Europa, 17.6 per 100,000 in Africa and 36.4 per 100,000 in Latin America (2). So we indeed live in a violent world, but there has been a downward trend between 1990 to 2000 from a violence related death rate of 35.3 to 28.8 per 100,000 (2,4). Each year, more than 1.6 million people worldwide lose their lives to violence (5). For every person who dies as a result of violence, many more are injured and suffer from a range of physical, sexual, reproductive and mental health problems. Violence places a massive burden on national economies, costing countries billions of US dollars each year in health care, law enforcement and lost productivity (5).

TRENDS IN ADOLESCENT HOMICIDE

In the years between 1985 and 1994 the adolescent homicide rates increased in many parts of the world. There was a sharp increase for males (it doubled), while the trend for females was steady. The increase was seen in developing countries and economies in transition with the most common method of attack by firearm. Dramatic increase was seen in the age group of 10-24 year olds in the Russian Federation after the collapse of communism with a 150% increase from 7.0% to 18.0 per 100,000. Decrease was seen in Canada and Australia, while both the United States and New Zealand had increase (2).

Between 1970 the early 1990s, the homicide rate for teens ages 15 to 19 more than doubled, from 8.1 to a peak of 20.7 per 100,000 in 1993 (7). The rate declined steeply during the late 1990s, then leveled out at around nine deaths per 100,000 between 2000 and 2004. Although the rate of homicides increased between 2004 and 2006, to 10.7 deaths per 100,000, it has since decreased. In 2010, the homicide rate was 8.3 deaths per 100,000, the lowest it has been since before 1980 (7).

Risk factors can be divided into four categories (8): Family factors such as a firearm at home, low income, domestic violence, teen parents or divorce; Social factors such as ethhnic heterogeneity, crowded housing, racial intolerance, lack of adult supervision and social acceptance of violence; Psychological factors suuch as depression, antisocial behavior, conduct disorder or aggression; and Personal factors such as male gender, alcohol or drug abuse, poor impulse control, previous gunshot injury and minority race.

TRENDS IN ADOLESCENT SUICIDE

Suicide is the third leading cause of death among adolescents with a fivefold increase seen for example in the United States for the period 1950-1990 (8). In 2010, rates of suicide among male teens were highest among American Indians (24.3 per 100,000) and whites (14.2), followed by Hispanics at 8.1, blacks at 6.8, and Asian or Pacific Islanders at 6.3 per 100,000 (7). Among females, American Indian teens had the highest rate at 11.0 per 100,000, followed by white teens at 3.5, Hispanic teens at 2.9, and Asian or Pacific Islanders with 3.1, with black teens at 1.1 per 100,000 (7).

Firearms and alcohol are also here important risk factors (4-7) and gender. Adolescent females attempt more suicided, but males have a higher completion rate due to the use of more leathal means (like a firearm).

TRENDS IN NON-FATAL VIOLENCE

For every adolescent homicide there is about 20-40 victims of non-fatal youth violence (2). Here still males are most often involved, but fewer firearm involvement and instead fists and feet and other weapons like knife and clubs (2).

TRENDS IN SCHOOL VIOLENCE

Research into school violence took off in Scandinavia and the United kingdom in the 1980s and together with the WHO croos national studies (37 countries) on health behavior in school aged children (HBSC) is conducted every fourth year (9). Bullying in schools varied from 15.7% in Sweden to 68.5% in Lithuania and with 50.0% in Israel (9).

According to the CDC's School Associated Violent Death Study, between 1% and 2% of all homicides among school-age children happen on school grounds or on the way to and from school or during a school sponsored event (10). In a 2011 nationally representative sample of youth in grades 9-12 (11):

- 12% reported being in a physical fight on school property in the 12 months preceding the survey
- 16% of male students and 7.8% of female students reported being in a physical fight on school property in the 12 months preceding the survey
- 5.9% did not go to school on one or more days in the 30 days preceding the survey because they felt unsafe at school or on their way to or from school
- 5.4% reported carrying a weapon (gun, knife or club) on school property on one or more days in the 30 days preceding the survey

- 7.4% reported being threatened or injured with a weapon on school property one or more times in the 12 months preceding the survey

EXAMPLES FROM OUR DAILY PRACTICE

We would like to share a few stories from our experience with adolescents on a daily basis:

- Two thirteen-year-old boys were arrested for breaking into air-conditioning units in the neighborhood to steal Freon. Obviously they use it for huffing, to get high. Upon interviewing them after being consulted by the social services, one of the boys said: "I am bored, my parents are working and I have nothing to do after school so we wanted to get high and forget about life's problems"
- A young man of 14 years of age was admitted after attempting suicide. He said his life was basically good, but he became worried that maybe he is not a real man, since he noticed that his breasts are growing and he is looking more like a girl
- Several young teens between the ages of 13-15 years were diagnosed with gonorrhea tonsillitis. They said they were not sexually active, but have participated in "head parties" with other peers. It was revealed that these parties referred to gathering of young teens to have oral sex.
- A 16-year-old girl was referred for evaluation of depression and weight loss. She disclosed that she had been sexually assaulted by her stepfather for the last two months. When we tried to line up her mother's help we got exactly the opposite: the mother threatened to kick the "liar" out of the home without even listening to the whole story.

We also see our fair share of good stories with teens doing good deeds and achieving high levels of success. It is the bad stories, however, that grab our attention, because of their sad and tragic consequences and our desire to understand why they happen. In countries like the United States of America the leading causes of mortality continue to be accidents, homicide, suicide, sexually transmitted infections and teen pregnancy. All are preventable yet they continue to happen. So whom should we blame? The parents for being busy and/or uneducated, the media for portraying sex, drugs and violence as a "normal" way of life, the school system for not educating our kids about real life, the health care industry that continues to deprive many of our teens access to health care, or our local and federal leaders both political and religious for giving bad examples with their continuing scandals of corruption and inappropriate sexual conduct!

It would be extremely simplistic to say that one or the other bears the blame. With the technological advances and the availability of modern communication systems including the internet, our teens are bombarded with a sea of information that is frequently inaccurate or age-inappropriate. The literature and real life experience are overall in agreement that improvement of all aspects of our societies is needed to help prevent many of our teens' problems. The parents should do their part in finding a way to spend quality time with their kids and to educate them on all aspects of life. Schools should do a better job of teaching real life skills and knowledge rather than purely academic subjects only. As a society, we should be able to provide better environment and health care for our adolescents. Our leaders should be providing good examples and so should the celebrities. If each one of us contributes, maybe we can improve our future by improving the current status of our adolescents who are our future.

HOME VISITATION

One type of prevention programs that has proven effective is home visitation. Such programs date back neary 100 years in Scandinavia, the United Kingdom and even in the United States with research showing the positive long-term effects (12). Prenatal and early childhood nurse home visitation (two years after birth) can reduce serious antisocial and criminal behavior shown by a 15 year closely follow-up study (12).

CONCLUSION

In recent years a growing body of research on adolescent violence has shown the epidemiology on a global basis and confirmed that we are talking about a major public health problem. Programs for intervention have also been researched and long-term follow-up (12) indicates that early intervention is working. Such programs would seem to demand a substantial economic investment, but proven cost-effective in the long run (13).

REFERENCES

[1]   World Health Assembly. World Health Assembly resolution –WHA 49.25. Prevention of violence: A public health priotity. Forty-ninth World Health Assembly, Geneva, 1996.
[2]   Krug EG, Dahlberg LL, Mercy JA, Zwi AB, Lozano R, eds. World report on violence and health. Geneva: World Health Organization, 2002.
[3]   WHO Global consultation on violence and health. Violence: A public health priotity. Geneva: WHO, WHO/EHA/SPI.POA.2, 1996.
[4]   Reza A, Mercy JA, Krug E. Epidemiology of violent deaths in the world. Inj Prev 2001;7:104-11.
[5]   WHO. Violence and injury prevention. URL: http://www.who.int/violence_injury_prevention /violence/en/
[6]   McIntosh G, Moreno M. Fatal injuries in adolescents. WMJ 2000;99(9):34-8.
[7]   Child trends. Data bank. Teen homicide, suicide and firearm deaths. URL: http://www.childtrends.org /?indicators=teen-homicide-suicide-and-firearm-deaths
[8]   Merrick J. Trends in adolescent suicide in Israel. Int J Adolesc Med Health 2000;12(2-3):245-8.
[9]   Merrick J, Kessel S, Morad M. Trends in school violence. Int J Adolesc Med Health 2002;14(1):777-80.
[10]   Centers for Disease Control and Prevention. Injury prevention and control. URL: http://www.cdc.gov/violenceprevention/youthviolence/schoolviolence/data_stats.html
[11]   Centers for Disease Control and Prevention. Youth violence. Fact at a glance 2012. URL: http://www.cdc.gov/violenceprevention/pdf/yv-datasheet-a.pdf
[12]   Olds D, Henderson CR, Cole R, Eckenrode J, Kitzman H, Luckey D, Pettitt L, Sidora K, Morris P, Powers J. Long-term effects of nurse home visitation on children's criminal and antisocial behavior. JAMA 1998;280(14):1238-44.

[13]   Olds D, Henderson CR, Eckenrode J. Preventing child abuse and neglect with prenatal and infancy home visiting by nurses. In: Browne KD, Hanks H, Stratton P, Hamilton C, eds. Early prediction and prevention of child abuse. A handbook. Chichester, UK: Wiley, 2002:165-82.

SECTION ONE:
BULLYING, AGGRESSION AND VIOLENCE

In: Children, Violence and Bullying
Editors: J Merrick, I Kandel and H A Omar

ISBN: 978-1-62948-342-9
© 2014 Nova Science Publishers, Inc.

Chapter 2

BOTSWANA: BULLYING VICTIMIZATION AMONG SCHOOL-GOING ADOLESCENTS

Patti Herring, PhD[1], Seter Siziya, BA (Ed), MSc, PhD[*2],
Sricharan Pasupulati, MD, MPH[3],
Emmanuel Rudatsikira, MD, MPH, DrPH[4]
and Adamson S Muula, MBBS, MPH, PhD[5]

[1]School of Public Health, Loma Linda University, Loma Linda,
California, US
[2]School of Medicine, The Copperbelt University, Ndola, Zambia
[3]School of Community and Environmental Health, Old Dominion University,
Norfolk, Virginia, US
[4]School of Health Professions, Andrews University, Berrien Springs,
Michigan, US
[5]Department of Community Health, University of Malawi, Blantyre, Malawi

ABSTRACT

Bullying victimization is a major public health problem among adolescents. It is associated with poor academic performance, anxiety, depression and suicidal behaviors. There are limited reports on victimization from bullying among Botswana adolescents. The purpose of this study was to determine the correlates for bullying victimization among school-going adolescents in Botswana. The 2005 Botswana Global School-based Health Survey (GSHS) data were obtained from the World Health Organization. A weighted analysis was conducted using statistical software (SPSS version 15.0). We estimated the prevalence of bullying victimization and conducted logistic regression analysis to estimate associations between the outcome (bullying victimization) and selected explanatory variables. Out of 2,165 in-school adolescents who participated in the study, 51.3% (54.2% males and 52.2% females; p=0.086) reported having been bullied in the last 30 days. In multivariate analysis, bullying victimization was positively associated

* Correspondence: Professor Seter Siziya, BA (Ed), MSc, PhD, The Copperbelt University, School of Medicine, Department of Clinical Sciences, Public Health Unit, Box 71191, Ndola, Zambia. E-mail: ssiziya@gmail.com.

with physical fighting (OR=2.17; 95% CI [1.73, 2.73]), truancy (OR=1.84; 95% CI [1.35, 2.50]), and alcohol drinking (OR=1.41; 95% CI [1.04, 1.91]). Victimization is prevalent among in-school adolescents in Botswana. Efforts to prevent and control bullying should take into consideration the factors identified in this study.

INTRODUCTION

Where data are available, bullying victimization is prevalent globally with significant regional variations in the rates of victimization (1-2). In a study on bully victimization among in-school adolescents from five continents, Due et al (2) reported the highest prevalence for bullying victimization among boys was in Zimbabwe (70.2%), while Zambia had the highest prevalence for girls (67%). Adverse conditions positively associated with victimization from bullying include serious injuries (3), alcohol and drug use (4), truancy (5), depression (6) and suicidal behaviors (7).

Bullying victimization is common in Botswana among school going adolescents. Fleming and Jacobsen (4) reports rates of being bullied as high as 53.0% with no sex difference (52.2% of females and 54.2% of males). They also considered factors (age, sex, symptoms of depression) associated with being bullied in their study but in their analysis they used the relative risk as a measure of the magnitude of association. Unfortunately the relative risk is not an appropriate measure of association in cross sectional studies. The purpose of this study was to re-analyze the data on correlates for bullying victimization among school-going adolescents in Botswana so that we may provide public health officers with correct results for use in interventions.

OUR STUDY

This study was based on a secondary analysis of data from the Botswana Global School-based Student Health Survey (GSHS) that was conducted in 2005. The 2005 Botswana GSHS was a school-based survey which included students in classes with the majority ages of 13-15 years. A two-stage cluster sampling design was used to produce data that was representative of students in the country. At the first stage, schools were selected with probability proportional to enrolment size. At the second stage, classes were randomly selected and all students in selected classes were eligible to participate. There was no replacement of students who were not available despite being in the selected schools. Students self-completed the questionnaires and the responses to questions were indicated on a computer scannable answer sheet.

In order to assess history of victimization from bullying, the question that was asked was: During the past 30 days, on how many days were you bullied? Possible responses included 0 days or any number of days. In terms of involvement in a physical fight, students were asked the question: During the past 12 months, how many times were you in a physical fight? Options included 0 times, one up to 12 or more times.

These data were obtained from the World Health Organization. The study was approved by the Botswana Ministry of Health. Parents were informed of the study through a letter, and students gave verbal consent to participate in the survey. To preserve individual confidentiality, the questionnaire was anonymously self-reported by the students.

Cases with missing values were not considered in the analysis. A weighting factor was used in the analysis to account for differences in the probability of selecting a school and classroom, and to account for differences in non response rates for various strata.

Data were first analyzed using SPSS version 11.5. Unweighted frequencies and their weighted percentages are reported. For the main outcome (bullying victimization), we recoded the responses in two categories: 0 for not having been victimized in the past 30 days, and 1 for having been victimized in the past 30 days. We conducted bivariate and multivariate logistic regression analyses in order to estimate associations between independent factors and the outcome variable. The hypotheses were "There were no significant associations between socio-demographic factors and bullying victimization". We report prevalence of bullying victimization as well as the unadjusted odds ratios (OR) and adjusted odds ratios (AOR) together with their 95% confidence intervals (CI).

FINDINGS

Table 1. Socio-demographic characteristics and bullying victimization of the study population

Factor	Male n (%)	Female n (%)	Total (%)
Age (years)			
< 14	78 (8.0)	131 (11.0)	209 (9.7)
14	190 (19.5)	302 (25.3)	492 (22.7)
15	319 (32.8)	372 (31.2)	6 (1.9)
16 +	385 (39.6)	388 (32.5)	773 (35.7)
Physical fight			
No	458 (47.1)	691 (58.3)	1149 (53.3)
Yes	514 (52.9)	494 (41.7)	1008 (46.7)
Parental supervision			
No	326 (34.5)	348 (30)	674 (32)
Yes	618 (65.5)	811 (70)	1429 (68)
Depression			
No	569 (59.6)	651 (55.7)	1220 (57.5)
Yes	385 (40.4)	518 (44.3)	903 (42.5)
Cigarette smoking			
No	817 (89)	1083 (95.2)	1900 (92.4)
Yes	101 (11)	55 (4.8)	156 (7.6)
Alcohol drinking			
No	596 (75.9)	795 (78.8)	1391 (77.5)
Yes	189 (24.1)	214 (21.2)	403 (22.5)
Drug use			
No	840 (86.3)	1138 (95.4)	1978 (91.3)
Yes	133 (13.7)	55 (4.6)	188 (8.7)
Truancy			
No	665 (70.2)	950 (80.3)	1615 (75.8)
Yes	282 (29.8)	233 (19.7)	515 (24.2)
Bullied			
No	377 (45.8)	481 (47.8)	858 (46.9)
Yes	446 (54.2)	525 (52.2)	971 (53.1)

A total of 2,165 students participated in the 2005 Botswana GSHS; and 1829 had information on whether they were bullied or not. Overall, 42.4% were depressed; 22.5% consumed alcohol; and 8.7% had used illicit drugs. More than 1 in five (22.5%) participants reported having missed classes without permission. Altogether, 53.1% (54.2% of male and 52.2% of female) participants reported having been bullied in the previous 30 days to the survey. Further description of the sample by gender is shown in Table 1.

Table 2 reports associations between being bullied and selected factors. Being bullied was positively associated with having engaged in physical fighting (OR=2.17; 95% CI [1.73, 2.73]), self reported feelings of depression (OR=1.40; 95% CI [1.16, 1.77]); truancy (OR=1.84; 95% CI [1.35, 2.50]); and alcohol drinking (OR=1.41; 95% CI [1.04, 1.91]).

Table 2. Factors associated with being bullied

Factor	Bullied n (%)	OR[1] (95% CI[3])	AOR[2] (95% CI)
Age (years)			
< 14	89 (9.2)	0.95 (0.67-1.35)	1.12 (0.76-1.67)
14	216 (22.3)	0.83 (0.59-1.16)	1.06 (0.79-1.43)
15	309 (31.9)	0.82 (0.59-1.14)	0.97 (0.74-1.28)
16+	355 (36.6)	1	1
Sex			
Male	446 (45.5)	1.08 (0.90-1.30)	0.92 (0.73-1.16)
Female	525 (54.5)	1	1
Physical fight			
No	409 (42.3)	1	1
Yes	557 (57.7)	2.89 (2.38-3.50)	2.17 (1.73-2.73)
Depression			
No	495 (52.2)	1	1
Yes	454 (47.8)	1.74 (1.44 - 2.10)	1.40 (1.16-1.77)
Cigarette smoking			
No	807 (88.8)	1	1
Yes	102 (11.2)	3.54 (2.31 - 5.40)	1.36 (0.77-2.40)
Drug use			
No	853 (88.1)	1	1
Yes	115 (11.9)	3.01 (2.06 - 4.42)	1.26 (0.7-2.26)
Truancy			
No	666 (69.1)	1	1
Yes	287 (30.1)	2.63 (2.10 - 3.33)	1.84 (1.35-2.5)
Parental supervision			
No	314 (33.1)	1	1
Yes	634 (66.9)	0.87 (0.70 - 1.10)	0.80 (0.85-1.37)
Alcohol drinking			
No	538 (69.7)	1	1
Yes	238 (30.7)	2.44 (1.90-3.13)	1.41 (1.04-1.91)

[1]OR Unadjusted odds ratio.
[2]AOR Adjusted odds ratio.
[3]CI confidence interval.

DISCUSSION

In a study of bullying victimization among in-school adolescents in Botswana, we found that 53.1% of the respondents were bullied in the last month. This prevalence is higher than the average (32%) for 66 countries and territories from five continents (2). In Africa, that prevalence is lower than 62.8% reported in Zambia (9), but higher than 40.1% in Ghana (8) and 39.6% in neighboring Swaziland (5).

We found that bullying victimization was positively associated with reported depression, having engaged in physical fighting, truancy, and alcohol drinking. In a study of the association between bullying and psychological health among senior high school students in Ghana, Owuso et al found that bullying victimization was positively associated with depression, suicide ideation, and loneliness (8). The association between bullying victimization and physical fighting was reported previously in other settings such as Zambia (9), Philippines (10) and China (11). In a study of the association between physical bullying victimization and physical fighting among Filipino school going adolescents, Rudatsikira et al reported a dose-response relationship between the two (10). Previous studies have reported the relationship between bullying victimization and alcohol use and other substances (12,13).

In this study, there was no significant gender difference in bullying victimization. Some studies have reported similar findings (8,10) while others have reported that males were more likely to be bullied than females (9,11). What is consistent in the literature is the gender difference in the types of bullying victimization; males are more at risk for physical victimization while females are more at risk of relational or emotional victimization (14-15).

The present study has several limitations and strengths. Data were collected through self-reports. To the extent that study participants mis-reported, intentionally or not, our findings may be biased. The study design was cross sectional which limits us from ascribing causation between the outcome and explanatory variables. It is also important to note that different studies have defined bullying differently. For instance, Sourander et al (16) defined bullying as "an aggressive act embodying an imbalance of power in which the victims cannot defend themselves accompanied by an element of repetition." Our study only asked whether students had been bullied. However, the sample size was large thus improving precision of the effect measure estimates. That this study is a secondary analysis of existing data can be both a strength and a weakness. A strength in that the subjects' responses could be accurate as study participants may not have anticipated any links between outcome variable and explanatory variables, hence truthful reporting; and a weakness in that there are likely to be several unmeasured confounders that a primary study could have planned to measure.

CONCLUSION

In this study, we found that bullying victimization was prevalent among school-going adolescents in Botswana. Efforts to prevent and control bullying should take into consideration the factors identified in this study.

ACKNOWLEDGMENTS

We thank the World Health Organization for availing the data for further analysis and the students for their participation in the survey.

REFERENCES

[1]   Craig W, Harel-Fisch Y, Fogel-Grinvald H, Dostaler S, Hetland J, Simons-Morton B, et al. A cross-national profile of bullying and victimization among adolescents in 40 countries. Int J Public Health 2009;54(Suppl 2):216-24.

[2]   Due P, Holstein BE, Soc MS. Bullying victimization among 13 to 15-year old school children: results from two comparative studies in 66 countries and regions. Int J Adolesc Med Health 2008;20:209-21.

[3]   Muula AS, Siziya S, Rudatsikira E. Prevalence and socio-demographic correlates of serious injuries among adolescents participating in the Djibouti 2007 Global School-based Health Survey. BMC Res Notes 2011;4:372.

[4]   Fleming LC, Jacobsen KH. Bullying among middle-school students in low and middle income countries. Health Promot Int 2010;25:73-84.

[5]   Siziya S, Muula AS, Rudatsikira E. Prevalence and correlates of truancy among adolescents in Swaziland: findings from the Global School-based Health Survey. Child Adolesc Psychiatr Ment Health 2007;1:15.

[6]   Fleming LC, Jacobsen KH. Bullying and symptoms of depression in Chilean middle school students. J Sch Health 2009;79:130-7.

[7]   Klomek AB, Sourander A, Niemela S, Kumpulainen H, Piha J, Tamminen T, et al. Childhoold bullying behavior as a risk for suicide attempts and complete suicides: a population-based birth cohort study. J Am Acad Child Adolesc Psychiatry 2009;48:254-61.

[8]   Owusu A, Hart P, Oliver B, Kang M. The association between bullying and psychological health among senior high school students in Ghana, West Africa. J Sch Health 2011;81:231-8.

[9]   Siziya S, Rudatsikira E, Muula AS. Victimization from bullying among school-attending adolescents in grades 7 to 10 in Zambia. J Inj Violence Res 2012;4:30-5.

[10]   Rudatsikira E, Mataya RH, Siziya S, Muula AS. Association between bullying victimization and physical fighting among Filipino adolescents: results from the Global School-Based Health Survey. Indian J Pediatr 2008;75:1243-7.

[11]   Hazemba A, Siziya S, Muula AS, Rudatsikira E. Prevalence and correlates of being bullied among in-school adolescents in Beijing: results from the 2003 Beijing Global School-Based Health Survey. Ann Gen Psychiatry 2008;7:6.

[12]   Swahn MH, Topalli V, Strasser SM, Ashby JS, Meyers J. Pre-teen alcohol use as a risk factor for victimization and perpetration of bullying among middle and high school students in Georgia. West J Emerg Med 2011;12:305-9.

[13]   Radliff KM, Wheaton JE, Robinson K, Morris J. Illuminating the relationship between bullying and substance use among middle and high school youth. Addict Behav 2012;37:569-72.

[14]   Hampel P. Direct and relational bullying among children and adolescents: coping and psychological adjustment. Sch Psychol Int 2009;30:474-90.

[15]   Frisen A, Jonsson A, Persson C. Adolescents's perception of bullying: who is the victim? Who is the bully? What can be done to stop bullying? Adolescence 2007;42:749-61.

[16]   Sourander A, Ronning J, Brunstein-Klomek A, Gyllenberg D, Kumpulainen K, Niemelä S, Helenius H, Sillanmäki L, Ristkari T, Tamminen T, Moilanen I, Piha J, Almqvist F. Childhood bullying behavior and later psychiatric hospital and psychopharmacologic treatment: findings from the Finnish 1981 birth cohort study. Arch Gen Psychiatry 2009;66:1005-12.

In: Children, Violence and Bullying
Editors: J Merrick, I Kandel and H A Omar

Chapter 3

INDIA: AGGRESSION AMONG HIGH SCHOOL STUDENTS

Manmeet Kaur Reen, BSC, MSC, APGDCGFC, B.ED[*] and Deepali Sharma, PhD

Department of Human Development and Family Relations,
Government Home Science College, Panjab University, Chandigarh, India

ABSTRACT

In this chapter we carried out a comparative study on a sample of 140 school going adolescents from class IX. A standardized questionnaire was administered to determine the prevalence of aggression in adolescents of private and government schools of Chandigarh. The results were analyzed using t-test. Regarding the school type, there were no significant differences between adolescents coming from government schools and those studying in private schools. Related to the sub scales of aggression, there was no gender difference except for the Anger scale (AngS) in which female respondents showed significantly higher scores as compared to their male counterparts. The findings highlighted the need of intervention aimed at anger management. Workshops and seminars can also be organized for parents, teachers and adolescents on adolescents' aggressive behavior.

INTRODUCTION

Adolescence is viewed as a period during which biological, cognitive, emotional and social changes and development takes place. Because of reorganization in all of the developmental areas, young children face various behavioral of adjustment problems (1). It is often assumed that this is a difficult period of life, with the adolescents being at risk of high stress, since they have to cope with enormous changes. Some of these changes are in the physical and sexual

---
[*] Correspondence: Manmeet Kaur Reen, BSC, MSC, APGDCGFC, B. ED, Department of Human Development and Family Relations, Government Home Science College, Panjab University, Chandigarh, Chandigarh, India. E-mail: manmeetreen@ymail.com.

behavior following puberty, some of the social and financial area, and some relate to decisions about the future .Thus, this period is certainly a period of change in which the adolescents are burdened by various pressures (2).

It is very important that adolescents pass through this stage successful otherwise problems may occur which may further lead to the formation of various kinds of deviant behavior like aggression, drug and alcohol use. Erikson (3) further argues that adolescents typically experience diffusion, a strong sense of uncertainty and need to achieve a sense of identity. But at this phase of life they find it hard to do this and are always perturbed about who they are and what their future will be? Such unanswered questions might lead to frustration and aggressive behavior among the adolescents (4,5). Further, biological or hormonal changes in adolescents (increased level of androgen and testosterone) are also associated with behavioral problems like rebelliousness, talking back to adults, and fighting with classmates (6).

Thus, emphasizing upon the critical nature of adolescent stage ,it is apparent that adolescence and aggression cannot be separated. Many studies tracing the problems of adolescence over several decades have shown an increase in the rate of aggression among the adolescents (7).

Aggression is defined as physical or verbal behavior intended to harm. Aggression can either be directed inward by self mutilation or directed outwardly at another person. Aggressive behavior is often used to claim status, precedents or access to an object or territory (8). According to Eysenck (2), two kinds of aggression are identified namely, person oriented and instrumental aggression. Person oriented aggression is designed to hurt someone else were causing harm in the main goal. In contrast, instrumental aggression has its main goal in obtaining some desired reward with aggression. Another category of aggression is based on the initiator of the aggression. Proactive aggression is aggressive behavior that is initiated by the individual to achieve some desired outcomes whereas reactive aggression in an individual reaction to someone else aggression.

These distinctions clearly revealed that aggression is not simple but a complicated aspect .It is not a single idea but it is of various types such as physical or verbal aggression.

Physical aggression

As the word indicates physical aggression is any response that produces or is intended to produce physical injury or physical pain in the victim or damage to an object. It involves the acts of hitting and kicking (9). The large body mass or higher physical development among the early adolescents is also an important predictor of the growing physical aggression among them. This is particularly supported by Trembley (10) who studied the association among the testosterone, physical development, and social behavior during early adolescence. He suggests that adolescents with larger body masses are more likely to be physically aggressive or socially dominant and tend to have higher testosterone levels, when provoked; adolescents tend to show physical aggressive behavior; like they would hit the person who irritates them.

Verbal aggression

Burbank (11) reports that children are involved in violence and physical aggression until they have attained the verbal skills but when these are developed, physical aggression is replaced by verbal aggression up to some extent. Infante (12) reveals that verbal aggression is a message behavior, which harms the self esteem of a person and thus produces psychological pain. Broadly speaking, verbal aggression is any response that produces psychological or social harm to the victim, hurt feelings, and damage to one's reputation, devaluation that could result in loss of prize, a job, and so forth. Nasty remarks, name calling are the active and verbal forms of verbal aggression whereas stony silence or sulking form a part of passive and non verbal aggression. In general terms verbal aggression is confined to yelling and screaming at others. Verbal aggression is a softer part than the physical aggression and is generally done for betterment. As Burbank (11) reports that verbal aggression is used for escape from demanding or difficult situations, and relief from stress. In the highly competitive world of today adolescents feel a threat to their identity, so in this process of getting the attention they always try to make others agree with their viewpoints. But when others disagree, they get into conflicts, indulge in heated arguments, and show verbal aggression.

Anger

Goodenough and Gesell (13, 14) report that infants and young children respond in anger in a direct and primitive manner, but as they develop the responses become less violent and more symbolic. In early school years anger reactions become more directed toward a single person and take the form of attempts to hurt the feeling rather than to injure the body of the offender. In middle school years, the anger is shown more on verbal plane. Anger reaction is displaced on others rather than on the person himself. The study also suggested that children think themselves as bosses if they shout or show violent reaction towards their peers.

Indirect aggression

Indirect aggression means telling untruth behind the back, starts being somebody else's friend in revenge, abuses, argues, sulks, take revenge in play (9).

THEORETICAL ORIENTATION

The study of aggression is a perfect example of nature-nurture debate, which is of central concern in many psychological arguments. The question being asked is whether aggression, as a characteristic of human being, is biologically determined or product of learning and environmental influences.

At this stage the aggression is shown mainly due to the situation or environmental conditions. So, frustration aggression theory and negative affect theory explains the behavior of the individual during early adolescent periods.

- *Frustration Aggression theory*
  Frustration always causes aggression and aggression is always the result of frustration. Aggression is therefore, triggered by frustrating situations and events. Therefore, people are driven to aggression in order to reduce frustration and thus to maintain a balanced internal state (15). Berkowitz (16) modified this original hypothesis to suggest that frustration actually produces a state of readiness for aggression, but that causes in the situation are also important. The key concept to grasp this theory is that an external stimulus leads to behavioral response. In this particular topic frustration is the stimulus which leads to an aggressive response.
- *Negative affect theory*
  It states that negative feelings and experiments are the main cause of anger and angry aggression. Sources of anger include: - pain, frustration, loud noises, foul odors, crowding, sadness and depression (16).
  The likelihood that an angry person will act aggressively depends on his or her interpretation of the motives of the people involved. It is most applicable to adolescents and adults, who think well and already know lots about the world.

Various other important theories that explain the aggression are:

- *Psychoanalytical Theory*
  Freud theorized that human are born with an instinct towards life (which he called Eros) and an instinct towards death (called Thanatos). The death instinct, Freud argued needs to be released through aggression. Freud also stated that there is a conflict between Eros and Thanatos, some of the negative energy of the Thanatos is directed towards others, to prevent the self destruction of the individual. Thus, Freud claimed that the displacement of negative energy of the Thanatos onto others is the basis of aggression (17).
- *Evolutionary theory or Ethnological and Socio-biological views*
  It states that humans are born with fighting instinct and aggression is built into our nature. Lorenz looked at instinctual aggressiveness as a product of evolution. In essence, he combined Freud's theory of aggression with Charles Darwin's natural selection theory (18).
- *Social Learning Theory*
  The theory is interested in observational learning and modeling. In this theory, aggression is initially learned from social behavior and it is maintained by operant conditioning (19, 20).

RATIONALE

Adolescence is a crucial stage that involves going through varied physical and emotional changes. One of the most important behavior aspects during adolescence is aggression which is likely to be influenced by gender, and school type. Limited work is available in this area thus suggesting the crucial need to understand the influence of these independent variables on the aggressive behavior of the adolescents.

Are boys more physically aggressive than girls? Are girls more verbally aggressive? How does school environment effect aggressive behavior? Based on study it will hopefully be possible to identify the areas of intervention further promotes the well being of the adolescent.

The following were the objectives of the study:

- To assess the prevalence and level of aggression among high school students.
- To examine gender differences among the respondents related to aggression.

OUR STUDY

The present research was planned as a comparative study on aggression carried out on a sample of 140 school going adolescents (70 Government and 70 from Private schools in Chandigarh. For the present study, aggression was the independent variable and gender and type of school were the dependent variables.

This study was conducted in Chandigarh and purposive sampling was done when it came to selection of the school and participants. In total four schools were selected which represented the government and private schools. Care was taken that these four schools represented the four geographical zones of Chandigarh. Within the government and private schools, the respondents were randomly selected. The sample was further segregated into the sub-category of gender i.e. boys and girls.

Assessment Measures

- Background information

A personal information sheet was prepared to collect the background information of the adolescents (Appendix A). It contained questions related to demographic factors such as age, school, gender, class, family type and birth order.

- The Aggression Questionnaire (2000)

A standardized questionnaire was administered to determine the prevalence of aggression in adolescents (Appendix A). The questionnaire had 34 items with the following areas: (i) general information (for example: name, age, gender, type of family, etc.); (ii) physical aggression (for example: I have threatened people I know, I get into fights more than most people); (iii) Verbal aggression (for example: my friends say that I argue a lot, I cannot help getting into arguments when people disagree with me); (iv) Anger (for example: some of my friends think I am short tempered, I have trouble controlling my temper); (v) Hostility (for example: I know that friends talk about me behind my back, I wonder what people want when they are nice to me); (vi) Indirect aggression (for example: I have been angry enough to bang a door when leaving someone behind in the room, I sometimes spread gossip about people I do not like).

The application of the test was discussed among the investigative team and accordingly changes were made. Certain statements or words in the tool that were not applicable in the Indian context were reworded.

The calculation of the level of aggression was done by converting raw scores into T scores by applying the formula given below:

$$T = 50 + 10(X-Y)/Z$$

where,

X=Raw scores of the students
Y=Average score of the whole cohort
Z=Standard deviation

The previous reports of reliability (coefficient alpha) suggest good to moderate reliability: Physical Aggression ($r = .88$), Verbal Aggression ($r = .76$), Anger ($r = .78$), Hostility ($r = .82$), Indirect Aggression ($r = .71$), and the Total scale ($r = .94$) (Buss & Warren, 2000).

Procedure

The students were contacted by taking an appointment from the school authorities and permission letters were granted by the Principal to conduct the tests. During the meeting with the Principals, the purpose of the study was also explained to them.

Class visits were made to meet the students and build rapport with them. The significance of the study was also explained. Their consent was taken and background information was collected from the students. Questionnaires were administered on both boys and girls and the doubts were clarified. The instructions about the questionnaire were given to students that for each statement they have to select the most preferred option amongst the given options.

Coding

The coding format was established and worked out by the team of investigators. The data was organized through coding. The purpose was to make it easier to tabulate the information and analyze the data for quantitative analysis. The coded data was entered using SPSS 16.0 version, which is standard statistical software, used for the purpose of analysis in the field of social sciences.

Plan of analysis

The data was analyzed by computing frequencies and percentages with the help of SPSS software to compare the responses of girls and boys from different government and private school. For analyzing the significant differences in the mean scores, t-test was employed.

FINDINGS

The study was conducted on boys and girls of different schools of Chandigarh. It aimed at studying aggression among adolescent: to know the prevalence and level of aggression in terms of gender. *Demographic characteristics:* There was a total sample of 140 students. Amongst them 77 were males and 63 were females. Most of the students constituting the sample were in the age group of 14 years. Most of them were from the nuclear family and the birth order was 1st or 2nd in majority of the sample. The study had following objectives: 1.To assess the prevalence and level of aggression among high school students. 2. To examine gender differences among the respondents related to aggression. Adolescents displayed average scores on aggression. There was no significant difference between the mean scores of the males and the females, on the overall aggression scores (see Table 1).Related to the sub scales of anger there were no gender differences noted on any of the sub scales except for the Anger scale (AngS) which had items like; "I get angry easily, but get over my anger quickly.", "At times I feel like a bomb ready to explode." etc. Female respondents showed significantly higher scores as compared to the males (see Table 2 and Figure 1).

Table 1. Mean aggression scores

Gender	N	Mean	Standard deviation	t score
Female	63	49.52	9.65	.05
Male	77	49.62	10.05	

Table 2. Mean aggression according to different sub scales

Sub Scale	Gender	N	Mean	Standard deviation	t score
Physical Aggression	Female	63	15.74	5.79	
	Male	77	16.83	6.18	1.06
Verbal Aggression	Female	63	13.09	3.82	
	Male	77	13.33	3.77	.37
Anger Scale	Female	63	19.50	4.70	
	Male	77	17.64	5.28	2.17
IRP	Female	63	17.57	5.65	
	Male	77	18.12	6.22	.55
Hostile reaction	Female	63	19.19	5.57	
	Male	77	18.67	5.52	.54
Indirect Anger	Female	63	15.17	4.47	
	Male	77	14.90	4.61	.34

*p< .05.

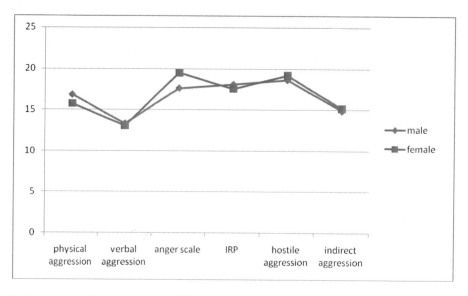

Figure 1. Mean aggression according to different sub scales of male and female respondents.

DISCUSSION

The purpose of the study was to assess the prevalence and level of aggression among Chandigarh high school students and to examine gender differences among the respondents related to aggression. The data was gathered using the standardized questionnaire. The average score on aggression and no significant difference between the mean scores of the males and the females are evident from the results of the present study. There were no gender differences found on any of the sub scales except the Anger Scale (AngS) for which many reasons can be attributed, which are as follows:

- *Changing role of society*
  Garg (21)attributes significantly higher score of the female respondents' to change in the pattern of Indian society in which appropriate sex role for females are being and replaced by more gender balanced behavior. Research has determined the anger is an important correlate of student aggression, and that there is a clear link between high levels of anger and problem behavior in school, poor academic performance, peer rejection, and psychosomatic complaints (22).Moreover, uncontrolled anger is cited as one of the factors linked to serious violence.
- *Early Maturation*
  The age of beginning of pubertal changes is gradually coming down and due to which adolescents go through varied physical and emotional changes .One of the most important behavior aspect during adolescence is aggression. As adolescence is a high stressful age, because of this adolescents become frustrated and thus show aggression (2).
- *Exposure to Mass Media*
  One of the reasons for no significant difference in the level of aggression in males and females could be exposure to mass media .Huesmann & Eron found increasing

rates of aggression for both boys and girls who are exposed to media (23). A high percentage of females prefer to watch family drama in comparison, to males, who prefer to watch action based programmes.

- *Maternal Employment*
  Maternal Employment could also be one of the reasons as there is lack of supervision and parent –child interaction due to maternal employment, the child might indulge in experimentation, risky behavior and delinquent acts (21).
- *Consumption of Junk Food*
  Due to the change in life style pattern and westernization the children are consuming more of junk food, which are high in carbohydrates .This results in high body mass index that leads to attainment of puberty at an early age due to which hormonal changes take place, which may lead to aggression (24).

These findings can be useful for providing information to the school teachers about the average level of aggression among adolescents .Necessary interventions can be provided on the basis of this research. Physical aggression (as well as property violation) uniquely contributes to each of the health risk behaviors from preschool onwards .This suggests that preventive interventions aimed at physical aggression could be initiated in early childhood in an effort to reduce the risk of each of these outcomes (25).The psychologist and educators should be aware of the peer group interactions that reinforce aggressive behaviors. The intervention programmes should extend beyond aggressive children to address the attitude and norms of the peer group that may support aggression and antisocial behaviors (26).

The intervention measures that include parents, peers and individual adolescents may help decrease the aggressive and conduct problems (27) .Some workshops can also be organized for parents, teachers and adolescents on anger management. Follow up activities focused on learning and practicing accepting alternatives to aggression. Focus may need to be placed on child's ability to maintain productive relationships with authority .It may also include opportunities to learn and practice constructive alternatives to non productive arguments and verbal assaults (28, 29).

The participants were only school going adolescents and therefore, it cannot be applicable to the same age children who do not go to school.

ACKNOWLEDGMENTS

For the successful completion of this paper, I express my deep gratification to Dr. Deepali Sharma, Assistant Professor, Department of Human Development and Family Relations, Government Home Science College, sector 10, Chandigarh, under whose guidance the present work was carried out. I am grateful for her whole hearted help, keen interest, constructive criticism and valuable suggestions. A special thanks to Dr. Suman Verma, Head of Department of Human Development and Family Relations, Government Home Science College, sector 10, Chandigarh, for her guidance and help. I thank the following people whose assistance made this study possible Vandana Vohra, Rashi, Tarneet, Harleen, Renu , Vandana, Kanika, Rishya, Sukhwinder, Kamaldeep, Sofina , Navdeep and Nriti. A word of thanks to all the principals of respective schools, for giving their kind permission to proceed with my research study. I will be failing in my duty if I do not pay my regards to all our respondents for giving me their precious time and cooperation.

(APPENDIX A)

Dear Students,

You are being provided with a battery of self report tests that will assist you gain greater insights into yourself. The goal of these tests is not to provide you with new information about yourself, but rather to help you achieve a better understanding of the barriers that might be standing in your way of a more satisfying and effective life .We hope you enjoy this process of self discovery and find information that will help you have a more satisfying and effective life.

Best wishes

Manmeet Kaur Reen

THE AGGRESSION QUESTIONNAIRE

Name: _____Age: _____
Gender: Male_____Female_____ Class: _____ Section: _____
School: _____
Birth order: 1st born _____ 2nd born _____ 3rd born _____
Type of family: Nuclear _____ Joint _____ Extended _____

Please ticks mark the appropriate response.
Answer Key:1= Not at all like me; 2= A little like me; 3=Somewhat like me ; 4=Very much like me; 5 = Completely like me

S.No	Statement	1	2	3	4	5
1.	My friends say that I argue a lot.					
2.	I let my anger show when I do not get what I want.					
3.	I wonder why sometimes I feel so unpleasant about things.					
4.	At times I feel like a bomb ready to explode.					
5.	I have threatened people I know.					
6.	If I am angry enough, I may spoil someone's work.					
7.	I get into fights more than most people.					
8.	I may hit someone if he or she upsets me.					
9.	At times I can't control the feeling to hit someone.					
10.	If somebody hits me, I hit back.					
11.	If I have to use violence to protect myself I will.					
12.	I get into fights more than the most people.					
13.	I have become so angry that I have broken things.					
14.	I can't help getting into arguments when people disagree with me .					
15.	I often find myself disagreeing with people.					

S.No	Statement	1	2	3	4	5
16.	When people annoy me ,I may tell them what I think of them .					
17.	I tell my friends openly when I am disagree with them.					
18.	I get angry easily, but get over my anger quickly.					
19.	I am a calm person.					
20.	Some of my friends think I am a short tempered.					
21.	At times, I feel that life has been unfair towards me.					
22.	I have trouble controlling my anger.					
23.	I do not trust strangers who are too friendly.					
24.	Other people are luckier than me.					
25.	At times, I feel that life has been unfair towards me.					
26.	I wonder what people want when they are nice to me.					
27.	I sometimes feel that people are laughing at me behind my back.					
28.	I know that "friends" talk about me behind my back.					
29.	At times, I am so jealous that I cannot think of anything else.					
30.	When people are bossy, I take my time doing what they want, just to show them.					
31.	When someone really irritates me, I might give him or her silent treatment.					
32.	I like to play practical jokes.					
33.	I have been angry enough to bang a door when leaving someone behind in the room.					
34.	I sometimes spread gossip about people I do not like.					

REFERENCES

[1] Suman EJ, Dorn LD, Schiefelblin VL. Puberty, sexuality, and health. In: Lerner RM, Brooks MAE, eds. Handbook of psychology: Developmental psychology. New York: Wiley, 2003:295-324.

[2] Eysenck, Michael W, Keane, Mark T. Cognitive psychology: A student's handbook, 4th ed. New York: Psychology Press, 2000.

[3] Erickson E. School literacy, reasoning, and civility: An anthropologist's perspective. Rev Educ Res 1984;54(4):525-46.

[4] Miller NE, Dollard J. Social learning and imitation. New Haven: Yale University Press, 1941.

[5] Glanz K, Rimer BK, Lewis FM. Health behavior and health education. Theory, research and practice. San Fransisco: Wiley, 2002.

[6] Hendry LB, Patrick H. Adolescents and television. J Youth Adolesc 1972;6(4):325-36.

[7] Zanden J. Human development, 7th ed. Boston: McGraw-Hill Higher Education, 2000.

[8] Muuss A. A concept analysis of relational aggression. J Psychiatr Ment Health Nurs 1995;14(5): 510-5.

[9] Davis JQ. Anger, aggression, and adolescents. New York: Pantheon Books, 2004.

[10] Underwood MK. Social aggression among girls. New York: Guilford, 2003.

[11] Tremblay R. Testosterone, physical aggression, dominance, and physical development in early adolescence. Int J Behav Dev 1998;22(4):753-77.

[12] Burbank VK. Cross-cultural perspectives on aggression in women and girls: An introduction. Sex Roles 1994;30:169-76.

[13] Infante DA. Teaching students to understand and control verbal aggression. Commun Educ 1995;44:51-63.

[14] 13. Goodenough FL. Anger in young children. Minnesota: Minnesota Press, 1931.

[15] Gesell A. Youth the years from ten to sixteen. New York: HarperCollins, 1956.

[16] Dollard J. Frustration and aggression. Yale: Yale University Press, 1939.

[17]   Berkowitz L. Aggression: Its causes, consequences, and control. New York: McGraw-Hill, 1993.

[18]   Freud S. The ego and the mechanisms of defense. London: Hogarth Press, 1937.

[19]   Lorenz K. On aggression. London: Methuen, 1996.

[20]   Bandura A. Imitation of film-mediated aggressive models. J Abnorm Soc Psychol 1963;66: 3-11.

[21]   Bandura A. Transmission of aggression through imitation of aggressive models. J Abnorm Soc Psychol 1961;63:575-82.

[22]   Garg R. A comparative study of aggression among adolescents with respect to gender and maternal employment. Dissertation. Panjab: Panjab University Dept Hum Dev Fam Relat, 2002.

[23]   Smith DC, Furlong MJ. Correlates of anger, hostility, and aggression in children and adolescents. In: Furlong MJ, Smith DC, eds. Anger, hostility, and aggression: Assessment, prevention, and intervention strategies for youth. New York: Wiley, 1994:15-38.

[24]   Huesmann LR, Eron LD, eds. Television and the aggression child: A cross national comparion. Hillsdale,NJ: Erlbaum,1986.

[25]   24. Reen M K: Sexual behavior, Knowledge and attitude towards reproductive health issues of college going girls in Chandigarh. Dissertation. Panjab: Panjab University Dept Hum Dev Fam Relat, 2009.

[26]   Timmermans M, Lier P, Koot HM. Which forms of adolescent external behaviors account for late adolescent risky sexual behavior and substance use? J Child Psychol Psychiatr 2008;49(4): 386-94.

[27]   Lee E. The relationship of aggression and bullying to social preference: Differences in gender and types of aggression. Int J Behav Dev 2009;33(4):323-30.

[28]   Barnow S, Lutch M, Freyberger H-J. Correlates of aggressive and delinquent conduct problems in adolescence. Behav Problems Adolesc 2005;31:24-39.

[29]   Buss AH, Warren WL. The aggression questionnaire. Los Angeles, CA: Western Psychological Services, 2000.

[30]   Buss A, Perry M. The aggression questionnaire. J Pers Soc Psychol 1992;63:452–9.

In: Children, Violence and Bullying
Editors: J Merrick, I Kandel and H A Omar

ISBN: 978-1-62948-342-9
© 2014 Nova Science Publishers, Inc.

Chapter 4

INDIA: MALTREATMENT OF ADOLESCENTS AMONG HIGH SCHOOL CHILDREN

Jyothi Manoj, MPhil and Josmy Thomas, MSc*

Kristu Jayanti College, Bangalore, Karnataka and St Joseph's Hospital,
Dharmagiri, Kothamangalam, Kerala, India

ABSTRACT

The purpose of this chapter was to retrospectively analyze the awareness of adolescents about child rights and assess the prevalence of maltreatment. Methods: 300 students from two schools in Calicut district participated in a cross sectional study. The participants were 153(51%) boys and 147(49%) girls with median age 14 years and range 3. Results: 53.67% of the children have poor awareness of child rights and maltreatment. The results provide baseline information on the prevalence and types of maltreatment children face. 47% were exposed to physical maltreatment, 47.6% has suffered emotional maltreatment, 16.7% sexual maltreatment, 29.7% neglect. There is no gender difference in exposure to the types of maltreatments (chi square $p > 0.05$) except sexual maltreatment where boys were found more vulnerable. Monthly income of the family and parents educational level has an influence on prevalence of maltreatment. Conclusion: Child maltreatment is highly prevalent among school children. We suggest schools must introduce interventions which incorporate personal safety, prevention of abuse and mental health issues for students and government and NGOs should develop programmes and counseling to create awareness among parents and teachers to build up a healthy generation.

INTRODUCTION

Child maltreatment is a state of emotional, physical, economic and sexual about meted out to a person below the age of eighteen and is a globally prevalent phenomenon. However, in India, as in many other countries, there has been no understanding of the extent, magnitude

* Correspondence: Jyothi Manoj, Assistant professor, Department of Statistics, Kristu Jayanti College, Bangalore-77, India. E-mail: jyothimanoj@kristujayanticollege.com.

and trends of the problem (1). Children are not recognised as subjects of human rights and adults play arbitrary limits on children's fundamental freedom. Teachers and parents have broad discretionary powers and can restrict children freedom with little accountability. Most of the restrictions that children face on a daily basis are not entrenched in law but are part of school or family rules (2). Discipline is something adults do with and for children, rather than to children to stop them from behaving in undesirable ways (3). Child abuse is more than bruises and broken bones. While physical abuse might be the most visible sign, other types of abuse, such as emotional abuse or child neglect, also leave deep, long lasting scars (4). The impact that child maltreatment leaves has long lasting effects throughout life, damaging a child's sense of self, ability to have healthy relationships, and ability to function at home, at work and at school. There is dearth of research done on the broad array of disciplining techniques adopted in schools of India. This study aims to analyze the awareness of high school children about their own rights that Indian Judiciary dictates for them which will help them protect themselves from being abused. The study also attempts to estimate the prevalence of maltreatment.

OUR STUDY

The study was carried out as a cross sectional survey 2 high schools in Calicut district of Kerala. The participants were recruited to in the study via a stratified random sampling technique with age as factor for stratification. A sample of 300 children was selected. A self-report questionnaire developed and piloted in collaboration with the adolescents, elicited information on socioeconomic status, demographic profile, knowledge regarding child rights and adolescent maltreatment and their experience of maltreatment at home and school. The participants were 150 (50%) rural and remaining urban, 153 (51%) were boys and 147 (49%) girls with median age 14 and range 3. After obtaining institutional ethical clearance, data was collected by the investigators. Statistical analysis was carried out by using SPSS version 17.

FINDINGS

Reliability test of the tool suggests that the items in the questionnaire are relevant and ensures the randomness of the data. (Chronback Alpha = 0.94). 50% of the children are from rural area and remaining urban. 83.3% [250] of the children have both their parents together while 14% [42] of their parents are abroad and stay with caretakers and 2.3% [8] have single parents. 75.7% [227] of the children come from nuclear family, 15% [45] of them from three generation families and remaining from joint families. 42% [126] of the families have monthly income less than 5000, 22% [66] have monthly income between 5000 – and 10,000 and the rest 36% earn more than 10000 as monthly income. Based on the response to the set of 15 questions on awareness of child rights, children were classified to have poor awareness about child rights if less than 6 answers were right, moderate awareness if 6 -10 answers were right and the rest to have good awareness. The information was elicited in table 1

Table 1. Distribution of awareness of children about maltreatment and child rights based on gender

Gender	Poor	Average	Good
Male	94(31.67%)	28(9.33%)	27(9%)
Female	63(21%)	35(11.67%)	49(16.33%)
Total	161 (53.67%)	63 (21%)	76(25.33%)

Percentage of adolescents who have awareness about child rights and various types ofmaltreatment, by gender (n = 300)

The analysis reveals that 161 (53.67%) of them had poor knowledge about their rights. Boys lack awareness (31.67%) than girls (21%). When urban and rural children were compared, it was found that among the urban children 19.67% (59) had good awareness about child rights while 23% [69] had poor knowledge (see table2). 30.67% (92) of rural children had poor awareness where as about 5.66% of responders [17] had good awareness.

Table 2. Distribution of awareness of children about maltreatment and child rights based on locality

Area of residence	Poor	Average	Good
Urban	69(23%)	22(7.33%)	59(19.67%)
Rural	92(30.67%)	41(13.67%)	17(5.66%)
Total	161 (53.67%)	63 (21%)	76(25.33%)

Table 3. Percentage of adolescents who has experienced the four types of maltreatments, by gender (n = 300)

Types of maltreatment	Male%	Female%	Chi square	p value
Physical	49.02	44.90	4.067	0.254
Sexual	18.30	14.97	23.715	0.000*
Emotional	49.67	45.58	4.732	0.193
Neglect	29.41	29.93	4.05	0.256

Table 4. The factors influencing the four types of maltreatment

Factors affecting maltreatment	Wilk's lambda	p value
Parents marital status(Single parent or not)	0.961	0.765
Location of residence(urban or rural)	0.988	0.482
Mother's education level	0.935	0.041[*]
Father's education level	0.894	0.001[*]
Monthly income of the family	0.898	0.001[*]
Level of knowledge of the children regarding maltreatment	0.913	0.004[*]
Type of family (Nuclear, three generation or joint family)	0.946	0.035

It was observed that children of both genders were vulnerable to the four types of maltreatment and gender had an influence in the case of sexual maltreatment (see table3). (Chi square p value = 0.00 for sexual maltreatment and for all others it is > 0.05). Boys are more in number who had responded of suffering from maltreatment which is against the usual belief that girl children are prone to abuse more than boys (1-4). The influences of various factors on the four types of maltreatment were analyzed by MANOVA. The result is presented in the table 4. The children's awareness, parent's education level, family's monthly income and type of family they belong showed significant influence in the prevalence of maltreatment.

DISCUSSION

The repercussions of various types of maltreatment were critically analyzed. Though various types of maltreatment were highly prevalent in Kerala, it was respite that the adolescents were able to cope up with stress. Less than 20% suffers from problems like sleeplessness, aggressive behavior, loneliness and difficulty in educational performance. The psychosocial problems expected to be present in the children exposed to maltreatment was comparatively less, might be due to the potency in the family bond. However, prevalence of maltreatment was correlated significantly with aggressive behavior ($R^2 = 0.036$, p- 0.001) and difficulty in educational performance ($R^2 = 0.12$, p= 0.00). The findings in the study highlight the need for more studies on the prevalence of all forms of child maltreatment. Also the authors suggest that schools must introduce interventions which incorporate personal safety, prevention of abuse and mental health issues.

Intervention programmes for parents and teacher emphasizing positive child disciplining practices are the need of the hour. The investigation revealed that 53.67% of children has poor awareness of child rights of which 31.67% are boys. Comparing with rural and urban children, lack of proper awareness is more among rural children. 19.67% of urban children have good awareness where as 5.66% of rural children have good awareness about child rights. There are various factors influencing the prevalence of maltreatment. The results show that monthly income of the family, parent's educational level and the child's awareness of maltreatment makes a significant difference in the prevalence of the four types of maltreatment. Children of parents with higher education reports no maltreatment. Children who knows about their rights have reported seldom or no exposure to maltreatment. Children from low income family and nuclear family have reported more exposures to multiple mal-treatment. MANOVA results show that the above mentioned factors provide an influential role in the prevalence of maltreatment. The significant consequences reported by the children who have suffered maltreatment are aggressive behavior, feeling lonely, sleeplessness and difficulty in academic performance.

REFERENCES

[1]   Study on Child Abuse: India 2007. URL: wcd.nic.in/childabuse.pdf
[2]   Derek K. Child social work policy and practice. London: Sage, 2009.
[3]   Tiwari J. Child abuse and human rights. New Delhi: Isha Books, 2011.
[4]   Child abuse and neglect. URL: www.helpguide.org/index

In: Children, Violence and Bullying   ISBN: 978-1-62948-342-9
Editors: J Merrick, I Kandel and H A Omar   © 2014 Nova Science Publishers, Inc.

Chapter 5

CANADA: SIBLINGS EXPOSED TO INTIMATE PARTNER VIOLENCE

Ashley Stewart-Tufescu*, PhD (candidate)
and Caroline C Piotrowski, PhD, MPH
Applied Health Sciences,
Faculty of Graduate Studies and Department of Family Social Sciences,
University of Manitoba, Winnipeg, Manitoba, Canada

ABSTRACT

In this chapter we investigate the influence of familial factors on child trauma symptoms in children exposed to intimate partner violence (IPV). Building upon past research, the trauma symptoms of siblings were compared, and the role of these familial factors, maternal stress and the quality of mother-child interactions, in relation to children's trauma symptoms was explored. Results indicated sibling trauma symptoms were significantly related, and that older siblings demonstrated significantly more trauma symptoms than younger siblings. Sibling trauma symptoms, maternal stress and the quality of mother-child interactions accounted for a significant amount of variance in trauma symptoms for both older and younger siblings. An exploration of maternal differential treatment indicated mothers directed significantly more positive behaviours towards older than younger siblings. Findings indicated that sibling trauma symptoms were mutually influential, and that some mothers may have compensated for stressful life circumstances with positive parent-child interactions.

INTRODUCTION

It is well documented that exposure to intimate partner violence (IPV) has numerous detrimental effects on children's developmental outcomes (1). In North America, the

---

*Correspondence: Ashley Stewart-Tufescu, PhD (candidate), Applied Health Sciences, Faculty of Graduate Studies, 212 Human Ecology Building, University of Manitoba, Winnipeg, Manitoba, R3T 2N2, Canada. E-mail: Ashley.Stewart-Tufescu@umanitoba.ca.

prevalence and incidence rates of childhood experiences of IPV vary greatly due to definitional, theoretical, and methodological issues (2). Regardless of this variation, IPV remains a serious and underestimated global public health concern affecting upwards of 275 million children worldwide (3). Childhood exposure to IPV may include seeing the consequences of violence, hearing the violence, witnessing the violence and/or becoming directly involved in the violence (4). Exposure to IPV has been linked to a wide variety of consequences, including but not limited to: negative emotional and behavioural functioning, compromised social competence and cognitive functioning, poor school achievement, internalizing and externalizing difficulties, and general health concerns (1,2). Some work has suggested that children exposed to IPV are also more likely to display symptoms consistent with post-traumatic stress disorder (PTSD); unfortunately, trauma symptoms have not been as widely studied as other behaviour problems and are not yet well understood (5,6). The first main goal of the present research was to better understand trauma symptoms in school-aged children exposed to IPV. Recent research has concentrated on better understanding the nature of heterogeneity in children's trauma symptoms, as well as identifying some of the mechanisms that may account for the range of variability in trauma symptomatology across children exposed to IPV (7).

Our research focuses on mechanisms that positively or negative influence children's well-being is consonant with a developmental psychopathology perspective. This theoretical framework is useful for understanding variability in adjustment, as it focuses on the origins and pathways of individual patterns of maladaptation (8). Risk and protective factors are given equal emphasis. Although risk factors that increase the likelihood of negative outcomes have been more widely studied to date, an understanding of protective factors that either reduce or eliminate adjustment difficulties is equally as important (2). Situating these differing risk and protective factors within specific contexts is vital, as the degree and nature of their influence is often context dependent. For example, some protective factors may be relevant only in certain situations, buffering children who face specific stressors but having a neutral or even negative effect in other situations (8). Lastly, the concept of developmental pathways seeks to explain the interaction of risk and protective factors at differing time points and contexts across the life course.

The body of work examining trauma symptoms of children exposed to IPV has identified several important mechanisms to date, including child and family characteristics; however, family relationships are another potentially important influence that are only just beginning to be investigated (9). From a developmental psychopathology perspective, family risk factors play a crucial role in influencing children's developmental trajectories (8). The quality of mother-child relationships are particularly important, in that they can either lessen or amplify child adjustment difficulties. A second main goal of the present research was to explore the association between the quality of mother-child relationships and child trauma symptoms.

Another issue commonly overlooked in the literature is that the majority of violent families have more than one child. Children within the same family can experience IPV quite differently. Unfortunately, the nature of the sibling experience within families is typically not considered. Siblings in violent families may or may not share exposure to the same stressful events. When exposure is shared, they may have quite different perceptions of such events given individual differences between them such as age and gender. An appreciable body of research on siblings with non-violent histories has demonstrated the influence of both shared and non-shared environments within families (10). In brief, shared factors are considered to contribute to sibling similarity on a given characteristic, while non-shared factors are seen as contributing to sibling differences, such as differential treatment by parents. One of the few studies that have addressed siblings exposed to IPV found that younger and older siblings demonstrated similar patterns of adjustment. (11) However, given the paucity of work on siblings to date, another important goal of the present study was to investigate similarities and differences in the trauma symptoms of siblings exposed to IPV.

In summary, the overall goals of the present study were to better understand trauma symptoms of school-aged children exposed to IPV, and to investigate a variety of family predictors that may mediate or moderate these symptoms. Several unique features of the present study make a substantial contribution to the literature. First, the trauma symptoms of more than one child within each family were investigated, allowing for a comparison of similarities and differences between siblings. Next, a multi-method approach was taken which included an observational assessment of the quality of mother-child relationships. Finally, other important family predictors such as maternal stress and sibling trauma symptomatology were also explored as potential mediators of trauma symptoms for IPV-exposed children.

REVIEW OF THE LITERATURE

Recent research suggests that children exposed to IPV are at an increased risk for post-traumatic stress disorder (PTSD) (6). They may experience symptoms which include traumatic re-experiencing, hyper-arousal, numbing, flat affect, dissociation, sleep disturbances, attention difficulties, cognitive problems, impulsivity and risk taking behaviours, and suicidal ideations (6). One study suggested that up to 50% of children exposed to IPV may meet the stringent criteria for clinical diagnosis of PTSD, while another study reported that clinically significant trauma scores among youth exposed to IPV ranged from 10-14% (5). Lang and Stover (12) suggested that the wide variability in rates of traumatic stress symptoms for children and youth exposed to IPV may be due to the fact that these symptoms receive much less research attention than internalizing and externalizing behavioural problems, and therefore may not be as clearly differentiated from other adjustment difficulties.

An additional challenge to understanding post-traumatic stress symptomatology among children exposed to IPV is the difficulty in differentiating between these symptoms and a specific clinical diagnosis of post-traumatic stress disorder (PTSD). Many of the studies that consider PTSD or PTSS in children exposed to IPV use proxy measures rather than the criterion from the Diagnostic and Statistical Manual of Mental Disorders (DSM-IV) (5). Moreover, the DSM criterion has been criticized for not being developmentally sensitive to children of a young age (6). In addition, co-morbid and secondary problems associated with PTSD may exacerbate symptomatology and/or lead to misdiagnoses; co-morbidity of PTSS is common with internalizing and externalizing difficulties (6). However, it is important to interpret these findings within the context of the methodological challenges of accurate measures of trauma symptoms, as well as the likelihood of co-morbidity with other difficulties such as the co-occurrence of witnessing IPV and experiencing child abuse directly. Given the above-mentioned methodological concerns, rates of traumatic stress in IPV-exposed children may be much higher than currently reported.

SIMILARITIES AND DIFFERENCES IN SIBLING TRAUMA SYMPTOMS

The degree of similarity and the differences in the adjustment of siblings exposed to IPV is under-studied. One of the few studies to date that has compared siblings from a shelter-based sample found no mean differences between younger and older siblings on internalizing or externalizing difficulties; however reports on child adjustment by differing family members were inter-related (13). More recently, Piotrowski (11) assessed patterns of adjustment in a community-based sample of siblings exposed to IPV, and found that younger and older siblings demonstrated the same five patterns overall, but that very few siblings matched exactly in terms of their patterns of adjustment. We know of no other work to date that has investigated or compared trauma symptoms in siblings exposed to IPV; given the paucity of attention paid to siblings in the literature, an important goal of the present research was to explore similarities and differences in sibling trauma symptoms.

MATERNAL STRESS

A variety of family factors have been suggested as potential mediators or moderators of trauma symptoms in children exposed to IPV. Some work has identified maternal stress as one potential influence, although linkages between maternal stress and child trauma symptoms remain unclear. Previous work reported that maternal parenting stress was found to mediate the relationship between IPV exposure and children's emotional and behavioural outcomes among low income, school-aged children (14). Unfortunately, this study did not include a measure of child trauma. More recently, research addressing the influence of maternal parenting practice and maternal stress on child internalizing problems in IPV-affected families concluded that maternal stress and observed parenting were not related, and found no evidence to support indirect effects of maternal stress on child internalizing difficulties (15). Given the limited research that has examined maternal stress and child trauma symptoms, another goal of the present study was to examine the relationship between maternal stress and child trauma symptoms in families exposed to IPV.

Mothers with a history of intimate partner violence often experience significantly greater levels of stress than mothers without such a history (16). In addition, their life circumstances are often more difficult, including lower socioeconomic status, less education and less available social support (17). Given these barriers, it is perhaps not surprising that some researchers have found their parenting to be negatively impacted. Maternal parenting stress has been reported to have a direct effect on child outcomes and behaviour problems following IPV-exposure (16). A recent study found that maternal distress was linked to parenting stress in IPV-affected families, and that maternal stress had a negative impact on the quality of the parent-child relationship. Moreover, it was parenting stress and not exposure to IPV that was found to be the strongest predictor of children adjustment in this study, including trauma symptoms (18).

In contrast, other studies have failed to report an association between maternal mental health, stress and parenting in IPV-affected families. These studies suggest that despite high levels of stress, mothers may utilize compensatory strategies to buffer their children's negative experiences (15, 17). Considering the conflicting nature of the current literature on maternal stress, and the lack of findings specific to the maternal stress and child trauma outcomes following IPV exposure, another goal of the present study was to investigate the potential influence of maternal stress on children's trauma symptoms.

THE ROLE OF MOTHER-CHILD RELATIONSHIPS

Mother-child relationships have also been identified as a significant influence on the adjustment of children exposed to IPV; however, there is currently no consensus as to the nature of this influence on children's trauma symptoms (16, 17). Some studies indicate that poor maternal mental health, particularly stress and depression, contributes to less optimal parenting behaviours (19). Other studies have shown that mothers may compensate for stressful circumstances with heightened sensitivity and attunement that may help protect and promote healthy emotional and developmental outcomes for children exposed to IPV (15, 17, 19). The buffering effects of supportive maternal caregiving have been linked with better child outcomes in violent families, including increased self-esteem and less externalizing behaviour. For example, Skopp and colleagues (13) found that higher levels of maternal warmth were associated with an attenuation of the relation between partner-to-mother aggression and children's externalizing problems. Others have found that mothers of asymptomatic children reported greater warmth than mothers of children with adjustment difficulties (9).

Given these findings, it was hypothesized in the present research that more negative mother-child interactions (e.g., characterized by more hostility, rejection and control) would be associated with more child trauma symptoms and greater maternal stress. Complementarily, it was also hypothesized that more positive mother-child interactions (e.g., characterized by more warmth, sensitivity and affection) would be associated with fewer child trauma symptoms and lower maternal life stress.

Clearly, positive mother-child relationships can play an important protective role in children's adjustment; they may be one crucial factor in understanding why some children exposed to intimate partner violence do not demonstrate trauma symptoms. Unfortunately, the quality of the mother-child relationships are often assessed by maternal self-report only, while observations of the quality of mother-child interaction and parenting are rarely conducted in IPV-affected families, with few exceptions (15,19). The present study addressed this gap in the literature by utilizing observational methodology to assess the quality of mother-child interactions.

In addition, to our knowledge no empirical work to date has addressed the role of differential maternal parenting on trauma symptoms of siblings with a history of IPV. Previous work investigating non-violent families has shown that differential parental treatment of siblings was significantly associated with negative mental health outcomes and behaviour problems in children, such as depressed mood, low self-esteem and conduct disorders (20). Clearly, further investigation into the potential influence of differential parenting on siblings exposed to IPV is needed. Therefore, the final goal of the present study was to describe differential maternal treatment of siblings exposed to IPV, and to explore linkages between differential treatment and children's trauma symptoms.

In summary, the overall goal of the present study was to address gaps in the literature by investigating the trauma symptoms of siblings exposed to IPV utilizing a community-based, multi-method research design. Our first goal was to explore similarities and differences in sibling trauma symptoms. Taking a developmental psychopathology approach, our second goal investigated if family predictors, such as maternal stress, the quality of the mother-child relationship, and sibling trauma symptoms were mediators of child trauma symptoms. The third and final goal of the present study was to explore the potential association maternal differential treatment of siblings and children's trauma symptoms in IPV-affected families.

OUR STUDY

A community-based sample of families was recruited from through newspaper advertising, mail flyers, and posters displayed in counseling & support centres. Inclusion criteria for families consisted of: a) at least two school-aged children between 5-18 years of age, b) fluency in English of all family members, and c) mothers self-identified as having a history of IPV. As required by the Research Ethics Board, all mothers were required to have some prior counseling for their abuse, which ranged from less than one month (9%) to more than one year (49%).

Mothers. Forty-seven mothers agreed to participate. Their average age was 35 years (*SD*= 5.30). This sample of mothers indicated their ethnic-cultural backgrounds as 62% Euro-Canadian, 30% Aboriginal, and 8% multiracial. The majority of mothers (75%) reported they were lone parents (separated, divorced, widowed or never married). Thirty families (64%) reported an income that fell below the Low-Income Cut-Off (LICO) for families of three members or more, which was $27,000 at the time of data collection (21).

Children. Younger siblings included 27 boys and 20 girls, with an age range from 4 to 14 years of age (*M*= 7.89, *SD*= 2.50). Older siblings included 29 boys and 18 girls with an age range from 6 to 17 years of age (*M*= 10.83, *SD*= 3.00). Sibling dyads had an average age spacing of 2.8 years (*SD*= 2.0) and included 18 brothers, 9 sisters, 8 older brother/ younger sister pairs, and 9 older sister/ younger brother pairs. The majority of mothers (62%) reported that their children had received or were currently receiving family counseling at the time of participating in the study.

After mothers signed an informed consent form and children provided oral assent, each family member was interviewed separately and privately. When age-appropriate, each family member was given the option of completing questionnaires on his or her own (with a Research Assistant available to answer questions). All interviewers were female, and whenever possible interviewers were of similar ethno-cultural origin to study participants. All families were provided $75 remuneration and information about local community resources (e.g., crisis hotlines) for participating in the study.

During the observational component of the study, family members were brought into an observation room equipped with a video camera and microphone. The observation room was furnished similarly to a home environment including couches, chairs, and a coffee table. A snack was also provided. Mothers were observed for ten minutes with each sibling separately. These interactions were semi-structured, in that mother-child dyads were provided with an Issues Checklist created by Robin and Foster (22), which consisted of a list of potential conversational topics that were likely to generate conflict. For example, participants may have discussed problems at home, school, or with friends. Each mother-child dyad was asked to choose any items from the checklist that they most wanted to discuss during the observation session. When a child was not participating in the observational session with their mother, they were asked to complete measures with a Research Assistant in a separate room.

Measures

Child Trauma Symptoms. The Child Behavior Checklist (CBCL) is a widely used tool for assessing externalizing and internalizing difficulties in children aged 4 to 18 years (23). A subset of items from this measure has also been widely used as a measure of post-traumatic stress disorder symptoms (PTSD) in children (24,25). This subscale consists of 20-items selected to reflect PTSD criteria as defined in the DSM-III-R (25). These items included: difficulties concentrating, obsessive thoughts, feelings of guilt, moodiness, difficulties sleeping, nightmares, irrational fears, clinging to adults, nervousness, anxiety, sadness or depression, withdrawal, secrecy, feelings of persecution, irritability, frequent arguing, and somatic complaints including: headaches, nausea, stomachaches, and vomiting. Each item was rated on a 3-point scale, ranging from 0 (not true), 1 (somewhat true) to 2 (often true). The CBCL-PTSD subscale has shown predictive power and incremental validity above and beyond the externalizing and internalizing behaviour scales of the CBCL-Total (24). Previous research using the CBCL-PTSD subscale for 4-18-year olds demonstrated good internal consistency, with a coefficient alpha of .87 (24). Similarly, good internal consistency was found for the CBCL-PTSD in the present study; coefficient alpha was .84.

Exposure to Intimate Partner Violence. Mothers were asked to estimate the length of their children's lifetime exposure to intimate partner violence. On average, younger siblings were exposed for 3.9 years (*SD*= 2.9) while older siblings were exposed for 4.8 years (*SD*= 3.6).

Maternal Violence History. The Physical Aggression scale of the Conflict Tactics Scale (CTS) was completed by mothers (26). The CTS asked about 9 violent behaviours that occurred within the context of a conflict in the past 12 months. Each violent behaviour was rated on a 7-point scale ranging from 0 (never) to 6 (more than 20 times). Mother reported on their own and their partner's behaviours; however, more mothers reported more often about themselves (n= 47) than their partner (n= 30). This subscale has been widely used to assess aggression in intimate partner relationships and has demonstrated adequate internal consistency, concurrent validity and construct validity (26). Alpha coefficients for this subscale in the present study were .90 and .85 for self-report and report on partner respectively.

Mothers in this sample reported experiencing moderate to high levels of intimate partner violence. Overall, 66% reported an intimate partner had directed violent behaviour towards them in the context of conflict at least once the past year (mild physical violence subscale *M*= 4.46, *SD*= 5.12; severe physical violence subscale *M*= 4.61, *SD*= 5.63; n= 30). Examples of these behaviours included: being pushed, grabbed or shoved (66%), kicked, bitten or hit (50%), beaten up (34%) or threatened with a weapon (28%). Sixty-eight percent of mothers also reported directing at least one violent behaviour towards an intimate partner in the context of a conflict during the year prior to the study (mild physical violence subscale *M*=

3.17 *SD*= 3.89; severe physical violence subscale *M*= 2.28, *SD*= 7.61, n= 47). Examples of these behaviours included: pushing, shoving or grabbing (62%), kicking, biting or hitting (34%), and threatening with a weapon (15%).

Maternal Stress. Mothers completed the Parenting Stress Index (PSI) which is a 101-item questionnaire designed to assess parent-child relationships and parenting stress (27). The Life Stress subscale was used to assess maternal stress in the present study; it is a 19-item subscale that provided an index of the amount of stress outside of the parent-child relationship experienced by the parent (27). High scores on the Life Stress subscale indicated stressful situational circumstances that were often beyond the control of the parent (e.g., death of a relative or loss of a job). The items of this subscale were scored dichotomously, with higher scores indicating greater stress. Previous work has shown the PSI has acceptable psychometric properties and good test-retest reliability for both clinical and non-clinical populations; coefficient alpha was .55 for this subscale in the present study (27).

Quality of Mother-Child Dyadic Interactions. The Parent-Child Relationship Coding Scheme, developed for the present study, consisted of six content codes (e.g., verbal content, nonverbal content, proximity, physical contact, compliance, and joint attention) designed to capture the quality of mother-child interaction; each content code was coded as positive, negative or neutral. Content codes were applied to the behaviour of each individual rather than to dyadic interaction at the end of every 15-second interval. Mother-child dyads were observed for a total of ten minutes. Inter-rater reliability was computed using Cohen's Kappa coefficients, and these were α =.87 for verbal content, α =.88 for nonverbal content, α=.96 for physical contact, α=.97 for proximity, α =.93 for compliance, α =.92 for joint attention, α=.99 for disengagement, α =.99 for uncodeable and α =.89 for emotional tone.

The six content codes of the Parent-Child Coding Scheme were combined into composite variables based on the proportion of positive, negative and neutral codes assigned to each of the six categories for each family member. By calculating proportional frequencies rather than raw frequencies, small differences in the length of observations were controlled. For example, the composite variable of positive interaction (e.g., warmth, affection, attention) consisted of positively coded content codes combined with positively coded emotional tone ratings for each family member. The composite variable for negative interaction was similarly constructed.

Statistical analyses

SPSS version 18 was used to conduct all analyses. Prior to hypotheses testing, descriptive statistics were conducted on all variables, as well as correlations between variables. All variables were normally distributed, and no outliers were detected. Missing data were not replaced or estimated for any analyses. The minimum alpha level used to test significant for all analyses in the present study was set at *p*< .05. Hierarchal regression analyses were conducted separately for older and younger siblings, using child trauma scores as the dependent variable in each of the models. Predictor variables included: sibling trauma scores, maternal life stress, and the quality of the mother-child interaction.

FINDINGS

Our analyses addressed the three main goals of our study: 1) to compare the trauma symptoms of siblings exposed to IPV; 2) to investigate family predictors of trauma symptoms of younger and older siblings, including maternal stress, sibling trauma symptoms, length of child exposure to IPV and the quality of mother-child interactions; and 3) to explore differential maternal treatment of siblings, and the linkages between differential treatment and the trauma symptoms of sibling exposed to IPV.

Comparison of sibling trauma symptoms

Younger and older siblings were first compared on several demographic characteristics, including age, sex, and length of exposure to IPV. Results indicated that older siblings were significantly older (younger M=8.5 years, older M=11.3 years, $t(46)$= -9.98, $p<$ .01) and exposed to IPV longer (younger M=46.9 months, older M=57.9 months, $t(46)$= -3.28 $p<$ .01) than younger siblings. Younger and older siblings did not differ in terms of the number of boys and girls; however, overall there were more brother dyads (n=18) than sister dyads (n=9) in this sample.

Two types of analyses were used to compare sibling trauma symptoms. First, the degree of association between younger and older sibling trauma symptoms was assessed; because of the significant demographic differences noted above, a partial correlation controlling for differences in sibling age and exposure to IPV was conducted. Results indicated that sibling trauma symptoms were significantly related $r(42)$ = .51, $p<$ .001. Next, an analysis of mean differences indicated that older siblings displayed significantly higher CBCL-PTSD trauma scores (M= 13.67, SD= 6.16) than younger siblings (M=10.75, SD= 5.98) on average, $t(43)$= -2.98, $p<$ .01 controlling for differences in sibling age and length of exposure.

Family predictors of child trauma symptoms

Pearson product moment correlations were first conducted to assess the degree of association between younger and older sibling trauma symptoms with family predictors including maternal stress, length of child exposure to IPV, maternal violence history, and the quality of mother-child interactions. Results are presented separately for each sibling in Tables 1 and 2.

For younger siblings, maternal stress was significantly and positively associated with younger sibling trauma symptoms. In addition, younger sibling trauma symptoms were positively and significantly related to the negative interactions mothers directed towards older siblings $r(32)$ = .43, $p<$ .05, and the negative interactions older siblings directed towards mothers $r(32)$ = .43, $p<$ .05. Maternal positive behaviour directed towards younger siblings was significantly related to positive behaviour by younger siblings directed towards mothers. Maternal negative behaviour towards younger siblings was also significantly related to negative behaviour by younger siblings directed towards them. Lastly, younger sibling lifetime exposure to IPV was significantly and positively related to positive behaviour by

Ashley Stewart-Tufescu and Caroline C Piotrowski

mothers towards them, and positively related to their positive behaviour directed towards their mothers.

Table 1. Correlations Between Younger Sibling Trauma Symptoms and Family Predictors

	1	2	3	4	5	6	7
Younger Siblings							
1. Trauma Score							
2. Child IPV	.03						
3. Mom IPV	.06	.73**					
4. Maternal Stress	.33*	-.12	-.10				
5. M-Y Positive	.04	.49**	.31	.08			
6. M-Y Negative	-.03	-.11	-.08	.17	-.26		
7. Y-M Positive	-.05	.43**	.26	.10	.78**	-.19	
8. Y-M Negative	.27	-.25	-.12	-.01	-.33*	.76**	-.44**

Note. N=46. M-Y=Maternal Interactions with Younger Siblings; Y-M= Younger Sibling Interactions with Mothers, $*p < .05$, $**p < .01$ level (2-tailed).

Table 2. Correlations between Older Sibling Trauma Symptoms and Family Predictors

Variable	1	2	3	4	5	6	7
Older Sibling							
1. Trauma Score							
2. Child IPV	.15						
3. Mom IPV	.16	.91**					
4. Maternal Stress	.13	-.06	-.10				
5. M-O Positive	.04	.17	-.01	-.33			
6. M-O Negative	.09	-.22	-.16	.13	-.64**		
7. O-M Positive	-.01	.10	-.09	-.33	.92**	-.59**	
8. O-M Negative	.13	-.26	-.17	.22	-.67**	.88**	-.68**

Note. N=44. M-O=Mother Interactions towards Older Siblings; O-M= Older Sibling Interactions with Mothers $*p < .05$, $**p < .01$ level (2-tailed).

For older siblings, there were no significant associations between trauma symptoms and family predictor variables. Similar to findings for younger siblings, maternal behaviours directed towards older siblings was significantly related to older siblings behaviour directed towards mothers, for both negative and positive interactions. No other significant associations were found for older siblings.

Next, hierarchical regression analyses were conducted separately for older and younger siblings, testing both main and interaction effects; these results are displayed in Table 3. In both models, the first step included the main effects of sibling trauma symptoms, maternal stress and negative mother-child interactions. The second step included the interaction term combining sibling trauma and maternal stress. All variables were centered prior to analysis as recommended by Aiken and West (28).

Table 3. Summary of Hierarchical Multiple Regression Analyses Predicting Younger and Older Siblings Trauma Scores From Sibling Trauma, Maternal Stress and Mother-Child Interactions

	Younger Sibling Trauma			Older Sibling Trauma		
Predictor	β	R^2	Adjusted R^2	β	R^2	Adjusted R^2
Model 1						
1. Sibling Trauma	.44[**]	.50	.45	.75[*]	.34	.27
2. Maternal Life Stress	.60			-.22		
3. Mother-Child Negative Interactions	21.88[**]			-14.93		
Model 2						
1. Sibling Trauma	.315[*]	.62	.56	.01[*]	.39	.30
2. Maternal Life Stress	.84[**]			.76		
3. Mother-Child Negative Interactions	21.77[**]			.29		
4. Interaction of Sibling Trauma X Maternal Life Stress	.11[**]			.16		

Note: $N=94$ mother-sibling dyads. [*]$p<.05$, [**]$p<.01$. Younger sibling Model 1 $F=9.13_{3,27}$[**] Model 2 $F= 10.55_{4,26}$[**]. Older sibling Model 1 $F= 4.70_{3,37}$[**], Model 2 $F=4.19_{4,26}$[**].

Younger Siblings. The model for younger sibling trauma symptoms accounted for a significant amount of the overall variance (adjusted $R^2= .56$). The main effects of older sibling trauma symptoms and maternal life stress were both significant, as was the interaction term between these two variables. The interaction was plotted in Figure 1; these results suggest that younger sibling trauma symptoms were more pronounced in the context of higher maternal life stress and higher older sibling trauma symptoms.

Older Siblings. The model for older sibling trauma symptoms also accounted for a significant amount of the overall variance (adjusted $R^2= .30$). While the main effect of younger sibling trauma symptoms was significant, all other main effects and interaction terms were not significant.

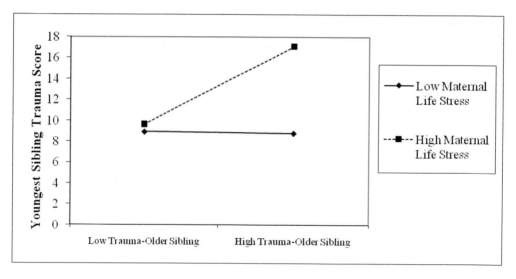

Figure 1. Depiction of interaction between older sibling trauma symptoms (low versus high) and maternal life stress (low versus high) in predicting younger sibling trauma symptoms.

Differential maternal treatment of siblings

The third and final goal of the present study was to explore differential maternal treatment of siblings exposed to IPV. To address this goal, correlational analyses were conducted to determine the degree of association between positive and negative mother-child interactions directed towards younger and older siblings. Results indicated that maternal positive and negative behaviours towards their younger and older children were significantly and negatively related $r(31)= -.58$, $p< .01$. A follow up comparison of mean differences indicated that mothers directed significantly more positive behaviours towards their older children ($M= .37$, $SD= .14$), than their younger children ($M= .31$, $SD= .15$), $t(32) = 2.96$, $p< .01$. No significant differences were found for negative behaviours mothers directed towards their younger and older children. Similarly, the positive and negative behaviours by siblings directed towards their mothers were also significantly and negatively related, $r(31)= -.64$, $p< .01$. A follow-up comparison of mean differences revealed that older siblings ($M= .37$, $SD=.16$) directed more positive behaviours towards their mothers compared with younger siblings ($M= .26$, $SD= .16$), $t(32)= 3.51$, $p< .001$. No significant mean differences were found between siblings concerning negative behaviours directed towards their mothers.

DISCUSSION

The findings of the present study contributed to our understanding of the trauma symptoms of children exposed to IPV in several major ways. First, older siblings demonstrated significantly more trauma symptoms than younger siblings, even when controlling for differences in age and exposure to IPV. Family variables, including maternal stress, the quality of mother-child interactions, and sibling trauma symptoms explained a significant amount of the variance in trauma symptoms for both siblings, but more so for younger siblings. And finally, mothers and older siblings engaged in more positive interactions with each other than mothers and younger siblings. These findings and their implications are discussed below.

Comparison of siblings

Our finding that older siblings demonstrated more trauma symptoms than younger siblings lends some support to the notion of non-shared environment, in that siblings may perceive or respond differently to their experiences within the family (10). Taking into account their differences in age and exposure to IPV, siblings in the present study may have experienced IPV differently; these differences may be attributable to a variety of factors. Exposure to IPV may have begun at a younger age for older siblings than younger siblings, or older siblings may have been aware of more violent events, or had a greater propensity to become involved in the violence while trying to protect/shield their mother and/or their younger sibling (13). It may also be the case that older siblings differed in their appraisal of the threat of IPV, including the degree of self-blame they engaged in (2,13). Some work has suggested that younger children may be partially protected from the full impact of violence because they may not be as cognizant of their experience and/or the potential risks associated with IPV exposure (29).

Differences in sibling trauma symptoms may also be influenced by the gender composition of the sibling dyad. Some previous work has found sex differences in sibling adjustment, while others have not (30,31). Although comparison of sex composition of sibling dyads was not possible for the present study due to sample size limitations, it is an important avenue for future research to pursue. Mean differences in sibling trauma symptoms may also be due to other factors not addressed in the present research, such as child temperament or regulatory functioning (32). However, it should be noted that sibling trauma symptoms were highly correlated in the present study, which supports previous work finding similarities between siblings in non-violent families on such characteristics as self-representation (30). This significant association may also reflect shared genetic inheritance between siblings, as shown in other work on externalizing symptoms (33). It may also reflect shared method variance, in that sibling trauma symptoms were measured solely by maternal report using the CBCL. In addition, mothers who have experienced IPV often demonstrate depressive symptoms and previous work has shown that mothers with mental health issues report on their child's behaviour differently from mothers without mental health issues (34).

The potential influence of maternal mental health issues such as depression and post-traumatic stress symptoms (PTSS) on maternal assessment of child trauma symptoms was not taken into account in the present study. A multi-method assessment of child trauma symptoms by a variety of reporters such as clinicians/therapists, teachers, siblings and by the child themselves would provide a more accurate assessment of their trauma symptoms. For example, in one study children exposed to IPV reported on their own trauma-related distress using a developmentally appropriate cartoon-based interview (15). Future research should utilize multi-method assessment from multiple reporters to further delineate the processes that contribute to similarities and differences in trauma symptoms of siblings exposed to IPV, and whether these change over time.

The role of familial factors

The present study is the first to our knowledge to investigate the role of sibling traumatology, maternal stress, and the quality of mother-child interactions on child trauma symptoms. Interestingly, the quality of observed negative mother-child interactions had a significant influence on trauma symptoms for younger, but not older siblings. This finding suggested that younger siblings may be more sensitive to negative maternal behaviours than their older counterparts. It should be noted that mothers engaged in significantly more positive behaviours with older siblings, which may have further heightened the sensitivity of younger siblings. This association between negative mother-child interactions and trauma symptoms is consistent with previous work, which found mother-child relationships to play an important role in the adjustment of children exposed to IPV (8,15).

Maternal stress was also a significant influence on trauma symptoms, and was found to interact with sibling trauma symptoms. Consistent with a developmental psychopathology perspective, the trauma symptoms of older siblings had a significant influence on younger siblings in the context of high maternal stress, while this pattern did not occur for older siblings. This finding supports previous work that older siblings bear greater influence on younger siblings than vice versa (31). However, the stronger influence of older siblings does not erase the impact of younger siblings; siblings did mutually influence each other in the present study. Sibling trauma symptoms were a significant predictor for both younger and older siblings, underlining the importance of sibling influence regardless of birth order. Social learning theory suggests that siblings may model or imitate one another. They may also influence each other through the quality of their interactions, whereby more conflictual interactions may exacerbate trauma symptoms, and more affectionate and nurturing interactions may attenuate trauma symptoms. Future research needs to address if the quality of interactions between siblings and their relationship overall influence trauma symptoms in children exposed to IPV.

In the present study, the older sibling trauma symptoms had a greater impact on younger siblings in the context of high maternal stress. It may be the case that children's trauma symptoms were aggravated by the stressful life events reported by their mothers, such as moving to a new location, death of family member, or change in employment status, which directly affected them as well. As noted above, it may also be the case that sibling interactions are more hostile or conflictual under circumstances of high maternal stress, which may further amplify trauma symptoms. Future work that directly considers these questions would be the next step in untangling the role of sibling influence on child trauma symptoms.

Maternal stress was not associated with the quality of the mother-child relationship for either older or younger siblings. These results contradict previous studies reporting adverse impacts of maternal distress on the parent-child relationship, but are consistent with other literature suggesting that despite stressful circumstances, mothers engage in positive interactions with their children and may use compensatory strategies to buffer children from the negative effects of IPV exposure (15,16). Our findings suggest that parenting can function independently of parental stress, and lend support to the conceptual model in which mothers effectively distinguish their roles as "parent" and as "person" (15). It should also be noted that mothers in the present study directed significantly more positive behaviours as compared to negative behaviours towards both younger and older siblings. It may be the case that this community-based sample of mothers was uniquely resilient in their parenting skills, in that they may have benefited from the treatment received concerning their abuse history.

In addition, we found no relation between maternal IPV history and child trauma symptoms, although other studies have documented a significant association between chronicity and severity of maternal IPV history and child adjustment problems (12). Although frequency of violent events were measured in the present study, type and severity of IPV were not, which may account for these differences. In addition, maternal treatment history may also have further attenuated this association. Future research addressing child trauma symptoms needs to addresses the different characteristics of IPV, as well as the exposure of family members to differing types of violence, such as in the media, in the schools and in the community.

Lastly, the present study explored the notion of differential maternal treatment of children exposed to IPV. Mothers were observed to direct more positive behaviours towards older siblings than younger siblings, but there were no significant differences in the negative behaviours they directed towards their children. However, since older siblings also directed more positive behaviours towards their mothers than their younger counterparts, it is unclear whether mothers or their older children were driving these positive interactions. These results are particularly interesting considering that older siblings demonstrated significantly more trauma symptoms as compared to younger siblings.

The concept of differential treatment should be distinguished from preferential treatment; differential treatment refers to treating each child within the family differently based on developmentally appropriate characteristics, such as age, gender, personality, etc. This is quite different from preferential treatment that is based on parental favoritism, in which one sibling feels disfavored while the other feels preferred, and which is commonly associated with negative sibling interactions (35). Past research has shown that even young children can understand and detect the difference between the two (36). In the present study, mothers were observed with each of their children separately, rather than with both children together. When alone with older siblings, mothers may have been more attuned to their more serious traumatology, and engaged in more positive interactions to more effectively meet their children's needs.

This notion of maternal attunement and compensatory strategies has been found in other studies primarily with mothers and their infants and younger children, although it clearly also has bearing for families with school-aged and adolescent children (17). Whether mothers engage in more positive interactions with older siblings when younger siblings are present is an important question for future research that may have important implications for child adjustment in IPV-affected families. It should be noted that the differences in mother-child interaction observed when mothers engaged with younger and older siblings separately in the present study were not associated with child trauma symptoms, lending further support to the notion that their differential treatment of siblings reflected sensitivity in parenting. Overall, these findings provide evidence for positive reciprocal dyadic interaction and mutual influence between mothers and children in families with a history of IPV.

The present findings underline the importance of using observational methods to assess the quality of mother-child relationships. While the observed micro-level interactions between mothers and their children were predictive of trauma symptoms for younger siblings, future research should include multi-method assessments of mother-child relationships that incorporate the perspectives of the mothers and children themselves. Future replication with larger heterogeneous samples, compared with samples without a history of IPV, would also strengthen the validity of these findings.

Sibling trauma symptoms were found to significantly influence one another; however, this was more pronounced for younger siblings in families with high maternal stress. Considering these findings from a developmental psychopathology perspective, younger siblings appeared to be more strongly influenced by negative mother-child interactions and older sibling trauma symptoms under these particular conditions.

Unfortunately, older sibling trauma symptoms were not adequately explained in the present study. Future research should explore other potential factors that may contribute to the trauma symptoms of older siblings, including individual characteristics such as temperament, personality, and co-morbidity with other adjustment problems such as depression and anxiety. Lastly, as noted earlier, future research should also include assessments of maternal functioning, such as post-traumatic stress symptoms (PTSS), depression or other health issues, which may also impact children's trauma symptoms.

In addition, children exposed to IPV are often exposed to violence in their communities and are victims of parental abuse and neglect as well as the impact of these serious risk factors may significantly influence children's trauma symptoms (37, 38).

In summary, the present study broke new ground by identifying maternal stress, the quality of the mother-child relationship and sibling symptoms as important mechanisms that account for variability in child trauma symptoms. Our findings lend support to a growing literature that suggests mothers may buffer the detrimental effects of IPV exposure through compensatory strategies including warmth, heightened sensitivity and attunement to their children.

The present study should be considered as a first step towards better understanding the influences of familial factors on the trauma symptoms of children exposed to IPV. Next steps should include how mother and sibling trauma symptoms interact to influence the adjustment of these children. Future work should also take a closer look at the quality of sibling relationships in IPV-affected families. Lastly, a comparison of mother-child interaction that involved both siblings simultaneously would provide a more depth examination of potential maternal differential treatment, and provide a more complete picture of how these unique relationships may influence child trauma symptoms in families with a history of IPV.

ACKNOWLEDGMENTS

This research was supported by Social Sciences and Humanities Research Council of Canada Grant 410-96-0311 awarded to Caroline C Piotrowski, Principal Investigator. This work also appeared in Dupont M, Renaud J, eds. Siblings: Social adjustments, interaction and family synamics. New York: Nova Science, 2012. The authors acknowledge the work of Ketan Tailor and Janelle Hoffman, for helping to establish inter-rater reliability. Conflict of interest: None.

REFERENCES

[1]   Carpenter GL, Stacks AM. Developmental effects of exposure to intimate partner violence in early childhood: a review of the literature. Child Youth Serv Rev 2009;31(8):831-9.

[2]   Evans S, Davies C, DiLillo D. Exposure to domestic violence: A meta-analysis of child and adolescent outcomes. Aggress Violent Behav 2008;13(2):131-40.

[3]   Pinheiro PS. World report on violence against children; Secretary-General's study on violence against children. New York: United Nations, 2006:257.

[4]   DeBoard-Lucas R, Grych J. Children's perceptions of intimate partner violence: causes, consequences, and coping. J Fam Violence 2011;26: 343-54.

[5]   Graham-Bermann SA, De Voe ER, Mattis JS, Lynch S, Thomas SA. Ecological predictors of traumatic stress symptoms in Caucasian and ethnic minority children exposed to intimate partner violence. Violence Against Women 2006;12(7):663-92.

[6]   Margolin G, Vickerman K. Posttraumatic stress in children and adolescents exposed to family violence: I. Overview and issues. Professional Psychol Res Pract 2007;38(6):613-9.

[7]   Gewirtz AH, Edleson JL. Young children's exposure to intimate partner violence: Towards a developmental risk and resilience framework for research and intervention. J Fam Violence 2007;22(3):151-63.

[8]   Cowan P, Cowan C. Developmental Psychopathology from family systems and family risk factors perspectives: implications for family research, practice, and policy. In: Cicchetti D, Cohen, D, eds. Developmental psychopathology, 2nd ed. Hoboken, NJ: Wiley, 2006:530-87.

[9]   Graham-Bermann SA, Gruber G, Howell KH, Girz L. Factors discriminating among profiles of resilience and psychopathology in children exposed to intimate partner violence (IPV). Child Abuse Negl 2009;33(9):648-60.

[10]   Scarr S, Grajek S. Similarities and differences among siblings. In: Lamb M, Sutton-Smith B, eds. Sibling relationships: their nature and significance across the lifespan. Hillsdale: Erlbaum, 1982:357–81.

[11]   Piotrowski CC. Patterns of adjustment among siblings exposed to intimate partner violence. J Fam Psychol 2011;25(1):19-28.

[12]   Lang JM, Stover CS. Symptom patterns among youth exposed to intimate partner violence. J Fam Violence 2009;23(3):619-29.

[13]   Skopp N, McDonald R, Manke B, Jouriles E. Siblings in domestically violent families: experiences of interparent conflict and adjustment problems. J Fam Psychol 2005;19(2):324-33.

[14]   Owen AE, Thompson MP, Kaslow NJ. Family variables that mediate the relations between intimate partner violence (IPV) and child adjustment. J Fam Violence 2006;24:433-45.

[15]   Gewirtz AH, DeGarmo DS, Medhanie A. Effects of mother's parenting practices on child internalizing trajectories following partner violence. J Fam Psychol 2011;25(1):29-38.

[16]   Huth-Bocks A, Hughes H. Parenting stress, parenting behavior, and children's adjustment in families experiencing intimate partner violence. J Fam Violence 2008;23:243-51.

[17]   Letourneau L, Fedick B, Willms D. Mothering and domestic violence: a longitudinal analysis. J Fam Violence 2007;22(8):649-59.

[18]   Zerk D, Mertin P, Proeve M. Domestic violence and maternal reports of young children's functioning. J Fam Violence 2009;24(7):423–32.

[19]   Levendosky AA, Graham-Bermann SA. Trauma and parenting in battered women. J Aggress Maltreat Trauma 2000;3(1):25-35.

[20]   Richmond MK, Stocker CM, Rienks S. Longitudinal associations between sibling relationship quality, parental differential treatment, and children's adjustment. J Fam Psychol 2005;19:550-9.

[21]   Statistics Canada. Income in Canada 1998 [internet] Ottawa, Ontario; 1998 [internet]. URL: http://www.statcan.gc.ca/pub/75-202-x/75-202-x1998000-eng.pdf.

[22]   Robin AL, Foster SL. Negotiating parent-adolescent conflict: a behavioral-family systems approach. New York: Guilford,1989.

[23]   Achenbach TM. Manual for the Child Behavior Checklist 4-18 and 1991 Profile. Burlington: University Vermont, 1991.

[24]   Dehon C, Scheeringa MS. Screening for preschool posttraumatic stress disorder with the child behavior checklist. J Pediatr Psychol 2006;31(4):431-5.

[25]   Wolfe VV, Gentile C, Wolfe DA. The impact of sexual abuse on children: a PTSD formulation. Behav Ther 1989;20(2):215-28.

[26]   Straus MA. Measuring intrafamily conflict and violence: The Conflict Tactics Scales. J Marriage Fam 1979;41(1):75–88.

[27]   Abidin R. Parenting Stress Index. New York, NY: Pediatric Psychology Press, 1995.

[28]   Aiken LS, West SG. Multiple regression: testing and interpreting interactions. Newbury Park, CA: Sage, 1991.

[29]   Osofsky JD. Prevalence of children's exposure to domestic violence and child maltreatment: implications for prevention and intervention. Clin Child Fam Psychol Rev 2003;6(3):161-70.

[30]   Gamble WC, Jin Yu J, Card NA. Self-representations in early adolescence: variations in sibling similarity by sex composition and sibling relationship qualities. Soc Dev 2009;19(1):148-69.

[31]   Tucker CJ, Updegraff K, Baril ME. Who's the boss? Patterns of control in adolescents' sibling relationships. Fam Relat 2010;59(5):520–32.

[32]   Cummings E, El-Sheikh M, Kouros C, Buckhalt J. Children and violence: the role of children's regulation in the marital aggression-child adjustment link. Clin Child Fam Psychol Rev 2009;12(1): 3–15.

[33]   Natsuaki MN, Ge X, Reiss D, Neiderhiser JM. Aggressive behavior between siblings and the development of externalizing problems: evidence from a genetically sensitive study. Dev Psychol 2009;45(4):1009-18.

[34]   Müller JM, Achtergarde S, Furniss T. The influence of maternal psychopathology on ratings of child psychiatric symptoms: an SEM analysis on cross-informant agreement. Eur Child Adolesc Psychiatry 2011;20(5):241-52.

[35]   Meunier JC, Roskam I, Stievenart M, van de Moortele G, Browne DT, Kumara A. Externalizing behavior trajectories: the role of parenting, sibling relationships and child personality. J Appl Dev Psychol 2011;32(1):20-33.

[36]   Kowal AK, Krull JL, Kramer L. Shared understanding of parental differential treatment in families. Soc Dev 2006;15(2):276–95.

[37]   Herrenkohl TI, Sousa C, Tajima EA, Herrenkohl RC, Moylan CA. Intersection of child abuse and children's exposure to domestic violence. Trauma Violence Abuse 2008; 9(84):84-99.

[38]   Kennedy A, Bybee D, Sullivan C, Greeson M. The effects of community and family violence exposure on anxiety trajectories during middle childhood: the role of family social support as a moderator. J Clin Chil Adolesc Psychol 2009;38(3):365-79.

In: Children, Violence and Bullying
Editors: J Merrick, I Kandel and H A Omar

ISBN: 978-1-62948-342-9
© 2014 Nova Science Publishers, Inc.

Chapter 6

AUSTRALIA: CHILD PROTECTION SERVICE DELIVERY DEVELOPMENT

Jing Sun, PhD[*1] *and Nicholas Buys, PhD*[2]
[1]School of Public Health and Griffith Health Institute. Griffith University,
Logan campus, Meadowbrook
[2]Health Group and Griffith Health Institute, Griffith University,
Gold Coast campus, Parkland, Australia

ABSTRACT

In this chapter we examine child protection service delivery model development in Australia. Child maltreatment and the need to protect children from harm and prevent child abuse and neglect has become a significant clinical and community concern in Queensland. In Queensland Health Strategic policy framework for children's and young people's health clearly provided strategic direction in which "collaborative whole of government policy development and implementation initiatives" will be supported. Queensland Health, as a key stakeholder in the child protection work, has provided services in identification and report suspicion of child abuse and neglect. To continue this role, a contemporary and effective service model to incorporate strategies and implementation plan in child protection is needed. The aim of the Child Protection Service Delivery Project is to develop a comprehensive and effective child protection service model. It is critical that this framework is evidenced-based and informed by the best evidence and practices in child protection. Griffith University was committed to undertake the literature review to support of the work of the project team in Service Framework development and implementation. This report presents the key findings from the literature review for use by the project team.

* Correspondence: Jing Sun, PhD, School of Public Health, Griffith University and Griffith Health Institute, Griffith University, Logan campus, Meadowbrook Q4131 Australia. E-mail: j.sun@griffith.edu.au.

INTRODUCTION

Child maltreatment remains a major public-health and social-welfare problem in high-income countries. Every year, about 4–16% of children are physically abused and one in ten is neglected or psychologically abused. During childhood, between 5% and 10% of girls and up to 5% of boys are exposed to penetrative sexual abuse, and up to three times this number are exposed to any type of sexual abuse. However, official rates for substantiated child maltreatment indicate less than a tenth of this burden. Exposure to multiple types and repeated episodes of maltreatment is associated with increased risks of severe maltreatment and psychological consequences. Child maltreatment substantially contributes to child mortality and morbidity and has long lasting effects on mental health, drug and alcohol misuse (especially in girls), risky sexual behaviour, obesity, and criminal behaviour, which persist into adulthood. Neglect is at least as damaging as physical or sexual abuse in the long term but has received the least scientific and public attention. The high burden and serious and long-term consequences of child maltreatment warrant increased investment in preventive and therapeutic strategies from early childhood.

While important advances have been made over the past 30 years in approaches to prevention of maltreatment and its associated impairment in the science of preventive health, these advances have paradoxically served to improve nurse-parents relationship or parenting skills at individual level and the effectiveness of the programmes have not been tested by the rigorous methodological design, such as RCT design.

There is insufficient evidence of the effectiveness of services in improving objective measures of abuse and neglect. The existing programs, for example, in Durham, NC, USA, a preventive system has been implemented based on principles of a system of care, defined as a comprehensive range of mental-health resources and other support services organised into a network to meet the needs of children and families. Researchers are proposing to use official rates of child maltreatment, with other indices, including visits to hospital emergency departments, injuries, and anonymous surveys of parents about parenting practices. A second example of a community-based intervention, Strong Communities for Children, is being assessed by Melton and colleagues in two South Carolina counties. This approach involves a comprehensive strategy of engaging all sectors of everyday life; it relies on volunteers and organisations to increase the support for families of young children. Community-based initiatives are attractive as a public-health approach to reducing child maltreatment, such programmes have not been evaluated. Whether such approaches reduce maltreatment is unclear, despite their promising theoretical foundation.

The aim of the Child Protection Service Delivery Project is to develop a comprehensive and effective child protection service model. It is critical that this framework is evidenced-based and informed by the best evidence and practices in child protection. This report presents the key findings from the literature review for use by the project team.

SECTION 1: PURPOSE, SCOPE AND METHODOLOGY

The literature was completed during the period June 2007 – June 2008 with the primary purpose of the literature review is to:

- Inform and support the development of child protection service delivery framework in Central Area Service District.
- Ensure the model is evidence-based and encompass the current effective practices around the world.

To achieve this purpose, the methods for the literature review included the following: An extensive national and international literature search has been conducted using a variety of databases including:

Academic databases:
- Medline from 1966 to December 2007
- ProQuest from 1980 to 2007,
- Sciencedirect 1980 to 2007,
- Balckwell Syndergy from 1966 to 2007.

Australian:
- Australian Institute of Family Studies Library Catalogue.
- Australian Public Affairs Information Service.
- Australian Family & Society Abstracts.
- CINCH (Australian Criminology Database).
- National clearinghouses in the fileds of child protection, health and domestic violence.

International:
- CareData
- Child Abuse, Child Welfare and Adoption (NISC).
- Educational Resources Information Clearinghouse.
- National Criminal Justice Reference Service.
- Sociological Abstracts.
- Social Services Abstracts.

For identifying research on organisational risk factors, management, recruitment and assessment, search words included:
- child and worker;
- staff and child;
- exploitation and institutions
- recruitment and child;
- actuarial and child; and
- actuarial and risk and assessment.

For identifying research on child-related and perpetrator-related risk factors, search words included:
- child abuse;
- child abuser;

Literature search criteria

The key words used for the searching were: Child abuse in conjunction with "physical" and "neglect". The results were filtered to exclude reports and articles published before 1980, those not relating people, and material not published in English. The articles found in the search were subdivided into the following categories:

- Clinical governance
- Workforce development
- Early prevention and intervention
- Partnership
- Communication and coordination
- Core activities
- Culturally and diverse background population

Articles with core activities were sought with the terms "case management" or "risk assessment". Additionally, the Child Abuse Quarterly Review was reviewed for research on child maltreatment and also the journal "Child Abuse and Neglect was searched from January 1995 to December 2007.

While the interface of child protection issues with health systems is a common concern, no service framework at district level is available either from literature review or from interstate. This suggests that there is no clear framework for the development of service model can be found. On the basis of this status, the research team was required to determine relevant topics and issues to guide the selection and examination of the literature. After consultation with Child Protection Project team, the concept of Child Protection Service Delivery Framework was interpreted and have the following two core dimensions:

1. Clinical governance
2. Workforce development
3. Early prevention and intervention
4. Partnership, communication and coordination
5. Core activities

These seven dimensions were used a guide in examining the literature for its relevance to the development and implementation of child protective service model in Central Health Service District in Queensland health. Further analyses were provided by consideration of key activities in child protection in clinical governance after reviewing clinical governance literature:

- Responsibilities articulated for district, organisation and individual level for child safety and quality
- Clinician and consumer involvement

These key activities are consistent with the Queensland Health *clinical Governance Domain (2005)* document that responsibilities across different levels were articulated.

This report presents seven messages from the literature considered critical to the development and implementation of a child protection service delivery model.

SECTION 2: LITERATURE REVIEW

Message 1: Clinical governance

The Australian Council of Healthcare Standards (1), in 2004, defined clinical governance as:

> "the system by which the governing body, managers and clinicians share responsibility and are held accountable for patient safety, minimising risks to consumers and for continuously monitoring and improving the quality of care"

Clinical governance is the set of processes and systems which ensure the safety and highest quality of the process of care. Clinical governance is both systems for accountability, oversight and systematic improvement of care and a set of checks and reviews whereby teams and communities of clinicians oversee and systematically improve the processes and practices of care (2). It has been introduced in the 1990s in the National Health Service in the United Kindom. It has become popular as a response to a series of concerns about the quality and safety of health care in the UK, Canada and Australia (3).

Clinical governance is associated more closed with the ward, unit, department, health centre and clinic. One key point is that governance of all types begins at the highest level, and it is a leadership issue to set organisational agendas for corporate, district and clinical governance. This means that boards and executive groups need to be highly vigilant. Having adequate reporting mechanisms and reviewing clinical and organisational performance through accurate data on a regular basis are preconditions for effective board and executive leadership. Board members and executives need to assure themselves that the organisation is performing effectively, that services are being delivered according to predefined standards and that mechanisms are in place to take remedial action when problems are encountered.

It has been recognised that describing the clinical governance framework for government, district and area service level in explicit terms is important for a number of reasons:

- It provides a clear and transparent communication to all stakeholders of the organisation's intentions and expectations in relation to the delivery of care.
- It clarifies roles and responsibilities of consumers and staff across the organisation but also explicitly demonstrates the value and contribution these people bring to the service, and the interdependence of each person's roles and responsibilities.
- It allows operationalization through the inclusion of relevant elements of the clinical governance framework in job descriptions, staff selection processes, performance review, education and training needs analysis, the building of staff and service capacity, and the testing and improvement of the framework's elements.

The application of clinical governance in a health care setting in Australia is new and the success of the implementation of the clinical governance framework has not been evaluated.

But a number of common principles have been proposed across Australia (4):

- **Collaborative relationship between clinicians and managers in which the specific roles and responsibilities of each are made explicit, are understood by the other and are complementary**. This can be understood as the highly trained and skilled clinicians provide increasingly complex, evidenced-based care to high-risk patients in collaboration with managers who have the high level training and skills to manage and to change highly complex, high-risk health systems (2). There are roles and responsibilities in relation to Clinical governance which range from the consumer of mental health services through to government jurisdictions. Specifically, consumer can drive clinical governance process through active participation in their own care, but also in their interaction with health services (e.g., through the complaints process and participation in health service committee). At the other end of the spectrum, the role of government is to develop policy and legislation that promotes and supports the notion of clinical governance, including the sharing of the risks involved as a system becomes more transparent and accountable (2).

- **Safeguarding principles in clinical risk management**. Doctors play a crucial role in protecting children from abuse and neglect (5). In a review undertaken in MPS in UK during 2007, 526 complaints made against practitioners in primary care during 2006 were analysed. Of these, 13 percent (66) were complaints about care given to a child or young person under the age of 18 years. The main reasons for complaints are: failure or delay in diagnosis; attitude or rudeness of the doctor, nurse or other practice staff; failure or delay in referral; and failure to examine or inadequate examination. Those complaints that involved problems with communication were predominantly in the age range of children under 11 years, suggesting parents-rather than children-experienced difficulties in communicating with doctors. There is a legal and professional duty for all doctors to consider the welfare of children and to ensure that advice provided, either to the child or young person or to their parents or carers, is appropriate and has taken into account any impact that this may have on the ultimate safety of the individual (5). The key message from the clinical governance framework for all practitioners is to seek advice when in doubt and at the earliest opportunity.

- **Roles and responsibilities of doctors and clinicians**. In most industrialised countries, reforming how health care is organised and monitored has become a political imperative. The English Department of Health (6) introduce a strategy to improve quality of health care services. 'Clinical governance' was identified as the mechanism to systematically improve standards of clinical care. Early guidance identified its components: evidence-based practice, audit, risk management, mechanisms to monitor the outcome of care, lifelong learning among clinicians and systems for managing poor performance. Health care providers were required to identify a clinician at board level with responsibility for clinical governance, supported by a board-level clinical governance committee.
Initial studies among managers and clinicians revealed some scepticism, especially as some components, such as clinical audit, were already perceived as having a limited effect on quality. Key barriers to successful implementation were identified:

lack of time, staff support and financial resources and issues related to organizational culture.

- **Monitoring, clinical supervision of nurses**: In the past decade, the importance of clinical supervision for nurses has been emphasized in a range of UK government and professional policy document (6).The literature which examines the function of supervision specially in the field of child protection is universally informed by reports of the inquiries into the deaths of children and the legislation and guidance which follow form these inquiries (7). The differing functions of supervision in the field of child protection are explored by Ruston and Nathan (8). Although their paper focuses on supervision in social work, their discussion of the complexities of supervision in pertinent to nursing and health professionals. Ruston and Nathan addressed that clinical supervision has management, support, educational and professional development functions. They argue that in the field of child protection, supervision both needs to be "inquisitorial", to ensure that attention is given to the detail of work, and at the same time must deal with the highly emotional nature of the work. This has major implications for the training of supervisors, who, simultaneously, hold the role of overseeing the investigation and holding line management responsibility for decision-making, being an 'expert adviser' and facilitating staff development. While nurses would not be primary investigators in child protection work, these functions of supervision would apply to those directly involved in child protection work. Many nurses felt that it was important that supervision be provided by a line manager in order to ensure accountability. While supervision will often involve discussion about particular case, a feature of clinical supervision should be the development of skills and knowledge across a range of practice situations (9).

- **Effectiveness of clinical governance**: Medical audits was the first type of quality improvement activity to be implemented widely in the National Helath Service in UK. A frequently used definition of audit is in the UK is " a quality improvement process that seeks to improve patient care and outcomes through systematic review of care against explicit criteria and the implementation of change. Where indicated, changes are implemented at an individual, team, or service level and further monitoring is used toe confirm improvement in health care delivery. While clinical audit is led by clinicians, boards and executives should ensure that regular and widespread clinical audit activity is occurring throughout health care organisations within their ambit of responsibility. Opinions about its effectiveness is mixed in UK (10). Many saw audit solely as an educational exercise for junior doctors. Its contribution was limited by lack of methodological rigours and the poor quality of recommendations that resulted. Moreover, the junior doctors who undertook audits had often moved on before the recommendations could be implemented, resulting in a loos of momentum. Among those with a more positive view, national audits were seen as especially useful. This was particularly true when they had been developed with clinical input. Others highlighted the benefits of audits that were able to identify areas of clinical risk or which explored a problem arising from a clinical incident in detail. Audit meetings were one mechanism for bringing together departments on different hospital sites, providing a building block for standardisation of services. Effective audits were seen as those that involved the whole team, including other health care professionals, and had consultant input into both the conduct of the audit and the implementation of the recommendations (10).

- **A more conducive cultural climate is facilitated by the use of a variety of approaches.** These include reviewing and aligning policies, structures and processes within a clear vision and framework of goals related to quality improvement, reviewing and celebrating positive behaviours, involving staff in the process of change with support for any training and development needs, improving the effectiveness of communication across the organization and providing teams with time and space to reflect on their performance. All have been shown to have a positive effect (11-13).

Evidence based management

Clinical governance is both the systems for accountability, oversight and systematic improvement of care (2). The trend towards debating the use of sound evidence as a basis for management of decision-making is growing. A study in Queensland in Australia found it has been effective to apply clinical governance principles to the development of enhanced systems of performance management for nursing, medical and technical staff in the local department. They focused on: staff appraisal and ensuring continuing professional development (2), so that all personnel associated with the initiative maintain current knowledge of clinical governance in which include professional performance/technical quality of care, resource use/efficiency, risk management, consumer/customer satisfaction. The strength of these initiatives is closely tied to developing an environment where blame is minimised and professional education maximised for all staff. For the Australian Council for Safety and Quality in Health Care, making arrangements to credential health professionals and improving health professional orientation programs seem consistent with the priority areas of "supporting those who work in the health care system" (14).

It is widely acknowledged that human errors in health care is inevitable and most human errors that occur are largely the consequences of deficiencies in the "system", rather that individuals. Clinical governances have been found critical to the successful development and implantation of an effective "system" approach to patient safety in health care (15). Whereas clinical governance at corporate level refers to a system by which companies are directed and controlled by boards of directors, shareholders, auditors. Clinical governance refers to a whole system cultural change which provides the means of developing organisational capability to deliver sustainable, accountable, patient-focused, quality-assured health care. Developing this organisational capability, in turn, rests on the following core processes: clinical audit, clinical effectiveness, clinical risk management, quality assurance, and organisational and staff development.

Clinical risk management is a key driver of patient safety processes within a clinical governance structure. There is a variation observed in the knowledge, beliefs and attitudes or experienced staff concerning clinical governance and clinical risk management processes because

- the clinical governance and CRM processes currently being operationalised in the Australian health care sector being relatively new in Australia.

- there is a lack of attention to these issues in the Australian child protection literature.
- a lack of education opportunities at both undergraduate and post registration levels in nurses to develop knowledge and skills relevant to clinical governance and CRM.
- the predictable resistance of a minority to change (3, 16).

Integrating this message with the daily work of district service work depends upon an identification for all staff and consumers their roles, expectations and contribution in regards to clinical governance. Reforming how health care is organised and monitored has become a political imperative in most industrialised countries, and concerns related to the medical professions abilities to ensure accountability among its members.

Role of health service

Child Protection Health Service in developed countries (e.g., U.S., Canada, Australia) provides child focused services to protect children and young people from significant harm as a result of abuse or neglect within the family unit and to ensure that children and young people receive services to deal with the impact of abuse and neglect on their well being and development. The Child Protection Health Service is based on the principle that the best protection for children is usually within the family, however the paramount consideration is the child's safety and well being. The role of the Child Protection Health Service is to:

- provide notifications to the child protection service or child welfare service.
- believe on reasonable grounds that a child is in need of protection because of abuse or neglect
- investigate matters where it is believed that a child is at risk of significant harm
- refer children and families to services that assist in providing the ongoing safety and well being of the children.
- take matters before the Children's Court if the child's safety cannot be ensured within the family.

Specifically, child protection health service have the following roles:

a. Assessment and diagnosis

Detection of child abuse is dependent on the clinician's ability to recognise suspicious injuries, do a careful and complete physical examination with the judicious use of ancillary tests, and to consider whether the history reasonably explains the physical findings. Absence of explanation for the injury, changing explanations, or one that is inconsistent with the child's developmental capabilities raises concern about abuse, and does delay in seeking medical care.

Bruises are the most common manifestation of physical abuse (17). Childhood burns, bone fractures, skull fractures, abusive head injury with subdural haemorrhage, retinal haemorrhages and brain injury might be the signs of child physical abuse (17).

Detection of abuse is dependent on the clinician's ability to recognise suspicious injuries, do a careful and complete physical examination with the judicious use of ancillary tests, and to consider whether the history reasonably explains the physical findings. Absence of explanation for the injury, changing explanations, or one that is inconsistent with the child's development capabilities raises concern about abuse, as does delay in seeking medical care. A detailed medical history should include previous trauma, admissions to hospital, chronic illness, and adherence to treatment. A family history of easy bruising or fracture is important to elicit. Questions about substance or alcohol abuse, mental illness, intimate partner violence, discipline practices, stressors or previous involvement of child protection services can be difficult to ask, but provide valuable insight into a family's functioning. Careful documentation, ideally with photographs, is necessary. An interdisciplinary approach is the best way to assess all possible risk factors; many hospital have developed interdisciplinary team for this purpose (17).

Bruises, bite marks, childhood burns are frequently due to abuse. Bone fractures are the second most common presentation of physical abuse after soft tissue injuries. Many of complex fracture of both sides of the skull and depressed or growing fractures are typical of abuse. The differential diagnosis of fractures due to abuse includes non-inflicted injury, trauma during delivery, osteogenesis imperfecta, rickets, copper deficiency, Caffey's disease, congenital syphilis, osteopenia of infancy, osteomyyelitis, and normal variants. The American Academy of Pediatrics recommends a mandatory skeletal survey in all cases of suspected physical abuse in children aged under 2 years. Follow-up skeletal surveys 10 or more days later can help to detect occult fractures that might not have been apparent on first images (18).

Abusive head injuries result from mechanisms including shaking, direct impact, penetration, and asphyxiation or hypoxia, alone or in combination. Hence, the term abusive head trauma is recommended. The findings of abusive head trauma, include subdural haemorrhage, retinal haemorrhages, and brain injury, particularly diffuse axonal injury, but these might not all be present. Eye examination by an ophthalmologist with indirect ophthalmoscopy and dilated pupils is essential to properly assess the retina. CT remains the initial imaging modality for the child with possible abusive head trauma.

Neglect is the most prevalent form of child maltreatment in USA, UK and other countries with potentially severe and long-lasting sequelae. Neglect has several manifestation that physicians might encounter. Initial question a physician should consider are: Is this neglect? Have the circumstances harmed the child, or jeopardised the child's health or safety? There are usually many interacting factors that contribute to neglect. This situation demands a comprehensive assessment of possible underpinning problems – with child, parent, family and community (19).

b. Reporting and documentation

Many countries have laws mandating physicians and nurses to refer suspicious of child abuse or neglect to designated child welfare agencies. The referrer does not need to be certain that maltreatment has taken place. The amount of suspicion that meets the threshold for reporting might be a judgment call. Consultation with an interdisciplinary team that is expert in child maltreatment, a pediatric expert, or the child welfare agencies, can help to make this decision. Reporting of child maltreatment is not easy (20, 21). But ensuring the child's safety is the priority. Physicians should inform families directly of their concerns and their report in a supportive manner. The referral can be explained as an effort to clarify the situation and provide help, or as a professional and legal responsibility. To explain what the ensuing process will probably include is useful. Physicians normally work cooperatively with the public agency to help ensure children's and families' needs are met.

c. Formal management of child care

Despite the overwhelming consensus that they would prefer to see the more difficult child care issues dealt with by other disciplines, particularly social work. Public health nurses they had to be involved to some extent in the formal handling of child abuse cases: their adherence to the Department of Health Child Abuse Guidelines and their involvement in case conferences. It did not appear as though the nurses say guidelines as particularly helpful or relevant. The case conference in child care cases, and particularly in cases of suspected or actual child abuse, is to create a forum for the exchange of information between all the relevant professionals and to facilitate decision-making for the future management of the case. The perception of case conferences were uniformly negative: it was suggested that they were poorly chaired, that clear decisions rarely emanated from them, that they wasted nurses time, and as often as not, responsibility for future management of the case would be allocated solely to the public health nurses. An example from UK study provided an example of clinical governance in child protection (22).

1. Roles and responsibilities of different staff groups in child protection. A common theme in many was the hierarchical approach with nurses being expected to refer their concerns to doctors, junior doctors to consultants, and emergency staff to paediatricians. Very few emphasised that each individual has a responsibilities for the welfare of children. Several protocols included contact details, most commonly for the named or designated professionals; paediatricians or community paediatricians, the child protection register and social work departments. The most common professional to provide liaison was a nurse practitioner or specialist nurse (31/51, 25.5%)

2. There is currently no scientific evidence to support the use of screening tools or checklists in identifying children at risk of abuse or neglect and no evidence from this or other studies to inform which procedure are effective at identifying children at risk. There was a lack of clarity about the purpose and appropriate use of indicators or concern to identify children at risk. For example, less than 50% of departments (35.2%, 25/71) reported that they used checklists to highlight concerns. Only nine respondents reported the factors they would use to highlight concern, and the median number of items listed was 7 (range 5-14). Some of the suggested items are perceived by professionals to be suggestive of abuse or neglect:
    a. on child protection register
    b. Inconsistent history
    c. Delay in attendance
    d. Parent-child interaction
    e. Child's appearance/behaviour
    f. History and examination do not match
    g. Direct allegation
    h. Injuries of different ages
    i. Frequent attendances
    j. Other features in history
    k. Other features in examination

3. In referral process, a few departments emphasised the importance of backing up referrals in writing, but few included an subsequent check of management. Some

protocols incorporated safeguard-for example, action to take if a child is taken from the department; informing the locality managers or information on contacting the social worker or police urgently if the child is perceived to be at immediate risk.

4. Subsequent management: the most common aspects of subsequent management incorporated in the protocols were guidelines on documentation, details on informing primary care, and action around discharge. However, most protocols provided very little detail beyond initial recognition and referral. Very few included any mention of dealing with the child's presenting complaint, or assessing their medical needs first. One protocol inappropriately commented that nurses should not undertake treatment of any injuries. None of the protocols gave any details on management in cases requiring admission and very few on closing the case if concerns are not verified.

5. There is a lack of interagency work. Effective child protection requires joint working of professionals from different agencies. Information sharing is essential in order to fully evaluate and appropriately respond to possible concerns. Staff should be encouraged to share concerns with other agencies, to respond to requests for information in relation to child protection, and to question other professionals where there are differences in opinion. Concerns about possible child abuse or neglect should normally be shared openly with the parents or carers unless to do so might further increase the risk to the child, or could compromise any criminal investigation. For example some protocols did not mention social service at all. One protocol emphasised that staff should not share information with other agencies until this had been approved by senior managers or professionals until this had been approved by senior managers or professionals. Some of the protocols provided helpful details on how to prepare a report for a case conference or statements for the police.

6. There is a little evidence of a child centred approach in hospital emergence/pediatric department. There were few protocols that retained an emphasis on the wellbeing of the child and none protocols gave any specific guidelines on listening to the child. Only two protocols mentioned the importance of abuse in disabled children, and none referred to cultural, ethnic or gender issues.

Message 2: Workforce development

Health care workers including pediatricians and nurses having been recognised as having a key role in the child protection service in Australia and internationally. Health care workers involved in child protection range from clinical staff who are responsible for conducting specialist medical investigations through to nurses working the community in positions such as school nurses, midwives and health visitors. While child abuse work may constitute one of many responsibilities, nurses and pediatricians are often the first professionals to identify children who have been or are at significant risk of child abuse and neglect. However, the potential for nurses and pediatricians to fulfil this role in many settings is hampered by a perceived lack of training around child protection (23).

1. Child protection training for all health professionals is not adequate in many countries

Most studies showed that the training for child protection workforce is not adequate across many countries. Most literature in workforce development in child protection have highlighted the need for adequate training of health professionals in identification, assessment and intervention in child protection.

Laming (24) recommended that all general practice staff and all those working health care services at primary health care and tertiary health care in regular contact with children, are lack of training in child protection.

Similarly, Hammond (7) commented that ongoing training, including interagency training, in child protection is required, for all health professionals. This suggests that training is not adequate not only by those professionals such as health visitors whose remit is to work with case of child abuse, but by all health staff who interact on a daily basis with the general public.

2. There is a necessity for qualifying training in child protection

The necessity for qualifying and post qualifying training in child protection is also a common recommendation from research which examines the role of all health professionals in child protection. For example, Lupton and colleagues (25) found that lack of child protection training was mentioned as a primary reason for health professionals failing to engage in collaborative work. The report recommends that all health staff should undertake training in this field:

- Training package should include improved standards for the prompt identification of all types of child abuse as well as greater understanding of recent legislation and an appreciation of the medical – legal implications of involvement in the child protection process.
- Training should also enhance understanding of thresholds for intervention, local referral processes, appreciation of roles of other agencies and the means of communicating with them as well as confidence in child protection work. Lupton et al. (2000) argued that differential approach to training is required and that "the content of training should be "assessed against the exposure of different health professionals to child protection issues".
- The findings from inquiries and research suggest that in order to provide an effective child protection service, primary care workers need both the skills and knowledge to identify cases of child abuse and to know their roles and responsibilities, as well as how to liaise with other agencies involved in child protection including social work services, police and legal system.

3. Qualifying and post-qualifying training in child protection for community nurses

The training needs of already qualified nurses in the field of child protection have been identified by a number of authors across the UK (26, 27). Theobald (27) identified that current training provided is minimal and suggested that mandatory qualifying training is required to assist nurses in the identification, assessment and referral procedures in child protection, and continuing education in child protection after registration is vital for children's nurses.

4. Ongoing policy development

There has been policy development in UK, which addresses the concerns in professional training. The Royal College of Nursing (28) has produced guidelines with regard to the extent and level of training required by nurses in child protection. It is suggested that there should be specific training for qualifying nurses and midwifes in child protection led by an identified university lecturer. The three levels of training of health staff is recommended (28):

- Level one would be aimed at all staff including ancillary an office workers in the identification of abuse and the process of child protection.
- Level two, a specialist training, would be aimed at staff who are in contact with children, for example, outpatient appointments.
- Level three, nurses, midwifes, and Accident and Emergency staff who are directly involved in child protection would receive specialist training.

In 2004, the importance of training was highlighted in the review of the role of midwifery and health visiting in the provision by the Chief Nursing officer for the Department of Health in UK (DoH, 2004). The necessity to develop core competences in identifying and supporting vulnerable families across the workforce, through training programs in child protection was acknowledged. Specialist training for school nurses and health visitors was recommended, alongside regular multi-disciplinary training for nurses, midwifes and health visitors regularly involved in child protection work.

In UK, the Health Care Commission said 60% of nurses received basic child protection training. However 58% of services nationally did not have enough trained nurses (28). Thirty-seven percent of nurses had received level two training in child protection. This training enables staff to recognise the signs and symptoms of abuse. It is particularly important that front line nurses are well trained so that they can draw the attention of designated child protection staff to any cases of concern. Seventy percent of services nationally did not have enough trained nurses at this level. This indicates practice nurses should be given more training in child protection with support from specialist children's nurses. Eight-five percent of services in Accident and Emergency departments did not meet the standard training in child protection service (29).

5. Pediatric training in child protection

The scope of millennial primary health care is expanding at a dizzying rate. Doctors' surgeries are expected to treat drug and alcohol dependency, and take on responsibility for child protection, while screening for domestic violence and child abuse and neglect. Given the rising scale of expectations placed on GPs, it is not surprising to find that various inquiries also find them deficient in satisfying the new demands – or indeed in fulfilling their traditional responsibilities, such as in relation to the child abuse and neglect issues. The solution is to provide them with the skill, knowledge, attitudes, and values for modern medical practice.

In Canada, child protection is a neglected area in pediatric training iut seems. The survey conducted by (30) found that among 16 medical schools, there are only three programs had mandatory clinical training for residents, and nine programs offered electives in child protection-but they were taken by only 4.7% of respondent during the previous year. Overall, only 26.8% of the residents said they'd had any kind of clinical instruction in child protection at any time during their medical training. There are 91.6% of residents and 85% of fourth-year residents indicated they needed further training in child protection.

The organisation in UK, UK General Medical Council does not understand child protection matters and has no system for dealing adequately with complaints submitted by parents who claim false allegations of abuse, according to Catherine Williams, from Shefield University.

In Australia

Within Australia and New Zealand, advanced training in child protection falls within the scope of Community Child Health. More recently advanced trainees who train under the Specialist Advisory Committee for Community Child Health, are required to complete three months of training in child protection. In multidisciplinary meetings, the child protection paediatrician may participate with other child protection agency stake-holders in decision aimed to achieve the best child protection outcome. In these forums, the child protection paediatrician is not simply acting in an impartial forensic role but participates in shared decision-making. In their clinical work, child protection paediatrician may be called upon to advocate for the child for services and assess the development and behaviour of children who come from vulnerable populations who may have experienced abuse or neglect (20, 31).

Doctors who take on these tasks need additional opportunities for training and professional development, and a means of accreditation that confirms their expertise to clinical and forensic colleagues and to the judiciary.

Most pediatricians are spending half of their allocated child protection time doing new assessments of children referred into the child protection system from health services. Only 13% of their working week is spent on the ongoing medical follow up of these children. In addition, only 50% of paediatrician continue to manage behavioural or developmental problems identified in these children beyond 6 months (20). This suggests that half these high-risk children receive long-term management elsewhere.

There were one-third of CP pediatrician who reported receiving no training at all, and there were two thirds of CP pediatricians having received less than 4 months of training in child protection prior to completing their FRACP. For those pediatricians who contribute to decisions with other child protection stake-holders in multi-agency meetings, they indicated that they had limited training for this role prior to FRACP, with 50% of pediatricians stating it as less than adequate (20, 31).

A major unmet need appears to be for specific training for staff in child protection work, especially the emotions that it arouses in workers, and what is realistic process to expect. Some staff feel the need for specialist training in therapeutic methods.

In Australia, nurses perceived that child protection was not part of their job responsibility. The nurses who have considerable contacts with children, such as midwives, school nurses and nurses in paediatric wards or acute hospitals did not provide service in child protection reflecting the fact that child protection services are provided by other service departments (23). There is great training need in nurses in Australia. The challenge to provide adequate training to nurses who have identified a need for further knowledge about child protection issues is great, especially given a lack of consensus among most groups of nurses as to what training they require.

Message 3. Early prevention and early intervention

The early identification of child abuse and neglect and early intervention to reduce the degree of harm to children is critical to child development physically and psychologically (29).

The following strategies in early identification and intervention were discussed in the literature review below:

Identify children and parents who fall into high risk parent group. Identification of risk factors: Child maltreatment seldom results from on cause; rather many risk factors usually interact. Factors such as child's disability (32) or a parent with substance abuse and depression (33) predispose children to maltreatment. Within a family, intimate partner violence increases children's risk of abuse (34). In communities, factors such as dangerous neighbourhoods or poor recreational facilities increase risk. Societal factors, such as poverty and associated burdens contribute substantially to risk of maltreatment (35).

Health service
The responsibility for making sure that the needs of children are met and that they are safe within their families is shared between the family, the community and the health department. When adults caring for children do not follow through with their responsibilities, are abusive or exploit their positions of power, then it is the wider child protection system that becomes responsible for taking action. Depending on how serious the risk and harm is to a child's safety and wellbeing will depend on the type of service provided. It is perhaps most useful to think about a continuum of service responses which are divided into primary, secondary and tertiary services. The overall goal of all the services is to prevent child abuse and neglect.

Primary Services
The goal of primary services is to provide support and education for children and families before problems arise. In many cases, primary services prevent abuse and neglect occurring. Primary prevention services are offered to everyone and include ante-natal services, maternal and child health services and human relationship education in schools.

Community attitudes towards violence, children's rights and physical punishment are associated with child abuse. Community education and awareness programs focus on addressing these issues by educating the public about alternatives to abuse, changing social attitudes towards violence, or encouraging community debate about issues such as censorship, family violence, substance abuse and drug use, etc.

1. Primary protection and intervention

Generally, medical response to child maltreatment happen after maltreatment has taken place; prevention is preferable. Physicians can help in several ways (36). A continuing relationship with a family offers opportunities to develop trust and knowledge of their circumstances. Astute observation of parent-child interaction can reveal useful information. For example, does the relationship seem warm and comfortable or tense and hostile?

In many countries, all new births are notified to the nurses and they have a minimum of five contacts during the first year of life which take place at prescribed times. There are minimum prescribed times, although in practice there may be more frequent visits if necessary (37). The school-going child is followed-up through the school nursing service. The routine contact with all young children and their families renders them important roles in the practice of child protection (38). For example, in Ireland, a breakdown of time spent on domiciliary child development visits shows that 82% of time is given over to developmental checks, 1.5% to ante-natal care, 14.7% to visiting vulnerable families and 2.1% to family surveillance (39). Although the pre-coding of these categories renders interpretation of these data difficult, it is likely that visits classified as development also included specific age appropriate advice relating to child care and parenting skills in addition to referral to local support services.

Parent education might help with child rearing, thus diminishing the risk of treatment. Hospital-based programmes for parents of new born babies educating about infant crying and risks of shaking seem to prevent abusive head trauma.

Screening for risk factors and tackling known problem, via referral to social or mental health services, can strengthen families and reduce maltreatment. This role for the physicians fits well with the broad view of health, and a professional mandate to help to ensure children's health and safety (40, 41). Check-ups (preventive care) offer opportunities to screen for psychosocial disorders. Its traditional focus on organ systems can be expanded to subjects such as feelings about the child, the parent's own functioning, possible depression, substance abuse, intimate partner violence, disciplinary approaches, and stressors and supports.

This primary role of advising and supporting parents in preventing poor child health care practices and therefore preventing child neglect and abuse has not yet evaluated. Gough (42) in an extensive review of the literature review on child abuse interventions, suggests that interventions less amenable to evaluation such as education and support may not be evaluated because of the difficulties inherent in measurement of their effectiveness.

Nurses can refer to statutory and voluntary agencies before any problems arise and it may be that in her role as a referral agent she is in some way effective in protecting children at a primary level (43). The Dublin-based Community Mothers' Programme provides an example of how nurses' work be effective, through the identification of community needs, initiation of support programmes and the subsequent referral of children and families to these (43).

2. Community level health service

There are four types of service provision for child protection at primary health care level (44):

1.   *Universal (core) health visiting*: The new birth visit was the cornerstone of the universal health visiting service. Availability of antenatal home visits predicted more postnatal home visits and more frequent group and community-based activities.
2.   *Teamwork delivering core service*: The core service was delivered, in most instances by the health visitor in conjunction with others, including members of the wider primary care team. Where health visitors led skill-mix team, fewer scheduled home visits occurred, but there were more group and community activities overall.
3.   *Extra health visiting:* services offered to individuals once a specific need has been identified, varied in the different areas described. Services included additional home visits by health visitors in 96% of areas and by other team member in 71%. People with postnatal depression could be offered program of visits of 83% and support group in 37% areas. Breast-feeding advisers, parenting education, sleep or behaviour group were available in most of the areas. You mum groups and stop smoking groups were run in 47% to 71% of places. Health visitors described a wide range of other services in pone responses, including domestic violence, drug users and support, menopause, weight management, men's health, language support, speech and language development, learning difficulties, mental health, multiple births, rural health and sexual health.

Secondary prevention

Secondary health services offer programs that identify and reduce the personal and social stresses on parents which can lead to family breakdown and/or child abuse. There are many community based agencies and organisations which support families and help them overcome significant problems. Services include in-home family support, counselling, respite care and various parenting and self-help groups.

Secondary prevention is concerned with the early identification and appropriate referral of families once there is evidence of risk of child abuse and neglect. This secondary orle of the nurses and pediatricians in the early detection of families at risk is grounded in their expertise (developed through education and professional experience) of normal emotional and physical development of children in the context of their families as well as in an in-depth knowledge and awareness of injuries or behaviour likely to be non-accidental in nature (41).

Currently, the formality of placing a child on an "at risk" register is not available in Australia although there have been strong recommendations to put one in place (40, 41). Criteria used by nurses and paediatricians to identify and differentiate between vulnerable and at-risk families need to be explored further. In the absence of an 'at risk' register, there is no formal mechanism for differentiating between 'vulnerable' and 'at-risk' children. Consequently, a family may remain vulnerable and/or 'at risk' indefinitely. In many Western Countries, the need to differentiate these criteria remain largely unarticulated. This has led nurses and paediatricians retaining responsibility for child protection in situations where they have indicated that specialist intervention is required. For example, in some cases, social worker intervention has not followed a request for intervention by the nurses.

For example, the primary and secondary protective interventions by the nurses in Ireland also included weighing the child, giving advice on nutrition, requesting consent form the parents for various medical checks, e.g., audiology, and encouraging parents to keep various appointments. Nurses also discussed the children who are vulnerable on a number of different occasions with the superintendent nurses, social worker, general practitioner, are medical officer and school. However, the monitoring role of the nurses is often limited by their continuing involvement in case conference on the family and the various contacts she made with other personnel involved in the case. A Canadian study which included 28 nurses concluded that they felt themselves powerless to bring about changes that could benefit clients because they

Tertiary health services

The study conducted by Greenwalt, Sklare, and Portes (45) in America has described the current practice of some mental health practitioners in the treatment of cases involving physical child abuse. The family is considered the primary client most frequently with the focus of the family therapy being to stop the abuse and to improve family relationships. Whether this focus should be considered the primary therapeutic goal needs further longitudinal research on the abused child.

One would expect physically abused children to receive the help needed to stabilize their lives and become productive members of society as soon as possible. However, while some authorities recognize the importance of providing treatment for the abused child (46), little can be found in the literature about the treatment actually provided the victim (47).

Table 1. Percentage of total treatment using each type of therapy

Therapy *M SD*	M	SD
Family Therapy	23.90	16.54
Individual Therapy for Abused Child	22.90	14.21
Individual Therapy for Perpetrator	21.26	14.37
Group Therapy for Perpetrator	8.36	11.97
Group Therapy for Abused Child	7.20	10.74
Couple Therapy	6.69	10.93
Individual Therapy for Non-offending Parent	5.27	7.10
Group Therapy for Non-offending Parent	2.80	6.19
Other Therapy	1.24	8.77

Greater emphasis appears to be placed on the treatment of the parents and the safety of the child (48) than on overcoming the effects of the abuse on the child. The literature is limited with publications that discuss a typical treatment plan of cases involving physical child abuse. Of those found, White (49) notes mental health services to the abused child only as a part of foster care, residential care, or day care (See Table 1) but not in the context of health service.

Over time, attitudes towards children have changed dramatically and we can understand much about how a society values its children by the laws and services it has to protect them. The child protection system both reflects and shapes community values and expectations. As such, each part of the child protection system—families, the general community, community agencies, professionals working with children, police and government— has a significant role to play to ensure that children are kept safe and well.

Message 4: Partnership, communication and coordination

1. Interagency coordination and collaboration
Ensuring effective interagency and inter-professional coordination and collaboration has been a common them and an ongoing, significant issue for the provision of both child protection and family support services of many years. A coordinated response to the problem of child maltreatment can produce:

- more effective in risk assessment
- greater efficiency in the use of resources
- improved service delivery by the avoidance of duplication and overlap between existing services
- clarification of agency or professional roles and responsibilities in frontier problems and demarcation disputes; and
- the delivery of comprehensive services

2. The mechanism of coordination
There is a potential for agencies to develop a large variety of inter-organisational links for the purpose of coordinated service delivery. There may range from low-key, unstructured, informal links between workers from different agencies, to the formalised interrelationships with may occur with agencies or professions in particular organistaional networks, to highly formalised, centralised coordinated structures (50). The formal structures or mechanisms that commonly facilitate interagency and interprofessional coordination are referral protocols, case conferencing, and the development of multidisciplinary teams. In Australia, formal referral protocols between health department and social work are perhaps the primary means of communication.

A number of authors have highlighted the important role that informal professional relationships and communication paths can play in combination with formal child protection structures (e.g., Challis et al., 1988). Although an over-reliance on informal communication methods and the circumventing of formal coordination and communication mechanisms may lead to the variety of interagency communication problems identified above, strong informal linkages operating in conjunction with more formal communication structures appear to lead to a more effective interagency network (50).

3. Interdisciplinary group work in the hospital management of child abuse and neglect
The interdisciplinary team at Children's Hospital in the US consisting of a paediatrician, attorney, psychiatric social worker, psychologist, nurse and occasional other consultant, all of whom assist in the management of child abuse and neglect cases seen within the institution. The group was organised in 1970. Since its inception, it has served to focus attention on child abuse and neglect at Children's hospital and an early evaluation suggested its effectiveness in promoting case management and in lessening re-injury. Child abuse and neglect involve many specialities, each of which has differing and unique definitions of the situation presented. For example, a child enters the emergency ward with a fracture, the physician might determine whether the nature of the break indicates inflicted trauma; the social worker interview the child's parents in order to evaluate their capacity to protect the child and to

forma relationship on which might be based a program to prevent the injury from reoccurring; and the attorney might consider the desirability of a restraining order to prevent removal of the child from the hospital prior to a full assessment.

The decision to seek medical evaluation for abuse in contact children generally falls to local child protection social (CPS) workers, so the rate of medical evaluations for contacts varies between respondents. More concerning is the frequency with which child abuse physicians disagree with local CPS workers on the need for medical evaluations of contact children. Frustration with CPS has been recognized as a barrier to appropriate reporting of suspected child maltreatment by general pediatricians.

It is frequent to find that even experts working with multidisciplinary teams report frequent disagreement. As child abuse medicine grows as a discipline, efforts to create and sustain ties between medical and social service teams are needed to improve care of children evaluated for abuse (51).

The research on group process indicates that social cohesion is a most important determinant of its functioning. There is a handbook written by the group which outlines the tasks each member is to perform. It also attempts to standardise decision-making by indicating when various procedures are appropriate. This handbook is felt important because it educates members and lessens arbitrariness, but a latent function is the reduction of conflict. Information sharing is another basis of team consensus. If all members agree that "a mother who was abused in more likely to abuse" then decision-making is simplified and group unity facilitated.

Norms: Group norms also encourage cohesion and harmony. They might be divided into two categories: the task-oriented and the social-emotional. The task emphasis is on consensus decision-making; that is, all members should agree with a particular course of action. If strong differences do occur, especially as between the medical and social work perspectives, nothing is done until they are resolved. If these competing positions seemed impossible to reconcile, the hospital administration was called upon to determine the nature and extent of team involvement. That is, when consensus was not reached, the administrator acted as a mediator, resolving the dispute in a way that was agreeable to all, and thus, lessening the likelihood of a protracted difference of opinion which would undercut group utility. The importance of consensus orientation is its impact on families. If a decision is reached because it flows from the factors of a case, then intervention can be rationally justified. But if a decision is made, not because of case data but because of team dynamics and group unity, then it might assist the team to the detriment of parents and children.

Social-emotional norms include the following: disagreement should be resolved through rational discussion and members should be supportive of one another. Social support is important because of the way the team is defined within the hospital setting. Generally hospital staff does not like trauma cases: they are complex, unpleasant and demanding. These two factors-nature of the cases and unclear relationship with personnel-strain communications and feelings between the team and others and make it more important for the team members to support their colleagues. Team disagreement which is private and that private division of opinion are healthy and lead to the education of individual group members as well as to more effective decision making. The conflicts are handled more privately not publicly, until they are resolved, is the more appropriate focus of the team work.

Roles: Implicit in decision making is the feeling that the person with the most first-hand information should play a pivotal role; that the opinions of outside staff should be respected, if not accepted, that participation should come from all members; that those who have seen the child and/or family describe, while the rest either question or suggest; that the lawyer is the sceptic probing conclusions and emphasising the need for objective data.

Status. Despite the fact that in the larger society, an in the hospital, a physician has greater status than a nurse or social worker that team operates under a norm of collegiality, ie., that all disciplines are equally important in decision-making; that the quality and logic of a suggestion is more important than the person offering it. that no person or role has the right to veto a recommendation acceptable to other group members.

4. Collaboration between organisations: Collaboration between child protection and mental health services in Australia

In the Australian Audit (52), service providers involved in approximately one-quarter of the 1814 programs could be said to be working collaboratively or in partnership with another agency. The partnerships generally involved a generic family support agency working with another, more specialist agency (for example, a drug rehabilitation service). However, in general, the partnerships involved only limited liaison between the agencies in order to refer cases and/or to share knowledge as a means of enhancing their service's response to particular groups of client families. Most of these arrangements did not appear to constitute cross-sectoral working arrangements.

A study was conducted in Queensland, Australia by Darlington and colleagues (53), where child protection and adult mental health are the responsibility of separate government departments-the Department of Families and Queensland Health, respectively. The study reported on data drawn from statutory child protection and mental health workers. The analysis of case-level data was based on information about 300 cases. Half the cases were reported by statutory child protection agency and half by workers in the state health departments. The cases reported include many families who required extensive support: just over half the cases had child protection orders in place or were receiving intensive family support, and three quarters of the cases involved a parent with a diagnosed mental illness.

The data regarding collaboration showed that workers engaged in collaboration to provide a wide range of services and supports focusing on

- adult mental health,
- child protection,
- family counselling and support,
- child health and mental health, and
- legal and financial assistance.

The provision of these various supports was delivered via a highly fragmented and decentralised network of over 100 government (federal, state and local) and community-based programs, services and agencies.

In some respects, the respondents' description of their experiences of interagency collaboration was encouraging: in half the cases reported by respondents, they identified either that no issues had arisen, or that collaboration had resulted in an improved outcome for the client or a positive collaborative process for the workers. This finding supports previous research, indicating that collaboration can be rewarding and beneficial for both workers and clients. It is important to note that there were difficulties in half the cases reported:

One problem is communication issue. In one-third of these cases communication was cited as a problem respondent had encountered. These data support previous findings (54-56) which indicate that information sharing, communication, and negotiating issues of confidentiality are crucial to a successful collaborative relationship.

The second most commonly cited difficulty for respondents was the need for role clarity, including boundaries and leadership. This result supports the findings of Mizrahi and Rosenthal's (57) work, which found leadership to be the most important factor for successful coalitions. This raises the questions of who the leader should be, how leaders should be chosen, and the scope of the authority to be bestowed.

It was clear there were specific pressure points at which problems concerning different understandings of child protection and mental health needs were most likely to cause disruptions. These pressure points appeared when child protection workers sought ongoing mental health intervention, but where mental health services did not perceive a clear mandate to act, and likewise, when mental health workers sought ongoing support from child protection services, but they did not there to be sufficient risk of harm to warrant this.

From this study, it can be seen that the effective communication and collaboration between heath professionals in child protection issues consists of the following issues. Aspect of effective communication were presented in the table below:

Table 2. Effectice communication (54)

Communication	Broad themes and specific elements
	Organisational level strategies
	Practice guidelines/formal protocols for interagency involvement
	Clarity for roles between services
	Clarity of confidentiality requirements
	Joint-agency meetings
	Key interagency liaison person in each service
	Case level strategies
	Joint case identification and management
	Sharing information
	Inter-professional relationship based on respect for persons, different professions and others knowledge
Professional knowledge and skills	*Staff training and supervision*
	Training
	Joint agency training
	Supervision and support for staff
	Types of knowledge required
	Procedural knowledge
	Substantial knowledge
	Understanding of the interdependent needs of parents and children
Resources	More staff/reduced case loads
	More services for parents with a mental illness and their children
	Greater emphasis on prevention and early intervention services

5. Purpose of collaboration: Policy and practice

The incidence study estimates that over 29,633 children were abused and neglected in Queensland in 2004-2005 (58). As a result, state department of health, hospital-based child protection teams, nurses, and medical practitioners are increasingly asked to evaluate and treat child abuse and neglect. However, many health professionals, including pediatricians, have not had formal training regarding child abuse and neglect and are uncomfortable evaluating cases of alleged abuse.

In an effort to mange increased caseloads, other disciplines have trained paraprofessionals and lay people to provide services to abusive families. Medical and community agencies have utilized parent aides, lay therapists, and lay health visitors. These trained paraprofessionals have been shown to be fully capable of identifying abusive situations, and have alleviated work loads and provided additional services.

Department of Health (DOH) in each state in Australia plays a coordinating role in addressing underlying issues of family violence and child abuse through the development of the Child and Adolescent Mental Health Policy. DOH undertook considerable intersectoral consultation with various community and government agencies in the development of this policy. As a commitment to improving local child protection strategies, DOH has proposed to engage with other agencies

The importance of inter-professional and inter-agency collaboration in identification, assessment and provision for children with abuse and neglect in Australia, England, Scotland and U.S. are recognised. The partnership embraces collaboration between service uses, professionals and organisations. The service encompasses many areas where children's social services and child health service must work in partnership for child protection work. The partnership was particularly in areas such as:

a. Multi-professional training: Department of Health and Child Safety made funds available for training the range of social and health services staff.
b. Service delivery: Health visitor work with the teams of social workers. Within these teams, the social workers undertake the usual range of social works tasks connected with the registration and inspection of early years provision. The health visitor has a role that includes health promotion and the health dimension of assessment and inspection.
c. Continuum of health and social services for families: one of the strategic aims of the Children Order is a shift towards greater family support at times of stress and difficulty, so that fewer families come into the child protection system, and fewer children need to be looked after by Health and Social Services. The key services areas comprise three components: universal services offered to all children and families, selective services depend on professional assessment of need and priority, and protection services for few children requiring major care or protection.
d. Referrals: A key element in the integrated service is the 'referral form' that summarises information about the potential recipient and the presenting need for a service.

6. Community level multidisciplinary team work

There have been concerns in the United States about the way in which health professionals have worked together in child abuse cases since child abuse re-emerged as a social problem in the 1950s and 1960s. In response to these concerns, professionals and agencies have been encouraged, persuaded and even sometimes mandated to cooperate and collaborate in order to improve the identification and assessment of abuse; to protect the child; to take the most appropriate civil and criminal legal action; and to ensure that the child and family receive the services and intervention they require.

One way of achieving closer cooperation among the various agencies involved in child protection work is through the establishment of 'multidisciplinary' or interagency teams or meetings (59). For example, one such system is the case consultation model. The case consultation team consists of professionals who meet on a regular basis to discuss a number of cases at each meeting. Most teams consist of social workers, public health nurses, peadiatricians, and others who deal with suspected or confirmed cases of abuse. They hold formal consultations to review critical decisions in specific cases. Most of the literature emphasizes the efficiency of this multidisciplinary approach to case consultation and its positive effect on service delivery (59).

- In all child maltreatment cases-those where there is a prosecution and also those where there is not-the child who has been subjected to maltreatment needs to have his or her medical, social and emotional needs assessed and addressed an the experts who can do this are health professionals and child welfare professionals. However, as studies suggested these professionals are not as fully involved in the team work as they might be. There is a real danger that the health and welfare needs of maltreated children are either being ignored or are determined by those who are not experts in child health and welfare.

7. Models of multidisciplinary team work
There are several guides to the development and implementation of a multidisciplinary child protection team.

- One model is case consultation teams. These teams focus on case conferences, service development, and work to enhance interagency collaborations (59).
- Second model is, treatment teams, often were in hospitals, collaborate on treatment plans for abused children and their families. They may also provide some long-term case management (60).
- The third model is resource development teams. Resource development teams address the issue of child abuse and neglect through public education and advocacy. Members may be professionals working in the field or other citizens. Miller and Whittaker (61), for example, describe a program that involves both professionals and 'lay' people working together. Their program strengthens natural support networks through self-help groups and skills training sessions. The literature also describes mixed model teams that combine the above functions.

8. Interdisciplinary child protection work in a hospital setting
Child maltreatment in all its manifestations constitutes a diagnostic and therapeutic problem to all hospital personnel caring for children and adolescents. To optimise practical procedures and to ensure child protection independent of decisions made by any single person, several Austrian hospitals have formed child protection teams or child abuse and neglect teams. In 1999, the Federal Ministry for the Environment, Youth and Family published a recommendation to install Child Protection Team (CPT) in all pediatric departments in Austria and provided a checklist set of guidelines to assist CPT in carrying out their work in

pediatric hospitals. These guidelines currently form the constitutional basis of CPT in 68% of all Austrian pediatric hospitals. The CPT team comprises the following professionals groups: pediatricains, pediatric surgeons, a child and adolescent psychiatrics, psychologists, psychotherapists, nurses, a social worker and a secretary. The CPT is available only to inpatient.

The CPT team was founded principally as a tool to provide support to the staff on the individual wards of the departments involved. During the weekly CPT meetings, physicians from the respective wards present specific cases. In the ensuring interdisciplinary discussion, the symptoms and history are discussed, and initial vote on the likelihood of maltreatment is taken. Necessary action – if any - and its implementation are discussed in a subsequent step. The nurse and physician in charge of the ward and a member of the CPT usually implement the recommended measures. In addition, since 1998 the CPT is legally required to notify the Youth Welfare Office of any child for whom the suspicion of maltreatment has been confirmed. Such cases also have to be reported to the police following the confirmation of a suspicion of maltreatment. Inpatient data from CPT functioning in hospitals are relatively scarce in the literature. The detailed data about the functioning and effectiveness of CPT are available only from the USA (62) and Canada (60). There are some data available from emergency rooms in the UK, but only one study from a European children's hospital in Switzerland provides a follow-up of patients diagnosed by the CPT 10 years earlier. Furthermore, there are significant differences in the definitions and categories different sets of diagnoses and different age group of child maltreatment across studies. Some studies cover only one type of maltreatment or concentrate on physical and sexual abuse only, others also include distinctive clinical diagnoses.

The analysis of clinical diagnoses revealed a high frequency of psychiatric diagnoses, which probably indicates the consequences of chronic maltreatment, even though the data can not prove this. The significantly higher mean age of children with psychiatric symptoms as compared with the whole group (12.8 vs. 8.8) might indicate that these symptoms can be viewed as the consequence of chronic maltreatment. Conversely, however, the risk of being maltreated might be greater in children with psychiatric illnesses or symptoms.

The diversity of the diagnostic features suggests an urgent need for a concise and common system of maltreatment categorisations to enable the assessment of CPTs to be compared.

The work of the CPT provides a suitable supportive measure for hospital staff dealing with the issue of maltreatment and abuse: the CPT is useful both improving the registration of relevant information and for undertaking suitable action for the purposes of child protection. unfortunately, in its current form it lacks a suitable quality assurance structure (both qualitative and financial-structural), as has also been documented in US CPTs. An improvement in which could ensure a better detection of maltreatment, a more appropriate handling of the whole problem and guaranteed protection of the children concerned.

Message 5: Core activities - Clinical assessment by developing detecting system and intervention

Nurses and paediatrician are the first contact of children who were abused and neglect. Their education provides them with a broad base in assessment, planning, implementing and evaluating health care and nursing care in holistic way for people who are sick. They are responsible for primary, secondary and tertiary level of protection.

Given the strong links between early experience of violence, abuse and harsh parenting regimes with later development of conduct disorder, it is important that children are protected effectively form harm. Health professionally, particularly paediatricians and health visitors, are crucial elements of the multi-agency child protection team. As the one service which links in with all pre-school children, either with in neonatal services or child surveillance, health professionals may be the only members of the multi-agency team who are in a position to recognise such harmful, or potentially harmful, situations and set in motion the child protection process. It is imperative that robust measures are taken which not only address immediate physical safety, but incorporate a long-term view of minimizing the emotional harm that accompanies domestic violence and other emotionally abusive family contexts.

1. Identification of children at risk

A number of indicators have been identified through a number of studies. Listed indicators used by UK and Australia emergency departments (ED) to identify children for suspicion of abuse can be seen in table 3.

Table 3. Suspicion of child abuse and neglect

Variables (22)	Indicators (63)
On child protection register	Incompatible or inconsistent history
Inconsistent history	All children under 1 year of age with a fracture
Delay in attendance	All patients with other suspicious injuries of abuse and a long bone fracture
Parent-child interaction	High-risk fracture Non-supracondylar humerus fracture under 18 months Femur fracture in children under 1 year
Child's appearance/behaviour	Previous presentation to ED with a long bone fracture
History and examination do not match	Unreasonable or unexplained delay in presentation
Direct allegation	All unwitnessed injuries
Injuries of different ages	Patients who presented to ED with more than one injury during the study period
Frequent attendance	Patients with more than one fracture during the study period
Other features in history	
Other features in examination	

Overall there was a lack of clarity about the purpose and appropriate use of indicators of concern. For example, in emergency departments (ED) physicians limited their documentation to a single parenting complaint, and it was difficult to be certain that a particular indicator was looked for and not found (e.g, whether the child had an unclothed examination or only the symptomatic limb was examined) (63). The documentation of childhood injuries in the ED is inadequate, making any assessment for abuse difficult. On review of the medical record, there was high percentage of children had one or more indicators that merited further analysis before a diagnosis of accident could be assigned, however, only 0.9% of children were referred to further examination. The poor referral rate in

ED, suggests that ED and orthopaedic staff are unaware of the significance of the indicators (see table 3 for indicators).

In a study conducted in UK (22), it has found that a large number of the protocols in ED department included long lists of signs and symptoms of abuse with no guidance on how to use these. Those felt to be of more practical value included a short checklist, with clear guidelines on what to do if concerns were identified. Some indicators were very specific (for example, children under 1 year with a fracture, burn or scale), while others were more descriptive (for example, the parents behaviour gives rise to concern). One included recognised risk factors (for example, teenage parents, low income, or prematurity) as well as signs and symptoms, but gave no indicator on how these were to be interpreted.

2. Therapeutic intervention

Tertiary protection is concerned with assessment of medical, behaviour and development of children entering the child protection system referred from health or police and social services. In Australian and New Zealand context, this consists of medical follow-up for children entering the child protection system, and monitor the development and behavioural progress in these children beyond six months; involvement of preventative child protection programmes which include programs on high-risk families with young infants and child protection research (64). Most paediatricians who are doing tertiary protection may also get involved in the advocate for the child for services through joining in multidisciplinary meetings, and participate with other child protection agency stake-holders in decisions aimed to achieve the best child protection outcomes (64).

It is in relation to tertiary protection that a discontinuity arises concerning the roles and responsibilities of different staff groups. A common theme in many was the hierarchical approach with nurses being expected to refer their concerns to doctors, junior doctors to consultants, and emergency staff to pediatricians. Very few emphasised that each individual has a responsibility for the wellbeing and safety of children. Several protocols in hospitals included contact details, most commonly for the names or designated professionals; paediatricians or community paediatricians; the child protection register and social work departments. Majority of emergency departments (77.5%) reported that there were opportunities for regular liaison on child protection matters, but these varied in both frequency and in the personnel involved. The most common professional to provide liaison was a nurse practitioner or specialist nurse (25.5%, 13/51).

In case of physical abuse, parents are usually the perpetrators (65). Such parents lack more effective and appropriate discipline methods than physical punishment. They may attribute negative intentions to their children's behaviour (66). They may have higher expectations for their children's behaviour then the child's developmental level would warrant. More over, they may lack problem-solving skills, so when overwhelmed by stress-often from poverty and social isolation-they may not see or be able to implement options, leading to frustration and possible loss of control (66).

For both sexual and physical abuse, cognitive-behavioural therapy (CBT) has dominated as the treatment with the most empirical validation. For physical abuse, CBT models have been represented among the strongest studies. Parent training-in which parents are taught how to behaviourally specify goals for change, to track target behaviors, to positively reinforce pro-social conduct, and to punish or ignore their children's aversive behaviors (67) – have also been extended to include coping skills, self control skills, communication skills training and psycho-education (67).

Some interventions have been developed specifically for children who have been physically abused. These include peer training, a school-based intervention that uses pro-social peers to help children who are withdrawn develop social skills (68). For very young children, between birth and five years of age, a therapeutic child development program has been developed to provide an intensive milieu of services, such as nutrition, health care, developmental therapies, case management, provided by responsive adults (69).

Group treatment has been a typical modality of intervention for sexual abuse given its potential to reduce stigma and for its cost effectiveness. The theoretical orientations of group therapy have varied widely and include most commonly eclectic treatment models comprising various combinations of the following components: psycho-education regarding sexual abuse and sexual abuse prevention, exploration of the abuse experience, exploration of feelings, art therapy, play therapy, role plays, problem solving, puppet work, writing exercises, and behaviour management" (70, p.674).

SECTION 3. RECOMMENDATIONS

It is recommended that every district and hospital is expected to have formal surveillance and accountability procedure or clinical governance framework for improving quality and safety despite uncertainty as to their effectiveness. To succeed, these frameworks must 1) devolve governance and performance monitoring to the level of clinical units or departments where care is provided and whose staff carry ultimate responsibility, 2) feature practice-relevant, data-driven agendas that actively seek involvement and innovation on the part of practising clinicians and 3) require hospital executives, clinical governance units and quality improvement coordinators to sponsor and support quality and safety activities within departments.

It is proposed to develop relevant action plan for improving quality and safety and implement the clinical governance framework incorporating work force development and early identification and early intervention into the implementation plan in child protection:

- *Define institutional service capacity*: each health service district, hospital and its respective departments should define their service capacity, that is, the clinical conditions and patient types for which each has the expertise, facilities and staff to manage well.
- *Implement district and department governance procedures:* State government executive in liaison with district and health area managers should formulate an action-based clinical governance framework that applies all hospitals and is linked to a timeline for its enactment and a commitment to provide required resources for achieving its objectives. Although the scope and number of specific governance actions will differ between institutions, a basic, generic framework should apply to all.
- *Provide professional training in quality and safety:* Health department, universities, and specialty colleagues and medical societies should collaborate in forging new

training programmes and career paths that focus on optimizing quality and safety. A key reform is to enable doctors, nurses and allied health professionals to more effectively undertake high-order bedside tasks that require specialised training by devolving distracting, low-order clerical and non-clinical procedural tasks to appropriately trained assistants. In times of future shortages of specific groups of skilled clinicians, professional boundaries will need some renegotiation in situations where evidence confirms that tasks previously considered as the exclusive province of one type of practitioner can be safely carried out by other groups.

- *Promote multi-disciplinary teamwork:* All hospitals should formulise and support multidisciplinary team activities that have been shown to lower risk of harm of children and promote interdisciplinary programmes of education and training in safety procedures, team skills and communication. Affiliated university schools of medicine, nursing and population health should implement interdisciplinary activities that cultivate attitudes or respect and cooperation among members of different professional streams.

- *Establish clinical orientation procedures:* All hospital departments should provide all newly appointed clinicians and nurses with a multidisciplinary orientation and information package that outlines departmental policies and procedures and personnel roles and responsibilities.

- *Formalise clinical handover and care coordination procedures:* All hospital departments should have clear procedures for 1) clinical handover between shifts for all disciplines and between different care teams, 2) accessing information and advice from external caregivers (e.g., general practitioner and specialists) with regards to the suspicion of children who are abused and neglected, 3) recording clinical information arising from emergency and pediatric department clinics, case conference and consultant visits and conveying it to others who need to know and 4) transferring structured child information (clinic identification and assessment and community referrals) to general practitioners and other clinicians involved in the clinical care.

- *Implement early identification and early intervention practices:* The health system is often the only infrastructure that reaches children younger than 3 years and therefore can initiate programmes to promote early development and prevent risks. In new born infant health check and health visits program, early detection of child abuse and neglect should be one of paediatrician and nurses' tasks. Once children are identified to be at risk of potential harm referrals to relevant early intervention program should be made. The parenting program (e.g., Triple P parenting program) should be made available in clinical and community settings. The educational system can promote child development by supporting comprehensive programmes for early child development. If the programmes are of high quality, have family involvement, and when needed provide health care and food supplementation or micronutrients, evidence suggests that disparities among the most disadvantaged children can be reduced before school entry. Linking early development programmes administered through the health system with programmes in the educational system increases the likelihood of building intervention follow-up for children at risk. To increase coverage of early child development programmes and improve their quality and effectiveness we need better advocacy strategies, coordination mechanisms, and improved policy. Research is needed on approaches to delivering feasible effective child protection programmes at scale and on the effects of synergies on child outcomes. Implement pre and in-service training for health professionals development.

Training local frontline health and social services professionals, and provide support and consultation in child protection is needed. Health professionals who were trained with knowledge and skills are related to increased rate of detection of child abuse and neglect (71).

Training strategies need to recognise the diversity of nurses' involvements in child protection work needs to be recognised through the development of training programmes which are appropriate for different workplaces and different occupational groupings. Due to the fact that the key role that nurses have in protecting children, specialist training in child protection needs to be provided all nurses including nurses who do not work with children or in settings where children are present, need to be able to access information on child protection issues as required. Many nurses work either directly with children or work in settings where children may be present (e.g., in private homes or in clinics where children accompany parents who are service users). This includes district nurses, community psychiatric nurses, and nurses working in the fields of learning disability and addiction. If they are to effectively contribute to the child protection agenda, they need to at least some basic training about child protection, particularly around identifying children at risk and how they should respond to any cases of suspected or alleged abuse of children. For new staff, participation in such training could become incorporated into their induction program, especially if an on-line training package is developed to provide basic knowledge about child protection issues.

REFERENCES

[1] Australian Council of Health Care Standards (ACHS). National report on health services accreditation performance, 2005. URL: www.achs.org.au.

[2] O'Connor N, Paton M. 'Governance of' and 'Governance by': Implementing a clinical governance framework. Australas Psychiatry 2008; 16(2): 69-73.

[3] Braithwaite J, Travaglia JF. An overview of clinical governance policies, paractices and initiatives. Aust Health Rev 2008;32(1):10-22.

[4] Scott IA, Poole PJ, Jayathissa S. Improving quality and safety of hospital care: a reappraisal and an agenda for clinically relevant reform. Intern Med J 2008;38:44-55.

[5] Cowan J. Children and young people: reviewing practice and policies. Clinical Governance 2008;13(1):73-8.

[6] Department of Health. The nursing, midwifery and health visiting contribution to health and health care. London: Department of Health, 1993.

[7] Hammond H. Child protection inquiry into the circumstances surrounding the death of Kennedy McFarlane. Edinburgh: Dumfries Galloway Child Protection Committee, 2001.

[8] Ruston A, Nathan J. The supervision of child protection work. Br J Soc Work 1996;26:357-74.

[9] Lister PG, Crisp BR. Clinical supervision in child protection for cummunity nurses. Child Abuse Rev 2005;14:57-72.

[10] Hogan H, Basnett I, McKee M. Consultant's attitudes to clinical governance: Barriers and incentives to engagement. Public Health 2007;121:614-22.

[11] Blumenthal D, Kilo C. A report card on continuous quality-improvement. Milbank Q 1998;76:625-48.

[12] Locock L. Redesigning health care: New wine from old bottles. J Health Serv R Policy 2003;8:120-2.

[13]   Morrison P, Heineke J. Why do health practitioners resist quality management. Qual Prog 1992;25: 51-5.

[14]   Australian Council for Safety and Quality in Health Care. A report on achievement and action for safety and quality improvement in Australian States and Territories. Canberra: Australian Council Safety Quality Health Care, 2002.

[15]   Johnstone M, Kanitsaki O. Patient safety and the integration of graduate nurses into effective organisational clinical risk management systems and processes: An Australian study. Org Manag Health Care 2008;17(2):162-73.

[16]   Swerissen H, Jordan L. Clinical governance in community health care settings: Evidence and issues. Aust J Prim Health 2005;11(2):26-31.

[17]   Dubowitz H, Bennett S. Physical abuse and neglect of children. Lancet 2007;369:1891-9.

[18]   Zimmerman S, Makoroff K, Care M, Thomas A, Shapiro R. Utility of follow-up skeletal surveys in suspected child psysical abuse evaluation. Child Abuse Negl 2005;29:1075-83.

[19]   Dubowitz H. The neglect of children's health care. In: Dubowitz H, editor. Neglected children: Research, practice and policy. Thousand Oaks, CA: Sage, 1999.

[20]   Flaherty EG, Sege R. Barriers to physician identification and reporting of child abuse. Pediatr Ann 2005;34:349-56.

[21]   Gunn VL, Hickson GB, Cooper WO. Factors affecting pediatricians' reporting of suspected child maltreatment. Ambulent Pediatr 2005;5:96-101.

[22]   Sidebotham P, Biu T, Goldsworthy L. Child protection procedures in emergency departments. J Accid Emerg Med 2008;24:831-5.

[23]   Crisp BR, Lister PG. Nurses' perceived training needs in chldr protection issues. Health Educ 2006;106(5):381-99.

[24]   Laming L. The Victoria Climbie Inquiry: Report of an inquiry by Lord Laming. London: HMSO, 2003.

[25]   Lupton C, Khan P, North N, Lacy D. The role of health professionals in the Child Protection process. Portsmouth: Social Services Research Unit, University of Portsmouth, 2000.

[26]   Powell C. Child protection: The crucial role of hte children's nurse. Paediatr Nurs 1997;9(9):13-6.

[27]   Thoebald S. Child protection. Why continuing education for nurses is important. Paediatr Nurs 2000;12(3):6-7.

[28]   Royal College of Nursing. Child protection. Every nurse's responsibility. London: RCN, 2003.

[29]   Quin G, Evans R. Accident and emergency department access to the child protection register: a questionnaire survey. J Accid Emerg Med 2002;19:136-7.

[30]   Murray T. Child protection neglected in pediatric training. Medical Post 2002;38(25):1.

[31]   Gunn VL, Hickson GB, Cooper WO. Factors affecting pediatricians' reporting of suspected child maltreatment. Ambulent Pediatri 2005;5:96-101.

[32]   Kendall-Tackett K, Lyon T, Taliaferrro G, Little L. Why child maltreatment researchers should include children's disability status in their maltreatment studies. Child Abuse Negl 2005;29:147-51.

[33]   Wilson SL, Kuebli JE, Hughes HM. Patterns of maternal behavior among neglectful families: implications for research and intervention. Child Abuse Negl 2005;29:985-1001.

[34]   Korbin JE. Neighborhood and community connectedness in child maltreatment research. Child Abuse Negl 2003;27:137-40.

[35]   Sedlack AJ, Bdroadhurst DD. Third national incidece study of child abuse and neglect: final report. Washington, DC: US Department Health Human Services, 1996.

[36]   Dubowitz H. Preventing child gengecta nd physical abuse: A role for pediatricians. Pediatr Rev 2002;23:191-6.

[37]   Kelly A. A public health nursing perspective. In: Fergusson H, Kenny P, eds. Behalf of the child: Child welfare, child protection and the child care act 1991. Bublin: AA Farmar, 1995:186-202.

[38]   Gilligan R. Irish child care services-Policy, practice and provision. Dublin: Institute Public Administration, 1991.

[39]   Burke TP. Survey of the workload of public health nurses. Dublin, Ireland: Institute Community Health Nursing, 1986.

[40] NSW Department of Health. Child Protection Service Plan 2004-2007. In: Health NDo, editor.: NSW Department Health, 2004.

[41] Queensland Health. Strategic Policy Framework for Children's and Young People's Health 2002-2007. Brisbane: Queensland Health, 2002.

[42] Gough D, Bell M. Providing services for children and young People who have experienced sexual abuse. Child Abuse Rev 2005;14:1-3

[43] Johnson Z, Howell F, Molloy B. Community mothers programme: randomised contorlled trial of non-professional interveniton in parenting. BMJ 1993;306:1449-52.

[44] Cowley S, Billings J. Resources revisited: salutogenesis from a lay perspective. JAN 1999;29:994-1004.

[45] Greenwalt BC, Sklare G, Portes P. The therapeutic treatment provided in cases involving physical child abuse: A description of current practices Child Abuse Negl 1998;22(1):71-8.

[46] Choy S. The psychological perspective. In: Untalan FF, Mills CS, eds. Interdisciplinary perspectives in child abuse and neglect. Santa Barbara, CA: Praeger, 1992.

[47] Graziano AM, Mills JR. Treatment for abused children: When is a partial solution acceptable? Child Abuse Negl 1992;16:217-28.

[48] Elmer E, Schultz BS. Social work evaluation and family assessment. In: D.C. Bross RDK, M.R. Lenherr, D.A. Rosenberg and B.D. Schmitt, editor. The new child protection team handbook. New York: Garland, 1988:136-49.

[49] White JC. The role of the social worker. In: Bross DC, Michaels LF, eds. Foundations of child advocacy: Legal representation of the maltreated child. Longmont, CO: Bookmakers Guild, 1987: 61-70.

[50] Tomison AM, ed. Interagency collaboration and communication in child protection cases: some findings from an Australian case tracking study. Paper presented at the Fifth ISPCAN Asian Conference on Child Protection; 26-28 November, 1999; Hong Kong: National Child Protection Clearing House, Australian Institute of Family Studies.

[51] Campbell KA, Bogen DL, Berger RP. The other children. A survey of child abuse physicians on the medical evaluation of children living with a physically abused child. Arch Pediatr Adolesc Med 2006;160:1241-6.

[52] Tomison A, Poole L. Preventing child abuse and neglect: Findings from an Australian audit of prevention programs. Melbourne: Australian Institute Family Studies, 2000.

[53] Darlington Y, Feeney JA. Collaboration between mental health and child protection services: Professionals' perceptions of best practice. Child Youth Serv Rev 2008;30(2):187-98.

[54] Bailey S. Confidentiality and young people: Myths and realities. In: Cordess C, ed. Confidentiality and mental health. London: Jessica Kingsley, 2001:71-84.

[55] Morrison T. Partnership and collaboration: Rhetoric and reality. Child Abuse Negl 1996;20(2):127-40.

[56] Pietsch J, Short L. Working together: Families in which a parent has a mental illness: Developing 'best practice' for service provision and interagency collaboration. Melbourne, Australia: Mental Health Research Institute, 1998

[57] Mizrahi T, Rosenthal BB. Complexities of coalition building: Leaders' successes, strategies, struggles, and solutions. Soc Work 2001;46(1):63-78.

[58] Commission for Children and Young People and Child. Commission for Children and Young People and Child Guardian Act 2000. Brisbane: Commission Children Young People Child, 2008.

[59] Crocker D. Innovative models for rural child protection teams. Child Abuse Negl 1996;20(3):205-11.

[60] Gentry T, Brisbane FL. The solution for child abuse rests with the community. Child Today 1982: 22-4.

[61] Miller JL, Whittaker JK. Social services and social support: blended programs for families at risk of child maltreatment. Child Welfare 1988;67.(2):161-74.

[62] Hochstadt NJ. Child death review teams: A vital component of child protection. Child Welfare 2006;85(4):653-70.

[63] Taitz J, Moran K, O'Meara M. Long bone fractures in children under 3 years of age: Is abuse being missed in Emergency Department presentations? J Paediatr Child Health 2004;40:170-4.

[64]   Cruickshanks P, Skellern C. Role of the tertiary child protection paediatrician: Expert and advocate. J Paediatr Child Health 2007;43:34-9.

[65]   Petit MR, Curtis PA. Child abuse and neglect: A look at the states. Washington, DC: CWLA Stat Book, 1997.

[66]   Azar ST, Barnes KT, Twentyman CT. Developmental outcomes in physically abused children: Consequences of parental abuse or the effects of a more general breakdown in caregiving behaviors? Behav Ther 1988;11:27-32.

[67]   Kolko DJ. Clinical monitoring of treatment course in child physical abuse: psychometric characteristics and treatment comparisons. Child Abuse Negl 1996;20:23-43.

[68]   Fantuzzo JW, Wray L, Hall R, Goins C, Azar S. Parent and social-skills training for mentally retarded mothers identified as child maltreaters. Am J Ment Retard 1986;91:135-40.

[69]   Moore E, Seattle WA, Armsden G, Seattle W, Gogerty PL. A twelve-year follow-up study of maltreated and at-risk children who received early therapeutic child care. Child Maltreat 1998;3(1): 3-16.

[70]   Reeker J. A meta-analytic investigation of group treatment outcomes for sexually abused children. Child Abuse Negl 1997;21(7):669-80.

[71]   Cerezo MA, Pons-Salvador G. Improving child maltreatment detection systems: a large-scale case study involving health, social services, and school professionals. Child Abuse Negl 2004;28(11): 1153-69.

In: Children, Violence and Bullying
Editors: J Merrick, I Kandel and H A Omar

ISBN: 978-1-62948-342-9
© 2014 Nova Science Publishers, Inc.

Chapter 7

UNITED STATES: VERBAL AGGRESSION IN ANIMATED CARTOONS

*Hugh Klein, PhD[*1] and Kenneth S Shiffman, MA[2]*
[1]Kensington Research Institute, Silver Spring, Maryland
[2]Cable News Network, Atlanta, Georgia, US

ABSTRACT

Relying upon a content analysis of one specific type of medium to which young people are exposed beginning at an early age, on a regular basis, and for many years (i.e., animated cartoons), the present study examines what types of messages are provided about verbal aggression. This research examines the following issues: 1) How prevalent is verbal aggression in animated cartoons? 2) Has this prevalence changed over time? 3) What characteristics tend to be associated with being a perpetrator of verbal aggression? 4) What reasons are given for why cartoon characters engage in verbal aggression? 6) What "types" of characters are yelled at, threatened, insulted, and so forth? Results indicate that verbal aggression is fairly prevalent in cartoons (it is the second most common type of antisocial behavior shown, ranking second only to violence) and that this prevalence has increased greatly over time. Cartoons tend to normalize verbal aggression, both by virtue of its frequency of occurrence and by the lack of patterning of characteristics associated with perpetrating this behavior. Although many (nearly half) of the reasons implied for being verbally aggressive are negative in nature, a substantial proportion of the time, this behavior is undertaken for positive reasons or for no reason at all. Characters of all types are equally likely to be verbally aggressive for negative reasons, although only certain types of characters (e.g., female, intelligent, "good guys," physically attractive) are shown to engage in this behavior for positive reasons.

* Correspondence: Hugh Klein, PhD, Kensington Research Institute, 401 Schuyler Road, Silver Spring, MD 20910 United States. Tel: 301-588-8875; E-mail: hughk@aol.com.

INTRODUCTION

For several decades now, there has been considerable public debate about the amount of antisocial content in the media. Numerous studies have demonstrated that the media are replete with antisocial content (1-3) and this has led to considerable public outcry over the years for action to be taken to reduce violent and aggressive content in the media. Many studies have demonstrated an association between media exposure and increased aggression and violence (3-6). There also appears to be a dose-response effect operating, such that people who have more exposure to the media are more affected by what they see, hear, and read than are their peers who are exposed to fewer media messages (6,7).

Interestingly, though, virtually all of the published literature and most of the public debate about antisocial media content has focused specifically on violence, the prevalence of violent content, and the potential harm resulting from exposure to violent media messages, with little attention having been devoted to other antisocial content that does not rise to a level of what might be deemed violence. By focusing almost exclusively on violence, media content researchers and public policymakers ignore a wide array of antisocial behaviors, such as property theft, yelling at others, vandalism, making threats to others' physical safety, grabbing or pushing/shoving others in a manner that is not truly violent in nature, lying and deceitfulness, frightening or intimidating others, among other examples. When violence is examined at the exclusion of these other negative behaviors, an important component of the "bigger picture" regarding media content and its effects on viewers is overlooked. Conceptually, therefore, a distinction can be made–and we contend, ought to be made– amongst violence, acts of physical aggression, acts of verbal aggression, and "other" types of antisocial content. Making this distinction would enable researchers and policymakers to study the prevalence of these different facets of antisocial media content, and to examine differences in the types of messages provided by the various types of antisocial content. It is quite likely, for example, that violence, verbal aggression, and physical aggression are not equally prevalent in the media. It is also probable that different characteristics are associated with the commission of these various types of behaviors, that different "types" of persons or characters are shown to perpetrate these different behaviors, that different reasons are presented to explain characters' involvement in these various actions, and that different consequences are shown to result from being a victim of violence versus verbal aggression versus physical aggression. By focusing only on violence, then, a sizable proportion of the total amount of antisocial content goes unexplored and, consequently, is not well-understood. Little is known about the messages provided to young viewers about a wide array of antisocial behaviors, particularly those that do not qualify as violence.

In the present paper, we differentiate amongst different types of antisocial content and focus our attention specifically on verbal aggression. Published research addressing this type of antisocial content has been sparse, making it relatively easy to summarize the main findings pertaining to this topic. In their research on gender roles in animated cartoons, Thompson and Zerbinos (8) found that male characters were more likely than female characters to be verbally aggressive and to be a victim of other characters' verbal aggression. Taking a somewhat different tack on studying the subject, Woodard (9) examined what he called "problematic language" in children's programs–that is, the use of "uncontradicted words or phrases as a form of disrespect (anything that fails to take into account the feelings of another or shows disdain for authority) or animosity where the intent is to be emotionally hurtful to specific characters in the program" (p. 20). Using this definition, Woodard (9) found that 45% of children's shows contained at least some problematic language, with one quarter of these containing what he termed "a lot" of this type of verbal aggression. Linder and Gentile (3) reported that verbal aggression was more prevalent in television programming aimed at children than it was in programming targeting general audiences. Based on their research on the content of television programming in the midwest, Potter and Vaughan (10) found that verbal aggression increased in prevalence during the mid-1990s. More recently, Glascock (11) reported that 95% of the prime-time television programs he studied included at least one instance of verbal aggression, and that an average of 38 acts of verbal aggression appeared in a "typical" hour of television viewing. He further noted that males tend to be more verbally aggressive than females on television, and that insults tend to be the most commonly portrayed of all types of verbal aggression. Sutil and colleagues (12) conducted a comparative analysis of Spanish, American, and Japanese television programming, and concluded that verbal aggression was greater on American television than it was in programs shown in the other countries. Studying television programming in the United States and Canada, Williams, Zabrack, and Joy (13) noted that verbal aggression and physical aggression occurred with almost equal frequency, at a rate of 1 act per 6-8 minutes of viewing. These authors also noted that, oftentimes, verbal aggression was shown to be humorous and it resulted in few consequences to the perpetrator. Other than these few studies, little else has been published on the subject of verbal aggression in the media.

It is important, we believe, to examine media portrayals of verbal aggression (and other non-violent types of antisocial content) in a systematic way, not only because it is a topic that, heretofore, has been studied very little, but also because of the great likelihood that exposure to verbal aggression in the media will lead to negative effects in viewers. There is a substantial body of theoretical work in the sociological, psychological, and media studies fields to account for and to anticipate the presence of adverse effects subsequent to exposure to verbally-aggressive media content. For example, social learning theory (14,15) posits that people acquire their beliefs, attitudes, and propensity to engage in behaviors, directly based on first-hand experiences they have with others who exhibit particular behaviors and/or indirectly, based on what they observe others—including others appearing in the mass media—doing or saying. As Kunkel et al. (2) put it, "through the observation of mass media models the observer comes to learn which behaviors are 'appropriate'—that is, which behaviors will later be rewarded, and which will be punished" (p. I-6). Accordingly, social learning theory would predict that people of all ages (and young people in particular) will learn a great deal about societal notions of aggression, social expectations for what is a "proper" situation that may be handled "appropriately" with verbal aggression, and the social consequences of being verbally aggressive just from being exposed to violence-related media content.

As another example, cultivation theory (16,17) states that media viewers' perceptions of social reality will be shaped by extensive and cumulative exposure to media-provided messages. This theoretical model assumes that people develop beliefs, attitudes, and expectations about the real world based on what they see and hear on television, on video, in film, in magazines, etc. Subsequently, they use the beliefs, attitudes, and expectations they have developed to make decisions about how they will behave in real-world settings and situations. Again, Kunkel et al (2) put it well when they stated, "The media, in particular television, communicate facts, norms, and values about our social world. For many people television is the main source of information about critical aspects of their social environment. . . . Whether television shapes or merely maintains beliefs about the world is not as important as its role in a dynamic process that leads to enduring and stable assumptions about the world" (pp. I-11 & I-13). In the context of the study of aggression-related media content (such as the present research, which focuses specifically on verbal aggression in one particular medium), then, cultivation theory would posit that media messages serve as agents of socialization regarding what to think about verbal aggression, situations in which it is (in)appropriate to yell at or threaten someone, verbally-aggressive persons, and victims of verbal aggression. This would be particularly true for young viewers who are exposed rather heavily to such media messages through the types of programming that they tend to view. Given the types of messages that many of the media provide about antisocial behaviors, cultivation theory would predict that the cumulative effect of exposure to these messages would provide young people with beliefs and attitudes that, ostensibly, reinforce social stereotypes that verbal aggression is omnipresent, that it is often acceptable to respond to situations aggressively, and so forth.

Taking these theoretical models' tenets and the aforementioned research studies on media effects to heart, the present study entails an examination of content pertaining to verbal aggression in a medium that, we contend, is likely to provide young people with some of their earliest notions regarding aggression-related standards/expectations: animated cartoons. We have chosen animated cartoons as the focal point of this research for a few reasons. First, people are exposed to this type of medium beginning at an early age. Therefore, messages provided by this particular medium are likely to be influential in the initial stages of developing beliefs and attitudes about aggression. Second, for most young people, this exposure continues for many years, and typically entails repeated and frequent media content exposures during that entire viewing period. Thus, animated cartoons also help to crystallize young people's beliefs and attitudes about verbal aggression, contexts in which verbal aggression is more/less acceptable, and verbally-aggressive persons, while helping to shape relevant behaviors through the repeated and consistent antisocial content-related messages they provide. Research has shown that early-life exposure to media messages does, indeed, affect the formation of attitudes and contributes to the crystallization of notions about a variety of aspects of young viewers' social worlds (18,19).

In this study, we address several research questions. First, how prevalent is verbal aggression in animated cartoons? To help place verbal aggression into greater context, the prevalence of this type of antisocial content will be compared to that of violence. Second, has this prevalence changed over time? Third, what "types" of characteristics tend to be associated with being a character that exhibits verbal aggression? Fourth, what are the purported reasons that cartoon characters engage in acts of verbal aggression? Fifth, what "types" of characters tend to be victimized most by verbal aggression in this medium? We conclude by discussing the implications of our findings and elaborating briefly upon some steps that might be taken in the future to provide viewers with what we consider to be more-positive content.

OUR STUDY

This study is based on an examination of the content of animated cartoons. For the present study, only animated cel cartoons are included in the sample (e.g., Bugs Bunny, Popeye, Mighty Mouse, Yogi Bear). This eliminates from the present study such types of animation as claymation (e.g., Gumby and Pokey, the California Raisins), pixillation (the type of animation usually seen at the end of *The Benny Hill Show*), and puppet animation (e.g., *Davey and Goliath*, George Pal's Puppetoons).

The cartoons chosen for the study sample were selected randomly from among all cartoons produced between the years 1930 and the mid-1990s by all of the major animation studios. Before drawing the final sample of cartoons that would be viewed and coded for this work, the researchers had to develop a comprehensive and inclusive sample frame of cartoons produced by the aforementioned animation studios. Published filmographies (20,21) provided the authors with a great deal of this information, and in some instances, the animation studios themselves were contacted and asked to provide comprehensive episode-by-episode lists of animated cartoons they had produced. Once the "universe" of cartoons had been identified, actual copies of the specific cartoons selected for viewing and coding as part of the random sampling approach had to be located. This was done in a wide variety of ways: by contacting animation fans and collectors and having them make copies of some of their cartoons for us, visiting film archives and repositories and viewing cartoons in their libraries/holdings on site, obtaining copies of the needed cartoons directly from the animation studios, purchasing sample-selected items from retail outlets and private sellers who advertised them in trade publications, renting videocassettes from retail outlets like Blockbuster Video, and videotaping from programs broadcast on television.

The origination date for this research [1930] was chosen for four reasons: 1) many major animation studios had begun operations by that time, 2) the era of silent cartoons had virtually ended, 3) cartoons produced prior to 1930 are not very accessible today, and 4) many cartoons produced during the 1930s are still broadcast on television and/or available for viewing on home video. Due to the fiscal constraints of the funding program, only animated cartoons with a total running time of 20 minutes or less were included in the sample frame.

A stratified (by decade of production) random sampling procedure was used to ensure that cartoons from all decades were represented equally in the study sample. This stratification procedure was necessary because very different numbers of cartoons have been produced during different decades (e.g., many more were produced during the 1980s than during the 1930s), thereby leading to the risk that a general random sample (as differentiated from this study's stratified random sample) might have led to an overrepresentation of certain decades during which greater- or lesser-than-average numbers of antisocial acts were portrayed.

Data collection

This study relied upon a content analysis approach to examine the types of messages that cartoons provide about verbal aggression (as well as other types of antisocial content). Data collection for this research entailed viewing the cartoons contained on the project's sample list and recording detailed information on predesigned, pretested, pilot tested, fixed-format coding sheets. Prior to beginning their viewing and coding work for this study, research assistants underwent an intensive training that familiarized them with the data that the study strived to collect, the rationale underlying the coding of each piece of information, and the decision-making procedures that should be used when recording information from each cartoon. To make sure that all people involved in the viewing/coding (i.e., data collection) process implemented the decision-making procedures in a similar manner, intercoder reliability coefficients were calculated periodically throughout the project. Reliability estimates consistently were above .80 for all major measures, and were at least .90 for all of the variables used in the analyses reported in this article, indicating a very high level of intercoder reliability for this research.

To understand the information that this study contains, it is best to conceptualize the database as consisting of two datasets. Dataset #1 focuses on the major characters in each cartoon (regardless of whether they are human characters, animals, personified inanimate objects [e.g., cars with the ability to growl or dance, telephone poles given human-like abilities to see or hear or sing], monsters, ghosts, etc.), providing detailed information that is of value when trying to interpret the types of messages that cartoons provide about who it is that is shown to be a perpetrator of verbal aggression. This dataset contains information about each major character's gender, age, race, ethnicity, marital status, level of intelligence, attractiveness, body weight, physique, occupational status, level of goodness or badness, and other demographic-type and descriptive information. In addition, Dataset #1 contains data about the number of acts of violence, aggression, and prosocial behaviors (and limited information about the types of these behaviors involved) that the characters have committed. This dataset's information is useful for examining such things as whether males/females or smart/dumb characters or attractive/unattractive characters are more likely to be verbally aggressive, whether characters of different "types" were more prosocial or more antisocial, and so forth. The sample size for this dataset was 4,201.

Dataset #2 contains information about all acts of violence, acts of aggression, and prosocial behaviors committed by major characters. This dataset provides information about the specific type of act involved (e.g., violence versus aggression versus prosocial act; specific type of violence committed or the specific type of aggressive or prosocial act performed); the purported reason(s) for engaging in the act; and characteristics of the victim of aggression. The information in this dataset can be linked to the information supplied by Dataset #1, so that detailed information (as described above) about the perpetrator is also available. The sample size for this dataset was 13,283, including 1,462 specific acts of verbal aggression.

Operational definitions of some key concepts

Perhaps the most important operational definitions to provide for this study are those used for violence and verbal aggression. In our research, we defined violence as "any behavior that is intended to harm any character or any character's property, or as any behavior that would reasonably be expected to cause harm to any character or any character's property." Distinctions were made in this research amongst violence, physical aggression (defined here as "any antisocial act that unintentionally leads to the physical injury of another character or another character's property"; "physical aggression" also included such behaviors as grabbing another character, pushing/shoving another character, and similar actions provided that they did not rise to the threshold established for labeling these behaviors as violence), and verbal aggression, and a considerable amount of time was devoted during training to make sure that coders understood the ways to differentiate these concepts from one another. Our definition of violence was adapted as a "best practices" hybrid based on the operational definitions used by several well-respected researchers who have studied violence in the media (9,22-25).

Regarding verbal aggression, coders were instructed to record all instances in which major characters interacted with one another or, with words, treated another character in a negative, antisocial manner. Yelling at another character with raised voice is one example of the type of behaviors included in our definition of verbal aggression. Threatening another character's safety or vowing revenge would be two other examples of verbal aggression. Purposely intimidating or taunting another character constitute other examples, as do ridiculing or insulting other characters' appearance, personality, or performance. Provided that the antisocial content was verbal rather than physical in nature, and provided that it did not meet the definition given above for violence, the act qualified as verbal aggression.

In this study, we collected detailed data only for major characters. We felt that it was important to distinguish between major and minor characters because the former have a much greater and much more consequential impact upon cartoons' storylines and messages, whereas the latter do not. Therefore, we adopted operational definition criteria that would enable the two character types (i.e., major and minor) to be differentiated easily and in a meaningful way. Coders were instructed to follow these rules in order to determine whether a character was "major" or "minor": First, all characters were supposed to be classified by default as minor, unless the conditions stipulated in one or more of the subsequent rules were met. Second, if a character appeared in an average of at least two camera cuts for each complete minute or additional partial minute of the cartoon's running time that was sufficient to label it a "major" character. For example, if a cartoon had a total running time of 8 minutes and 10 seconds, a character would have to appear at least 18 times (i.e., in 18 or more camera cuts, [that is, two per minute or partial minute of running time, multiplied by nine minutes/partial minutes increments]) throughout the duration of the cartoon in order to be considered "major" using this criterion. Third, a character could be considered "major" if it spoke an average two sentences or phrases counting as sentences per minute or partial minute of the cartoon's total running time. Fourth, a character could be considered "major" if it had an average of three or more camera cuts in which it appeared and sentences or phrases counting as sentences per minute of the cartoon's running time. This criterion was implemented to take into account that many consequential characters in the cartoons do not appear a lot and do not say a lot, but their cumulative visual and verbal presence in the cartoon merits "major" character status even though the two previous rules would have prevented such a designation from being made.

Finally, a character could be considered "major" if it appeared on screen for at least 20% of the cartoon's total running time, regardless of the number of camera cuts and sentences or phrases counting as sentences spoken. Generally speaking, although these rules may seem to be somewhat convoluted, determining whether a character was a major or minor one was an easy, straightforward, and relatively-obvious process.

Analysis

Some of the findings reported in this paper are based on descriptive statistics, particularly where prevalence estimates are used, as was the case for addressing Research Question 1. Descriptive statistics are also used, at least in part, for answering Question 4, pertaining to the frequency of depicting certain types of reasons for being verbally aggressive. Changes over time in the prevalence of verbal aggression (Question 2) are examined using logistic regression, since the dependent variable was dichotomous and the predictor variable was a continuous measure. Tests of curvilinearity were performed to determine whether observed changes were linear in nature or whether they demonstrated periods of significant upswing followed by periods of significant downswing (or vice-versa). The analyses examining the characteristics associated with which "types" of characters were more/less likely than others to exhibit verbal aggression (Question 3) or were more/less likely to be victims of verbal aggression (Question 5) entailed the computation of odds ratios (ORs), with 95% confidence intervals (CI95) presented for each estimate. Odds ratios were selected for these analyses because they facilitated direct comparisons of the messages provided about characters of different types, whereas other statistical tests do not lend themselves so easily to such comparisons and interpretation. Due to the large sample size used in this research, results are reported as statistically significant whenever $p<.01$ and as marginally significant whenever $p<.05$.

FINDINGS

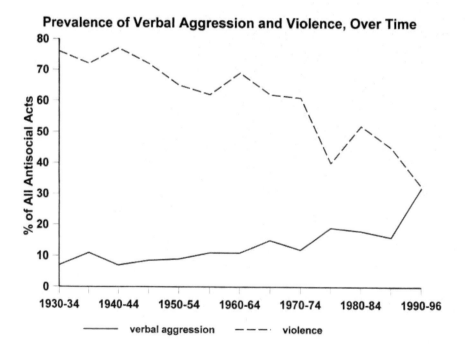

Figure 1. Prevalence of verbal aggression and violence, over time.

Of all antisocial content in the cartoons studied, 14.1% took the form of verbal aggression. This makes it the second-most common type of antisocial content contained in cartoons, ranking only behind violence (which accounted for 59.7% of all antisocial content). As Figure 1 shows, this percentage increased steadily and quite sharply over the years (p<.0001), from about 7% of all antisocial content during the 1930s and 1940s, to about 11% during the 1950s and 1960s, to about 15% during the 1970s and 1980s, and to more than 33% during the 1990s. During the same period, the prevalence of violence declined steadily and sharply (p<.0001), from approximately 75% during the 1930s and 1940s, to about 66% during the 1950s and 1960s, to about 50% during the 1970s and 1980s, to 33% during the 1990s.

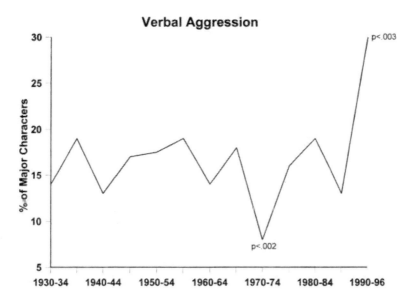

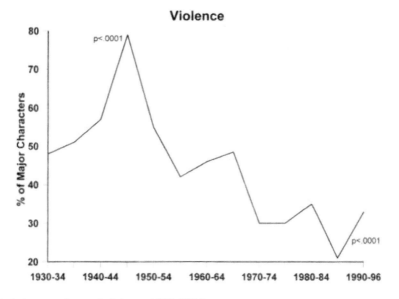

Figure 2. Verbal agresssion and violence 1930-1996.

Moreover, approximately 1 major character in 6 (17.6%) engaged in at least one act of verbal aggression. This percentage dropped from the 1930s and 1940s (16%) until the 1970s (12%) (p<.002) and then increased thereafter (to 20% during the 1980s and 1990s) (p<.0003). As Figure 2 demonstrates, quite a different pattern was observed for violence. From the early 1930s until the later 1940s, cartoon characters became significantly more likely to perpetrate violence (p<.0001), with a very sharp decline in this prevalence thereafter (p<.0001).

Characteristics associated with being verbally aggressive

On most of the dimensions examined, cartoon characters of different "types" were equally likely to engage in verbal aggression. For example, males and females were equally likely to be verbally aggressive (p<.48). As another example, youths, adults, and elderly characters did not differ in their likelihood of engaging in verbal aggression (p<.06). The same was true with respect to race (p<.30) and physical attractiveness (p<.25) as well. On one dimension– namely, intelligence–cartoons provided a mixed message about verbal aggression. Intelligent characters were nearly twice as likely as dumb or ordinary-intelligence characters to be verbally aggressive (OR = 1.89, CI_{95} = 1.34–2.66, p<.0002). At the same time, however, analyses also revealed that characters that were below-average in intelligence were somewhat more likely than ordinary-intelligence and smart characters to be verbally aggressive (OR = 1.48, CI_{95} = 1.04–2.13, p<.03). These seemingly-contradictory findings resulted because it was the characters of average intelligence that were significantly less likely than their smarter and dumber counterparts to engage in verbal aggression. On only one dimension, body weight, did characters differ in a single, consistent way with respect to verbal aggression: Overweight characters were more than twice as likely to engage in verbal aggression as their thin or normal weight counterparts (OR = 2.10, CI_{95} = 1.64–2.69, p<.0001).

Reasons for engaging in verbal aggression

The most common type of reason for being verbally aggressive was anger, accounting for 27.0% of all instances of verbal aggression. The second most common explanation underlying characters' verbal aggression was for no apparent/discernible reason, accounting for 12.4% of all instances of verbal aggression. The third most common reason for exhibiting verbal aggression was as an expression of concern for another character's physical or emotional well-being, which was observed in 11.3% of all instances. The fourth most common reason for being verbally aggressive was to frighten or intimidate another character, which explained 9.7% of all acts of verbal aggression. All other types of explanations (e.g., self-preservation, doing one's job, due to frustration, and more than 30 others) were observed with much lesser frequency.

When examining the purported reasons that were implied as to why cartoon characters engaged in verbal aggression, one finding surprised us: the large number of instances in which positive reasons were given for engaging in this antisocial behavior. Consequently, we decided to collapse the reasons for being verbally aggressive into three categories: negative reasons (e.g., anger, revenge, inherent meanspiritedness, frustration, dislike for another character, and so forth), positive reasons (e.g., out of concern for another character's well-being, due to kindness, as an expression of admiration, out of friendship, and so forth), and neutral reasons (e.g., doing one's job, following orders, to get attention, among others). When collapsed together like this, nearly half (48.0%) of all instances of verbal aggression could be attributed to negative reasons. Although fewer in number, a not-inconsequential proportion (26.5%) of the verbally aggressive acts were performed for positive reasons.

Further analysis of these positive-versus-negative-reasons data revealed one interesting pattern of findings: Characters of all types were equally likely to be verbally aggressive for negative reasons, but only certain types of characters were verbally aggressive for positive reasons. For example, females were somewhat more likely than males to be verbally aggressive for a positive reason (OR = 1.35, CI_{95} = 1.06–1.72, p<.02). Physically-attractive characters were more than twice as likely as their less-good-looking counterparts to engage in verbal aggression for a positive reason (OR = 2.12, CI_{95} = 1.37–3.26, p<.0004). Similarly, intelligent characters were nearly twice as likely to be verbally aggressive for a positive reason as were their less-intelligent counterparts (OR = 1.97, CI_{95} = 1.31–2.97, p<.001). Finally, "good guys" were nearly three times as likely as characters that were not considered to be "good guys" to be verbally aggressive for a positive reason (OR = 2.93, CI_{95} = 2.14–4.02, p<.0001).

Characteristics associated with being a victim of verbal aggression

The analyses pertaining to the characteristics associated with being a victim of verbal aggression revealed a few significant differences. For example, females were about 50% more likely to be victims of verbal aggression than were males (OR = 1.53, CI_{95} = 1.30–1.81, p<.0001). As another example, racial differences were found with regard to the likelihood of being a victim of verbal aggression (χ^2 [5df] = 24.49, p<.0002). In particular, Caucasians were found to be somewhat more likely than members of other races to be victims of verbal aggression (OR = 1.33, CI_{95} = 1.01–1.75, p<.05). With respect to age, as age went up, the likelihood of being a victim of verbal aggression went down (χ^2 [3df] = 158.69, p<.0001). Youths were more than twice as likely as their adult and elderly counterparts to be a victim of verbal aggression (OR = 2.11, CI_{95} = 1.86–2.39, p<.0001) whereas elderly characters were about half as likely as those that were children, adolescents, or adults to be victimized by verbal aggression (OR = 0.51, CI_{95} = 0.34–0.76, p<.0001). We also discovered that characters classified as "good guys" were less likely than others to be portrayed as victims of verbal aggression (OR = 0.66, CI_{95} = 0.58–0.75, p<.0001). On two dimensions–namely, body weight and intelligence–cartoons provided a mixed message with respect to being a victim of verbal aggression. Overweight characters were more likely to be victims of verbal aggression when compared to their thinner-than-average and ordinary weight counterparts (OR = 1.63, CI_{95} = 1.41–1.89, p<.0001). At the same time, underweight characters were also more likely to be victims of verbal aggression than their normal-weight and overweight counterparts (OR = 1.97, CI_{95} = 1.57–2.49, p<.0001). As with intelligence as a characteristic associated with perpetrating verbal aggression, here, the seemingly contradictory findings are the result of the ordinary-weight characters being less likely to be victimized by verbal aggression than their thinner-than-average or overweight counterparts. For the same type of reason, we found that intelligent characters were more likely than those that are dumb or of ordinary intelligence to be victims of verbal aggression (OR = 2.73, CI_{95} = 2.26–3.30, p<.0001) and that characters of below average intelligence were also more likely to be victims of verbal aggression when compared to their average-intelligence and smart counterparts (OR = 1.83, CI$_{95}$ = 1.51–2.20, p<.0001).

DISCUSSION

Before discussing the implications of our main findings, we would like to acknowledge a few potential limitations of the present study. First, this research was based on animated cartoons with running times of 20 minutes or less, thereby excluding longer-form animated cartoons from consideration. We do not know whether or not short-form and long-form animated cartoons are similar to one another with respect to the types of messages they convey, and therefore cannot assess the extent to which the exclusion of the latter may affect this study's findings. Conducting research such as ours with the longer cartoons would be a worthwhile endeavor for future researchers to undertake. Second, our sample ends during the middle-1990s. It would be helpful and, we believe, interesting to have this research extended to the present, so that the most up-to-date trends possible are studied and analyzed. Third, as with any content analysis research study, some scholars might prefer to see different operational definitions of the key concepts used. There is no "gold standard" in content analysis research with regard to defining major versus minor characters, violence, verbal aggression, and so forth. The definitions that we adopted were chosen on the basis of common sense, so that they would foster face validity, and on the basis of simplicity and clarity of implementation, so that they would maximize interrater reliability. Moreover, our approach to defining violence was based on a synthesis of the definitions used by several leading media content researchers (cited earlier), thereby lending additional credibility to the operational definition selected for the current research. We believe that our operational definitions are well-conceptualized and justified; but as with any content analysis study, there is no way to know the extent to which the use of different definitions might have led to different research findings.

Despite these potential limitations, we still believe that the present research has much to contribute to our understanding of cartoons' messages about verbal aggression. First, verbal aggression is a common occurrence in cartoons and, indeed, is the second most commonly shown type of antisocial behavior (with violence ranking first). More than one-sixth of all major characters engaged in at least one act of verbal aggression and more than one-sixth of all cartoons contained at least some verbal aggression. Moreover, verbal aggression became increasingly commonplace as time went on, making it more of a problem in the more recent years studied than in earlier years. This increase took place throughout a long period during which the prevalence of other types of antisocial content–particularly violence–demonstrated a sharp, steady decline in prevalence. The message that this sends to viewers is that yelling at others, threatening others, insulting others, and so forth are "ordinary" behaviors and that they are commonplace. By including so much verbally-aggressive content, animated cartoons convey the message that this behavior is normatively acceptable.

This message about the normalcy of verbal aggression is, we believe, reinforced by the fact that characters of all types were equally likely to engage in verbal aggression. This finding surprised us greatly because, on most dimensions that we have examined in conjunction with our research on animated cartoons, strong patterns of differences are found.

For example, in one report (26), we noted that cartoons provide very different messages about what it means to be male and what it means to be female. In another published report (27), we discussed the fact that cartoons tend to reinforce social stereotypes based on being overweight and the importance of being thin. In other recent works we have developed, we have reported on strongly-patterned findings pertaining to cartoons' messages about prosocial behaviors (28), physical attractiveness (29), and gun violence (30). Given cartoons' overwhelming tendency to supply viewers with repeated, patterned messages about various social groups and social behaviors, our general finding of "no difference" with respect to the commission of verbal aggression surprised us. When it comes to this particular type of antisocial behavior, it seems that pretty much everyone is equally likely to be verbally aggressive. In the world of animated cartoons, verbal aggression is an equal opportunity behavior.

That many of the reasons underlying cartoon characters' verbal aggression are motivated by negative feelings or desires (e.g., anger, revenge, intimidation, inherent meanspiritedness, etc.) came as no surprise to us. After all, what more-predictable justification could there be for yelling at someone or threatening or intimidating him/her than as a manifestation of one's anger, frustration, or basic meanness?! Two of the other findings pertaining to cartoon characters' reasons for perpetrating verbal aggression did, however, strike us as being interesting and worth discussing further.

The first of these was the finding pertaining to no reason at all–that is, the commonness of engaging in verbal aggression without apparent reason. Essentially, these acts, which accounted for approximately 1 of every 8 instances of verbal aggression (making them the second most common "reason" for being verbally aggressive), entailed yelling for yelling's sake, threatening others purely because one could, insulting others for no discernible reason, and so forth. We contend that this presents viewers with a particularly negative and particularly dangerous message about verbal aggression: that it is so acceptable and so normal (as mentioned before) that one may elect to engage in this behavior for no reason whatsoever, simply because one wishes to do so. It is a very antisocial world in which yelling, threatening, insulting, and the like occur for no apparent reason; and such oftentimes is the world in which animated cartoon characters live and present themselves to viewers.

The second point we would like to make with respect to the purported reasons underlying cartoon characters' verbal aggression is that, a sizable proportion of the time (about one-quarter), characters demonstrated verbal aggression for positive reasons. In many of these instances, the verbal aggression was undertaken in an effort to prevent a character from harm, yet in the context of the cartoons' storylines, the raised voices were not presented as "Hey, watch out!" types of remarks. Had that been the case, they would have been coded as prosocial behaviors, despite the elevated voice volumes, not as acts of verbal aggression. Likewise, in many other instances, verbal aggression was done as an expression of friendship or out of a sense of duty or obligation to another character, but not in a way that enabled it to be coded as being prosocial in nature. In the contexts of the storylines in question, even though they were motivated by positive things, coders deemed them to be antisocial (i.e., verbally aggressive) in nature rather than as prosocial acts (which were also coded as a part of our research study, whenever deemed appropriate).

It is quite intriguing to us that so many of the instances in which cartoon characters were verbally aggressive were performed for benevolent reasons. It seems to us that, in order to understand verbal aggression in the media more completely (and in the process, advance thinking and knowledge in the media studies field), it would be wise to conceptualize verbal aggression as being comprised by different types, rather than placing all acts of verbal aggression into a single category. If, for example, verbal aggression were to be classified on the basis of the implied justification for the act, we might be able to look for differences in the messages provided about "negative verbal aggression" or "hostile verbal aggression" versus "positive verbal aggression" or "benevolent verbal aggression," or however else one might wish to name the constructs.

Our findings about the characteristics associated with verbal aggression undertaken for positive versus negative reasons underscore the importance of considering the development, implementation and scientific study of just such an approach. Although characters of all "types" were found to be equally likely to engage in verbal aggression for negative reasons, specific characteristics were found to be associated with being verbally aggressive for positive reasons. In the cartoons studied in conjunction with the present research, several positive traits such as intelligence, physical attractiveness, and being a "good guy" were found to be associated with being verbally aggressive for positive reasons. These findings merit further examination in future studies. We believe that future researchers examining verbal aggression in the media might wish to consider classifying verbal aggression into different types, since viewers are presented with quite different messages about the behavior depending upon who is doing it and why it is being performed. To some extent, Glascock (11) took this approach in his work examining the verbal aggression content of television programming, and we believe that it is a line of inquiry well worth exploring and expanding upon in future studies.

ACKNOWLEDGMENTS

This research was supported by a grant by the National Institute on Alcohol Abuse and Alcoholism (R03-AA09885). The authors wish to acknowledge, with gratitude, Denise Welka Lewis, Scott Desmond, Lisa Gervase, and Thomas Lambing for their contributions to this study's data collection efforts.

REFERENCES

[1]   Diefenbach DL, West MD. Violent crime and poisson regression: A measure and a method for cultivation analysis. J Broadcast Electronic Media 2001;45:432-45.

[2]   Kunkel D, Wilson BJ, Linz D, Potter J, Donnerstein E, Smith SL, et al. Violence in television programming overall: University of California Santa Barbara Study. In: Mediascope, National Television Violence Study 1994-1995. Studio City, CA: Mediascope, 1996:I1-172.

[3]   Linder JR, Gentile DA. Is the television rating system valid? Indirect, verbal, and physical aggression in programs viewed by fifth grade girls and associations with behavior. J Appl Dev Psychol 2009;30:286-97.

[4]   Anderson CA, Berkowitz L, Donnerstein E, Huesmann LR, Johnson JD, Linz D, Malamuth NM, Wartella E. The influence of media violence on youth. Psychol Sci Public Interest 2003;4:81-110.

[5]   Chory-Assad RM. Effects of television sitcom exposure on the accessibility of verbally aggressive thoughts. West J Commun 2004;68:431-53.

[6]   Singer MI, Slovak K, Frierson T, York P. Viewing preferences, symptoms of psychological trauma, and violent behaviors among children who watch television. J Am Acad Child Adolesc Psychiatry 1998;37:1041-8.

[7]   Shrum LJ, Wyler RSJr, O'Guinn TC. The effects of television consumption on social perceptions: The use of priming procedures to investigate psychological processes. J Consum Res 1998;24:447-58.

[8]   Thompson TL, Zerbinos E. Gender roles in animated cartoons: Has the picture changed in 20 years? Sex Roles 1995;32:651-73

[9]   Woodard EHIV. The 1999 state of children's television report: Programming for children over broadcast and cable television. Philadelphia, PA: Annenberg Public Policy Center, University of Pennsylvania, 1999.

[10]   Potter JW, Vaughan M. Antisocial behaviors in television entertainment: Trends and profiles. Commun Res Rep 1997;14:116-24.

[11]   Glascock J. Direct and indirect aggression on prime-time network television. J Broadcast Electronic Media 2008;52:268-81.

[12]   Sutil CR, Esteban JL, Takeuchi M, Clausen T, Scott R. (1995). Televised violence: A Japanese, Spanish, and American comparison. Psychol Rep 1995;77:995-1000.

[13]   Williams TM, Zabrack ML, Joy LA. The portrayal of aggression on North American television. J Appl Soc Psychol 1982;12:360-80.

[14]   Akers RL. Deviant behavior. Belmont, CA: Wadsworth, 1973.

[15]   Bandura A. Social learning theory. New York: General Learning Press, 1971.

[16]   Gerbner G, Gross L. Living with television: The violence profile. J Commun 1976;26:173-99.

[17]   Signorielli N, Morgan M. Cultivation analysis: New directions in media effects research. Newbury Park, CA: Sage, 1990.

[18]   Greenberg BS. Television and role socialization: An overview. In: D Pearl, L Bouthilet, J Lazar, eds. Television and behavior: Ten years of scientific progress and implications for the eighties–Volume II: Technical reviews. Rockville, MD: Natl Inst Mental Health, 1982.

[19]   Tiggeman M, Pickering AS. Role of television in adolescent women's body dissatisfaction and drive for thinness. Int J Eat Disord 1996;20:199-203.

[20]   Lenberg J. The encyclopedia of animated cartoons. New York: Facts on File, 1991.

[21]   Maltin L. Of mice and magic: A history of American animated cartoons. New York: Plume, 1980.

[22]   Gerbner G, Signorielli N. Violence profile 1967 through 1988-89: Enduring patterns. Philadelphia, PA: Annenberg School Communication, 1990.

[23]   Hickey N. New violence survey released. TV Guide August 13 1994;42:37-9.

[24]   Nichols P, Dabbs D, Chester K. Landmark research reports on the nature of violent portrayals, ratings and advisories, and anti-violence messages on television. Press release by Mediascope, Los Angeles, CA, February 7 1996.

[25]   Cole J. The UCLA television violence report 1996. Los Angeles, CA: UCLA Center Communication Policy, 1996.

[26]   Klein H, Shiffman KS, Welka DA. Gender-related content of animated cartoons, 1930 to the present. Adv Gender Res 2000;4:291-317.

[27]   Klein H, Shiffman KS. Thin is 'in' and stout is 'out': What animated cartoons tell viewers about body weight. Eat Weight Disord 2005;10:107-16.

[28]   KIein H, Shiffman KS. Prosocial content of animated cartoons. In: HV Kovacs (Ed.). Mass media: Coverage, objectivity, and changes (pp. 23-45). Hauppauge, NY: Nova Science Publishers, 2011.

[29]   Klein H, Shiffman KS. Messages about physical attractiveness in animated cartoons. Body Image 2006;3:353-63.

[30]   Klein H, Shiffman KS. Bang bang, you're . . . NOT dead and you're . . . NOT even hurt?! Messages provided by animated cartoons about gun violence. Int J Child Adolesc Health 2011;4:265-76.

In: Children, Violence and Bullying
Editors: J Merrick, I Kandel and H A Omar

ISBN: 978-1-62948-342-9
© 2014 Nova Science Publishers, Inc.

Chapter 8

UNITED STATES: MESSAGES PROVIDED BY ANIMATED CARTOONS ABOUT GUN VIOLENCE

Hugh Klein, PhD[*1] *and Kenneth S Shiffman, MA*[2]

[1]Kensington Research Institute, Silver Spring, Maryland, US
[2]Cable News Network, Atlanta, Georgia, US

ABSTRACT

Relying upon a content analysis of animated cartoons, this study examines the messages provided about gun violence, focusing on the following questions: 1) How prevalent is gun violence in animated cartoons? 2) Has this prevalence changed over time? 3) What characteristics are associated with being a perpetrator of gun violence? 4) What types of effects are shown to result from the perpetration of gun violence? 5) What reasons are given for why cartoon characters use guns? 6) What "types" of characters are victimized by firearms? Results indicate that gun violence is prevalent in cartoons and the prevalence has not diminished over time. Cartoons provide inaccurate information about the characteristics associated with perpetrating or being a victim of gun violence. Oftentimes, the use of firearms is shown to result in no negative consequences to the perpetrator or the victim, and this is true even when victims are shown to be shot. When effects are shown, they tend to be minor in nature. Anger, revenge, and inherent meanspiritedness are the most common reasons implied for why characters commit acts of gun violence.

INTRODUCTION

According to figures compiled by the US Bureau of Justice Statistics, 13% of all violent crimes committed in the United States can be attributed to the use of handguns (1). Each year, between 90,000 and 100,000 persons are either injured (two-thirds) or killed (one-third) in this country as a result of handgun use (2,3). Males are nearly seven times as likely as females

* Correspondence: Hugh Klein, PhD, Kensington Research Institute, 401 Schuyler Road, Silver Spring, MD 20910 U.S.A. Tel: 301-588-8875; E-mail: hughk@aol.com (primary) or hughkhughk@yahoo.com (secondary).

to be killed as a result of gun violence and they are more than eight times as likely as females to be injured nonfatally by a gun (2,3). Youths are the least likely of all age groups to be killed as a result of gun violence, with fatality rates approximately one-quarter those noted for adults and elderly persons (2). Conversely, elderly people are the least likely to be injured nonfatally by a gun, with rates one-sixth those of youths and one-ninth those of adults (3). In terms of racial differences, African Americans are the most likely to be harmed as a result of gun violence, with double the national average fatality rate and more than triple the national average nonfatal injury rate (2,3).

Information about the perpetrators of gun violence is, surprisingly, less available. The Federal Bureau of Investigation (4) is perhaps the best source of information on crimes, through its Uniform Crime Reporting system. Data from this source suggest that weapons crime rates are more than 12x greater for males than for females, 3x greater for African Americans than for Caucasians (and 11x greater among African Americans than among other racial minority groups), and about 50% greater among youths than adults, both of which outpace elderly persons by a very wide margin (4).

Numerous sources are usually blamed for the high rates of gun violence in American society: poverty, gang activities, illegal drug abuse and drug trafficking, to name but a few of the major sources that are often mentioned. In addition to these, the mass media are often cited for helping to incite violence and escalate the propensity toward aggressive and violent behaviors in our culture. The media are replete with antisocial content (5, 6), and this has led to considerable public outcry over the years for action to be taken to reduce violent and aggressive content in the media. Many research studies have demonstrated an association between media exposure and increased aggression and violence (7-9). There also appears to be a dose-response effect operating, such that people who have more exposure to the media are more affected by what they see, hear, and read than are their peers who are exposed less significantly to media messages (9,10).

Conceptually, this makes perfect sense and there is a substantial body of theoretical work in the sociological, psychological, and media studies fields to account for–and to anticipate the presence of–these types of effects. For example, social learning theory (11,12) posits that people acquire their beliefs, attitudes, and propensity to engage in behaviors, directly based on first-hand experiences they have with others who exhibit particular behaviors and/or indirectly, based on what they observe others—including others appearing in the mass media—doing or saying. As Kunkel et al. (6: I-6) put it, "through the observation of mass media models the observer comes to learn which behaviors are 'appropriate'—that is, which behaviors will later be rewarded, and which will be punished." Accordingly, social learning theory would predict that people of all ages (and young people in particular) will learn a great deal about societal notions of violence and aggression, social expectations for what is a "proper" situation that may be handled "appropriately" with violence, and the social consequences of being aggressive or violent just from being exposed to violence-related media content.

As another example, cultivation theory (13,14) states that media viewers' perceptions of social reality will be shaped by extensive and cumulative exposure to media-provided messages. This theoretical model assumes that people develop beliefs, attitudes, and expectations about the real world based on what they see and hear on television, on video, in film, in magazines, etc. Subsequently, they use the beliefs, attitudes, and expectations they have developed to make decisions about how they will behave in real-world settings and situations. Again, Kunkel et al. (6: I-11, I-13) put it well when they stated, "The media, in particular television, communicate facts, norms, and values about our social world. For many people television is the main source of information about critical aspects of their social environment. . . . Whether television shapes or merely maintains beliefs about the world is not as important as its role in a dynamic process that leads to enduring and stable assumptions about the world." In the context of the study of violence-related media content (such as the present research, which focuses on gun violence in one particular medium), then, cultivation theory would posit that media messages serve as agents of socialization regarding what to think about violence, violent situations, violent persons, and victims of violence. This would be particularly true for young viewers who are exposed rather heavily to such media messages through the types of programming that they tend to view. Given the types of messages that many of the media provide about antisocial behaviors, cultivation theory would predict that the cumulative effect of exposure to these messages would provide young people with beliefs and attitudes that, ostensibly, reinforce social stereotypes that violence is omnipresent, that it is often acceptable to respond to situations aggressively or violently, and so forth.

Taking these theoretical models' tenets and the aforementioned research studies on media effects to heart, the present study entails an examination of content pertaining to gun violence in a medium that, we contend, is likely to provide young people with some of their earliest notions regarding violence-related standards/expectations: animated cartoons. We have chosen animated cartoons as the focal point of this research for a few reasons. First, people are exposed to this type of medium beginning at an early age. Therefore, messages provided by this particular medium are likely to be influential in the initial stages of developing beliefs and attitudes about violence and aggression. Second, for most young people, this exposure continues for many years, and typically entails repeated and frequent media content exposures during that entire viewing period. Thus, animated cartoons also help to crystallize young people's beliefs and attitudes about violence, violent situations, and violent persons, while helping to shape relevant behaviors through the repeated and consistent antisocial content-related messages they provide. Research has shown that early-life exposure to media messages does, indeed, affect the formation of attitudes and contributes to the crystallization of notions about a variety of aspects of young viewers' social worlds (15,16).

In this study, we address several research questions. First, how prevalent is gun violence in animated cartoons? Second, has this prevalence changed over time? Third, what "types" of characteristics tend to be associated with being a perpetrator of gun violence? Fourth, when gun violence occurs in cartoons, what effects are shown to result? Fifth, what are the purported reasons that cartoon characters engage in gun violence? Sixth, what "types" of characters tend to be victimized most by gun violence in this medium? We conclude by discussing the implications of our findings and elaborating briefly upon some steps that might be taken in the future to provide viewers with what we consider to be more-positive content.

OUR STUDY

This study is based on an examination of the content of animated cartoons. For the present study, only animated cel cartoons are included in the sample (e.g., Bugs Bunny, Popeye, Mighty Mouse, Yogi Bear). This eliminates from the present study such types of animation as claymation (e.g., Gumby and Pokey, the California Raisins), pixillation (the type of animation usually seen at the end of *The Benny Hill Show*), and puppet animation (e.g., *Davey and Goliath*, George Pal's *Puppetoons*).

The cartoons chosen for the study sample were selected randomly from among all cartoons produced between the years 1930 and the mid-1990s by all of the major animation studios. Before drawing the final sample of cartoons that would be viewed and coded for this work, the researchers had to develop a comprehensive and inclusive sample frame of cartoons produced by the aforementioned animation studios. Published filmographies (17,18) provided the authors with a great deal of this information, and in some instances, the animation studios themselves were contacted and asked to provide comprehensive episode-by-episode lists of animated cartoons they had produced. Once the "universe" of cartoons had been identified, actual copies of the specific cartoons selected for viewing and coding as part of the random sampling approach had to be located. This was done in a wide variety of ways: by contacting animation fans and collectors and having them make copies of some of their cartoons for us, visiting film archives and repositories and viewing cartoons in their libraries/holdings on site, obtaining copies of the needed cartoons directly from the animation studios, purchasing sample-selected items from retail outlets and private sellers who advertised them in trade publications, renting videocassettes from retail outlets like Blockbuster Video, and recording programs broadcast on television.

The origination date for this research (1930) was chosen for four reasons: 1) many major animation studios had begun operations by that time, 2) the era of silent cartoons had virtually ended, 3) cartoons produced prior to 1930 are not very accessible today, and 4) many cartoons produced during the 1930s are still broadcast on television and/or available for viewing on home video or DVD. Due to the fiscal constraints of the funding program, only animated cartoons with a total running time of 20 minutes or less were included in the sample frame.

A stratified (by decade of production) random sampling procedure was used to ensure that cartoons from all decades were represented equally in the study sample. This stratification procedure was necessary because very different numbers of cartoons have been produced during different decades (e.g., many more were produced during the 1980s than during the 1930s), thereby leading to the risk that a general random sample (as differentiated from this study's stratified random sample) might have led to an overrepresentation of certain decades during which greater- or lesser-than-average numbers of violent acts were portrayed.

Data collection

This study relied upon a content analysis approach to examine the types of messages that cartoons provide about gun (and other types of) violence. Data collection for this research entailed viewing the cartoons contained on the project's sample list and recording detailed information on predesigned, pretested, pilot tested, fixed-format coding sheets. Prior to beginning their viewing and coding work for this study, research assistants underwent an intensive training that familiarized them with the data that the study strived to collect, the rationale underlying the coding of each piece of information, and the decision-making procedures that should be used when recording information from each cartoon. To make sure that all people involved in the viewing/coding (i.e., data collection) process implemented the decision-making procedures in a similar manner, intercoder reliability coefficients were calculated periodically throughout the project. Reliability estimates consistently were above .80 for all major measures, and were at least .90 for all of the variables used in the analyses reported in this article, indicating a very high level of intercoder reliability for this research.

To understand the information that this study contains, it is best to conceptualize the database as consisting of three datasets. Dataset #1 focuses on the cartoon itself as the unit of analysis and contains macro-level variables that provide prevalence-type information. Among several others, this dataset includes such measures as the cartoon's length; number of characters of each gender, race, age, body weight group, and so forth; number of times using or making reference to various legal and illegal drugs; and number of prosocial and antisocial acts committed. This dataset facilitates analyses indicating the proportion of cartoons containing at least one violent act, how that proportion changed over time, or identifying the rate per hour of seeing violence. The sample size for this dataset is 1,221.

Dataset #2 focuses on the major characters in each cartoon (regardless of whether they are human characters, animals, personified inanimate objects [e.g., cars with the ability to growl or dance, telephone poles given human-like abilities to see or hear or sing], monsters, ghosts, etc.), providing detailed information that is of value when trying to interpret the types of messages that cartoons provide about who it is that is shown to be a perpetrator of gun violence. This dataset contains information about each major character's gender, age, race, ethnicity, marital status, level of intelligence, attractiveness, body weight, physique, occupational status, level of goodness or badness, and other demographic-type and descriptive information. In addition, Dataset #2 contains data about the number of acts of violence, aggression, and prosocial behaviors (and limited information about the types of these behaviors involved) that the characters have committed. This dataset's information is useful for examining such things as whether males/females or smart/dumb characters or attractive/unattractive characters are more likely to perpetrate violence, whether characters of different "types" were more prosocial or more antisocial, and so forth. The sample size for this dataset is 4,201.

Dataset #3 contains information about all acts of violence, acts of aggression, and prosocial behaviors committed by major characters. This dataset provides information about the specific type of act involved; (if violence) the effect(s), if any, that the violent act caused on its victim; whether or not the act backfired on the perpetrator (and if so, the effects it had); the purported reason(s) for engaging in the prosocial, aggressive, or violent act; and characteristics of the victim of violence or aggression or the beneficiary of the prosocial act. The sample size for this dataset is 13,283, including 6,191 separate acts of violence.

Operational definitions of some key concepts

Perhaps the most important operational definition to provide for this study is that used for violence. In our research, we defined violence as "any behavior that is intended to harm any character or any character's property, or as any behavior that would reasonably be expected to cause harm to any character or any character's property." Distinctions were made in this research amongst violence, physical aggression and verbal aggression, and a considerable amount of time was devoted during training to make sure that coders understood the ways to differentiate these concepts from one another. Our definition of violence was adapted as a "best practices" hybrid based on the operational definitions used by several well-respected researchers who have studied violence in the media (19–23). In the analyses conducted for the present paper, we focus specifically on gun violence, regardless of the type of gun used (e.g., handgun, rifle, automatic assault weapon, etc.).

In this study, we collected detailed data (i.e., the information collected in Dataset #2 and Dataset #3) only for major characters. We felt that it was important to distinguish between major and minor characters because the former have a much greater and much more consequential impact upon cartoons' storylines and messages, whereas the latter do not. Therefore, we adopted operational definition criteria that would enable the two character types (i.e., major and minor) to be differentiated easily and in a meaningful way. Coders were instructed to follow these rules in order to determine whether a character was "major" or "minor": First, all characters were supposed to be classified by default as minor, unless the conditions stipulated in one or more of the subsequent rules were met. Second, if a character appeared in an average of at least two camera cuts for each complete minute or additional partial minute of the cartoon's running time, that was sufficient to label it a "major" character. For example, if a cartoon had a total running time of 8 minutes and 10 seconds, a character would have to appear at least 18 times (i.e., in 18 or more camera cuts, [that is, two per minute or partial minute of running time, multiplied by nine minutes/partial minutes increments]) throughout the duration of the cartoon in order to be considered "major" using this criterion. Third, a character could be considered "major" if it spoke an average two sentences or phrases counting as sentences per minute or partial minute of the cartoon's total running time. Fourth, a character could be considered "major" if it had an average of three or more camera cuts in which it appeared and sentences or phrases counting as sentences per minute of the cartoon's running time. This criterion was implemented to take into account that many consequential characters in the cartoons do not appear a lot and do not say a lot, but their cumulative visual and verbal presence in the cartoon merits "major" character status even though the two previous rules would have prevented such a designation from being made. Finally, a character could be considered "major" if it appeared on screen for at least 20% of the cartoon's total running time, regardless of the number of camera cuts and sentences or phrases counting as sentences spoken. Generally speaking, although these rules may seem to be somewhat convoluted, determining whether a character was a major or minor one was an easy, straightforward, and relatively-obvious process.

Analysis

Some of the findings reported in this paper are based on descriptive statistics, particularly where prevalence estimates are used, as was the case for addressing Research Question 1. Descriptive statistics are also used, at least in part, for answering Questions 4 and 5, pertaining to the frequency of depicting certain types of effects resulting from gun violence and the purported reasons given for perpetrating gun violence. Changes over time in the prevalence of gun violence (Question 2) are examined using logistic regression when the dependent variable was dichotomous and the predictor variable was a continuous measure. Tests of curvilinearity were performed to determine whether observed changes were linear in nature or whether they demonstrated periods of significant upswing followed by periods of significant downswing (or vice-versa). The analyses examining the characteristics associated with which "types" of characters were more/less likely than others to perpetrate gun violence (Question 3) or were more/less likely to be victims of gun violence (Question 6) entailed the computation of odds ratios (ORs), with 95% confidence intervals (CI_{95}) presented for each estimate. Odds ratios were selected for these analyses because they facilitated direct comparisons of the messages provided about characters of different types, whereas other statistical tests do not lend themselves so easily to such comparisons and interpretation. Due to the large sample size used in this research, results are reported as statistically significant whenever $p < .01$ and as marginally significant whenever $p < .05$.

FINDINGS

Questions 1 and 2: Prevalence of gun violence

Averaged over time, gun violence accounted for 13.0% of all violent acts coded in conjunction with this research, making it the second most common type of violence depicted. Figure 1 shows that there have been very substantial changes in the prevalence of gun violence in the cartoons over the years ($p < .0001$), with several significant upsurges and downsurges noted, but no general trend overall in the direction of this phenomenon.

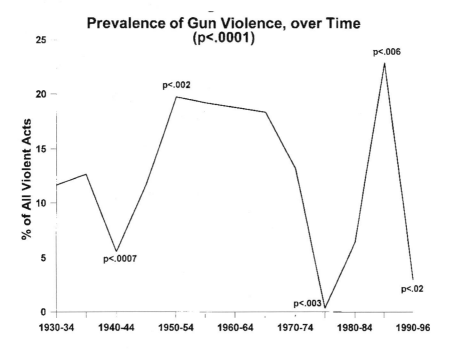

Figure 1.

Question 3: Characteristics associated with perpetrators of gun violence

Numerous differences were found with respect to who it is that perpetrates gun violence in animated cartoons. For example, males were twice as likely as females to perpetrate gun violence (OR = 1.97, CI_{95} = 1.47–2.64, p<.0001). With respect to age, youths were far less likely than other age groups to perpetrate gun violence (OR = 0.35, CI_{95} = 0.25–0.49, p<.0001). The likelihood of perpetrating gun violence was not found to differ on the basis of race, however (e.g., for Caucasians versus non-Caucasians, OR = 0.74, CI_{95} = 0.48–1.13, p<.17). Characters that were below average in intelligence were less likely than those that were of average or above-average intelligence to perpetrate gun violence (OR = 0.24, CI_{95} = 0.12–0.49, p<.0001). Several physical appearance variables also differentiated gun violence perpetrators from characters who did not engage in this practice. For instance, characters that were thin/underweight were far less likely than characters that were normal weight or overweight to perpetrate gun violence (OR = 0.12, CI_{95} = 0.06–0.25, p<.0001). As another example, ugly characters were twice as likely as those that were average-looking or attractive to perpetrate gun violence (OR = 1.95, CI_{95} = 1.52–2.52, p<.0001). As a third example, characters that were not well-built were less likely to perpetrate gun violence when compared to their counterparts who were of ordinary physique or who were well-built (OR = 0.54, CI_{95} = 0.37–0.81, p<.003).

Question 4: Effects resulting from gun violence

Approximately 4 times out of 5 (78.4%), gun violence was shown to lead to at least some type of effect on a victim. Compared to other types of violence, this particular type of violence was more than three times as likely to be shown to result in harm (OR = 3.56, CI_{95} = 2.52–5.05, p<.0001). When effects were shown to result from gun violence, characters were most likely to experience pain, which was observed in 16.1% of gun violence victims. Although pain was the most common result of gun violence, characters were equally likely to experience pain as a result of this type of violence as they were from any other type of violence they befell (OR = 0.83, CI_{95} = 0.56–1.24, p<.37). The second most common effect of gun violence was death, accounting for approximately 1 gun violence portrayal in 9 (10.9%). Compared to other types of violence, gun violence was almost 20x more likely to result in another character's death (OR = 18.87, CI_{95} = 10.30–34.57, p<.0001). The third most common effect shown to result from gun violence were cuts or scrapes (8.8%). As was the case for violence-induced death, violence-induced cuts and scrapes were far more common among victims of gun violence than among victims of other types of violence (OR = 17.93, CI_{95} = 9.23–34.82, p<.0001). The fourth most common consequence of gun violence was a character becoming dazed (6.7%). This particular type of adverse effect of violence was about half as common among victims of gun violence as it was among victims of other types of violence (OR = 0.51, CI_{95} = 0.29–0.90, p<.02).

All other types of effects potentially resulting from gun violence, such as losing limbs, losing consciousness, having bones broken, being burned, and bleeding (among others) were all shown to occur much less frequently.

In terms of consequences for the perpetrator, our data revealed that gun violence was somewhat less likely than other types of violent acts to backfire on the perpetrator (OR = 0.71, CI_{95} = 0.51–1.00, p<.05). Approximately 95% of the time (94.7%), cartoon characters that used a firearm against another character did not have their violence backfire on them.

Question 5: Reasons for perpetrating gun violence

Compared to other types of violence, gun violence was less likely to be perpetrated for no reason whatsoever (OR = 0.34, CI_{95} = 0.23–0.50, p<.0001). By far the most common reason underlying cartoon characters' perpetration of gun violence was anger, accounting for 54.5% of all shooting incidents observed. This rationale for engaging in violence was more than twice as common for gun violence as it was for other types of violent acts (OR = 2.16, CI_{95} = 1.85–2.52, p<.0001). Revenge was the second most common explanation for a character perpetrating gun violence, explaining 20.6% of such acts. This was no more or less common a reason for perpetrating gun violence than it was for committing any other type of violent act (OR = 0.97, CI_{95} = 0.80–1.17, p<.73). Inherent meanspiritedness was the third most common justification for gun violence, accounting for 19.2% of these acts. Compared to other types of violence, characters were somewhat less likely to perpetrate gun violence for this particular reason (OR = 0.80, CI_{95} = 0.66–0.98, p<.03). The only other reason cited with any frequency regarding gun violence was self-defense, which was noted as a reason for 16.7% of all acts of gun violence. This percentage was comparable to that found for other types of violent acts (OR = 1.13, CI_{95} = 0.92–1.40, p<.25). Other reasons for perpetrating gun violence– for example, as an act of jealousy, as a result of greed, to win something, to save another character or another character's property–were all cited much less frequently.

Question 6: Characteristics of victims of gun violence

In this study, some information is available about the types of characters that are victimized by violence, including their gender, age classification, race, body weight, physique, physical attractiveness, and their classification as a "good guy" versus a "bad guy." No differences were found based on gender, physique, or physical attractiveness. Youths (i.e., children and adolescents) were less likely than adults and elderly characters to be shown as victims of gun violence (OR = 0.33, CI_{95} = 0.22–0.49, p<.0001). Caucasians were somewhat more likely than nonwhites to be victims of gun violence (OR = 1.88, CI_{95} = 1.07–3.30, p<.03). With respect to body weight, overweight characters were less likely than their normal weight and underweight counterparts to be victims of gun violence (OR = 0.53, CI_{95} = 0.36–0.76, p<.0005). Finally, "good guys" were almost twice as likely as characters that were not "good guys" to be victims of gun violence (OR = 1.94, CI_{95} = 1.63–2.31, p<.0001).

DISCUSSION

Before discussing the implications of our main findings, we would like to acknowledge a few potential limitations of the present study. First, this research was based on animated cartoons with running times of 20 minutes or less, thereby excluding longer-form animated cartoons from consideration. We do not know whether or not short-form and long-form animated cartoons are similar to one another with respect to the types of messages they convey, and therefore cannot assess the extent to which the exclusion of the latter may affect this study's findings. Conducting research such as ours with the longer cartoons would be a worthwhile endeavor for future researchers to undertake. Second, our sample ends during the middle-1990s. It would be helpful and, we believe, interesting to have this research extended to the present, so that the most up-to-date trends possible are studied and analyzed. Third, as with any content analysis research study, some scholars might prefer to see different operational definitions of the key concepts used. There is no "gold standard" in content analysis research with regard to defining major versus minor characters, violence, and so forth. The definitions that we adopted were chosen on the basis of common sense, so that they would foster face validity, and on the basis of simplicity and clarity of implementation, so that they would maximize interrater reliability. Moreover, our approach to defining violence was based on a synthesis of the definitions used by several leading media content researchers (cited earlier), thereby lending additional credibility to the operational definition selected for the current research. We believe that our operational definitions are well-conceptualized and justified; but as with any content analysis study, there is no way to know the extent to which the use of different definitions might have led to different research findings.

Despite these potential limitations, we still believe that the present research has much to contribute to our understanding of cartoons' messages about gun violence. First, the use of firearms is a common type of violence shown in animated cartoons, comprising 13% of all violent acts depicted. This makes it the second most common type of violent act portrayed, only ranking behind punching or hitting other characters with one's hand(s). Despite legislators' numerous attempts over the years to find ways to reduce the public's exposure to violent media content (24–27), gun violence has remained a frequent occurrence over the many decades spanned by this research (although it did vary greatly from time period to time period, as Figure 1 shows). It is particularly noteworthy that gun violence has not diminished significantly over time even though the likelihood of a cartoon containing at least one act of violence decreased dramatically over time (data not shown, $p<.0003$) and the total amount of violence contained per cartoon also dropped sharply over time (data not shown, $p<.0001$). The presence of gun-related violence, it seems, has been impervious to such changes and its prevalence has not diminished even in the wake of scientific research and regulatory action taken to reduce its existence.

In this research, we also discovered that animated cartoons tend to provide relatively unrealistic and inaccurate information about what "kinds" of persons/characters perpetrate gun violence. For example, in the cartoon world, males are about twice as likely as females to perpetrate gun violence; in the "real world," the ratio is about 12:1. In the cartoon world, members of all racial groups were about equally likely to perpetrate gun violence, whereas in the "real world," African Americans are 3x likelier than other groups to do so. In the cartoon world, young persons were one-third as likely as their adult and elderly counterparts to use a gun; in the "real world," youths have the highest rates of weapons violations. Similarly, animated cartoons tend to provide unrealistic and inaccurate information about what "kinds" of persons/characters are victimized by gun violence. For example, in the cartoon world, males and females were about equally likely to be shown as a shooting victim, whereas in the "real world," males outnumber females by more than 7:1. In the cartoon world, Caucasians are nearly twice as likely as nonwhites to be victimized by gun violence; in the "real world," in contrast, it is African Americans who outpace other racial groups in these statistics. Numerous other researchers have commented on the tendency for the media to provide unrealistic portrayals of a variety of social groups and social phenomena (28–30). Our research complements their findings and adds two more ways in which inaccurate information is provided: by misconstruing both who it is who perpetrates gun violence and who it is who is victimized by gun violence in animated cartoons.

Another important finding derived in the present research is that animated cartoons tend to provide a rather dangerous series of messages to viewers about the consequences of gun violence. One-quarter of the time when shooting is shown, nothing happens, implying that this behavior is often a harmless one with few, if any, consequences. When characters are shown to be shot, the large majority of them experience no pain (83.9%), none of them bleeds, very few of them are rendered unconscious (4.2%) or dazed (6.7%), they rarely die (10.9%), and a sizable proportion of them suffer no consequences whatsoever of the gun violence befalling them (21.7%). This finding is similar to that reported by other researchers (6) who also observed that a sizable proportion of violent incidents in the media result in no harm. Moreover, the perpetrators of gun violence in animated cartoons rarely experience negative consequences as a result of their use of firearms (5.3% of the time). Based on these findings, we conclude that the message that cartoons convey to viewers that using guns is not very dangerous and that shooting others typically carries with it serious negative consequences neither for the shooter nor his/her victim. We concur with Kunkel and associates (6: I-121), who remarked that "programs do not portray any physical, emotional, psychological, or financial consequences of violence. When such consequences are shown, they are for the most part depicted as short-term in nature." This, we believe, is a risky message to convey, particularly where young viewers are concerned, because they are probably learning about guns and the possible consequences of gun use via their exposure to media content such as that presented in media like animated cartoons (as well as other programs or films they watch). If their early socialization about guns entails learning that gun use is rarely serious and typically causes no harmful effects even if one is shot–as was the case in the cartoons studied in the present research–then a healthy respect for and fear of the dangerous aspects inherent in gun use may not be developed. This, in turn, could lead some youths to come to think of guns as toys, rather than as weapons, and might lead to an increased risk of accidental use of firearms.

A fourth main finding of our research is that, when cartoon characters use guns, they almost always have a reason (or several reasons) for doing so. The most common reasons for using guns in the cartoons we studied were anger, revenge, and meanspiritedness. Our finding for anger resembles that obtained by Kunkel and associates (6), who also noted that anger was a common reason for television characters to perpetrate violence. Once again, we believe that these reasons underlying gun use in cartoons provide a potentially-dangerous message to viewers: If one is angry, or if one feels that one has been wronged and wishes to exact vengeance upon the perceived wrongdoer, or even if one is simply feeling mean or nasty at a particular moment in time, one acceptable way to handle these feelings is with the use of firearms. Story writers and animators of cartoons need to be made more keenly aware of the message that they are sending to viewers, particularly young viewers, with respect to the use of guns. In the absence of that awareness and a subsequent willingness on the part of the writers and animators to take action on the basis of that information, it is likely that viewers will continue to be confronted with–and presumably affected by–story content suggesting that anger and/or the desire for revenge justifies the use of guns.

What might be done based on these findings?

There are a number of things that might be done in an attempt to improve on the situation outlined above. First and foremost, studios producing new animated cartoons and the story-writers and producers of such cartoons could begin to develop storylines that are less violent, particularly where the use of guns is involved. Such cartoons can be entertaining without (or with significantly less) violence, and whenever violent content is deemed essential to the plot, it can be included in such a manner as to convey responsible messages (e.g., violence causes harm, perpetrators of violence may suffer consequences for their actions). We believe that one excellent way to begin to improve cartoons' content vis-a-vis gun violence would be, quite simply, to provide animated cartoon content that minimizes violence as much as possible. This has been done with great success in recent years with cartoon programs such as *Arthur* and *The Adventures of Little Bear*, among others.

Providing counter-programming amidst televised animated cartoon episodes (or alongside such cartoons made available to consumers on home video and DVD) might also be an avenue worth exploring. One way that counter-programming could be implemented–one that we think might be worthwhile and cost-effective for the television and cable industries to consider–would be through the addition of interstitial segments in existing animated cartoon programs. Interstitials are small program segments, usually having running times ranging from 30 seconds to about 3 minutes, that can be inserted between cartoon episodes within a given program if the episodes are short enough or that can be inserted between programs during the commercial blocks that occur before and after scheduled programming is broadcast. As short-form segments, interstitials would be inexpensive to create, and their short running times would allow them to be added to a variety of children's programs without requiring the broadcaster to edit these programs for time. The interstitials could be made so that they feature the same cartoon characters shown in the original (i.e., "problematic") cartoons, but with short vignettes that are simultaneously entertaining, enlightening, and prosocially-oriented. In this manner, the original, entertaining cartoons containing larger amounts of gun violence can remain intact and be broadcast intact while being combined with newer content that is designed to be equally entertaining but more prosocial in nature. Over the years, some studios (most notably Hanna-Barbera and Warner Brothers) and some television networks (most notably the American Broadcasting Company [ABC]) have implemented educational and/or prosocial interstitial segments into their animated cartoon programming, and these programs have been entertaining and positive in their content. We applaud these efforts. Moreover, some research has been conducted on the effects of counter-programming, generally showing at least some measure of success in accomplishing its goals (31). We believe that this type of approach to the issues pertaining to gun violence that we have outlined in this paper merits further exploration in the years to come.

Coinciding with this idea, a series of animated educational interstitial cartoons could be developed specifically to address a variety of issues pertaining to violence. The goal of the program series would be to educate young people about different types of violence and about ways that matters can be handled in an appropriate, rather than in a violent, manner. One program in the series could focus specifically on guns, the dangers associated with the improper use of guns, and so forth. Others might deal with issues like nonviolent conflict resolution, bullying, and vandalism, as well as other topics that are relevant to young persons' lives. The key with all such programming is to make it entertaining, so that viewers will watch the programs willingly and eagerly and pay attention to them and their messages.

ACKNOWLEDGMENTS

This research was supported by a grant by the National Institute on Alcohol Abuse and Alcoholism (R03-AA09885). The authors wish to acknowledge, with gratitude, Denise Welka Lewis, Scott Desmond, Lisa Gervase, and Thomas Lambing for their contributions to this study's data collection efforts.

REFERENCES

[1]   Rand MJ. Guns and crime: Handgun victimization, firearm self-defense, and firearm theft. Washington, DC: Bureau Justice Stat, 2002.

[2]   National Center for Injury Prevention and Control. Web-based injury statistics query and reporting system (WISQARS): Injury mortality reports. Atlanta, GA: CDC, 2004.

[3]   National Center for Injury Prevention and Control. Web-based injury statistics query and reporting system (WISQARS): Nonfatal injury reports. Atlanta, GA: CDC, 2004.

[4]   Federal Bureau of Investigation. Age-specific arrest rates and race-specific arrest rates for selected offenses. Washington, DC: US Gov Printing Office, 2003.

[5]   Diefenbach DL, West MD. Violent crime and poisson regression: A measure and a method for cultivation analysis. J Broadcasting Electronic Media 2001;45:432-45.

[6]   Kunkel D, Wilson BJ, Linz D, Potter J, Donnerstein E, Smith SL, et al. Violence in television programming overall: University of California Santa Barbara Study. In: Mediascope, National Television Violence Study 1994-1995. Studio City, CA: Mediascope, 1996:I1-72.

[7]   Anderson CA, Berkowitz L, Donnerstein E, Huesmann LR, Johnson JD, Linz D, et al. The influence of media violence on youth. Psychol Sci Public Interest, 2003;4:81-110.

[8]   Chory-Assad RM. Effects of television sitcom exposure on the accessibility of verbally aggressive thoughts. West J Commun 2004; 68:431-53.

[9]   Singer MI, Slovak K, Frierson T, York P. Viewing preferences, symptoms of psychological trauma, and violent behaviors among children who watch television. J Am Acad Child Adolesc Psychiatry 1998;37:1041-8.

[10] Shrum LJ, Wyler RSJr, O'Guinn TC. The effects of television consumption on social perceptions: The use of priming procedures to investigate psychological processes. J Consumer Res 1998;24:447-58.

[11] Akers RL. Deviant behavior. Belmont, CA: Wadsworth, 1973.

[12] Bandura A. Social learning theory. New York: General Learning Press, 1971.

[13] Gerbner G, Gross L. Living with television: The violence profile. J

[14] Commun 1976;26:173-99.

[15] Signorielli N, Morgan M. Cultivation analysis: New directions in media effects research. Newbury Park, CA: Sage, 1990.

[16] Greenberg BS. Television and role socialization: An overview. In: Pearl D, Bouthilet L, Lazar J, eds. Television and behavior: Ten years of scientific progress and implications for the eighties--Volume II: Technical reviews. Rockville, MD: Natl Inst Ment Health, 1982.

[17] Tiggeman M, Pickering AS. Role of television in adolescent women's body dissatisfaction and drive for thinness. Int J Eat Disord 1996;20:199-203.

[18] Lenberg J. The encyclopedia of animated cartoons. New York: Facts on File, 1991.

[19] Maltin L. Of mice and magic: A history of American animated cartoons. New York: Plume, 1980.

[20] Gerbner G, Signorielli N. Violence profile 1967 through 1988-89: Enduring patterns. Philadelphia: Annenberg Sch Commun, 1990.

[21] Hickey N. New violence survey released. TV Guide 1994;42:37-9.

[22] Nichols P, Dabbs D, Chester K. Landmark research reports on the nature of violent portrayals, ratings and advisories, and anti-violence messages on television. Press release by Mediascope, Los Angeles, CA 1996 Febr 07.

[23] Cole J. The UCLA television violence report 1996. Los Angeles, CA: UCLA Center Commun Policy, 1996.

[24] Woodard EH. The 1999 State of Children's Television report: Programming for children over broadcast and cable television. Philadelphia, PA: Annenberg Public Policy Center, 1999.

[25] Federal Communications Commission. Telecommunications act of 1996. Washington, DC: US Gov Printing Office, 1996.

[26] Pearl D, Bouthilet L, Lazar J, eds. Television and behavior: Ten years of scientific progress and implications for the eighties—volume II: Technical reviews. Rockville, MD: Natl Inst Ment Health, 1982.

[27] US Congress. House Committee on Interstate and Foreign Commerce: Hearings and report. Investigation of Radio and Television Programs. Washington, DC: US Gov Printing Office, 1952.

[28] US Surgeon General's Scientific Advisory Committee on Television and Social Behavior. Television and growing up: The impact of televised violence. Washington, DC: US Gov Printing Office, 1972.

[29] Paek HJ, Shah, H. Racial ideology, model minorities, and the "not-so-silent partner": Stereotyping of Asian Americans in U.S. magazine advertising. Howard J Commun 2003;14:225-43.

[30] Spitzer BL, Henderson KA, Zivian MT. Gender differences in population versus media body sizes: A comparison over four decades. Sex Roles 1999;40:545-65.

[31] Stern SR. Self-absorbed, dangerous, and disengaged: What popular films tell us about teenagers. Mass Commun Soc 2005;8:23-38.

[32] Power JG, Murphy ST, Coover G. Priming prejudice: How stereotypes and counter-stereotypes influence attribution of responsibility and credibility among ingroups and outgroups. Human Commun Res 1996;23:36-58.

In: Children, Violence and Bullying
Editors: J Merrick, I Kandel and H A Omar

ISBN: 978-1-62948-342-9
© 2014 Nova Science Publishers, Inc.

Chapter 9

SWEDEN: CHILDREN IN UNSAFE ENVIRONMENTS AND LIFE SITUATIONS

Jane Brodin, PhD[*]

Department of Child and Youth Studies, Stockholm University,
Stockholm, Sweden

ABSTRACT

This chapter is based on a project studying children growing up in precarious environments and life situations in Sweden. Data have emerged from the explorative study "Children in precarious life situations". Regardless of Sweden's long tradition in the social welfare field many children have difficulties and do not feel mentally well. The aim of this chapter is to increase the knowledge of children in precarious environments and life situations and to explore the existence of exposed arenas where many children spend their everyday lives. The chapter is based on previously conducted studies, official documents from UNICEF, Save the Children and WHO and on newly published research. The number of children who are maltreated is increasing in spite of the fact that they live in a welfare state. This has been highlighted both in research and the mass media; for some time the injustices and wrongdoing that many children experience have been highlighted. It is evident that despite Sweden's ratification of the United Nation's Convention on the Rights of the Child (CRC), it seems difficult to follow its intentions. Twenty years after Sweden's ratification of the CRC, it is now high time to listen to the voices of children in order to give them the opportunity of influencing their own lives. Many adults neglect to take responsibility for children's emotional and mental well-being. The power of teachers to protect children against harassment, abuse and insulting treatment is undervalued. Children need adults to rely on.

[*] Correspondence: Professor Jane Brodin, Department of Child and Youth Studies, Stockholm University, 10691 Stockholm, Sweden. E-mail: Jane.Brodin@buv.su.se.

INTRODUCTION

The UN Convention on the Rights of the Child (CRC) (1) was in 2009 celebrating its 20th anniversary, and all countries in the world (except the US) have ratified the convention. This means that the UN member states have undertaken to legally conduct its intentions. As a result of this the CRC has got a fairly strong penetrating power and this is due to several reasons. One reason is that many governments have considered it politically correct to have a global convention with focus on children, another that media has highlighted the injustices and wrongdoing that many children in the world experience today. The CRC is the first document of international law in which children's rights are recorded (2). The convention gives a general definition of which rights children have in all societies regardless of religion, culture or social structure. The convention includes financial, social, cultural and political rights, as well as the right of all children to the satisfaction of their basic needs of love, warmth, shelter, food and sleep (3). The convention is founded on the assumption that children have the right to have their basic needs satisfied and to be respected as individuals. Its four main principles are that all children have equal worth, that the child's best should have priority, that children have the right to life and development, and that children shall be able to influence their own situations, that is, to have their voices heard (1,4). If the member states had succeeded in living up to the goals in the convention, then it is reasonable to believe that reality would look different than it does for many children today.

BACKGROUND

Children in Scandinavia have materially better lives than children in many other countries; this is revealed in reports from Save the Children (5) and UNICEF (6). At the same time, it appears from media reports and research that many children do not feel mentally well and are unhappy despite growing up in a welfare society (7-9). The same reality has been observed in research from other countries (10-14). It appears that many children are maltreated by parents, relatives, peers and/or teachers, i.e. adults who are normally expected to protect them. What does it mean when we say that a child is maltreated? The World Health Organization (WHO) (15) states that the concept "maltreated children" refers to children who are subjected to physical abuse, sexual abuse, improper care and neglect, psychological insults and exploitation. However, maltreated and insulted children are not responsible themselves for their difficult situations; instead it is the environment around each individual child that leaves them exposed – an exposure that is especially problematic for children who are vulnerable (9). The main focus in intervention should therefore not be on the child, but on factors in their immediate environment (16,17). Maltreated children are often children who are found in precarious environments or in vulnerable life situations. An example constitutes children with neuro psychiatric disorders e.g. ADHD (Attention Deficits Hyperactivity Disorder), who are often placed in remedial classes in school because they are regarded as bully and disturbing, instead of regarding the environment.

PREVIOUS RESEARCH

The multidisciplinary project BASTA (Basic skills, social interaction and training of the working memory) involved 41 pupils between 8 and 12 years with difficulties in attention and concentration and their parents. The results from the project showed that children with neuro psychiatric diagnosis often experience difficulties in cooping with peers and consequently fail in social interaction and turn up in conflicts (18,19). These children will get nothing but negative feedback but many researchers mean that a negative response is better than no response at all (20). Jaudes and Mackey-Bilaver (21) conducted a study aimed at examining to what extent chronic health conditions place young children under age six at risk of maltreatment. They reported that children with behavioural and mental health conditions of low-income families, i.e. children with poor socio-economic background, were at the highest risk of abuse or neglect. However, the results also showed that intellectual disabilities did not increase the risk of maltreatment, while chronic physical conditions increased the risk slightly. Their conclusion was that early detection of mental or psychosocial conditions is of vital importance in order to prevent that children are maltreated and abused, and that child protection agencies should be trained to identify children at risk (ibid.). The same observations have been highlighted in Bulgaria by Stancheva-Popkostadinova and O'Connor (22).

OUR STUDY

The aim of this chapter is to increase the understanding and knowledge of children in precarious environments and life situations. Based on our previous studies (18,20) four main topics appeared: adult's responsibility for children's well-being, the school setting as a vital arena for children and adults, stress on children who are vulnerable and finally how adults in the immediate environment can help children who are maltreated and precarious. These topics have in the above mentioned studies appeared to be essential. This paper is thus based on previously conducted studies and official documents from UNICEF, Save the Children and WHO as well as newly published research. The approach is explorative and descriptive and the aim is to increase the understanding of children who are often labelled as bully and disorderly.

FINDINGS

Children act in many different arenas in their everyday lives, and one of the most frequent and extremely important arena is the school (6). Adults (parents, teachers and other professionals) in the child's immediate environment must be aware of and interpret the child's emotional and psychical reactions. Teachers in pre-school and school who notice that a child is maltreated, abused or insulted, must be observant and report the inconveniences to the social authorities in order to protect the child. But also other persons close to the child may notice that a child does not feel well (13,23,24). The teacher is often a role model for the children in the class, and therefore possesses great power in supporting children who are maltreated. The teacher's attitude shows the children in the class what is accepted in the way of speech and action, and the teacher must therefore act professionally (see the IRIS-project, 2009, www.irisproject.eu). By showing the classmates of a pupil with disorder that all children are accepted as the individuals they are, an attentive professional teacher can bring out something positive about each child (18). Thus the teacher makes the school into a safe environment even for those children who otherwise might feel that they are not supported by their teachers and classmates. The results from the IRIS-project show that seeing each child must be a natural part of a teacher's work. This will minimize the risk of each child with difficulties of being exposed to bullying; this is highlighted by many researchers (25-27).

Teachers in Sweden as in many other countries have, at the least suspicion that a child is abused, an obligation to report that suspicion to the social authorities (20,28). First of all this is a question of giving a child protection and shelter (1), secondly this is an ethical issue that must be taken into consideration. The result showed that there are many different reasons for adults not to report their suspicions about a child being maltreated. One reason reported was that it was painful for the teachers to see that children were maltreated, and they identified with the parents. Another reason was that the teachers lacked the professional knowledge about how to approach children who have difficulties (29). Listening to the children, trying to understand what they are actually saying, being able to see that a child is not feeling well, and being able to form an idea of how the children see their own situations are ways of observing the child's reactions and needs, and of showing the child respect (30). In this context it is also important to highlight the parents' responsibility towards their children. Children need parents, but if the parents do not have the strength or ability to carry out their parenthood in a loving and reliable way, then it is important that there is some other adult in the child's immediate environment with whom the child can talk if he or she has difficulties (4,22). The child cannot be left alone and it is not reasonable that children are forced to bear their problems themselves. However, if parents have social, emotional or psychiatric problems in their own lives they may be unable to give their child the support that the child needs so much in order to do well. The best of the child must thus be taken into consideration (1,3).

THE SCHOOL AS ARENA FOR CHILDREN AND ADULTS

The school is an arena both for children, teachers and other professionals. Children are sometimes subjected to bullying and harassment in school by teachers and/or pupils. The role and power of the teacher is often undervalued but research has showed that the teacher is a role model for the peers in the class (25). As a result of negative experiences and harassment in school some children and young people feel insulted and avoid to attend school and in the long run drop out of school. At the same time research has shown (7) that many adults do not feel well today and some parents are substance abusers, unemployed, unhealthy, or have other problems and therefore experience difficulties in giving the child a good home and to support the child in schoolwork. Some children experience difficulties in attending school as they feel uncomfortable to talk about their home situation. In 2006 the Act on discrimination and other insulting treatment of children and pupils (31) was passed in Sweden. This law was meant to counteract discrimination on the grounds of gender, ethnicity, functional disability, or religion and other beliefs. It confirms the responsibility that teachers, head teachers, and municipal authorities have for creating environments in which children and young people can feel secure and be treated equally. The law is applicable to education according to the Swedish Education Act (32). Many of these pupils find it difficult to carry out their schooling and fail in their studies which will in the long run influence their future opportunities. In some cases the parents are not aware that their child is frequently absent from school and perhaps the child does not talk about how he or she is doing at school (25). Sometimes all involved, i.e. parents, teachers, and the head teachers are unaware of the child's problem (29,2). From reports in mass media it appears that many children avoid talking to their parents about harassment and insulting treatment in school. They feel unsure that their parents would understand or even worse that their parents would diminish their problems. They believe that they are themselves responsible for the occurred situation (20). Alin Åkerman stated (7) that many young people with serious suicidal thoughts or even suicide attempts have been subjected to bullying during their middle school years. The feeling of vulnerability leaves deep scars that often remain into the upper secondary school period. The overall mental health during the past decade seems to have deteriorated all over the world, and a symptom of this is that some have developed a self-destructive behaviour. Boys often react with aggressiveness, while girls develop eating disorders or self-mutilation tendencies (ibid.).

Benjaminson (8) argued that school can be a secure place for many children and adolescents, and that their security is often based on the fact that unpredictable things cannot happen in school. She reports, though, that school can for other children become an extra burden, especially if they are not supported by their teachers and classmates. Benjaminson focused on children in precarious emotional situations and shows that many children cannot get any help from their parents with their homework, or are sometimes unable to do their homework because their home environments are too chaotic. These children cannot talk about this in school, and therefore appear to be careless and uninterested in their schoolwork. A relatively large segment of the pupils at the senior level of compulsory school do not manage to leave school with passing grades in the core subjects. This means that, in the short term, they are not accepted into the upper secondary school programmes that they wish to enter, and in the long term that they have difficulties in choosing what work they want to do. They fail often in their schoolwork, blame themselves, and feel that they have been treated unfairly and without justice (ibid.). These adolescents can all too easily be dissociated from school, as they have no control over the situation anyway.

Children react differently to the experiences they are submitted to depending on their varying conditions. Some children are born vulnerable and fragile, while others develop vulnerability by being in risky environments. However, most children and young people are resilient and have resistance and irrepressibility that allows them to repair difficulties and injustices that they have experienced during childhood (24,33).

CHILDREN WHO ARE VULNERABLE

The family is another arena in which children spend much of their daily lives. The Scandinavian family was earlier a core family consisting of a man, a woman and often one child. In southern Europe the family is often an extended family consisting of parents, siblings and relatives. The general concept of the family has changed over time and the number of single parents with children is growing. A family can today consist of many different constellations, and children grow up under various conditions (2). Most children have good developmental conditions, but there are still children growing up in destructive environments. Parents have the main responsibility for their children, in compliance with the Children and Parents Code (34), but what happens when parenthood is flawed, for example when parents have intellectual disabilities, mental illness or severe physical disorders? The Swedish National Board of Health and Welfare (35) states that parents who have intellectual disabilities often need a great deal of support in order to be able to care for their children. Bager (36) reports that every year 160 children are born in Sweden to single mothers with intellectual disabilities and fathers with psychosocial problems. Many of these children follow the normal development curve, but the parents, and especially the mothers, often need and require extensive support. Nevertheless, it has been found that most of the children who are taken into social care are not children of parents with intellectual disabilities, but with other problems (36).

Many children are vulnerable from birth, while others live in environments that are precarious and make them vulnerable. Which children are in the risk zone for ending up in a precarious life situation or living environment? Sommer (24) has stressed that some children are resilient and learn to cope with and handle difficult conditions. For this reason all children are not designated to bad living conditions although they are considered to be children at risk. Some children grow up as beautiful lilies in the asphalt and the only way to explain this phenomenon is by the concept resilience – they are resistant and recover from the difficulties. We know that the family's living conditions affect the children's situation; their financial position, health/ill health, work/unemployment, good or dubious social situations are some factors that have significance to the child's vulnerability. Children who have functional impairments can be in the risk zone if they have difficulties in communicating and making their opinions heard (9) as well as children with behavioral and mental health conditions (21). The risk of being excluded if the children cannot participate in the activities that their peers do, also entails the possibility that they can be excluded or bullied (2). Children who come from another ethnic background than the dominant Swedish one can sometimes be vulnerable, as their parents may have ideas that differ from the common ones about child-raising and what can be expected of a child. The collision between the two cultures (the Swedish and the ethnically different) often leads to both misunderstanding and condemnation of the families' way of acting (35).

Some children have heavy demands placed on them in their everyday lives, especially when it comes to schoolwork. This can lead to stress, which in the long term can result in ill health. Another form of vulnerability can be found in families where the child is abused mentally or physically. In 1979 Sweden passed a law against corporal punishment, but despite the law the abuse of children of all ages has increased. The greatest increase (from 758 cases in 1981 to 7455 cases in 2006) reports on abuse of children between 7 and 14 years (38). In many cases the perpetrator of these crimes are very young, but abuse of children under six years of age is often committed by a family member – a parent or step-parent.

Reflections on how adults can help children who are maltreated

Research has as mentioned above shown that the number of children in Sweden, who are maltreated is growing despite the law (7,8,20). The trend is the same all over the world. Several reasons are evident, and in this article only a few examples of children who are in precarious living environments or living situations are mentioned. These children are often subjected by adults or older children to physical or sexual abuse, neglect or improper care, mental insults and exploitation, but they can also be cases of children who are subjected to harassment or bullying in school by peers. This is a global problem and it appears that children are neglected and abused also in other parts of the world (e.g. 4,11,32). Some of these children have no close adults to confide their problems to. Their vulnerability is thus extensive, and it is easy for these children to take the burdens of responsibility upon themselves and blame themselves for their situation (8).

Parents are the most significant people in the child's life, and they are expected to give their children unconditional security and love (1). Children's right to have parents is irrefutable, and for most children their parents are of great importance to their health and well-being. Children who have difficulties need parents who can support and help them and the parents are often children's role models in life. Parents have responsibility, and even though the parents may themselves have difficult life situations, they are still important to their children (9). If a child has parents who do not have the stamina to carry out their parental roles, it is important that the child have some other adult to confide in but they can never shift the responsibility for their children over to the school. The school is the arena that includes all children, and therefore the school can be seen as a complement to the home, one that compensates the child for what he or she cannot get at home. A good school environment is important for all children, as it can provide security for the child (29, www.irisproject.eu). Teachers are role models in school, and therefore it is important that they offer all pupils a good environment. Teachers have a great responsibility to observe what happens in the class and in the schoolyard; in the school world there are no parents present who can protect the child. For many children the parents represent security, but as mentioned previously other adults can step up to listen to the child and give support in a difficult situation (18,20). If it is apparent that a child is maltreated despite this action, reporting the situation to authorities must be considered. It can be difficult to know when a report should be made, but the law in Sweden for instance says that as soon as there is a suspicion that a child is maltreated, it should be reported to the social authorities. In reality, however, it has been shown that many adults avoid reporting as they feel unsure about whether they *see or interpret a situation correctly*.

Many children in today's school are subjected to bullying, harassment and discrimination, and as a result do not want to go to school. In 2006 a Swedish law was passed (31) and its purpose is to create good, secure environments for children and young people. If children do not feel secure, they may decide to play truant and thus fall behind and fail in their schoolwork. For some children this can become a vicious circle in which the situation for the child eventually becomes intolerable if the child has no support from his or her parents, schoolteachers or other adults in his or her close environment (27).

School should be a good educational environment, one that takes advantage of a child's interests and supports his or her development. Even though the school's primary task is not to raise children but rather to educate them, teachers must take responsibility for providing opportunities for all children to feel that they are taking part. The teacher must therefore take notice of, listen to and *see* each child, and thus offer the child a secure environment.

Despite the ratification of the CRC twenty years ago the goals are not yet attained. The member states need to reconsider the convention seriously and try to find out how to meet the needs of children and give them a voice to express themselves and influence their daily living. The convention concerning persons (including children) with disabilities from 2008 stress "nothing about us without us".

CONCLUSION

The global increase of children not feeling well must be stopped. The teachers' role as a gatekeeper to stop bullying and insulting treatment in school need to be stressed as the power of teachers is undervalued. Efforts to stop harassment, abuse and insulting treatment of children must be regarded as a step towards prevention of maltreatment. The main result showed that adults in general must take increased responsibility for children's mental well-being.

REFERENCES

[1]   The Convention of the Rights of the Child. New York: United Nations, 1989.
[2]   Brodin J, Lindstrand P. Perspektiv på en skola för alla. [Perspectives on a school for all]. Lund: Studentlitteratur, 2010. [Swedish]
[3]   Hollenweger J. The Convention on the Rights of Persons with Disabilities. New York: United Nations, 2008.
[4]   Brodin J, Stancheva-Popkostadinova V. Ethical considerations in child research in light of the convention on the rights of the child. Divisions of global affairs, Rutgers University. J Global Change Governance 2009;2(2):1-16.
[5]   "Några räknas som bättre än andra" 25 berättelser från unga i Sverige om mobbning, rasism och diskriminering.["Some count as better than others". 25 stories of young persons in Sweden about bullying, racism and discrimination"]. Stockholm: Save the Children Sweden, 2002. [Swedish].
[6]   UNICEF . Innocenti Report Card No. 5: A league Table of Child Maltreatment Deaths in Rich Nations. Florence: Innocenti Research Centre, 2003.
[7]   Alin Åkerman B. Att skada sig själv – ett uttryck för ångest och identitet [To hurt oneself – a reaction of regret and identity]. In Bjärvall (Ed.). Utsatta barn – allas ansvar [Exposed children – responsibility of all people]. Stockholm: FAS, 2006.(Swedish).
[8]   Benjaminson C. Ungdomars erfarenheter av emotionell utsatthet under uppväxten. [Adolescent's experiences of emotional exposure when growing up]. Dissertation. Stockholm University: Dept Child Youth Stud, 2008.
[9]   Brodin J. Barn i utsatta miljöer och livssituationer [Children in exposed environments and living situations]. Socialmed Tidskr 2009;2:185-91. [Swedish]
[10]   Attar-Schwartz S. School functioning of children in residential care: The contributions of multilevel correlates. Child Abuse Neglect 2009;3(7):429– 40.
[11]   Browne KD. Focus on Asia. Child Abuse Rev 1993;2:127–9.
[12]   Crittenden PM, Hartl Claussen A. The organization of attachment relationships: Maturation, culture and context. New York: Cambridge Univ Press, 2003.

[13]   Glaser D. Emotional abuse and neglect (psychological maltreatment): a conceptual framework: Child Abuse Neglect 2002;26(6-7):697–714.

[14]   Mudaly N, Goddard C. The truth is longer than a lie: Children's experiences of abuse and professional intervention. London: Jessica Kingsley, 2006.

[15]   Child abuse and neglect by parents and other caregivers. World report on child and adolescent injury and prevention. Geneva: World Health Organization, 2006..

[16]   Bandy T, Moore KA. Non-participation of children and adolescents in out-of-school time programs: Child, family, and neighbourhood factors. Research-to-Results, 2009, Child Trends (ED506014)

[17]   Dutro E.. Children writing 'hard times': lived experiences of poverty and the class-privileged assumptions of a mandated curriculum. Language Arts 2009;87(2):89–98.

[18]   Brodin J, Ljusberg A-L. Teaching children with attention deficit hyperactivity disorder in remedial classes. Int J Rehabil Res 2008;31(4):351–5.

[19]   Westerberg H. Working memory: Development, disorders and training. Dissertation. Stockholm: Karolinska Inst, 2004.

[20]   Ljusberg A-L. Pupils in remedial classes. Dissertation. Stockholm: Dept Child Youth Stud, 2009.

[21]   Jaudes PK, Mackey-Bilaver L. Do chronic conditions increase young children's risk of being maltreated? Child Abuse Neglect 2008;32(7):671–81.

[22]   Stancheva-Popkostadinova V, O'Connor B. Teamwork between professionals and parents of children in the field of intellectual disabilities: Learning exchange between students in Bulgaria and Australia. Science, Culture and Education, Blagoevgrad, Bulgaria: South-West University, 2008.

[23]   Cumming S, Visser J. Using art with vulnerable children. Support Learning 2009;24(4):151–8.

[24]   Sommer D. Barndomspsykologi. Utveckling i en förändrad värld.[Childhood psychology. Development in a changeable world]. Malmö: Runa Förlag, 2005. [Swedish]

[25]   Hjörne E. Excluding for inclusion? Negotiating school careers and identities in pupil welfare settings in the Swedish school. Dissertation. Göteborg: Acta Universitatis Gothoburgensis, 2004.

[26]   Lareau A. Unequal Childhoods. Class, race and family life. Berkeley, CA: Univ Calif Press, 2003.

[27]   Strander K. Goda pedagogiska miljöer – fristad och utmaning, [Good pedagogical environments – room for relaxation and challenge]. In: Brodin J, ed. Barn i utsatta livssituationer.[Children in exposed living situations]. Malmö: Gleerups, 2008:49-78. [Swedish]

[28]   Ljusberg A-L, Brodin J, Lindstrand P. Ethical issues when interviewing children in remedial classes. Int Rehabil Res 2007;30:203–7.

[29]   Brodin J. Support systems in preschool and school for children with disabilities. IRIS-project, CD-rom. www.irisproject.eu. 2009b.

[30]   Grugel J, Peruzzotti E. Claiming rights under global governance: Children's rights in Argentina. Global Governance 2007;13:199–216.

[31]   SFS 2006:67. The act prohibiting discrimination and other insulting treatment of children and pupils. Stockholm: Min Educ, 2006.

[32]   SFS 1985:1100 Swedish Education Act. Ministry of Education, 1985.

[33]   McGloin JM, Spatz Widom C. Resilience among abused and neglected children grown up. Dev Psychopathol 2001;13:1021-38.

[34]   SFS 1949:381. Children and parents code. Stockholm: Min Soc Affairs, 1949.

[35]   Högdin S. Utbildning på (o)lika villkor: om kön och etnisk bakgrund i grundskolan.[Education on (un)equal conditions: about gender and ethnical background in school]. Dissertation. Stockholm: Dept Soc Work 2007. [Swedish]

[36]   Bager B. Barn till mödrar med utvecklingsstörning – en inventering. Liten riskgrupp som behöver stort stöd under otrygg uppväxt. [Children of mother's with intellectual disabilities – a survey]. Läkartidningen 2003;100(1-2):22–5.

[37]   National Board of Health and Welfare [Socialstyrelsen] Barn och Unga: insatser år 2006. [Children and young people: efforts in 2006]. Stockholm: Natl Swedish Board Health Welfare, 2007. [Swedish]

[38]   Swedish National Council for Crime Prevention. Stockholm: Brå, 2007.

In: Children, Violence and Bullying
Editors: J Merrick, I Kandel and H A Omar

ISBN: 978-1-62948-342-9
© 2014 Nova Science Publishers, Inc.

Chapter 10

BEHAVIORAL PARENT TRAINING PROGRAMS FOR REDUCTION OF CHILD PROBLEM BEHAVIOR

Cynthia L Boyle, MA and John R Lutzker, PhD[*]

Applied Behavioral Science, University of Kansas, Lawrence,
Kansas and Center for Healthy Development, School of Public Health,
Georgia State University, Atlanta, Georgia, US

ABSTRACT

In order to produce durable behavioral change over time, effective behavioral parent training programs should demonstrate that parenting skills generalize to various situations outside the training setting, as well as improve child problem behaviors in those situations over time. However, there is a paucity of studies that demonstrate such outcomes because many empirically-based behavioral parent training programs are typically assessed in controlled research settings, rather than in "real world" settings where behavior change is intended. The limited body of literature that has reported investigations of the effects of parent skill generalization on child problem behavior in nontraining settings is examined here. Specifically, a quantitative analysis of generalization outcomes was conducted. In this analysis, amount of generalization found in nontraining settings was quantified by calculating a "generalization score" for parent skills evaluated in each study. The formula used to compute a generalization score was "percent change." Generalization scores were calculated by dividing percent change scores for the nontraining setting by percent change scores for the training setting. Although generalization was not consistently shown across all parents, children, and/or variables in a number of studies, results suggest that parents can generalize skills to nontraining settings. However, knowledge of critical variables that produce generalization, techniques that reliably increase its likelihood, and individual variables that influence its occurrence, is incomplete. Recommendations for future research to increase parent skill generalization in real world settings are discussed.

[*] Correspondence: John R Lutzker, PhD, Director, Center for Healthy Development, College of Health and Human Sciences, Professor of Public Health, Georgia State University, POBox 3995, Atlanta, GA 30302-3995, United States. E-mail: jlutzker@gsu.edu

INTRODUCTION

Research has shown that behavioral parent training programs can produce changes in parent skills to decrease child problem behaviors (1). In order to produce durable behavior change over time, effective programs should also demonstrate that parenting skills generalize to various situations outside the training setting, as well as improve child problem behaviors in those situations over time. Parent generalization of skills occurs when parents correctly implement strategies with new children, across different nontraining settings, or for novel child problem behaviors without additional training or when supplemental training is less than that provided in the initial training setting (2). Because such programs aim to teach parents skills that decrease child problem behaviors in the natural rather than clinical environment, studies in which change is not documented outside the training setting limit conclusions about the practicality and clinical/social validity of behavioral parent training programs.

However, there is a paucity of studies that demonstrate such outcomes because many empirically-based behavioral parent training programs are assessed in controlled research settings, rather than where behavior change is intended, that is, home and community settings (3). In contrast, when generalization in these settings has been examined, studies neglect to include data across training and nontraining settings. Such data would demonstrate that parenting skills in the clinic sufficiently generalized and were responsible for reductions in child problem behavior in the home. Unless such measurements are conducted, it is difficult to conclude that behavioral parent training produces durable and socially valid behavior change.

Thus, the purpose of this brief review was to examine the limited body of literature that has investigated the effects of parent skill generalization on child problem behavior in nontraining settings and to quantify the level of generalization that has been found in those settings. To this end, a PsychoInfo database search using terms such as "parent training," "parent education," "parenting program" "generalization," "transfer," "child problem behavior," and child disruptive behavior," yielded 46 studies. Studies with interpretable pre and posttest data from training and nontraining settings on parent skills and child outcomes targeted for change were included. Of these, 16 evaluated the extent to which skills taught to parents through behavioral parent training were implemented in nontraining settings, and included data on child problem behavior in those settings.

OUR STUDY

Many of the studies that met inclusion criteria analyzed outcomes using single-case research designs. These designs report outcomes for individuals and thus do not allow for calculations such as effect size which can quantify the magnitude of change that occurred for a particular variable, setting, or group of participants. Although effect size calculations have been reported for single case research designs (4), the studies included in this review did not provide the type of data required for these calculations. All studies measured outcomes using direct observations by trained observers. To provide a meaningful analysis of parent generalization in nontraining settings, the amount of generalization found in these settings was quantified by calculating a "generalization score" for parent skills evaluated in each study.

Thus, conclusions could be made about if and how much skill generalization occurred compared to changes that occurred in training settings. The formula used to compute a generalization score was "percent change." This calculation was chosen because it indicates the extent to which a variable has increased or decreased in magnitude from an initial value (baseline). Percent change was calculated for training and nontraining settings. Generalization scores were calculated by dividing percent change scores for the nontraining setting by percent change scores for the training setting.

In theory, generalization scores quantify if change in nontraining settings was less than (<99%), equal to (=100%), or greater than (>100%) change that occurred in training. To examine the extent to which skill generalization produced reductions in child problem behaviors in nontraining compared to training settings, this score was also calculated for child outcomes. When direct observation data were only presented graphically and not reported in the text of reports, data points from graphs were used to procure numbers; hence, calculations may represent rough estimates for some studies. Generalization scores (see table 1) were grouped into categories: poor (0% to 25%), fair (25% to 49%), moderate (50% to 79%), high (80% to 100%), and very high (>100%). Studies that introduced generalization promotion components sequentially have data in table 1 to reflect multiple phases (i.e., posttreatment 2).

FINDINGS

The focus here is on studies producing high/very high levels of skill generalization and speculation regarding variables that appear to influence generalization outcomes. Overall, 13 of 16 (81%) studies showed fair to very high levels of skill generalization. In 19% of studies, greater levels of skill change occurred at posttreatment in nontraining settings than in training settings. Moderate to high and fair levels of skill generalization in nontraining settings were found in 38% and 25% of studies, respectively; poor generalization was found in 19%. These data suggest that generalization of parent skill is a predictable outcome of behavioral parent training programs.

Does generalization of parent skill also produce desirable changes in child behavior in nontraining settings? Where skill generalization levels were moderate or higher, equivalent or greater levels of change were also observed in child problem behavior (see table 1). As would be expected, poor or fair levels of skill generalization produced lower levels of change in child problem behaviors in nontraining settings (5-7). However, in six studies, poor or fair levels of parent skill generalization were able to produce moderate to high levels of change in child problem behaviors in nontraining settings at posttreatment. In three of these studies (8-10), generalization scores accurately reflect that the degree of skill change in nontraining settings was considerably less than that found in training settings. However, in all cases the percentage of skill change (see table 1) in nontraining settings was over 100%; this accounts for corresponding changes in child problem behavior.

Table 1. Percentage of change and generalization scores for parent skill and targeted child behaviors across training and generalization settings

Authors	N	Training Setting	GEN Setting	Mastery Criteria	% Change Training Setting Child			% Change GEN Setting Child			% Change Training Setting Parent			% Change GEN Setting Parent			GEN Score Child			GEN Score Parent		
					PTTX		FU	PTTX		FU	PTTX		FU	PTTX		FU	PTTX		FU	PTTX		FU
					1	2		1	2		1	2		1	2		1	2		1	2	
Peed, Roberts, & Forehand, 1977 (8)	6	CL	H	Y	30			17			301			103			*M					*F
Sanders, 1982 (7)	2	H	CM	N	56	69	97	5	60	84	64	73	77	14	73	78	P	*H	H	P	*VH	H
Sanders & Dadds, 1982 (26)	5	H	H&CM	N	26	57		36	61		120	118		64	81		VH	*VH		M	*M	
Bauman, Reiss, Rogers, & Bailey, 1983 (27)	9	CM	CM	N	61			75			67			64			VH			H		
Dachman, Halasz, Bickett, & Lutzker, 1984 (5)	1	H	H	Y	65			28			1900			0			F			P		
Zangwill, 1984 (10)	5	CL	H	N	51			42			363			122			H			F		
Sanders & Christensen, 1985 (28)	10	CL&H	H	N	4		46	30		43	23		20	41		35	VH		H	VH		VH
Dadds, Sanders, & James, 1987 (Study 1) (6)	6	CL&H	H&CM	N	56		24	6		18	53		44	14		17	P		M	F		F
Dadds, Sanders, & James, 1987 (Study 2) (6)	4	CL&H	H&CM	N	62	67	67	44	70	74	39	43	46	36	47	40	M	*VH	VH	H	*VH	H
Cordisco, Strain, & Depew, 1988 (11)	3	S	H	N	79		81	65	188	71	128		105	44	84	63	H	*VH	H	F	*M	M
Sanders & Plant, 1989 (29)	3	H	H	N	80		69	71		72	48		40	32		32	*H		VH	*M		H
Powers, Singer, Stevens, & Sowers, 1992 (9)	3	H	H&CM	N	64		75	64		75	2039		2255	188		388	*H		H	*P		P
Powers & Roberts, 1995 (15)	9	CL	H	Y	88	181		157	160		151	275		483	540		VH	*H		VH	*VH	
Delaney & Kaiser, 2001 (30)	4	CC	H	Y	62			33			119			80			M			M		
Bencit, Edwards, Olmi, Wilczynski, & Mancial, 2001 (13)	3	CL	H	Y	234			142			245			38			M			P		
Hancock, Kaiser, & Delaney, 2002 (12)	5	CC	H	Y	119			79			126			50			M			F		

Notes: N=Number of participants; Gen=Generalization; CL=Clinic; H=Home; CM=Community; S=School; CC=Childcare center; Y=Yes; N=No; PTTX=Posttreatment; FU=Follow up; *= Generalization promotion strategy used: Poor=P; Fair=F; Moderate=M; High=H Very high=VH.

The remaining studies (11-13) show a similar pattern; however, percentage of change scores for parent skills in nontraining settings ranged from 38% to 50%, suggesting that even modest parent skill generalization produced what might be considered adequate changes in child problem behavior. Alternatively, it is possible that children generalized responding from training to nontraining settings. These findings bring questions for research such as, what is the minimum level of parent skill generalization that produces socially valid changes in child behavior? Is more or less parent skill generalization required for certain populations? Are existing measures sensitive to changes in parent skill?

Overall, these data suggest that changes in parent skill in nontraining settings produced measurable changes in child problem behavior. Notably, five out of seven studies that conducted follows-up showed maintenance of moderate to very high levels of skill generalization with similar levels of improvement in child problem behaviors. One exception was the work of Powers et al. (1992), when a parent failed to generalize skills, 1:1 training to mastery criteria in the nontraining setting was provided. Yet, skill gains were of questionable utility as child behavior was unaffected. One possibility is that behavioral functions differed across training and nontraining settings. Thus, correct implementation of parent strategies might be hampered if contingencies applied across settings did not address function in both settings. This example suggests that a functional analysis or, minimally a descriptive analysis (14) should be conducted so that parents can learn to apply contingencies correctly once the formal intervention ends.

Generalization promotion components

The speculation that including specific strategies or training techniques to promote skill generalization would result in greater levels of parent skill generalization and improved child problem behavior in nontraining settings was partially supported. Of the eight studies that did so, three described high or very high levels of skill generalization as well as high or very high levels of improvement in child problem behavior.

For example, Sanders (7), mediated generalization (2) by introducing parent self-monitoring. This procedure increased parent skill and desired child behaviors from poor to very high and high, respectively. The Dadds et al (6) data showed that skill levels improved from high to very high with the introduction of planned activities training (PAT) and partner support training (PST); the former taught sufficient exemplars (2) by targeting multiple activities and situations that commonly set the occasion for problem behaviors. Parents learn to plan activities in advance, discuss rules and consequences with children, and provide feedback.

Generalization is further mediated by instructing parents to implement PAT in all new situations in which they face problem behavior. PST targeted family conflict, quality discussions, and problem-solving. Ceiling effects precluded definitive conclusions about effects of PAT and PST on skill generalization, though concurrent improvements (from moderate to very high) in child behavior suggested that additional skill generalization occurred outside of experimental observations. Future studies examining multiple generalization strategies should be designed to test each separately such that programs can be tailored for efficiency by including only effective strategies.

Training techniques (15) were examined in an evaluation of parent generalization in structured (task demand) and unstructured (play, household routines) nontraining settings by comparing standard (ST) to simulation training (SIM) techniques. The latter added role-playing in three clinic simulations: wake-up/dressing, mealtime, and clean-up/bedtime. One difference emerged between training techniques that is not captured in table 1: child compliance and praise ratios in unstructured nontraining settings were significantly greater for SIM compared to ST from pre-to posttest. Thus, practicing skills in multiple contexts with stimuli closely approximating those found in nontraining settings effectively promoted skill generalization. Provision of multiple exemplars also appears to effect parents' ability to perform in less predictable conditions such as when they are completing household routines. Increased levels of skill generalization and improved child behaviors were clearly shown after training was systematically scheduled in nontraining conditions in which generalization did not occur (11). For two of three parents, an instruction to generalize and teaching similar to that provided in training was provided; one parent received graphic feedback on her own and her child's performance. Thus, generalization promotion involved additional training in the nontraining setting that was slightly less intense than that provided in training; this is called sequential modification (2).

In sum, in studies with high/very high levels of parent skill generalization and corresponding levels of child improvement, techniques such as training sufficient exemplars, programming common stimuli, and mediating generalization, lead to positive outcomes.

Similarity of training to nontraining setting. Another speculation was that training conducted in settings similar to the natural environment would produce higher levels of generalization. High to very high levels of skill generalization and corresponding levels of improvement in child problem behaviors were found in 38% of studies in which training was conducted and generalization assessed in the same/similar setting; 25% of studies in which training was conducted in a setting much different than where generalization was assessed also produced these robust outcomes. Thus, similarity of training setting as a factor in promoting skill generalization was not strongly supported.

Use of mastery criteria. Another question, if use of mastery criteria for parent skills would improve skill generalization in nontraining settings, was only weakly supported. If parenting procedures are not learned to mastery criteria in the training setting, parents may incorrectly implement these procedures when faced with novel stimulus conditions. Thus, analyzing parent skill generalization in nontraining settings should only occur after it has been established that skills have been learned to mastery criteria. In this study sample, percentage of change scores for parent skill generalization were 80% or more for 3 of 6 studies using mastery criteria; 1 of these showed comparable levels of improvement in child problem behaviors. In the 10 studies in which mastery criteria were absent, only 2 showed parent skill changes of 80% or more and neither showed the same magnitude of change in child problem behavior. Small sample size limited conclusions about the value of mastery criteria; however, data suggest that examining competency as a factor in skill generalization is warranted. Future research could compare parents who have met and have not met mastery criteria to determine if skill competency is a factor affecting generalization.

Training techniques and parenting strategies employed. Did certain training techniques and parenting strategies improve generalization? Seven of 20 training techniques (e.g., discussion, modeling, instructions, role-play with therapist, and verbal feedback) with high/very high generalization scores used by at least 3 studies were identified. However, all but two (i.e., rehearsal, written feedback) were also used by interventions that produced poor/fair skill generalization. A similar pattern emerged with 6 of 27 parenting strategies identified (praise, timeout, response cost, contingent responding, behavior compliance routine, delivering instructions). These data suggest that training techniques and parenting strategies used in studies in which there was high/very high generalization were not unique to successful programs. A meta-analysis conducted to pinpoint training techniques and parent strategies predictive of positive parent and children outcomes found that role-playing skills with their children was a significant predictor of large effect sizes (16). Strategies predictive of large effect sizes included teaching parents communication skills such as active listening and decreasing negative comments/questions, increasing positive parent-child interactions such as attending and praising, and disciplinary consistency, especially timeout. Exploring if such findings are applicable to improved parenting skills and child problems outside of training is needed.

DISCUSSION

Details regarding individual studies that were not shown in table 1 warrant further discussion. First, generalization was not consistently shown across all parents, children, and/or variables in a number of studies. Commentary on generalization failure in the articles reviewed here mostly fell into two categories: individual differences and design problems. The former focused on incorrect parent implementation, differences in parent skill ability, at-risk parents with competing contingencies, and poor attendance. The latter included small sample size, ceiling/floor effects, coding sensitivity problems, and reactivity. These problems are common to parent training research in general; thus, more sophisticated research designs with larger samples could address some of these issues, as well as questions such as: does lack of social support, type of observational procedure, or access to professionals via webcams or other technology affect the likelihood of generalization?

To further pursue research on parent generalization, a number of methodological and experimental design limitations should be addressed. First, some studies implemented multiple generalization strategies at the same time; thus, the relative effect of each on parent skill, if any, could not be determined. Other studies did not analyze variables operating when generalization was unprogrammed. Such analyses should be incorporated into research where generalization has been shown (2). Whether mastery criteria increases skill generalization, if failure to meet such criteria predicts poor generalization, and if use of mastery criteria affects the likelihood of skill maintenance should be examined.

Also, fewer than half of studies examined generalization over time. Maintenance data are essential to learn the full impact of programs, and should be planned by design. Another pattern that emerged was the absence of comparative data on parent and child behaviors in training versus nontraining settings; 31 studies were excluded from this review due to insufficient data. Including direct observation measures of parent and child behaviors across settings, different behaviors, and siblings when possible would allow for a comprehensive analyses of parent skill generalization. These measurements should be practical. For example, clinic-based parent training programs might arrange for single probes at baseline, during training, and at posttest via video observations to provide a snapshot of parent skill and child problem behaviors in the natural environment. Video technologies installed in the home, such as wireless webcams could be used to record behavioral observations that are transmitted via the internet to a centralized location for review (17). Such methods would save programs on time and resources typically devoted to scheduling observational appointments and staff time and travel expenses.

Directions for future research

One promising strategy to bolster skill generalization is general case instruction (18). This involves strategic selection of contexts for teaching from the entire range of opportunities in which the skill can used in the natural environment (19). Teaching exemplars sample the range of response and stimulus variations the learner will contact including possible exceptions. Exemplars are sequenced such that easy and difficult situations are represented. Teaching employs procedures such as shaping, prompting, and differential reinforcement. Performance is tested in multiple nontraining contexts to monitor generalization. General case instruction has been effective in training parents discrete trial training techniques (19); thus, it may also be useful in training parents behavior management strategies. For example, teaching exemplars for use of planned ignoring could sample the range of response variations (e.g., whining, tantrums, throwing objects) for which the function of child problem behavior is to contact positive reinforcement including exceptions (e.g., when to use planned ignoring in combination with response blocking for spitting).

In a related area, it was found that teaching various procedures for a range of behaviors was a more effective methodology for increasing generalized use of skills and targeted child behaviors than teaching parents to apply those skills narrowly to specific target behaviors (20). This strategy, referred to as "training loosely" (2), was effective for parents that participated in Triple P (21). Generalization techniques involved teaching behavioral principles through tip sheets, videos, parent designed behavior plans, use of sufficient exemplars, goal-setting, and self-monitoring. Using the parent participatory model, parents were verbally prompted to use the parenting information to which they were exposed to make choices and solve problems related to their own and their child's behavior. Parents were asked to think of other situations in which the parenting strategies might be helpful instead of being directly instructed to generalize certain procedures to specific behaviors. Feedback from the therapist allowed for discussions of behavioral function as parents were brainstorming when to use procedures across a range of situations. Investigators (21) found statistically significant decreases in child problem behavior across training and nontraining settings. Future research could identify the relative effectiveness of training in which parents learn to apply behavior management procedures "loosely" versus for specific targeted problem child behaviors.

An obstacle to generalization research is the cost of conducting multiple observations to establish that parenting skills have generalized to the natural environment. However, if resources devoted to implementation of programs could be reduced, programs could focus on evaluation of outcomes in home and community settings. New technologies applied to the delivery of a variety of health promotion programs that reduce staffing resources required for face-to-face programming may provide promise in reducing the overall cost of these interventions. For example, programs targeting the reduction of child behavior problems are being delivered successfully via video-based interventions (22), multimedia online training courses (23), and CD-ROM technology (24).

In other fields, virtual reality computer-based systems are being used to teach social skills (25), and educational video games are being used in youth violence prevention efforts (17). Virtual reality methods might be a promising strategy for families to learn parenting skills, for example, by practicing skills with virtual children (17). Educational video games could teach parents decision-making and problem-solving skills important for management of child behavior problems. For example, the object of a video game might focus on parents obtaining game points based on the number of times parents use time-out correctly, praise appropriate child behaviors, or use planned ignoring for minor child behavior problems. These methods bring an inherent novelty and entertainment value to what has previously been purely instruction and practice-based learning. However, such methods should be clinically and socially valid; thus, evaluation of outcomes in the natural environment is essential.

CONCLUSION

In conclusion, there is evidence that parents generalize skills to nontraining settings; however, knowledge of critical variables that produce generalization, techniques that reliably increase its likelihood, and individual variables that influence its occurrence, is incomplete. Moreover, technology-based interventions should strategically plan for evaluation of generalization in their initial stages of development to add weight to the advantages they offer in terms of their promised efficiency and cost-effectiveness. Such analyses will improve the technology of generalization and warrant further study.

ACKNOWLEDGMENTS

The authors would like to thank Dr James Sherman for his assistance.

REFERENCES

[1]   Lundahl BW, Risser HJ, Lovejoy MC. A meta-analysis of parent training: Moderators and follow-up effects. Clin Psychol Rev 2006;26(1):86-104.

[2]   Stokes TF, & Baer, D. M. An implicit technology of generalization. J Appl Behav Analysis 1977;10:349-67.

[3]   Long N, Edwards MC, Bellando J. Parent training interventions. In Matson JL, Andrasck F, Matson ML, eds. Treating childhood psychopathology and developmental disabilities. New York: Springer, 2008:79-104.

[4]   Swanson HL, Sachse-Lee C. A meta-analysis of single-subject-design intervention research for students with LD. J Learn Disabil 2000;33(2):114-36.

[5]   Dachman RS, Halasz MM, Bickett AD, Lutzker JR. A home-based ecobehavioral parent-training and generalization package with a neglectful mother. Educ Treat Child 1984;7(3):183-202.

[6]   Dadds MR, Sanders MR, James JE. The generalization of treatment effects in parent training with multidistressed parents. Behav Psychother 1987;15(4):289-313.

[7] Sanders MR. The generalization of parent responding to community settings: The effects of instructions, plus feedback, and self-management training. Behav Psychother 1982;10(3):273-87.

[8] Peed S, Roberts M, Forehand R. Evaluation of the effectiveness of a standardized parent training program in altering the interaction of mothers and their non-compliant children. Behav Modif 1977;1(3):323-50.

[9] Powers LE, Singer GH, Stevens T, Sowers JA. Behavioral parent training in home and community generalization settings. Educ Train Ment Retard 1992;27(1):13-27.

[10] Zangwill WM. An evaluation of a parent training program. Child Fam Behav Ther 1983;5(4):1-16.

[11] Cordisco LK, Strain PS, Depew N. Assessment for generalization of parenting skills in home settings. J Assoc Pers Sev Handicaps 1988;13(3):202-10.

[12] Hancock TB, Kaiser AP, Delaney EM. Teaching parents of preschoolers at high risk: Strategies to support language and positive behavior. Topics Early Child Spec Educ 2002;22(4):191-212.

[13] Benoit DA, Edwards RP, Olmi DJ, Wilczynski SM, Mandal RL. Generalization of a positive treatment package for child noncompliance. Child Fam Behav Ther 2001;23(2):19-32.

[14] Wood BKK. Young children with challenging behavior: Function-based assessment and intervention. Topics Early Childhood Spec Educ 2009;29(2):68-78.

[15] Powers SW, Roberts MW. Simulation training with parents of oppositional children: Preliminary findings. J Clin Child Psychol 1995;24(1):89-97.

[16] Kaminski JW, Valle LA, Filene JH, Boyle CL. A meta-analytic review of components associated with parent training program effectiveness. J Abnorm Child Psychol 2008;36(4):567-89.

[17] Self-Brown S, Whitaker D. Parent-focused child maltreatment prevention: Improving assessment, intervention, and dissemination with technology. Child Maltreat 2008;13(4):400-16

[18] Horner, RH, McDonald RS. A comparison of single instance and general case instruction in teaching a generalized vocational skill. JASH 1982;7(3):7–20.

[19] Kashinath S, Woods J, Goldstein H. Enhancing generalized teaching strategy use in daily routines by caregivers of children with autism. J Speech Lang Hear Res 2006;49(3):466-85.

[20] Koegel, RL, Glahn TJ, Nieminen GS. Generalization of parent-training results. J Appl Behav Analysis 1978;11(1):95-109.

[21] Boyle CL, Sanders MR, Lutzker JR, Prinz RJ, Shapiro C, Whitaker DJ. An analysis of training, generalization, and maintenance effects of Primary Care Triple P for parents of preschool-aged children with disruptive behavior. Child Psychiatry Hum Dev 2010;41(1):114-31.

[22] Webster-Stratton C, Hollinsworth T, Kolpacoff M. The long-term effectiveness and clinical significance of three cost-effective training programs for families with conduct-problem children. J Consult Clin Psychol 1989;57(4):550-3.

[23] Pacifici C, Delaney R, White L, Cummings K, Nelson C. Foster parent college: Interactive multimedia training for foster parents. Soc Work Res 2005;29(4):243-51.

[24] Gordon DA. Parent training via CD–ROM: Using technology to disseminate effective prevention practices. J Prim Prev 2000;21(2):227–51.

[25] Schwebel DC. Pediatric pedestrian safety in virtual reality. In: Harper KST, ed. University of Alabama at Birmingham, Injury Control Research Center Biennial Report. Birmingham, AL: Univ Alabama, 2007.

[26] Sanders MR, Dadds MR. The effects of planned activities and child management procedures in parent training: An analysis of setting generality. Behav Ther 1982;13(4):452-61.

[27] Bauman KE, Reiss ML, Rogers RW, Bailey JS. Dining out with children: Effectiveness of a parent advice package on pre-meal inappropriate behavior. J Appl Behav Analysis 1983;16(1):55-68.

[28] Sanders MR, Christensen AP. A comparison of the effects of child management and planned activities training in five parenting environments. J Abnorm Child Psychol 1985;13(1):101-17.

[29] Sanders MR, Plant K. Programming for generalization to high and low risk parenting situations in families with oppositional developmentally disabled preschoolers. Behav Modif 1989;13(3):283-305.

[30] Delaney EM, Kaiser AP. The effects of teaching parents blended communication and behavior support strategies. Behav Disord 2001;26(2):93-116.

In: Children, Violence and Bullying
Editors: J Merrick, I Kandel and H A Omar

ISBN: 978-1-62948-342-9
© 2014 Nova Science Publishers, Inc.

Chapter 11

DATING VIOLENCE IN ADOLESCENCE

*Anuja Bandyopadhyay, MBBS, Amit Deokar, MD and Hatim A Omar, MD, FAAP**

Division of Adolescent Medicine, Department of Pediatrics,
Kentucky Children's Hospital, University of Kentucky,
Lexington, US

ABSTRACT

Adolescent dating violence is a health and social problem, worldwide. The objective of this chapter was to identify the risk factors and consequences of dating violence, assess the prevention measures taken to increase awareness regarding it and provide an overview of the screening and interventional tools used to support the teens involved in dating violence. Methods: A review of the literature, published in the last 29 years, was conducted and the content was critically analyzed. Conclusions: There is an increasing trend of dating violence in a younger population. Consistent definitions, comprehensive assessment tools and focused screening are required to assess the actual prevalence of dating violence. Dating history, context of the date, peer influence, prior history of abuse, alcohol and drugs have been identified as significant risk factors for dating violence. Dating violence has acute as well as long term effects on the body and mind. Since, victims may not report it or even may not identify dating violence as a hazard, the responsibility of screening for it lies heavily on health care providers. Interventional measures should be implemented in a non-judgmental manner, giving due importance to the safety of the adolescents. Primary prevention programs are the key feature to reduce dating violence and require the co-operative participation of several components of the community including school personnel, health care providers, parents and the youth.

* Correspondence: Hatim Omar, MD, FAAP, Professor of Pediatrics and Obstetrics/Gynecology, Chief, Adolescent Medicine and Young Parent programs, J422, Kentucky Clinic, University of Kentucky, Lexington, KY 40536 United States. E-mail: haomar2@uky.edu.

INTRODUCTION

This article provides a critical overview of the concept of adolescent dating violence and risk factors associated with victimization and perpetration. It discusses the existing literature on the prevalence of dating violence and its health outcomes. It provides a summary of the techniques used to screen teen dating violence along with the different approaches towards managing the patients reporting it. It enumerates the measures that have been adopted till date to prevent adolescent dating violence and provide support for its survivors. It attempts to explore the potential avenues to create a more effective strategy for adolescent dating violence and the need for a formal policy to address teen dating violence. This review is intended to create an awareness regarding adolescent dating violence and help health care providers customize their approach towards the problem in their own clinical settings.

Defining dating violence has always been a difficult task. The term 'dating' may have different significance, when defining relationships between adolescents. Further, the term 'violence' may imply any shade of the spectrum varying between a seemingly harmless 'calling names' to the horrifying act of rape. The most popular definition, modeled around the article by Sugarman and Hotaling (1) stated that dating violence is "the perpetration or threat of an act of violence by at least one member of an unmarried couple on the other member within the context of dating or courtship (same sex or opposite sex)" (1). The Centers for Disease Control and Prevention- Intimate partner violence surveillance (2), further divided the acts of violence into four categories:

1) Physical violence: The intentional use of physical force with the potential for causing death, disability, injury, or harm
2) Sexual violence: This has again been divided into three types,
    a). Use of physical force to compel a person to engage in a sexual act against his or her will, whether or not the act is completed
    b). Attempted or completed sex act involving a person who is unable to understand the nature or condition of the act, to decline participation, or to communicate unwillingness to engage in the sexual act, e.g., because of illness, disability, or the influence of alcohol or other drugs, or because of intimidation or pressure
    c). Abusive sexual contact
3) Threat of physical or sexual violence: use words, gestures, or weapons to communicate the intent to cause death, disability, injury, or physical harm
4) Psychological and emotional violence: Although any psychological/emotional abuse can be measured by the intimate partner violence surveillance system, the expert panel recommended that it only be considered a type of violence when there has also been prior physical or sexual violence, or the prior threat of physical or sexual violence

The Intimate Partner Violence Surveillance: Uniform Definitions and Recommended Data Elements, Version 1.0 (2) by Centers for Disease Control and Prevention gives a uniform definition for each of the terms associated with dating violence.

A consistent definition is needed to monitor the incidence of intimate partner violence and examine trends over time and jurisdictions. Lack of consistent definitions has led to a wide array of prevalence rate of dating violence. For example, researchers have found rates as low as 9% (3) and, when verbal aggression is considered, as high as 65% (4). This is further challenged by the teen's varying interpretation of what is being asked of them. Gender-based differences may exist at the level of item interpretation. For instance, males may interpret "hit" as a closed-fisted behavior, whereas females may include an open-handed slap (5). Coercive behavior items usually include the element of force; however, males tend to describe force as psychological pressure, whereas females describe physical force (6). Widespread usage of consistent definitions would help in assessing the magnitude of dating violence and assist in directing efforts towards prevention and intervention.

IMPORTANCE OF DATING VIOLENCE

The period of adolescence is one of continual change and transition (7). Adolescents begin to search for relationships outside the family in an attempt to develop their autonomy and identity. Dating is a prominent activity during adolescent years. In 2000, 89% of adolescents ages 13 to 18 years reported this type of relationship (8). Barely eight years later, Liz Claiborne Survey (9) showed that more than one in three 11-12 years olds (37%) have acknowledged in being in a relationship; while nearly three in four 11-14 years olds (72%) say boyfriend/girlfriend relationships usually begin at age 14 or younger.

Wekerle and Wolfe (5) postulated that adolescent dating violence begins to emerge between the ages of 15 and 16 years. Recent studies show that dating violence has an earlier onset than predicted. Liz Claiborne Survey showed that one in five 13-14 year olds in relationships (20%) said they knew friends and peers who had been struck in anger (kicked, hit, slapped, or punched) by a boyfriend or girlfriend. Two in five 11-14 year olds in relationships (41%) knew friends who had been verbally abused-called names, put down, or insulted-via cellphone, IM, social networking sites (like MySpace and Facebook). More than a third of 11-14 year olds in relationships (36%) knew friends and peers of their age who had been pressured by a boyfriend/girlfriend to do things they didn't want to do. Yet half of all 11-14 year olds (49%) claimed that they did not know the warning signs of a bad/hurtful dating relationship. This may be interpreted as an evidence of inadequacy of the current interventions undertaken to spread awareness regarding this serious health problem. It was also pointed out a disturbing trend of increasing dating violence in a younger age group. The younger they are, the more vulnerable they will be to the consequences of dating violence.

Liz Claiborne Survey found a correlation between early sexual experience and teen dating violence. The survey reported that among all teens age 15-18, one in ten (10%) indicate they have been physically abused by an angry partner (kicked, punched, choked, slapped or hit). By contrast, an alarming one out of three 11-14 year olds who had sex by age 14 (33%) said they have endured such beatings. Teens who were exposed to dating violence were at higher risk for intimate partner violence later in adulthood (10,11). Hence, this rising trend of dating violence at a younger age necessitates introspection.

Apart from vulnerability, another problem posed by teen dating violence is failure to recognize it. Pushing, hitting, and verbal threats may be mistaken for signs of love and caring and younger girls dating older boys may interpret these actions as a deeper commitment to the relationship that will result in long-term positive benefits (5). Adolescents involved in aggressive dating relationships supported this perception, with 25% to 35% interpreting the violence as an act of love (3,12). One study showed that many girls thought that accepting abuse was a good way to secure the interest of a man with whom they were seeking a relationship (12). This distorted perception of dating violence is definitely alarming.

Dating violence is typically not a single event (13,14). In studies of severe abusive behavior in intimate relationships, chronicity has been related to patterns of alternating cruel and kind behaviors, attachment insecurity, personality disorder (15), expectations that relationships might improve (thus barring exit from it) and a process of adaptation or accommodation to violence that blocks exit (12,16). Appraisals of perceived control may place the victims at increased risk for abuse in the long run, as victims are unlikely to be able to control the violence as it escalates in both severity and frequency over time (16). Apart from its chronic pattern, teen dating violence has been considered to be a "potential mediating link between violence in the family of orientation and violence in the later family (the family of procreation)" (17). If this holds true, then, intimate relationship development during adolescence may offer an important window of opportunity to thwart the continuation of violence and abuse and to learn more adaptive, nonviolent alternatives (5).

VICTIMS

According to National Youth Risk Behavior Survey in 2007 (18), percentage of students between 9th to 12th grade who were hit, slapped or physically hurt on purpose by their boyfriend or girlfriend during the 12 months before the survey was found to be 9.9 (8.9-11.1). Tracing the prevalence from 1999, we see the trend rise from 8.8 (1999) to 9.5 (2001) to 8.9 (2003) to 9.2 (2005) and now to 9.9 (2007).

Overall, the prevalence of dating violence was higher among male (11.0%) than female (8.8%) students and higher among 9th-grade male (10.5%) and 12th-grade male (14.1%) than 9th-grade female (6.3%) and 12th-grade female (10.1%) students, respectively. Overall, the prevalence of dating violence was higher among black (14.2%) and Hispanic (11.1%) than white (8.4%) students; higher among black female (13.2%) and Hispanic female (10.1%) than white female (7.4%) students; and higher among black male (15.2%) than white male (9.3%) students. Overall, the prevalence of dating violence was higher among 11th-grade (10.6%) and 12th-grade (12.1%) than 9th-grade (8.5%) and 10th-grade (8.9%) students; higher among 11th-grade female (10.2%) and 12th-grade female (10.1%) than 9th-grade female (6.3%) students; and higher among 12th-grade male (14.1%) than 9th-grade male (10.5%) and 10th-grade male (9.1%) students.

Nationwide, 7.8% of students had ever been physically forced to have sexual intercourse when they did not want to. Overall, the prevalence of having been forced to have sexual intercourse was higher among female (11.3%) than male (4.5%) students; overall, the prevalence of having been forced to have sexual intercourse was higher among 11th-grade (8.5%) and 12th-grade (8.3%) than 9th-grade (6.6%) students.

Although the prevalence of dating violence among gay, lesbian or bisexual adolescents is similar to that of heterosexuals (19) rural status has been associated with a lower risk of dating violence and higher risk of early sexual debut for sexual-minority girls and a higher risk of dating violence and lower risk of early sexual debut for sexual-minority boys (20).

Another study (21) indicated that students in rural school districts are at greater risk for participating in dating violence than suburban and urban students, with rural female students at greatest risk.

PERPETRATORS

Interestingly, girls have a significantly higher prevalence than boys of reporting violence perpetration within dating relationships (22,23) even when asked to exclude violence perpetrated in self-defense (23). Specifically, girls have a significantly higher prevalence of psychological aggression perpetration within dating relationships than boys do (22). Boys are significantly more likely to perpetrate injuries on their dating partners than girls are. Therefore, the severity and consequences of violence perpetration need to be considered in addition to the prevalence of involvement in violent behaviors (22). It has also been seen that girls were more likely than boys to report forced sex victimization within dating relationships, while boys were more likely than girls to report forced sex perpetration within dating relationship (22).

UNDER-REPORTING OF DATING VIOLENCE

Studies of college-aged populations suggest that a significant portion of young adult victims do not report acquaintance rape, specifically because of the relationship (24). It has been postulated that adolescent victims may be even more reluctant to report acquaintance rape due to past intimacy with the perpetrator or to date-specific behavior such as the use of alcohol or drugs (24). This suggests that the data on dating violence may suffer due to under-reporting. Another reason for inconsistencies in prevalence rate has been suggested by Betz (25) in an article by giving the example of two national surveys, YRBSS (Youth Risk Behavior Study Survey, 2005) and the National Crime Victimization Survey (NCVS) illustrating the differences in methodological approaches. YRBSS data are collected from students via survey in the school setting; the NCVS is completed using an interview format in the presence of family members (26), which may not provide the privacy required to disclose such information.

NEW APPROACH FOR ASSESSMENT OF PREVALENCE

Most of the information regarding dating violence prevalence has been found through surveys relying on self-report questionnaires. It has been suggested that assessment tools need to capture the sequential nature within which violence is embedded. The emotional consequence of the behavior should be measured not only by self-report, but also by other objective methods that measure the immediate response (e.g., distress) and the longer-term effects (5). Rather than focusing on 'unwanted' sexual behavior from a victim or perpetrator's standpoint, an assessment of the couple's sexual parameters may provide a different interpretation of dating violence. It has been suggested that it may be useful to measure acts of violence as well as violence "misses" (e.g., the number of times the partner was turned down when sexual advances were unwanted, the number of times the partner "accepted" such direct communication, etc) (5).

Tracing the history Table 1 summarizes some of the studies done on adolescent dating violence over the past two decades.

Table 1. Prevalence of adolescent dating violence in various studies

First author (year)	Study design	Study settings	Subject particulars	Age group	Measure of violence and prevalence
Makepeace (17) (1981)	Cross-sectional; Using questionnaires	Medium-sized mid-western university	202 subjects 49% M 51% F	College students	1 in 5 students experienced physical violence 5.1% cases were reported to legal authorities
Henton (83) (1983)	Using self reported questionnaire	Oregon	644 54.5% M 45.5% F	High school students (mean age=17)	12.1% experienced premarital abuse
Roscoe (3) (1985)	Self report	High school in central Michigan	204	Juniors and seniors in high school	Remarkable similarity between high school and college students 'dating violence', suggestive of a pattern
Symons (84) (1994)	Cross-sectional study; using questionnaires	Rural North Carolina	561 77% F 23% M	Age range = 15-20 years	60% reported dating violence; many denied abusive relationships but recorded abusive events
Foshee (76) (1996)	Self administered questionnaire	Rural North Carolina county	1967 49.6% M 50.4% F	8th and 9th graders	25.4% reported as victim of non sexual violence, 8% reported as victim of sexual violence; 14% as perpetrator of nonsexual and 2% of sexual violence
Spencer (21) (2000)	Retrospective study	2 rural, 1 suburban and 2 urban schools of upstate New York	2094 497 (rural) 441 (suburban) 1156 (urban)	7th,9th and 11th graders	Rural students were more prone to dating violence (18%), female students being at increased risk
Swart (85) (2002)	Cross-sectional survey using questionnaires	Eldorado Park, South Africa	928	9th-12th graders	35.3% males and 43.5% females reported as perpetrators; 37.8% males and 41.7% females reported as victims
Ackard (86) (2003)	Cross-sectional survey	Nationally representative sample of United States	3533	9th to 12th graders	17% girls and 9% boys reported as victims; nearly 50% of victims reported staying in the relationship out of fear of physical harm
Smith P.H. (87) (2003)	Longitudinal survey	University of North Carolina	1569	18-19 year old women entering college	Women who were physically assaulted as adolescents were at greater risk for revictimization during their freshman year
Decker M.R.(88) (2005)	Cross sectional survey	Massachusetts	1641	9th to 12th female graders	51.6% girls diagnosed with STD/HIV reported dating violence
Marquart (89) (2007)	Cross sectional survey	National sample (United States)	20,274	Rural adolescents	16% adolescents reported as victims
Rivera-Rivera (40) (2007)	Cross-sectional survey	Mexico	7960 57.63% F 42.37% M	Age range= 12-21 years	Victims: 9.37% (female) and 8.57% (male) for psychological violence; 9.88% (female) and 22.71% (male) for physical violence
Wolitzky-Taylor K.B.(90) (2008)	Telephone-based interview	Nationally representative sample (United States)	3614	12-17 year olds	2.7% girls and 0.6% boys reported as victims of dating violence

RISK FACTORS

Looking at the studies identifying the risk factors for teen dating violence, considerable overlap may be seen between the factors responsible for perpetration and victimization. Although we may attempt to separately identify the risk factors at the individual, family and community level, in reality teen dating violence is a conglomeration of the factors co-existing at all levels.

Dating history: Multiple dating and sexual partners, earlier age at menarche and/or first date, history of dating violence are identified risk factors (27)

Context of the date: The context in which the date occurs may also have an impact on the probability of assault. If the male partner initiates the date, pays for the date, and drives, the possibility of sexual assault increases (28). Going to the perpetrator's house alone and increasing age discrepancy between victim and perpetrator (27) are relevant risk factors.

Abuse and prior violence history: History of sexual victimization before age 18 is a risk factor for sexual dating violence (27). Research has shown that young adult women with a history of sexual abuse may have difficulty in accurately perceiving risk in potentially harmful sexual situations, and therefore may be vulnerable to more repeated victimization (29). Childhood emotional abuse has been uniquely predictive of teen dating violence (30). Exposure to violence during childhood, both in the form of child abuse and family violence, has been linked to dating violence victimization and perpetration (31).

Alcohol, tobacco and drugs: Alcohol and drug use have been consistently associated with teen dating violence in most studies across the world (32-34). Early alcohol use has been found to be an important risk factor for dating violence victimization, independent of both peer and parental influences (35). Riding with a drinking driver has been regarded as a factor as well (36). Amongst the drugs, special mention may be made of the "date rape drugs", a term coined by the media to label a few specific drugs (i.e. Rohypnol, GHB and ketamine), because of the frequency with which they are used by men to facilitate rape (37). The use of these drugs for the purpose of inducing amnesia and rapid sedation of the victim is becoming more common (38). Interestingly, it has been seen that women's voluntary consumption of drugs prior to a sexual assault reduces perpetrator responsibility and blame and increases blame to the victim compared to other situations (39). Tobacco use has been implicated as a risk factor for perpetration, particularly in case of males (36).

Peer influence: Gang membership has been significantly associated with dating violence victimization in boys and perpetration in both genders (40). A sexually active peer group has been implicated as a risk factor for sexual dating violence (27).

Prior criminal history: Studies have found that history of prior criminal acts is associated with an increased probability of assaulting a partner. The relationship was greater when there was prior violent crime compared to property crime, when there was early onset of criminal behavior, and when the offender was female (41).

Parent education: At all ages, the lower the parent education, the greater the acceptance of dating abuse, likelihood of gender stereotyping, and exposure to family violence (42).

Community: Exposure to weapons and violent injury in the community was correlated to teen dating violence (43). Students in rural school districts are at greater risk for participating in dating violence than suburban and urban students, with rural female students at greatest risk (21).

Role of media: Media has a powerful influence on young minds. A study reported that exposure to violent music led to normalization of the use of violence (including violence against women) among listeners (44). Controlling for public financial assistance, relative to adolescents not experiencing dating violence, those who did were 1.9 times more likely to have viewed X-rated movies (45). The relationship between watching wrestling on television and being the perpetrator of dating violence was also stronger among females and remained consistent over a 6- to 7-month time period (46). Studies have assessed media use as a risk factor for dating violence (47).

Others: For males, having low self-esteem and having a friend who has been a victim of dating violence predicted chronic victimization while for females, living in a single parent household, having a friend who has been a victim of dating violence and being depressed predicted chronic victimization (34).

CONSEQUENCES

Studies examining dating violence and adolescents have focused primarily on physical and mental health outcomes for female victims. Limited research has examined health outcomes for adolescent male victims or for perpetrators (girls and boys) of dating violence (48).

Important sex differences have been observed in the risk behaviors associated with date violence, indicating that if girls have been involved in physical fighting with a dating partner as opposed to someone other than a dating partner, they are at particularly increased risk of attempting suicide, engaging in sexual and HIV risk behaviors, getting pregnant, and riding in a car with a drunk driver (49).

Physical impairment: Physical aggression decreased significantly across the age groups, but health consequences become more severe with age. A study found that broken nose, black eye, broken bone, went from 1% at 16 years to 4.5% at 20 years of age (50). Severe physical dating violence may cause profound physical injury.

Victims of sexual violence: Consequences of adolescent sexual violence has been considered separately, due to its wide spectrum of manifestations. Apart from the physical injury, women who are sexually assaulted experience a dramatic negative impact on their functioning. Up to 50% of rape victims develop post traumatic stress disorder as well as other psychological problems (51). In addition, victims tend to have more somatic complaints and chronic pains.

In 1974, Ann Burgess and Lynda Holmstrom described 'rape trauma syndrome' in context to the varied behavioral, somatic and psychological reactions occurring after forcible rape or attempted forcible rape. The period after sexual assault was divided into:

- Acute phase-Disorganization: It comprises of impact reactions (within hours) and immediate effects (within weeks). Impact reactions may manifest in expressed style (such as sobbing, restlessness or even smiling) or controlled style (calm, composed or subdued effect). Immediate effects may be seen as somatic manifestations (skeletal muscle tension, genitourinary disturbances) or emotional reactions (guilt, powerlessness, loss of trust, disbelief, shame, depression, denial).

- Reorganization phase: It comprises of short term effects up to 3-4 months (like generalized anxiety and fear, impaired social functioning, eating disorders) and intermediate effects up to 1 year (like phobia, sleep disturbance, increased dependence)
- Long term reactions: It comprises of reactions up to 4 years like anger, continued sexual dysfunction, hyper vigilance to danger

Furthermore, dating violence was associated with a number of risky attitudes, beliefs, and norms among sexually active girls (52), including being more than twice as likely to have a perceived risk of acquiring an STD, being more than twice as likely to have norms nonsupportive of a healthy relationship, and being 2½ times as likely to perceive themselves as having limited control over their sexuality (52).

Psychological impairment: Adolescent dating violence increases nonspecific risk toward behavioral and psychological impairment in youth, particularly female adolescents (53,54). Dating violence was associated with higher levels of depression, suicidal thoughts, and poorer educational outcomes (54). Physical dating violence was associated with poorer psychosocial functioning, substance dependence and comorbid Axis I diagnoses (55). Abusive experiences during dating relationships may disrupt normal developmental processes, including the development of a stable self-concept and integrated body image during adolescence (56). This may give rise to higher rates of eating disorders and a low sense of emotional well-being (56).

LEGAL ASPECTS

Although, there are laws regarding intimate partner violence, a specific law regarding 'dating' violence does not exist. Restraining orders are a common legal alternative by which to seek protection from an abusive partner. A study revealed that most female intimate partner homicide victims did not have a restraining order when they were killed hinting that restraining orders may protect victims of intimate partner violence (57). However, in most states of United States, one can apply to get a domestic violence restraining order only if one is above 18 years; if one is under 18 years, then one must have an adult's name on the court papers and that adult must ask for the order on one's behalf. This may restrict the teen's options to seek help from the jurisdiction, if the teen does not want to involve an adult.

If a victim is identified after screening, they may turn to the health care providers for further information and advice. As health care providers, it may be pertinent to be well-informed about the state legal recourses for dating violence. According to the book on the "Impact of domestic violence in your legal practice: A Lawyer's Handbook" (58), providing information regarding protective order should be accompanied by a discussion with the teen of the repercussions of a legal action. Often a civil or criminal case may be followed by a violent retaliation by the abuser. In such cases, a non-legal action to keep the teen safe may be a better option. In such a situation, the responsibility for safe intervention lies heavily on the health care system. As health care providers, it is also important to familiarize oneself with the child abuse law of one's state. If the abuser be an adult, then it may be a case of child abuse. Sexual relationships between an adult and a minor partner may constitute child abuse or sexual assault depending on jurisdiction's treatment of 'statutory rape'.

Apart from legal measures, health care providers should be aware of the community resources which may be mobilized to assist the minor victims and perpetrators. Non-legal remedies utilizing combined support from health care providers, social workers, school teachers, school security, guardians, and counselors may be as effective as legal remedies in preventing recurrence of dating violence and providing support to the teens involved in it.

INTERVENTIONAL MEASURES

Screening: Studies reveal that spontaneous disclosure of dating violence is an infrequent occurrence (59,60). According to Brown et al (59) this secrecy may be because of several factors. First, adolescents may want to keep their dating/romantic lives private and feel shy or reluctant to divulge details. Secondly, as discussed before, they may not recognize the behavior as abusive, and may even view it as a demonstration of love. Finally, the term 'dating' may be outdated. Sex and intimacy may happen in a variety of relationship contexts, and the details may be missed if the interview is focused on dating.

The study by Brown et al (59) showed that forced sex was screened more commonly even though it may be easier for the adolescents to disclose incidents of verbal or physical abuse rather than sexual abuse. The study found that hospital settings and female clinicians were more likely to screen for dating violence. The strongest predictor of screening was screening for other risk behaviors. Although it has been recommended that all female patients over age 14 years be screened regardless of symptoms, signs or suspicion of abuse (61) the actual screening rates remain low (59,62). One study showed that that 52% of women reported that they had never been screened for sexual violence by a health care professional (51).

Regarding health care provider's failure to screen patients for dating violence a review of studies identified several barriers. Potential barriers include lack of training specific to this topic, lack of awareness of the prevalence of dating violence and lack of time. In a study (63), residents in pediatric training programs reported that they would not routinely screen for or manage appropriately their adolescent patients in violent dating relationships. Residents believed that although it is a physician's role to discuss adolescent dating violence, they felt that they were not adequately trained to do so. Another barrier is the provider's concern about patient's non-disclosure, fear of repercussions and non-compliance (62). However, contrary to this belief, a study reported that women find discussions of sexual violence by their health care providers to be helpful and nonintrusive. Educational, linguistic, and cultural factors appear to affect the likelihood that health care providers discuss sexual violence with their patients (51).

Several studies (48,64) have tried to overcome these barriers and have suggested means to improve screening for teen dating violence. A few salient points have been mentioned in table 2.

Table 2. Measures to be taken while screening for teen dating violence

• To maximize safety and comfort it is important to interview in private, without the partner or parents
• Create an environment of trust and assure confidentiality • Make eye contact • Use specific phrases of questions which would create a comfortable disclosure climate Example: Asking a girl whether she has been abused by her boyfriend may elicit a "no", whereas asking the girl if she has felt threatened or scared in the company of her boyfriend may facilitate the truth • Avoid words like "dating violence" or "abuse" or any such words that sounds demeaning or judgmental or anything technical and so, beyond the comprehensibility of people without professional health care training Example: Use simple questions like "At any time, has a partner hit, kicked or otherwise hurt, frightened, threatened or demeaned you?" • If time permits it is better to use multiple open-ended questions to allow more opportunities for patients to disclose • Do not put any blame or judgment on the victim; make it clear that you are someone they can look to for guidance • Be aware of the symptoms of dating violence such as injuries in various stages of healing, pattern injuries where the imprint of an object, like a belt is present on the body, pelvic pain, insomnia, depressive symptoms. • Injured patients should always be asked to explain how it happened and clinicians must be alert for answers that don't explain the injuries • Express compassion Example: "I'm sorry this happened" • Show respect Example: "You did not deserve such a treatment. This violence is not your fault. You have a right to be respected." • Assess the patient's perception of abuse Example: "Some people think that such treatment is a way of expressing love. What do you think?" • Screen for violence using gender neutral term, do not assume perpetrator is male

Protocols that provide guidelines about what types of questions to ask patients regarding dating violence are available (64). A study (59) suggested the use of HITS screening tool with the questions "Has your partner ever":

• Hurt you physically?
• Insulted you or talked down to you?
• Threatened you with harm?
• Screamed at you or cursed you?

A study by Brown et al (59) suggested inclusion of screening procedures as a part of training program for students, interns and residents to promote screening by health care providers. It said that board exams could emphasize the importance of dating violence by including relevant items. According to the study, health care professionals could be sensitized to detect dating violence by symposia and seminars at conferences.

Table 3. Measures to be adopted after identifying a victim of adolescent dating violence

- Listen to the victim without expressing shock or judgment
- Determine the nature of the relationship with the perpetrator, and whether the victimization occurred in the distant/recent past or is ongoing
- Assess for exposure to multiple forms of violence (parental, guardian, sibling, community)
- Explain the victim's rights and options with regards to reporting, prosecution and treatment
- Assure dating violence will not be revealed to the parents or the perpetrator without consent. However, try to involve the victim's parents when possible and appropriate, if victim allows doing so.
- Perform a physical examination, if appropriate, including tests for sexually transmitted infections and pregnancy.
- Be familiar with emergency contraception for rape victims and with the facilities that provide rape counseling in your area so that immediate referral can be implemented
- Help the patient assess danger
  Assess for risk factors associated with intimate partner homicide utilizing a valid risk assessment instrument such as the Danger Assessment (DA) (91)
  Assess specifically for threats to kill, access to firearms, severity of physical and sexual violence, controlling and jealous behavior, stalking and harassing behavior, children in the home that perpetrator is not biological parent to, substance use (victim and perpetrator), perpetrator suicidal ideation/attempts
- Be familiar with your state's mandatory reporting laws (child abuse and intimate partner violence). Determine if adolescent is an emancipated minor and not legally reportable under child abuse laws
- Assess whether the victim feels entrapped. Being isolated from support other than the abuser can interfere with medical access and complicate discovery of future abuse. Assess whether it is safe to go home on that day.
- Promote planning for safety
  Asking questions like "What steps can you take in the future to keep yourself safe?"
  "Some young people choose to date with a group of friends they trust. Would that be an option?"
  "If someone hurt you again, where could you go in an emergency? How would you get there?"
- Make a safety plan for emergency
- Offer information about legal resources, such as restraining orders, mandatory arrest, police/911
- Assist in identifying trusted individuals (teacher, counselor, family member, friend)
- Assist in identifying appropriate community-based resources, programs that target adolescents including the following: Emergency housing and long-term housing advocacy, resident and nonresident counseling (individual and group) legal options (criminal justice relief, civil protection, peace order, child custody, and visitation orders), job training program
- Offer information on dating violence through brochures, internet resources (give safety alerts that computer use can be monitored)
- Offer counseling
- Assess need for referral to a medical or mental health specialist
- Mobilize intervention measures for the perpetrator
- Assess need for substance abuse treatment if needed
- Offer follow-up
- Schedule a follow-up appointment
- Document all findings in medical records.
  S- Document what the victim Said, using exact words
  O- Document whatever you observed. Documentation using forensic techniques—body map with site and injury and date, photographs of injuries with written description of size and appearance, name of perpetrator, concise and objective statements
  A-Your assessment of potential dating violence
  P-Describe safety planning, mandatory reporting and follow-ups

SURVIVING DATE VIOLENCE

Once dating violence has been recognized, it is important to proceed in a cautious manner, since the issue is sensitive. Several studies have outlined subsequent measures which may be adopted (48,64,65). A few key points have been mentioned in Table 3.

Support groups have emerged as a key element in promoting health and providing support to the teens involved in dating violence. The groups provide a trusting and safe environment for members to share feelings and experiences and support the group members as well as encourage healing and introspection of the mind. School based support groups target the at-risk population and is tailored to students at schools who have experienced abuse. School-based support group programs, like the Expect Respect Program(66) have shown to expand awareness of abuse in the peer group, increase relationship skills and increase self-awareness. Safe Dates Program is another school and community based program which has a secondary preventive component. Secondary prevention activities target cognitive factors which influence the decision to take preventative measures; for instance, to seek help with leaving an abusive partner or to stop perpetrating dating violence. The program increases the awareness of the participants regarding their options while seeking help in the community (67).

PRIMARY PREVENTION

Apart from secondary and tertiary prevention efforts, in the form of support groups, there has also been considerable attempt to mobilize awareness and encourage primary prevention of dating violence.

Although most of these programs are based on curricula with 4 to 10 sessions that are delivered in a classroom setting (68-71), researchers have urged that prevention programs should also be made available in non-traditional settings such as housing complexes, community centers and clinics (72). Programs in special care systems like the Girl Talk 2 intervention in the juvenile justice system has found relative success in promoting protective behavior amongst the girls in the system (73).

A study by Cornelius et al (74) revealed that, commonly used scare tactics designed to highlight the deleterious effects of dating violence often employed in encouraging participation in prevention programming, are ineffective in recruitment for dating violence prevention program. Instead, potential participants should be informed about the high prevalence of dating violence and about personal and relationship risk factors. The benefits of the prevention program should be emphasized as well, such as learning nonviolent communication, problem solving skills, and increases in relationship satisfaction (74). There is also some evidence that making programs as convenient as possible and minimizing concerns about the revelation of sensitive material by marketing programs as education rather than counseling, for example, may also be fruitful recruitment strategies (74).

A review of published literature reveals that only a few evaluations of the preventive programs have been conducted till date. Nearly all used design without random assignment to experimental and control group (68,70,71,75) and measured attitude, knowledge and skills but not behavior (68,70,71). The Safe Dates Program evaluation (67,69,76-78) was randomized, controlled, evaluated behavior in addition to other aspects and was conducted at baseline, at 1 month and then yearly for 4 consecutive years. Another study by Wolfe and associates (79) was also randomized, controlled and it had a follow up of two years.

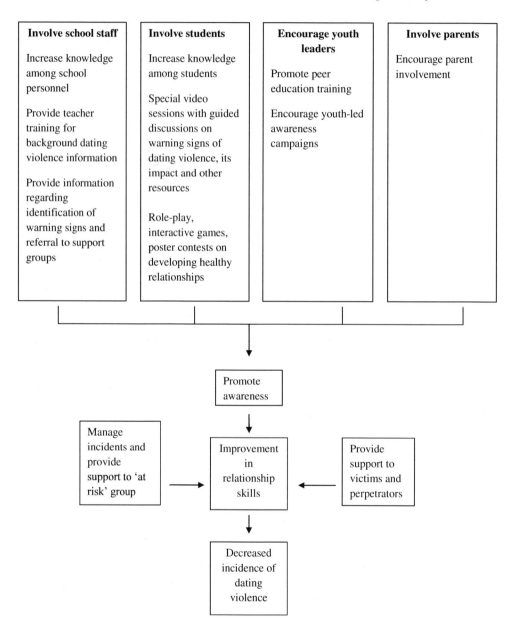

Figure 1. Basic model for school based dating violence prevention program.

Safe Dates program provides an example of primary prevention of teen dating violence. It is based on the Safe Dates conceptual Model (78). The theoretical base for the model revolves around the key concepts of changing norms and improvising conflict management skills. Norms are instruments of social control and thus have a significant effect on behavior and conformity (80). Safe Dates program activities were designed to alter dating violence norms by increasing the adolescent's perception of negative consequences associated with dating violence and altering peer responses to dating violence. Activities were also designed to decrease adolescent acceptance of tradition gender-role norms which put females in a submissive position relative to males and males in position of power and authority. An evaluation of Safe Dates showed that the program was effective in preventing and reducing dating violence in adolescents as many as three years post intervention. Program effects were not moderated by gender or race but some effects were moderated by prior involvement in dating violence. Although it found that the design holds promise, the evaluation suggested modification in the content focusing on teaching conflict resolution skills and altering beliefs in the need for help (78).

A basic model for school based dating violence prevention program based on the examples of the Expect Respect Program (66) and Safe Dates Program (69) has been presented in figure 1, with emphasis on primary prevention of teen dating violence. Schools are ideally best equipped to promote primary prevention of dating violence. It requires development and implementation of simple strategies requiring participation of teachers, students as well as parents.

NEW APPROACHES

Newer studies suggesting methods to improve prevention program measures are warranted. A recent study identified that outcomes of school programs may be affected by format (classroom vs. small group), group type (single gender vs. mixed gender) as well as combination of these characteristics (81). A study had pointed out that no program targets couples, in part due to the flux of mid-adolescent partnership (5). It might be useful to explore these new channels while developing prevention programs to create a more effective means of intervention.

CONCLUSION

Despite the widespread prevalence of dating violence, a study showed that 60 % of victims and 79% of perpetrators did not seek help for dating violence (60). It is consistent with the Liz Claiborne Survey (9), which showed that most children are unaware of the warning signs of dating violence. This has contributed in making teen dating violence an important social and public health problem. As health care providers, we are ideally placed to promote prevention of adolescent dating violence as well as support for the victims and perpetrators due to our regular contact with the adolescents during well-check examinations and sports physicals.

Prevention of adolescent partner violence can begin as early as age 3 or 4 years by educating patients to distinguish good touch from bad touch and to seek adult help, if they are uncomfortable with the way another child or adult is touching them. Preadolescent and early adolescent well-child examinations can include a positive discussion of how to demonstrate caring, show respect, and resolve conflicts nonviolently (64). Clinic newsletters, pamphlets, posters may help to disperse knowledge regarding healthy dating relationships.

The role of media is essential in creating an awareness of this health problem. Studies have found that adolescents use media as a potential source of health information (82). Most dating violence prevention programs make use of theatre to enact plays promoting awareness. Internet plays a major role in providing information to teens regarding warning signs of dating violence and forming support groups for the victims and perpetrators. Media has assumed this role in a responsible manner, ensuring the safety of the teens, who access this information, by deleting the traces of access on the computer, in case of possible cyber stalking.

There is a need of awareness and commitment at all levels of the society across all ages. It is the responsibility of the entire community to join hands and mobilize resources from all realms to recognize and eradicate teen dating violence and teach the young minds that love can't mean violence.

REFERENCES

[1]   Sugarman DB, Hotaling GT. Dating violence: A review of contextual and risk factors. In: Levy B, ed. Dating violence:Young women in danger. Seattle, WA: Seal Press, 1991:100-18.
[2]   Saltzman LE. Intimate partner violence surveillance: Uniform definitions and recommended data elements: Version 1.0. Atlanta, GA: Centers Dis Control Prev, Natl Center Inj Prev Control, 2002.
[3]   Roscoe B, Callahan JE. Adolescents self-report of violence in families and dating relations. Adolescence 1985;20(79):545-53.
[4]   Laner MR. Courtship abuse and aggression: Contextual aspects. Sociol Spectrum 1983;3;69-83.
[5]   Wekerle C, Wolfe DA. Dating violence in mid-adolescence: theory, significance, and emerging prevention initiatives. Clin Psychol Rev 1999;19(4):435-56.
[6]   Muehlenhard CL, Cook SW. Men's self-reports of unwanted sexual activity. J Sex Res 1988;24:58-72.
[7]   Lerner RM, Galambos NL. Adolescent development: challenges and opportunities for research, programs, and policies. Annu Rev Psychol 1998;49:413-46.
[8]   Wolfe DA, Feiring C. Dating violence through the lens of adolescent romantic relationships. Child Maltreat 2000;5(4):360-3.
[9]   Unlimited TR. Liz clairborne Inc. Survey on Teen Dating Abuse, 2008. URL: http://www. loveisnotabuse.com/statistics.htm.
[10]   Smith PH, White JW, Holland LJ. A longitudinal perspective on dating violence among adolescent and college-age women. Am J Public Health 2003;93(7):1104-9.
[11]   Taylor CA, Sorenson SB. Injunctive social norms of adults regarding teen dating violence. J Adolesc Health 2004;34(6):468-79.
[12]   Johnson SB, Frattaroli S, Campbell J, Wright J, Pearson-Fields AS, Cheng TL. "I know what love means." Gender-based violence in the lives of urban adolescents. J Womens Health (Larchmt) 2005;14(2):172-9.
[13]   Katz J, Kuffel SW, Coblentz A. Are there gender differences in sustaining dating violence? An examination of frequency, severity, and relationship satisfaction. J Fam Violence 2002;17(3):247-71.
[14]   Marcus RF. Youth violence in everyday life. J Interpers Violence 2005;20(4):442-7.
[15]   Dutton DG. The abusive personality : violence and control in intimate relationships. New York: Guilford, 2007.
[16]   Pape KT, Arias I. Control, coping, and victimization in dating relationships. Violence Vict 1995;10(1):43-54.
[17]   Makepeace JM. Courtship Violence among College Students. Fam Relat 1981;30(1):97-102.
[18]   Eaton DK, Kann L, Kinchen S, Shanklin S, Ross J, Hawkins J, et al. Youth risk behavior surveillance--United States, 2007. MMWR Surveill Summ 2008;57(4):1-131.

[19]   Freedner N, Freed LH, Yang YW, Austin SB. Dating violence among gay, lesbian, and bisexual adolescents: results from a community survey. J Adolesc Health 2002;31(6):469-74.

[20]   Poon CS, Saewyc EM. Out yonder: sexual-minority adolescents in rural communities in British Columbia. Am J Public Health 2009;99(1):118-24.

[21]   Spencer GA, Bryant SA. Dating violence: a comparison of rural, suburban, and urban teens. J Adolesc Health 2000;27(5):302-5.

[22]   Swahn MH, Simon TR, Arias I, Bossarte RM. Measuring sex differences in violence victimization and perpetration within date and same-sex peer relationships. J Interpers Violence 2008;23(8):1120-38.

[23]   Foshee VA, Linder F, MacDougall JE, Bangdiwala S. Gender differences in the longitudinal predictors of adolescent dating violence. Prev Med 2001;32(2):128-41.

[24]   Rickert VI, Wiemann CM, Vaughan RD. Disclosure of date/acquaintance rape. Who reports and when. J Pediatr Adolesc Gynecol 2005;18(1):17-24.

[25]   Betz C. Teen dating violence: An unrecognized health care need. J Pediatr Nurs 2007;22(6):427-9.

[26]   Hickman LJ, Jaycox LH, Aronoff J. Dating violence among adolescents: prevalence, gender distribution, and prevention program effectiveness. Trauma Violence Abuse 2004;5(2):123-42.

[27]   Rickert VI, Wiemann CM, Vaughan RD, White JW. Rates and risk factors for sexual violence among an ethnically diverse sample of adolescents. Arch Pediatr Adolesc Med 2004;158(12):1132-9.

[28]   Megan J. Jenkins FHD. The attribution of date rape: Observer's attitudes and sexual experiences and the dating situation. J Appl Soc Psychol 1987;17(10):875-95.

[29]   Terri L. Messman-Moore ALB. Risk perception, rape and sexual revictimization: A prospective study of college women. Psychol Women Quart 2006;30(2):159-72.

[30]   Wekerle C, Leung E, Wall A-M, MacMillan H, Boyle M, Trocme N, et al. The contribution of childhood emotional abuse to teen dating violence among child protective services-involved youth. Child Abuse Negl 2009;33(1):45-58.

[31]   Gover AR, Kaukinen C, Fox KA. The relationship between violence in the family of origin and dating violence among college students. J Interpers Violence 2008;23(12):1667-93.

[32]   Easton A, Kiss E, Mowery P. Budapest Student Health Behavior Survey--Budapest, Hungary, 1999. Findings on unintentional and intentional injuries, alcohol use, and sexual activity. Cent Eur J Public Health 2004;12(2):94-101.

[33]   Ramisetty-Mikler S, Goebert D, Nishimura S, Caetano R. Dating violence victimization: associated drinking and sexual risk behaviors of Asian, Native Hawaiian, and Caucasian high school students in Hawaii. J Sch Health 2006;76(8):423-9.

[34]   Foshee VA, Benefield TS, Ennett ST, Bauman KE, Suchindran C. Longitudinal predictors of serious physical and sexual dating violence victimization during adolescence. Prev Med 2004;39(5):1007-16.

[35]   Swahn MH, Bossarte RM, Sullivent EE, III. Age of alcohol use initiation, suicidal behavior, and peer and dating violence victimization and perpetration among high-risk, seventh-grade adolescents. Pediatrics 2008;121(2):297-305.

[36]   Champion H, Foley KL, Sigmon-Smith K, Sutfin EL, DuRant RH. Contextual factors and health risk behaviors associated with date fighting among high school students. Women Health 2008;47(3):1- 22.

[37]   Ian Hindmarch RB. Trends in the use of alcohol and other drugs in cases of sexual assault. Human Psychopharmacol Clin Exp 1999;14(4):225-31.

[38]   Pope E, Shouldice M. Drugs and sexual Assault: A review. Trauma Violence Abuse 2001;2(1):51-5.

[39]   Girard AL, Senn CY. The role of the new "date rape drugs" in attributions about date rape. J Interpers Violence 2008;23(1):3-20.

[40]   Rivera-Rivera L, Allen-Leigh B, Rodriguez-Ortega G, Chavez-Ayala R, Lazcano-Ponce E. Prevalence and correlates of adolescent dating violence: baseline study of a cohort of 7,960 male and female Mexican public school students. Prev Med 2007;44(6):477-84.

[41]   Straus MA, Ramirez IL. Criminal history and assault of dating partners: the role of type of prior crime, age of onset, and gender. Violence Vict 2004;19(4):413-34.

[42]   Foshee VA, Karriker-Jaffe KJ, Reyes HL, Ennett ST, Suchindran C, Bauman KE, et al. What accounts for demographic differences in trajectories of adolescent dating violence? An examination of intrapersonal and contextual mediators. J Adolesc Health 2008;42(6):596-604.

[43] Malik S, Sorenson SB, Aneshensel CS. Community and dating violence among adolescents: perpetration and victimization. J Adolesc Health 1997;21(5):291-302.

[44] Johnson JD, Adams MS, Ashburn L, Reed W. Differential gender effects of exposure to rap music on African American adolescents' acceptance of teen dating violence. Sex Roles 1995;33(7):597-605.

[45] Raiford JL, Wingood GM, DiClemente RJ. Prevalence, Incidence, and predictors of dating violence: A longitudinal study of African American female adolescents. J Women's Health 2007;16(6):822-32.

[46] DuRant RH, Champion H, Wolfson M. The relationship between watching professional wrestling on television and engaging in date fighting among high school students. Pediatrics 2006;118(2):265-72.

[47] Manganello JA. Teens, dating violence, and media use: A review of the literature and conceptual model for future research. Trauma Violence Abuse 2008;9(1):3-18.

[48] Glass N, Fredland N, Campbell J, Yonas M, Sharps P, Kub J. Adolescent dating violence: prevalence, risk factors, health outcomes, and implications for clinical practice. J Obstet Gynecol Neonatal Nurs 2003;32(2):227-38.

[49] Kreiter SR, Krowchuk DP, Woods CR, Sinal SH, Lawless MR, DuRant RH. Gender differences in risk behaviors among adolescents who experience date fighting. Pediatrics 1999;104(6):1286-92.

[50] Munoz-Rivas MJ, Grana JL, O'Leary KD, Gonzalez MP. Aggression in adolescent dating relationships: prevalence, justification, and health consequences. J Adolesc Health 2007;40(4):298-304.

[51] Littleton HL, Berenson AB, Radecki Breitkopf C. An evaluation of health care providers' sexual violence screening practices. Am J Obstet Gynecol 2007;196(6):564.e1-.e7.

[52] Wingood GM, DiClemente RJ, McCree DH, Harrington K, Davies SL. Dating violence and the sexual health of black adolescent females. Pediatrics 2001;107(5):E72.

[53] Ackard DM, Eisenberg ME, Neumark-Sztainer D. Long-term impact of adolescent dating violence on the behavioral and psychological health of male and female youth. J Pediatr 2007;151(5):476-81.

[54] Banyard VL, Cross C. Consequences of teen dating violence: understanding intervening variables in ecological context. Violence Against Women 2008;14(9):998-1013.

[55] Brown A, Cosgrave E, Killackey E, Purcell R, Buckby J, Yung AR. The longitudinal association of adolescent dating violence with psychiatric disorders and functioning. J Interpers Violence 2008 Dec 19, epub ahead of print.

[56] Ackard DM, Neumark-Sztainer D. Date violence and date rape among adolescents: associations with disordered eating behaviors and psychological health. Child Abuse Negl 2002;26(5):455-73.

[57] Vittes KA, Sorenson SB. Restraining orders among victims of intimate partner homicide. Inj Prev 2008;14(3):191-5.

[58] Goelman DM, Lehrman FL, Valente RL, American Bar Association. Commission on Domestic V. The Impact of domestic violence on your legal practice: A lawyer's handbook. Washington, DC: Am Bar Assoc, Commission Domestic Violence, 1996.

[59] Brown LK, Puster KL, Vazquez EA, Hunter HL, Lescano CM. Screening practices for adolescent dating violence. J Interpers Violence 2007;22(4):456-64.

[60] Ashley OS, Foshee VA. Adolescent help-seeking for dating violence: prevalence, sociodemographic correlates, and sources of help. J Adolesc Health 2005;36(1):25-31.

[61] Saltzman LE, Green YT, Marks JS, Thacker SB. Violence against women as a public health issue: Comments from the CDC. Am J Prev Med 2000;19(4):325-9.

[62] Waalen J, Goodwin MM, Spitz AM, Petersen R, Saltzman LE. Screening for intimate partner violence by health care providers. Barriers and interventions. Am J Prev Med 2000;19(4):230-7.

[63] Forcier M, Patel R, Kahn JA. Pediatric residents' attitudes and practices regarding adolescent dating violence. Ambul Pediatr 2003;3(6):317-23.

[64] Hamberger LK, Ambuel B. Dating violence. Pediatr Clin North Am 1998;45(2):381-90.

[65] Griffin MP, Kossn MP. Clinical screening and intervention in cases of partner violence. Online J Issues Nurs 2002;7(1):3.

[66] Ball B, Kerig PK, Rosenbluth B. "Like a family but better because you can actually trust each other": the expect respect dating violence prevention program for at-risk youth. Health Promot Pract 2009;10(1 Suppl):45S-58S.

In: Children, Violence and Bullying   ISBN: 978-1-62948-342-9
Editors: J Merrick, I Kandel and H A Omar   © 2014 Nova Science Publishers, Inc.

Chapter 12

GERMANY: TREATMENT OF JUVENILE DELINQUENCY AND YOUNG OFFENDERS

Thomas Ross, PhD and María Isabel Fontao, PhD*

Forensic Psychiatry and Psychotherapy, Psychiatric Centre Reichenau,
Reichenau, Germany

ABSTRACT

Correctional research has shown that young offenders have different treatment and programming needs than adult offenders. A large number of specific treatment and violence prevention programs for young offenders have been developed and applied in many countries. The majority of these programs are of the "cognitive skills type", i.e. they aim at enhancing cognitive and social skills, which are often deficient in young offenders. Modern treatment programs attend to the criminogenic needs of offenders, such as impulsivity or poor affect control, empathy deficits, low levels of socio-moral reasoning, substance use and poor problem-solving skills; a style of delivery that young offenders will find interesting and engaging; and flexibility in its administration in order to take into account potentially small custodial sentences. Programs of this type teach young offenders cognitive-behavioral skills that enable them to take their time, i.e. to stop and think before they act, in order to resolve socially complex and potentially "dangerous" situations. Focussing on treatment programs, this review provides a brief overview of the history of (young) offender treatment and some of the most common treatment and violence prevention models for young offenders.

INTRODUCTION

The Austrian psychiatrist August Aichhorn was the first seriously to concern himself with the treatment of young delinquent individuals (1). Working with delinquent youth at the city borders of Vienna about 100 years ago, he developed an influential treatment concept which

---

* Correspondence: Thomas Ross, PhD, Forensic Psychiatry and Psychotherapy, Psychiatric Centre Reichenau, Feursteinstrasse 55, D-78479 Reichenau, Germany. E-mail: thomas.ross@uni-ulm.de.

has later been described as the corrective emotional experience (2), now an indispensable terminus technicus in psychoanalytical treatment (3,4). From a theoretical point of view, he proposed a dual deficit model. He posited a failure of progression from the pleasure principle to the reality principle in conjunction with a malformation of the superego in his developmental account of the disorder. This basically accounts for lack of impulse control in delinquent individuals, as a tendency for immediate gratification persists and remains unchallenged. Excessive strictness and overindulgence were both seen as causes of the child´s or youth's failure to renounce the pleasure principle. He saw psychosocial deprivation as the primary reason for impeding the renunciation of the pleasure principle and for disrupting the internalisation of parental norms. This and the internalisation of poor parental norms in delinquent families were put forward as explanations of superego dysfunction (3). Before the "cognitive revolution" in the 1950s brought about a different theoretical view about the antecedents of delinquent and violent behavior, British, Dutch, and many German forensic psychiatric and social therapeutic facilities had worked in correspondence with the ideas laid out above. Aichhorn´s approach to treatment included a phase of getting the patient involved in the treatment process. Instead of re-enacting punishment, he would frustrate the patients´ wishes for punishment later in the process, i.e. in the case of recidivism, he tried to understand what the delinquent act actually meant for the individual, and what it stood for in the individual´s mind. Aichhorn believed that in order to renounce their narcissistic position and give up the pleasure principle in favour of the reality principle, delinquent individuals had to establish an idealizing relationship with their therapist. To establish a relationship stable enough to make positive treatment effects possible, the therapist had to be able to indulge the patient and compromise traditional views on psychoanalytic treatment techniques.

Drawing on Aichhorn´s early work, Kurt Eissler, a US-American psychoanalyst of Austrian origin, suggested that delinquents, due to their narcissistic position, are not able to establish positive transference with their therapists (5). He described the technical difficulties in treating a delinquent as a consequence of his lack of desire to change. Delinquents have no need or motive to tell the therapist what is going on in them, and their symptoms are painful not to them but to others in their environment. Furthermore, he postulated that delinquents will not be able to differentiate sources of external and internal danger, and to consciously experience and cope with anxiety stemming from these sources. Instead, in order to cope with anxiety, they tend to engage in destructive acting-out. In order to reduce anxiety, the attitude of the therapist should be characterized by qualities such as warmth, firmness, and high expectations of the person combined with clear guidance. Implicit in this is the therapist´s positive regard for the delinquent, his or her own sense of integrity and authority and belief in the possibility of change. Furthermore, he stressed the importance of capturing the imagination and curiosity of the resistant patient. Instead of applying classical psychoanalytic technique such as analysis and interpretation of thought and behavior, he stated that from time to time, real gratification should be granted. Eissler was convinced that a basic treatment of this sort is a necessary condition for aggression to translate in anxiety, and the fruitful application of psychoanalytic technique on offender patients.

Modern psychodynamic offender treatment highlights the need for establishing well structured therapeutic regimes that can support the patient´s needs to overcome resistance. This is also true for the psychodynamic treatment of young offenders. Good staff management, support and consultation are empathized; the patients need an empathetic, encouraging, and challenging therapeutic relationship and a therapeutic team that is able to convey (psychological) security. The latter is seen to be important in order to help a patient recognize and cope with his conflicts and eventually to facilitate effective prosocial conflict resolution. Recent work informed by attachment theory and its application to the treatment of offenders has generally empirically supported the notions laid out above (6,7).

Historically, there was a second approach to offender treatment, derived from behavior therapy. In the 1960s, behavioral researchers began to aversively condition unwanted sexual fantasies, reactions, and behaviors in adults, i.e. they tried to extinguish these by means of well recognized learning mechanisms such as classical conditioning. Electric shocks or aversive olfactory stimuli were applied, for example, for the reconditioning of sexual deviant arousal. Aversion therapy was reported to be effective, at first, but scientific enthusiasm for these approaches faded quickly in the light of new findings that were more promising. Today, there is scientific consensus that, in the long run, aversive reconditioning aggravate rather than extinguish deviant sexual preferences, i.e. patients tend to get worse (8). This is not to say that general learning principles do not work in offender populations. The principle of positive reinforcement, for example, is unquestioned as an important means of enhancing prosocial behaviors in virtually all psychotherapeutic approaches to treatment, including treatments of young patients. It is important to note, however, that classical approaches to positive reinforcement such as "token economies", i.e. the simple gratification of "correct" behavioral responses, have been abandoned in recent years. This is true for both adult and young offender groups. A detailed account of the history of cognitive-behavioral approaches to the treatment of (sexual) offenders can be found in Laws and Marshall (9) and Marshall and Laws (10).

TREATMENT PROGRAMS

Beginning in the early 1970s, and in the tradition of early behavioral therapy for offenders and especially sexual offenders, scientists in Canada and the United States started to develop more complex programs aiming at the enhancement of more prosocial attitudes and skills in order to counteract antisocial behaviors. These programs replaced older ones which had mainly focussed on symptom reduction as a means of relapse prevention. In order to be effective, treatment interventions had to shift towards cognitive processes facilitating delinquent behavior and/or recidivism, i.e. denial and minimization, prosocial norm building, victim empathy, self-regulation, splitting, and the enhancement of self assertiveness. Therefore, modern offender treatment programs address a range of cognitive and social elements often found in offender populations: cognitive distortions, social skills, and low self-esteem, lack of empathy, and, especially but not exclusively in the case of sexual offenders, intimacy deficits and deviant sexuality (11,12).

Today, numerous programs exist worldwide, and many of them are manualized, albeit not all to the same degree. By the time this paper was written in late 2009, the United States alone had several repositories of model programs and systematic reviews on the Internet, e.g. published by the US National Registry of Effective Programs and Practice (SAMHSA's National Registry of Evidence-based Programs and Practices [NREPP] at http://nrepp.samhsa.gov; a model programs guide, published by the US Office of Juvenile Justice and Delinquency Prevention (OJJDP Model Program guide -Developmental Services group at http://www.ojjdp.gov/mpg/www.dsgonline.com/mpg2.5/mpg_index.htm; or a web page with valuable information on blueprint programs including programs for violence prevention (Blueprints f: Center for the study and prevention of violence at http://www.colorado.edu/cspv/blueprints/modelprograms.htmlor healthy youth development at http://www.blueprintsprograms.com). Individual programs comprise different types of intervention for different offender types aiming at a range of life domains among various settings: Program types are prevention, intervention, and suppression programs; Settings can be structured along a continuum of institutionalisation: Correctional (highly institutionalised) programs; mental health programs, and non-institutionalised community programs. Offender types are grouped by age, risk (violent/non-violent), and degree of offender organisation, i.e. programs primarily devised for individuals or gang-related programs; school and after-school programs, and specialized interventions on individual, family, and peer group levels.

PRINCIPLES OF EFFECTIVE INTERVENTION

Drawing on the intensive research conducted predominantly by Andrews and colleagues since the beginning of the 1990s, a number of principles of effective correctional intervention have been formulated (13-15):

- Correctional intervention should make use of structured and validated risk-assessment. The implementation of a complete system of continuous offender risk screening and need assessments is better than the application of isolated instruments or procedures. Assessing offenders in a reliable and valid manner is regarded as a prerequisite for effective treatment, management and supervision of offenders. Furthermore, assessments should be made by staff who is well trained in the administration of tools and instruments; and there should be written accounts or protocols of the procedures that are applied.
- Clients should be assigned to treatment according to the risk principle, i.e. intensive services should be reserved for moderate and high risk cases, and never for low risk cases. Treatment targets must be strongly related to the criminogenic needs of the target group (need principle) Criminogenic needs are defined as individual dynamic factors empirically associated with risk for (re)-offending, e.g. antisocial attitudes and values, lack of problem solving skills, substance abuse, employment status, or low educational and vocational achievement.
- Cognitive behavioral interventions are the methods of choice, if they are administered in a way that matches the intellectual and emotional skills of their clients (responsivity principle).
- Managers and supervisors should attend to the relationship and structural skills of service delivery staff.
- Reinforcement of relationship and structural skills on a regular basis will help maintain primary treatment effects.
- The dosage of service delivery must be sufficiently high. For example, high risk offenders need significantly more initial structure and services than low-risk offenders. This claim is especially true for the management of day time activities,

which should be occupied with delineated routine (employment, education, therapy) and other appropriated services (physical exercise, etc).

- Treatment will work better if the management policy is supportive. Monitoring, feedback, and corrective action routine should be active ingredients of the management strategy in correctional services.
- Staff should relate to offenders in interpersonally sensitive and constructive ways to enhance intrinsic motivation because lasting behavioral change will not occur if intrinsic motivation for change is low. In recent years, motivational interviewing has been described as a technique to help clients enhance motivation for treatment. Feelings of ambivalence that usually accompany both phases of the decision process that eventually results in adherence to treatment and treatment itself, can be explored by motivational interviews. Essentially, methods of communication (e.g. Socratic questioning) are used to help clients think about why they feel that treatment is not what they want. There is reason to assume that motivational interviewing reaches its ends, i.e. helps effectively enhance motivation for initiating and maintaining self-referential processes that might eventually lead to more pro-treatment attitudes (16).
- The probability for change to occur is strongly influenced by the quality of relationship experiences an offender is making in his present environment, i.e. with probation officers, treatment providers, and institution staff. Therefore, ongoing positive reinforcement of perceived behavioral change both in correctional institutions and natural communities is regarded as a cornerstone of the maintenance and improvement of treatment effects coming from different sources, i.e. cognitive behavioral therapy, individual and/or counselling and therapy, or interpersonal skills training.

It is not far-fetched to say that there is a general rule to potential effectiveness of intervention programs. The outcome of intervention depends on the degree to which individual risk factors for violence match with the treatment components offered by the program. Treatment effects are additive. For example, programs taking into account two Andrews principles tend to have better outcomes than those focussing on one, and those who focused on three principles were better than others focussing on only two (17-19). Thus, there is a statistical relationship in the number of risk factors under treatment and the potential outcome of the program. Furthermore, the effectiveness of treatment programs depends on the quality of the program itself (evidence based treatment with well trained mental health personnel), the availability of supplemental services (e.g. individual psychotherapeutic treatment), the optimal service amount (50 or more contact hours), appropriate clients (according to risk-needs analyses). In comparison with untreated controls with average recidivism rates of 40%, Lipsey and co-workers (18,20) expect roughly 20% recidivism for youth under the best available treatment conditions. In other words, if all relevant known factors are taken into consideration, and optimal treatment can be delivered, recidivism may be reduced by approximately 50%.

BEST PRACTICE PROGRAMS

The vast majority of treatment programs for young offenders to date is of a cognitive-behavioral type. In a meta-analysis of 509 juvenile justice programs, Lipsey (21) identified five main features of effective juvenile delinquency prevention and treatment programs:

- The primary service, i.e. the therapeutic element in it is effective, independent of its use with another intervention. In other words, the therapeutic program used must be effective for the target group.
- Supplementary services: Adding another service component to primary service often increases the effectiveness of the intervention.
- Treatment amount: The amount of service frequency must be sufficient, as indicated by service frequency, program duration, and program quality.
- Treatment quality: Service quality and the quality of implementation influence effectiveness.
- Youth risk level: Programs are generally more effective with high-risk offenders than for low-risk offenders.

Lipsey´s work also makes clear that the configurations of programs have a considerable impact on their effectiveness. Since many juvenile delinquency prevention and treatment programs are not large-scale and multi-systemic including a combination of effective individual, family, educational and vocational interventions, these programs will be less effective, even if they use single components which are typically regarded as adequate treatments for young offenders.

There are three major program effectiveness criteria: The type of program, fidelity of program implementation, and risk level. About 40% of the variation in recidivism is associated with the type of program, another 40% of the total value of a program is associated with the quality of program implementation, which is measured in terms of frequency and duration of the program (25%), and quality of service (15%). The risk level accounts for roughly 20% of the variation, i.e. programs addressing high-risk subjects are usually more effective than those addressing youth with low risk of delinquency and/or violence.

Based on his meta-analyses of programs for general delinquents, Lipsey grouped programs according to their relative effectiveness for prevention subjects, juvenile offenders on probation, and institutionalised offenders. For example, for juvenile probationers, he divided his database into three main categories, on the basis of their average effects: above-average effects, average effects, and below-average effects. Among the services with above average effects count cognitive-behavioral therapy, group counselling, vocational training, mentoring, and some forms of sex offender treatment and drug abuse treatment. Average effects are associated with family counselling or therapy, individual counselling or therapy, life skills enhancement, multi-systemic therapy, and educational intervention. Below average effects score all programs with recreation components, challenge programs, intensive supervision, and restitution. Finally, there is a number of interventions that will at best render no rehabilitative effects at all, or make things even worse. Among these count punishment regimes for juvenile offenders, scared straight programs, boot camps, large custodial facilities, long terms of confinement, curfew laws, and restrictive out of home placement for mental health treatment, psychiatric hospitalisation, and placements in residential treatment centres (22).

ADULT AND YOUTH OFFENDER PROGRAMS

While adult and young offender treatment including cognitive-behavioral treatment approaches using manualized programs have the same roots, different developmental paths have been pursued especially after Andrews published his principles of effective correctional intervention in the early 1990s (13). It has since been clear that young offenders have somewhat different treatment and programming needs than adult offenders. As both juvenile and adult offender programs draw on essentially the same knowledge base in criminology and forensic psychology, similarities prevail, especially as far as the structural makeup of best practice programs is concerned. For example, key structural components of cognitive-behavioral programs for both adults and young offenders include a shared set of criminogenic needs, such as impulsivity or poor affect control, empathy deficits, low levels of socio-moral reasoning, substance use and poor problem-solving skills. A style of delivery that participants will find interesting and engaging is not only important for young offenders, because offender groups tend to suffer from boredom, especially when they are in custody. However, owing to the ground breaking conceptual work of Andrews and co-workers (13-15), the application of meta-analysis as a method for the comparison of large samples of treatment studies (23), and the pioneering scientific work of key researchers in the field it has recently been possible to describe an array of age-related risk factors for violence and general delinquency in youth (see the paragraphs above, for relevant literature). These risk factors must be met if a program is to operate effectively. Therefore, programs aiming at the prevention and reduction of crime and violence in juveniles must be broader than those of adult offenders, using several structural elements related to the current developmental stage of the young person. In youth, parallel, where possible multi-systemic interventions on individual, vocational, peer group, community and family levels are indicated. In adult offenders, some target areas of intervention will inevitably differ from those aimed at juveniles, i.e. family (especially parents) and peer group interventions, and schooling or vocational training. Furthermore, the level of legal sanctioning is generally higher with adults than with youth, and offender careers are more visible. Adults will therefore spend more time in correctional facilities with lesser chances to participate in effective community programs.

AN EXAMPLE

The Reasoning and Rehabilitation Program (24) is a multifaceted, cognitive-behavioral program designed to teach juvenile and adult offenders cognitive skills and values that are essential for prosocial competence. The program was devised about 30 years ago and continuously updated with research findings. It is based on more than 100 studies that have yielded substantial reductions of re-offending. To date, the program has been delivered to more than forty thousand offenders world-wide. It has its roots in Canada, where about 8000 serious offenders in 47 penitentiaries have participated in the program. R&R has been applied across the spectrum of offender types: children in schools deemed at risk for offending; chronically recidivistic adult offenders; alcohol and drug-abusing offenders; violent offenders; property offenders; car thieves; child and spouse abusers; sex offenders, and white collar criminals. R&R is now being conducted in secure forensic psychiatric facilities all over the English speaking world, Germany, Spain, the Netherlands, and the Baltic States.

The program consists of nine interrelated modules: problem solving, social skills, values enhancement, critical reasoning, negotiation skills, creative thinking, the management of emotions, cognitive exercises, and skills in review. Program targets are:

- The enhancement of self-control: offenders are taught to stop and think before they act; to consider all the consequences before making decisions; to formulate (future) plans; to use thinking techniques to control their emotions and their behavior.
- Meta-cognition: Offenders are encouraged to critically assess their own thinking; to realize that how they think determines what they think, how they feel and how they behave. Thinking strategies are taught as a means of self-regulating their behavior.
- Critical reasoning: Offenders are instructed how to think logically, objectively, and rationally without distorting the facts or externalising the blame.
- Social skills: Utilizing a modification of a structured learning therapy program (25), skills are taught which will help offenders achieve positive reinforcement rather than rejection in social situations (e.g. responding to criticism or negotiating instead of demanding).
- Interpersonal cognitive problem solving skills: offenders are taught how to analyse and to understand the emotional content of interpersonal problems, how to consider other people's values, behavior and feelings, and how to recognize how their behavior affects other people and why others respond to them as they do.
- Creative thinking: offenders often have a rather rigid thinking style (conceptual rigidity). They are thus taught alternative thinking, i.e. how to consider alternative, prosocial rather than antisocial ways of responding to the problems they experience.
- Social perspective taking: the emphasis is on other people's views, feelings, and thoughts, i.e. the development of empathy.
- Values enhancement: group discussion techniques are used and a number of commercially available games to teach values. The aim is to move the offender from a rather egocentric world view to a consideration of the needs of others.
- Emotional management: Anger management techniques were adapted to help offenders down-regulate excessive emotional arousal. The focus is on control of negative and the build-up of positive emotions.

The content of R&R is taught in 35 group sessions of two hours duration, the frequency is between two to four sessions a week. Some sessions require preparation on behalf of the participants. The encouragement of group activities based on great variety of working materials is the core technique to promote behavioral change: role-playing, thinking games, learning exercises with and without video-feedback, and related cognitive exercises.

There is a considerable body of empirical evidence for the effectiveness of the R&R program. As an example of the most compelling evidence of its effectiveness, Tong and Farrington (26) provided a meta-analysis of sixteen evaluations in four countries, involving

26 separate comparisons in which experimental and control groups were compared. Overall, there was a 14% reduction of recidivism for program participants compared with controls. The program was effective in community and institutional settings, and for relatively low-risk and high-risk offenders.

PROGRAMS BASED ON OTHER THAN COGNITIVE-BEHAVIORAL THEORY

The vast majority of anglo-american research on psychological treatment programs of juvenile and adult offenders encompass programs devised and delivered in the cognitive-behavioral tradition. This is not surprising given the fact that cognitive-behavioral research and treatment have been stimulating an impressive bulk of data on treatment effectiveness. Research on programs with other theoretical underpinnings, including the psychodynamic group approach, has been lagging behind. There are good reasons for this, as we will demonstrate on the example of psychodynamically oriented treatment. Personal factors of potential program tutors might play a role. Psychodynamic as compared to cognitive-behavioral therapists are on average less research oriented. Issues related to the scientific integrity of the research process have been described in this context, i.e. there has been an ongoing debate about adequate operationalizations of psychodynamic concepts. Furthermore, there might be a bias toward the publication of large-scale quantitative studies which have typically been conducted by cognitive-behavioral research personnel as compared to small qualitative individual case studies which are often preferred by psychodynamic researchers and therapists. During the last 20 years, however, psychodynamically oriented research groups have developed both individual (27,28) and group treatments for patient groups with personality disorders who are usually regarded as difficult to treat, i.e. patients with borderline and antisocial personality disorders. The group treatment with probably the highest propensity to be effective with juvenile offender samples is mentalization based treatment (MBT) (29).

TRANSFERENCE FOCUSED PSYCHOTHERAPY (TFP) (27)

TFP is a highly structured psychodynamic individual treatment based on Otto Kernberg´s object relations model of Borderline Personality Disorder (27,30). Although originally conceptualised as an individual treatment, TFP elements have recently been adapted to a group format in forensic settings. The results are promising in that the concepts of TFP apparently help promote an understanding of individual patients as they relate to others in complex group settings (31).

In TFP, the focus is on the interaction between the patient and the therapist, and an emphasis is placed on the current moment rather than the past. Based on early relationships with caregivers and related attachment figures, the patients´ unintegrated and/or split off internal representations of self and others will be activated, made conscious and reflected upon. The aim is to help the patient integrate these representations into a more complex, i.e. a more mature structure of personality. Ideally, TFP helps patients create a more coherent sense of self, to overcome splitting and to build more positive representations of self and others. The therapist´s role is to perceive and experience the patient´s representation of the interaction in the transference relationship, and to neutrally observe and command on it without normative evaluation, or judgment. TFP has been adapted for offender populations (TFFP; Transference Focused Forensic Psychotherapy) and there are a number of pilot studies suggesting positive effects for both patients and institutional staff (32).

There is a growing body of research supporting the efficacy of TFP. For example, Clarkin et al (28) examined the efficacy of TFP in comparison with Dialectical Behavior Therapy and Dynamic Supportive Treatment. The results indicated that although all three therapeutic approaches were effective in fostering global improvement in the symptoms ob borderline personality disorder, TFP was effective in more borderline characteristics examined than either of the other two approaches. There are limitations, however, to the interpretation of these results, because patients in the TFP-condition received more individual therapy than those in the other two research groups.

MENTALIZATION BASED TREATMENT (MBT) (29)

MBT is a manualized psychodynamic group and individual treatment program for patients with borderline personality disorder, developed by Fonagy and Bateman (29,33). The core concept of this treatment is mentalization, i.e. the capacity of humans to interpret actions of oneself and others on the basis of intentional states such as beliefs, goals, purposes, reasons, feelings, or desires. Due to disorganized attachment representations, which are often found in patients with borderline personality disorder, they tend to have limited mentalization capacity. This is also thought to be true for most offender patients.

The aim of treatment is to increase mentalization in order to improve affect regulation, interpersonal functioning, and the ability to pursue life goals. The therapeutic focus is on the patient´s current present state rather than the past. During sessions the therapist seeks to activate the patients´ attachment systems, and to encourage them to create and to emotionally experience safe bonds with both the therapist and the other group members. If these processes are made accessible for conscious reflection, a psychological basis for the formation of a secure attachment relationship is provided. Thus, it will be safe for the patient to explore the mind of the other, to confront negative affect, and to understand the intentional nature of interpersonal relationships.

According to mentalization theory, the improvement of mentalization capacity of offender patients will help them perceive others as intentional psychological beings who do not pose a threat to their psychological integrity. Mentalization is also thought help them reflect the destructive nature of their violence on the mind of others. Thus, MBT will eventually enhance empathy and thus impede offenders from engaging in violence as a means of interpersonal conflict resolution, or from acting out negative mental states otherwise. Fonagy and co-workers have conducted extensive outcome research on MBT for borderline personality disorder. Compared to treatment as usual, MBT is clearly superior (34). Furthermore, MBT is without doubt a promising approach to the prevention of violence and the treatment of offender groups, including juvenile offenders (35-38).

TREATMENT EFFECTS

The effectiveness of treatment for the reduction of recidivism has been shown in hundreds if not thousands of studies, and the magnitude of effects at least equals those of many other treatments in somatic medical science (39,40). The average effect size of all approaches to offender treatment is approximately $r = .10$, i.e. a reduction of recidivism in treated offenders of 10% as compared to untreated offenders (8,13,41-46). Although this effect size is rather moderate compared to the average effect of psychotherapy with other in- and outpatient groups (approximately $r = .80$)(47), it is highly significant with respect to the avoidance of serious harm inflicted upon victims and societies at large. Furthermore, treatment is cost-effective. For example, Welsh and Farrington's (48) study on the cost-benefit ratio of offender treatment reported a ratio of 1 to 1.13 - 7.14 in favour of the treatment condition. Offender treatment programs that take into account the principles of risk, need, and responsivity (13) usually do better than other approaches, approximating average effect sizes of $r = .30$ (17,21,49-52). Sexual offender treatment is probably even more effective than the treatment of other (violent) offenders. For example, the meta-analysis of Lösel and Schmucker (52) included 69 studies on N = 22,181 sexual offenders and reported a reduction of recidivism in sexual delinquency of roughly 40% in treated compared to untreated individuals. There is good reason to assume that treatment of offenders is most effective when they are treated as youth, regardless of the type of index crime they have committed (20,53). Recent research on the treatment of juvenile delinquents show high average effect sizes between $r = .30$ (49), $r = .37$ (51), and $r = .43$ (54). Effect sizes under the best theoretically available treatment conditions approximate $r = .50$ (21).

LIMITATIONS

Although there can be no doubt that the cognitive-behavioral group program approach to the prevention and treatment of juvenile offenders has been effective, there are several limitations to this approach. For example, programs tend to focus on the reduction and elimination of dynamic risk factors by teaching offenders how to avoid recidivism (avoidance goals). They usually do not focus on the flipside of the same coin, namely on the positive human goals or goods all humans seek in order to live satisfying and good lives (approach goals; Ward and co-workers have conceptualised this idea in a theory emphasising goal-directed behavior and they have put forward ten primary human goods, sought by all humans and needed for psychological well-being; for details on this theory see Ward and Brown (55); Ward and Gannon (56). The inclusion of such approach goals in existing best practice programs might help open up new perspectives on improving manualized treatments for young and adult offenders.

We also know that some (early) intervention programs could not maintain initial positive effects in the long run. One reason for this was that they tended to be repetitious and boring, with too many predefined manualized elements to be complied with and too little space for spontaneous individual input. Although modern program makers have learned from these problems and have therefore introduced systematic elements to keep participants interested, some of these problems remain. Furthermore, programs are better when implemented from and monitored by researchers rather than practitioners (18,20,21). It is obvious, however, that for practical reasons not all programs can be accompanied by research personnel.

Rather than a critique of manualized cognitive-behavioral programs as such, we see a rather self-made limitation to the effective development of potential alternative treatment strategies for young and adult offenders. Although conceptual work in treatments of other than the cognitive-behavioral type is quite elaborate and well advanced, these approaches are still underrepresented in the modern treatment literature.

FUTURE PERSPECTIVES

In order to make offender treatment programs even more effective than they are, the following main options should be taken into account. First, research on the selective effectiveness of individual program components should be intensified. If new programs are designed, they should be tested based on intervention components that are significantly associated with effect sizes across studies. We know that not all program components are equally effective. For example, Landenberger and Lipsey (17) reported that in order to be effective, (cognitive-behavioral) programs must contain modules teaching interpersonal problem solving skills and anger control techniques, whereas unsuccessful programs employed activities aimed at getting offenders to consider the impact of their behavior on their victims (victim impact) and simple reward and penalty schemes designed to reinforce appropriate behavior (behavior modification).

Second, if adequately adapted for the needs of young offender treatment, and implemented in a supplementary and innovative way, programs might profit from the findings of general psychological science (57).

Third, prevention and treatment programming priorities should be defined with respect to current advances in the study of age-related risk factors (58-61). From these it follows that early intervention with young children should target early delinquent behaviors associated with individual risk factors (i.e. hyperactivity, impulsivity, and attention problems), drug use, aggressive behavior, family poverty, and effective parenting with antisocial parents. Interventions for adolescents should work towards loosening offender's affiliation to antisocial peers; one focus should lie on the reduction of general involvement in delinquency, another one on the avoidance of physical violence. Pro-social ties should be strengthened at this time, improvement of mental health and relationships with parents are other issues to be taken into account. From a programmatic point of view, programs for adolescents must be systemic and multi-topic, i.e. it should comprise specific interventions on the individual, family, school, peer, and, where possible, on community level (18).

Fourth, program makers should also take a look on potential protective factors for delinquency. For example, Loeber and colleagues have conceptualised factors that predict a low probability of offending among youth exposed to risk factors and they describe factors that promote desistance. In their latest analyses, they demonstrate how protective or promotive factors have main effects in essentially the same way as risk factors, i.e. the presence of protective factors can counter-balance the detrimental effects of risk factors (61). In a study about common risk and protective factors in successful prevention programs, Durlak (62) reviewed a total of 1,200 prevention studies. Among the most important protective factors for behavior problems, school failure, physical health, physical injury and abuse and adolescent pregnancy count personal and social skills and self-efficacy (individual level), general (pro-social) support, high social norms and effective social policies (community level), good parent-child relationship (family level), high quality schools (school level), and positive role-models (peer level).

Fifth, it should be borne in mind, that treatment effects accumulate with the inclusion of individual treatment, and other supplemental services are a necessary condition for maintaining long term effects of offender treatment. In addition to sound psychological in-patient treatment, an elaborated model of after-care after release from prison or from forensic psychiatry is indispensable.

Finally, effective comprehensive strategies on preventing crime and treating juvenile offenders need to be supported by scientists and further developed. Best practice programs will not be as effective as they could be if they are not embedded in a well functioning and benevolent network of care-takers on different levels of intervention. Therefore, a strong involvement of scientists and practitioners in the development and application of social prevention and treatment policies is needed.

REFERENCES

[1]   Aichhorn A. Verwahrloste Jugend; Die Psychoanalyse in der Fürsorgeerziehung: 10 Vorträge zur ersten Einführung (11. ed., 2005). [Neglected Youth; Psychoanalysis in child care and education: 10 introductory papers] Bern: Huber, 1925. [German]

[2]   Alexander F, French TM. Psychoanalytic therapy: Principles and application. New York: Ronald Press, 1946.

[3]   Cordess C, Cox M, eds. Forensic psychotherapy. Crime, psychodynamics and the offender patient. (Vol. I and II). London: Jessica Kingsley, 1998.

[4]   Welldon E, van Velsen C, eds. A practical guide to forensic psychotherapy. London: Jessica Kingsley, 1997.

[5]   Eissler, R. The effect of the structure of the ego on psychoanalytic technique. J Am Psycho-analytic Assoc 1953;1:104-43.

[6]   Fonagy P. Towards a developmental understanding of violence. Br J Psychiat 2003;183:190-2.

[7]   Fonagy P. The developmental roots of violence in the failure of mentalization. In: Pfäfflin F, Adshead G, eds. A matter of security. The application of attachment theory to forensic psychiatry and psychotherapy. London: Jessica Kingsley, 2004:13-56.

[8]   Hall GN. Sexual offender recidivism revisited: a meta-analysis of recent treatment studies. J Consult Clin Psychol 1995;63:802-9.

[9]   Laws DR, Marshall WL. A brief history of behavioral and cognitive behavioral approaches to sexual offenders: Part 1. Early developments. Sex Abuse 2003;15:75-92.

[10] Marshall WL, Laws DR. A brief history of behavioral and cognitive behavioral approaches to sexual offender treatment: Part 2: The modern era. Sex Abuse 2003;15:93-120.

[11] Marshall WL, Fernandez Y, Hudson S, Ward T, eds. Sourcebook of treatment programs for sexual offenders. New York: Plenum Press, 1998.

[12] Hollin C, ed. The essential handbook of offender treatment and assessment. Chichester: John Wiley, 2004.

[13] Andrews D, Zinger I, Hoge RD, Bonta J, Gendreau P, Cullen FT. Does correctional treatment work? A clinically relevant and psychologically informed meta-analysis. Criminology 1990; 28:369-404.

[14] Andrews DA. Enhancing adherence to risk-need-responsivity. Crim Public Pol 2006;5:595-602.

[15]   Andrews DA, Dowden C. Risk principle of case classification in correctional treatment: A meta-analytic investigation. Int J Offender Ther 2006;50:88-100.

[16]   Miller WR, Rollnick S. Motivational Interviewing: preparing people for change, 2nd ed. New York: Guilford, 2002.

[17]   Landenberger NA, Lipsey MW. The positive effects of cognitive-behavioral programs for offenders: A meta-analysis of factors associated with effective treatment. J Experimental Crim 2005;1:451-76.

[18]   Lipsey MW. The evidence base for effective juvenile programs as a source for best practice guidelines. Nashville, TN: Vanderbilt Univ, Center Evaluat Res Methodol, 2006.

[19]   Hanson RK, Bourgon G, Helmus L, Hodgson S. A meta-analysis of the effectiveness of treatment for sexual offenders: Risk, need, and responsivity. Corrections Research User Report No. 2009-01. Ottawa: Public Safety Canada, 2009.

[20]   Lipsey MW, Cullen FT. The effectiveness of correctional rehabilitation: A review of systematic reviews. Annu Rev Law Soc Sci 2007; 3: 297-320.

[21]   Lipsey MW. A standardized program evaluation protocol for programs serving juvenile probationers. Nashville, TN: Vanderbilt Univ, Center Evaluat Res Methodol, 2007.

[22]   Howell JC. Preventing and reducing juvenile delinquency: A comprehensive framework, 2nd ed. Thousand Oaks, CA: Sage, 2009.

[23]   Durlak JA, Lipsey MW. A practitioner´s guide to meta-analysis. Am J Community Psychol 1991;19:291-332.

[24]   Ross RR, Fabiano EA, Ross RD. Reasoning and Rehabilitation: A handbook for teaching cognitive skills. Ottawa: Centre Cognit Dev, 1986.

[25]   Goldstein AP, Sprafkin R, Gershaw NJ, Klein P. Skillstreaming the adolescent. Champaign, IL: Res Press, 1980.

[26]   Tong LSY, Farrington DP (2006). How effective is the "Reasoning and Rehabilitation" programme in reducing reoffending? A meta-analysis of evaluations in four countries. Psychol Crime Law 2006;12:3-24.

[27]   Clarkin JF, Yeomans FE, Kernberg OF. Psychotherapy for Borderline Personality. New York: John Wiley, 1999.

[28]   Clarkin JF, Levy KN, Lenzenweger MF, Kernberg OF. Evaluating three treatments for borderline personality disorder: A multiwave study. Am J Psychiat 2007;164:922-8.

[29]   Bateman AW, Fonagy P. Mentalization-based treatment of BPD. J Pers Disord 2004;18:36-51.

[30]   Yeomans FE, Clarkin JF, Kernberg OF (2002). A primer on transference-focused psychotherapy for the borderline patient. Northvale NJ: Jason Aronson, 2002.

[31]   Mattke D, Dammann G, Martius P. Der Transfer von einzel-therapeutischen Behandlungskonzepten auf Gruppenformate: Das Beispiel der Übertragungsfokussierten Psychotherapie (TFP) [The transfer of individual treatment concepts on group settings. The example of Transference Focused Psychotherapy (TFP)]. Gruppenpsychother GR 2007; 43: 161-80. [German]

[32]   Fontao MI, Pfäfflin F, Lamott F. Anwendung der TFP auf die Behandlung von Maßregelvollzugspatienten. Eine Pilotstudie. [Application of TFP in the treatment of forensic psychiatric patients - a pilot study] In: Lackinger F, Dammann G, Wittmann B, eds. Psychodynamische Psychotherapie bei Delinquenz. Stuttgart: Schattauer, 2008: 395-405. [German]

[33]   Fonagy P, Bateman AW. Mechanisms of change in mentalization-based treatment of BPD. J Clin Psychol 2006;62:411-30.

[34]   Bateman AW, Fonagy P. 8-Year follow-up of patients reated for borderline personality disorder: Mentalization-based treatment versus treatment as usual. Am J Psychiat 2008;165:631-8.

[35]   Twemlow SW, Fonagy P, Sacco FC. An innovative psychodynamically influenced approach to reduce school violence. J Am Acad Child Psy 2001;40:377-9.

[36]   Twemlow SW, Fonagy P, Sacco FC. The role of the bystander in the social architecture of bullying and violence in schools and communities. In: Devine J, Gilligan J, Miczek KA, Shaikh R, Pfaff D, eds. Youth violence: scientific approaches to prevention. New York: NY Acad Sci, 2004:215-32.

[37] Twemlow SW, Fonagy P. Transforming violent social systems into non-violent mentalizing systems: an experiment in schools. In: Allen JG, Fonagy P, eds. The handbook of mentalization-based treatment. Hoboken: John Wiley, 2006:289-306.

[38] Bateman AW, Fonagy P. Comorbid antisocial and borderline personality disorders: mentalization-based treatment. J Clin Psychol 2008;64: 181-94.

[39] McGuire J. Criminal sanctions versus psychologically based interventions with offenders: a comparative empirical analysis. Psychol Crime Law 2002;8:183-208.

[40] Marshall WL, McGuire J. Effect sizes in the treatment of sexual offenders. Int J Offender Ther 2003;47:653-663.

[41] Lipsey MW. The effect of treatment on juvenile delinquents: Results from meta-analysis. In: Lösel F, Bender D, Bliesener T, eds. Psychology and Law. International Perspectives. Berlin: De Gruyter, 1992:131-43.

[42] Lipsey MW, Wilson DB. The efficacy of psychological educational and behavioural treatment. Am Psychol 1993;48:1181-1209.

[43] Lösel F. The efficacy of correctional treatment: A review and synthesis of meta-evaluations. In: McGuire J, ed. What works: Reducing re-offending: Guidelines from research and practice. Chichester: John Wiley, 1995: 79-111.

[44] Redondo S, Sanchez-Meca J, Garrido V. The influence of treatment programmes on the recidivism of juvenile and adult offenders: A European meta-analytic review. Psychol Crime Law 1999;5:251-78.

[45] Egg R, Pearson FS, Cleland CM, Lipton DS. Evaluation von Straftäterbehandlungsprogrammen in Deutschland: Überblick und Meta-Analyse. [Evaluation of offender treatment programmes in Germany: An overview and meta-analysis]. In: Rehn G, Wischka B, Lösel F, Walter M, eds. Behandlung gefährlicher Straftäter. Grundlagen Konzepte Ergebnisse. Herbolzheim: Centaurus, 2001:321-47 [German]

[46] Hanson RK, Gordon A, Harris AJ, Marques JK, Murphy W, Quinsey VL, Seto MC. First report of the collaborative outcome data project on the effectiveness of psychological treatment for sex offenders. Sex Abuse 2002;14:169-94.

[47] Lambert M, ed. Bergin and Garfield's Handbook of psychotherapy and behavior change. New York: John Wiley, 2004.

[48] Welsh BC, Farrington DP. Correctional intervention programs and cost benefit analysis. Crim Justice Behav 2000;27:115-33.

[49] Pearson FS, Lipton DS, Cleland CM, Yee DS. The effects of behavioural/cognitive behavioural programs on recidivism. Crime Delinquency 2002;48:476-96.

[50] Dowden C, Antonowicz D, Andrews DA. The effectiveness of relapse prevention with offenders: a meta-analysis. Int J Offender Ther 2003;47: 516-28.

[51] Walker DF, McGovern SK, Poey EL, Otis KE. Treatment effectiveness for male adolescent sexual offenders: a meta-analysis and review. J Child Sex Abuse 2004;13:281-93.

[52] Lösel F, Schmucker M. The effectiveness of treatment for sexual offenders: A comprehensive meta-analysis. J Experimental Crim 2005;1: 117-46.

[53] Sherman LW, Farrington DP, MacKenzie DL, Welsh BC. Evidence based crime prevention. New York: Routledge, 2006.

[54] Reitzel LR, Carbonell JL. The effectiveness of sexual offender treatment for juveniles as measured by recidivism: A meta-analysis. Sex Abuse 2006;18:401-21.

[55] Ward T, Brown M. The Good Lives Model and conceptual issues in offender rehabilitation. Psychol Crime Law 2004;10:243-57.

[56] Ward T, Gannon TA. Rehabilitation etiology and self-regulation: the comprehensive good lives model of treatment for sexual offenders. Aggress Violent Behav 2006;11:77-94.

[57] Ross T. Current issues in self regulation research and their significance for therapeutic intervention in offender groups. Int J Behav Consultation Ther 2008;4:68-81.

[58] Farrington DP (2003). Key results from the first 40 years of the Cambridge Study in Delinquent Development. In: Thornberry TP, Krohn MD, eds. Taking stock of Delinquency: an overview of findings from contemporary longitudinal studies. New York: Kluwer/Plenum, 2003: 137-84.

[59] Loeber R, Farrington DP, eds. Serious and violent juvenile offenders: Risk factors and successful interventions. Thousand Oaks, CA: Sage, 1998.
[60] Loeber R, Farrington DP, eds. Child delinquents. Development Intervention and service needs. Thousand Oaks CA: Sage, 2001.
[61] Loeber R, Farrington DP, Stouthamer-Loeber M, White HR. Violence and serious theft: Development and prediction from childhood to adulthood. New York: Routledge, 2008.
[62] Durlak JA. Common risk and protective factors in successful prevention programs. Am J Orthopsychiat 1998;68:512-20.

In: Children, Violence and Bullying ISBN: 978-1-62948-342-9
Editors: J Merrick, I Kandel and H A Omar © 2014 Nova Science Publishers, Inc.

Chapter 13

WORKPLACE AND BULLYING

*Said Shahtahmasebi, PhD**

The Goodlife Research Centre Trust, Rangiora, New Zealand

ABSTRACT

A working environment is bullying and unsafe as long as your manager believes that being a 'team player' means loyalty to your manager and doing as you are told. Unfortunately, the literature on bullying concentrates on the characteristics of victims and the impact of bullying on their lives. The literature offers very little on how to prevent and eradicate bullying. Instead, the literature's solution is to offers ways of preparing potential victims. The problem with this approach is that while it does not address bullies and bullying it can also lead to confrontation and more bullying especially covert bullying. The literature on bullying in the workplace describes the mental and physical ill-health suffered by the victims and their families. The literature also discusses methods of bullying such as overt and covert, as well as physical and psychological abuse. The implications are that the consequences of abuse go far beyond the intended target; from the impact on the working environment to an individuals' health to economic and financial loss. The literature suggests various recommendations to employers and managers to combat bullying at work. However, the common assumption within the literature has been that the bullying is done by a colleague, a line manager or middle manager. Furthermore, it is often, wrongly, assumed that the executive/vice-chancellor, human resources, the trustees or the governing body are unaware of bullying in their workplace. Rate of workplace bullying is consistently highest in the Education and health sectors. This high rate of bullying can only be sustained if the management culture, wittingly or unwittingly, is one of bullying. In this chapter it is argued that cases of bullying whether due to isolated individuals, competition, rivalry, power or pure meanness as reported in the literature, can only thrive in a bullying management culture. Therefore, debate and policy formulation must be directed at government level in the first instance. The case reported is intended to raise some relevant issues to stimulate a debate and more research in this area.

---

* Correspondence: Said Shahtahmasebi, The Good Life Research Centre Trust, 4 Orkney Street, Strowan, Christchurch 8052, New Zealand. E-mail: radisolevoo@gmail.com.

INTRODUCTION

Much of the bullying literature is based on the premise of a bully with at least one victim, and offering suggestions on how parents, teachers, authorities, employers, and workforce can identify bullies in order to combat bullying. Very few authors discuss the possibility that bullies thrive when the workplace culture together with employment laws is conducive to supporting and encouraging bullying. For example, in some organisaitons, the executive management believes that loyalty means that staff must do what they are told i.e. loyalty to the executive rather than the organisation's goals, this will have a major impact on how senior and middle management behave and manage their staff. In this chapter the main issues of workplace bullying is raised and demonstrated through a case report.

Much has been written about the consequences of bullying as a social problem both in school and the workplace. The literature covers the various aspects of bullying e.g theoretical considerations (1), management environment and gender (2), psychological violence, misplaced loyalty and methods of bullying (e.g overt: visible physical and mental abuse, and covert: subtle abuse) (3), the effects of bullying (4-7), bullying at school (8), (9-11), and causes of bullying (12,13). McAvoy and Murtagh (14) provide a brief description of workplace bullying. An example of overt and covert abuse by an employer is demonstrated in a case narrative (15). Various authors make recommendations to the employers in order to combat bullying in their work environment (16). Glendinning (17) suggests that it is the role of human resources to deal with bullying and administer relevant policies in the workplace which often has tremendous implications for the organisation.

Most studies of bullying have concentrated on the victims' characteristics. Very few people ever victimise themselves; to have a victim there must be a seeker (18). Human interaction is a process and therefore is governed by dynamic codes of conduct. Some individuals, for whatever reasons, breach these codes to inflict suffering on others with whom they are bound by and share a common goal; through the organisational policy objectives and contracts. Very few studies have paid attention to studying the characteristics of the organisations, the bullies or the environments where bullies thrive. An important question to ask is what governs these individuals' behaviour? Without a proper study design to treat bullying as a process and to include the dynamics of human behaviour, our understanding of bullying behaviour could be vague and confused and at best one-sided. For example, Einarsen (12) in attempting to address the nature and causes of bullying on the one hand reports that the victims of harassment are more oversensitive, suspicious and angry, have low self-esteem and are anxious. On the other hand Einarsen argues that the personality of the victim may provoke aggression in others. Einarsen quotes competition, envy and the aggressor's own self doubt as three main reasons for bullying. However, these results were based on a subjective survey of the victims. The author, quite correctly, reports that without longitudinal studies personality factors may well be the outcome of bullying. It is not surprising then that assertiveness in the workplace is advised (19). Indeed, most employers, through their human resources (HR) division, offer staff self-development/assertiveness courses.

There are a number of problems with this strategy. There are no clearly defined boundaries for when assertiveness becomes aggression and bullying. What good will assertiveness or any anti-harassment policy do in a working environment and culture based on fear amongst staff, rumours, lies, falsifying of facts and misinformation and so on often referred to as predatory bullying (12)? And what are the implications of implementing recommendations from poorly designed studies and lack of real evidence? For example, Manthei's (20) comparison of methods of teaching assertiveness is flawed and lacks academic rigour; it appears to breach ethics regulations, is a badly designed and poorly conducted study with an inappropriate methodology that does not relate to the aims of the study. The author's conclusions appear to be her own views and do not relate to the results. Therefore, policies developed based on such studies will create more problems for the organisations rather than resolving.

For practical purposes, perhaps, the brief discussion by McAvoy and Murtagh (14) provides a more comprehensive collection of issues from the prevalence of morbidity in the individual victims to the morbidity of the workplace environment. They also report that apart from the negative effects on physical and mental well being, bullying can have negative cognitive effects e.g lack of initiatives. Such practices will not be without economic and other social consequences. For example, McAvoy and Murtagh report that statistics from the UK national workplace bullying advice line suggest 20% of the cases are from the education sector, 12% from health care followed closely by 10% from social services. It is not therefore surprising that the associated costs of bullying in the UK alone is estimated at £2-30bn per annum. Similarly, a Canadian report (21) suggests a cost to employers of $3.5bn and when the costs of wage replacement, health and medical care are included the costs are estimated at $16bn. See also Sheehan for the Australian experience (22).

Bullying and harassment, though studied as one phenomena, take different forms and shape. However, it is argued that bullying thrives in an environment where the organisation has a bullying culture (4,12). Examples of harassment may include belittling opinion, public humiliation, withholding of access to training, unnecessary disruption, obstruction, threats of dismissal, shifting of goalposts, removal of responsibility, undue pressure to produce work (4). Sheehan (22) reports psychological abuse in the workplace and discusses the damage caused, and the legal and economic risks to organisations that fail to address the problems.

A STORY

Unsurprisingly, the case report concerns a tertiary education institution. The subject has kindly given permission to outline some of the main events representing unprofessional behaviour by the institution – in order to maintain anonymity details of events have been kept to a minimum.

The subject accepted an offer of a post from an educational establishment. The subject was brought in with the specific mandate to carry out research and development (R & D), consultancy with a small teaching component. The advertisement and the bumph gave a positive picture of the institution using phrases such as a highly supportive, friendly and dynamic working environment, teaching staff expert in their fields, high quality research and researchers with international standing and so on. A quick internet search established that the claims about international standing was standard hype and by dynamic it was meant a high staff turn-over. The subject's final choice over other job offers was influenced by the challenges of the post.

One of the subject's mandates was to identify problem areas and report them to the management. Initially, things got onto a flying start and despite the negative rumours about the institution and the management a number of initiatives got underway. These initiatives proved popular with staff. Within the first few weeks of starting work, the subject realised that the institution had huge problems in terms of culture, management style, staff and above all vision. All the management posts had been filled via internal promotions despite attracting credible and well-qualified external candidates and against the wishes of staff members who participated in the selection process. Most of the managers/staff had been in the same institution for many years. The existence of tribalism suggested the divide and rule style of management. Access to resources in particular to do research is the privilege of those belonging to the right tribe. Symbolism appears the central driving force in management style and staff perceptions of status. For example, office size and position and job title (e.g team leader) signifies academic status as opposed to experience, qualification and performance. The institution is being administered by staff without relevant management experience (in particular people skills) and qualifications. These internal appointments were apparently made after open competition with staff competing with credible, well-qualified and highly experienced candidates. Clearly, such a management style is a recipe for disaster particularly where new blood is recruited to carry out the education developmental work and delivery. The subject reported that the frustration of experienced and qualified staff working under such management had soon given way to friction and confrontation which quickly turned to hostility, abuse and harassment.

The subject made a report to the management based on the above observations and suggested that for the institution to achieve its goals a more supportive management practice was essential. In the report the subject further suggested that change in practice and recruitment of new blood at senior level to be a necessity. Moreover, the report recommended that as a first step the institution needed to consider a retraining programme for its current managers. With hindsight, the management did not want to see that kind of report! What followed next was months (nearly three years) of a sustained campaign against the subject. The initiatives one by one, without justification and in breach of the institution's own policies, were cancelled, the subject was excluded from input and contribution, workload was increased, rumours about the subject were spread. Consultations with the HR and their promise of resolving the situation was not only fruitless but also led to further campaigns. Included in the arguments with the management was the treatment of staff. However, the subject underestimated the fear amongst the staff; their unwillingness to demand their own rights and were prepared to be passive by-standers grateful for having a job, summarised the workplace culture of the institution. Managers with no track record and experience in R & D suddenly became experts and criticised the subject. Needless to say that the subject was quick and efficient in dismissing such criticism, which appeared to make the matters worse and help the campaign against the subject to intensify. Delaying tactics and obstruction also included intrusion, not processing of forms until after the closing date, access to personal files/materials without the knowledge or permission of the subject, interfering with processes, contacting external agencies with the specific view of obstructing the subjects progress. The subject reported these as the institution's immoral activities and malpractice by design.

The subject reported wondering if the management was so critical why would they not call a meeting with a view of terminating the contract. Not surprisingly, some material and statistics that became available through the unions revealed an unwritten policy of not to terminate contracts for fear of legal repercussion, that the senior management including HR had a history of aggressive behaviour and harassment against staff, were engaged in spreading rumours, setting up colleagues against colleagues, obstruction, positive support for the subject from other heads of department being falsified as negative, threatening behaviour, instead of following complaint procedures the management met every complaint with a counter complaint, and, the use of their external social contacts to obstruct. It also revealed consistent complaints against the same managers and pattern of behaviour by the institution (similarly using humiliation, threats, undermining, belittling etc): the victims were either silenced, had to leave their posts or on long-term sick leave whilst the offending mangers received promotion! In fact, during a face-to-face conversation about the structure of the institution and procedures with the head of department, the subject was told that the head was the real decision maker pointing out that there was no point contacting even the executive/vice-chancellor.

The subject was a confident and professional individual with a capacity to articulate and debate a point of view with evidence. The irony was that the employer consistently used this virtue negatively against the subject first covertly and then overtly in the statements of complaints. Examples of false assertion by the managers included that staff find the subject is aggressive, intimidating and putting the institution at risk!

The consequences of working under such a working environment are multi-dimension. First of all the effects on the subjects personal life can be categorised as individual and family. The individual effects include health, financial, career and family problems: the subject suffered mental and emotional stresses manifesting as physical and emotional symptoms. Quite apart from the emotional suffering, the combined effect of ill-health was debilitating, led to a loss of confidence, reduced output, and financial loss in fees for GP/consultant/psychiatrist/medicine. The effect on the subject's family was most unforgivable. The family also suffered severe emotional stress and ill-health which strained the relationship between the subject and the rest of the family leading to separation.

For the employer, it is the loss of an active dedicated employee who put institution goals ahead of personal objectives. Lost productivity. Lost progress. Lost market. Therefore, lost long-term investment and possible lost returns. Unnecessary expenditure in lawsuit(s) that could be invested in the institution for its staff and students' future.

DISCUSSION

Recommendations to combat bullying in the workplace are directed at the employer (16,23), e.g employers must educate their line managers, and should investigate claims thoroughly. By the end of the last century, most western governments acknowledged bullying and its consequences as a major problem, and have issued policy statements holding employers responsible for managing a stress-free working environment. This is no different to the executive/vice-chancellor's passing of the problems to the source of the problem to resolve! It is not, therefore, surprising that the number of cases post government legislations for stress-free working environment including this one (15,22-24) demonstrate that the offending employers continue to show a disregard for the law let alone implementing anti-harassment recommendations. The politicians, the trustees, the auditors, the legal community, staff, the community they all know who the offending organisations are – the question is why do we allow bullying behaviour to continue?

Clearly, it is not as easy to study perpetrators or organisations. Any references to the bully or organisation characteristics are usually obtained from the victims' accounts. Most studies also rely on surveys of victims or legal/court case notes. However, very few cases make it to the courts and a majority accept out of court settlements (for obvious reasons e.g low levels of self-esteem, stressed and depressed, ill-health). However, the settlement comes with a gagging order preventing the victims from discussing any aspects of the case with anyone! Therefore, we know very little about the victims and in particular the effect on their families; the untold damage to health and mental well being in particular the emotional well-being of the children. In addition, our information on bullying is collected after the event; after a period of sustained bullying and stressful working environment. Thus, although the data set will have contained historical information it is essentially cross-sectional information on an individual exhibiting low self-esteem, uninterested, depressed and unable to articulate. It is not surprising that some authors recommend self-development training (e.g. assertiveness) models to combat bullying! This type of models accepts bullying in the workplace and places the onus on the employee to prepare for it.

In attempting to understand why certain senior managers who already hold positions of power and have established "empires" behave in such a manner in today's society, the subject reported that almost all the comments received from other colleagues pointed to the insecurity and low confidence of the management due to their lack of experience. These comments appear in line with the literature quoted in the introduction. However, they do not explain the treatment of other teaching staff who did not pose a threat to anyone and simply wanted to do their jobs. One simple explanation could come from the literature. Such a management style is reminiscent of school yard/playground bullying. There is some evidence to suggest school bullies suffer from psychological and mental health problems which go undiagnosed and untreated (10,11), furthermore, school bullying may be transferred to adulthood and workplace (8). On the other hand legal risks may have influenced management behaviour. The literature provides examples of the legal precedent of employees being awarded damages against employers who failed to provide due care and support for appointing inexperienced staff into management roles (22).

An important issue arising from the case report and which did not feature in the literature is the effects on the victim's family quality of life i) sudden change in the family, and ii) sustained strained family relationship and stress, and iii) the workforce as passive observers.

It is commendable to see that McAvoy and Murtagh (14) suggest that the medical profession ought to take a serious role in preventing bullying in the workplace. This would be a good idea if it wasn't for the fact that health services have one of the highest rates of bullying. Denying that bullying or racism does not exist in 'our society' has never or will never resolve the issue. In the absence of solid evidence to explain the reasons for bullying, societies where bullying is common must acknowledge it rather than deny it and eradicate it from politics, home, school yards and the workplace. In other words, we cannot wait for a political solution and society must own and solve the bullying problem e.g. see Shahtahmasebi (27). As long as your manager believes that being a 'team player' means doing what you are told then bullying will be part of the culture.

REFERENCES

[1]   Rayner C, Sheehan M, Barker M. Theoretical approaches to the study of bullying at work. Int J Manpower 1999;20(1/2):11.

[2]   Lee D. Gendered workplace bullying in the restructured UK Civil Service. Pers Rev 2002;31(1/2):205.

[3]   Crawford N. Conundrums and confusion in organisations: the etymology of the word "bully". Int J Manpower 1999;20(1/2):86.

[4]   Cusack S. Workplace bullying: icebergs in sight, soundings needed. Lancet 2000;356(9248):2118.

[5]   Hollinghurst A. Bullying in the workplace: its effect on job satisfaction, stress and anxiety amongst NHS nurses. Nurs 2 Nurs 2000;1(8):34-5.

[6]   Kivimaki M, Virtanen M, Vartia M, Elovainio M, Vahtera J, Keltikangas-Jarvinen L. Workplace bullying and the risk of cardiovascular disease and depression. Occup Environ Med 2003;60(10): 779-83.

[7]   Vartia MA. Consequences of workplace bullying with respect to the well-being of its targets and the observers of bullying. Scand J Work Environ Health 2001;27(1):63-9.

[8]   Smith P, Singer M, Hoel H, Cooper C. Victimization in the school and the workplace: Are there any links? Br J Psychol 2003;94:175.

[9]   Chesson R. Bullying: The need for an interagency response. BMJ 1999;319(7206):330.

[10]   Forero R, McLellan L, Rissel C, Bauman A. Bullying behaviour and psychological health among school students in New South Wales, Australia: cross sectional survey. BMJ 1999;319(7206):344.

[11]   Kaltiala-Heino R, Rimpel M, Marttunen M, Rimpela A, Rantanen P. Bullying, depression, and suicidal ideation in Finnish adolescents: school survey. BMJ 1999;319:348-51.

[12]   Einarsen S. The nature and causes of bullying at work. Int J Manpower 1999;20(1/2):16.

[13]   Zapf D. Organisational, work group related and personal causes of mobbing/bullying at work. Int Manpower 1999;20(1/2):70.

[14]   McAvoy BR, Murtagh J. Workplace bullying: the silent epidemic. BMJ 2003;326(7393):776-7.

[15]   Wornham D. A descriptive investigation of mortality and victimisation at work. J Business Ethics 2003;45(1):29-36.

[16]   Johnson H. Big bad bullies. Training 2002;39(9):22.

[17]   Glendinning PM. Workplace bullying: Curing the cancer of the American workplace. Public Pers Manage 2001;30(3):269.

[18]   Brodsky CM. The harassed worker. Toronto: Lexington Books DC Heath, 1976.

[19]   Yeung R, Cooper D. Business: Bullying in the Workplace - Beat the BULLY. Accountancy 2002;129(1301):1.

[20]   Manthei M. A comparison of the effectiveness of professionals, nonprofessionals, and self-help groups in teaching assertiveness. Dissertation. University of Massachusetts, 1982.

[21]   Rosolen D. Stress test. Benefits Canada 2002;26(2):22.

[22]   Sheehan M. Workplace bullying: responding with some emotional intelligence. Int J Manpower 1999;20(1/2):57.

[23]   Seward K, Fahy S. Tackling workplace bullies. Occup Health 2003;55(5):16-8.

[24]   Bernardi LM. The legal case against bullying in the workplace. Canadian HR Reporter 2001;14(19):10.

[25]   Vandekerckhove W, Commers MSR. Downward workplace mobbing: A sign of the times? J Business Ethics 2003;45(1):41.

[26]   Yandrick RM. Lurking in the shadows. HRMagazine 1999;44(10):60.

[27]   Shahtahmasebi S. De-politicizing youth suicide prevention. Front Pediatr 2013;1(8); URL: http://www.frontiersin.org/Journal/Abstract.aspx?s=1411&name=child_health_and_human_developm ent&ART_DOI=10.3389/fped.2013.00008 .

SECTION TWO: SUICIDE

In: Children, Violence and Bullying
Editors: J Merrick, I Kandel and H A Omar

ISBN: 978-1-62948-342-9
© 2014 Nova Science Publishers, Inc.

Chapter 14

UNITED STATES: ADOLESCENT OUTCOMES ASSOCIATED WITH EARLY MALTREATMENT AND EXPOSURE TO VIOLENCE

Richard Thompson, PhD[*1], Alan J Litrownik, PhD[2], Cindy Weisbart, PsyD[3], Jonathan B Kotch, MD, MPH, FAAP[4], Diana J English, PhD[5] and Mark D Everson, PhD[6]

[1]Department of Research, Juvenile Protective Association, Chicago
[2]Department of Psychology, San Diego State University, San Diego
[3]Department of Psychiatry, University of British Columbia, Canada
[4]Department of Maternal and Child Health, University of North Carolina, Chapel Hill
[5]School of Social Work, University of Washington, Seattle, US
[6]Department of Psychiatry, University of North Carolina, Chapel Hill, North Carolina, US

ABSTRACT

Early adverse experiences such as witnessing violence and child maltreatment are associated with many negative psychosocial outcomes. Early suicidal ideation may mark children at particular risk of these negative outcomes. In this chapter we examine whether early suicidal ideation mediates the link between early adverse experiences and adolescent child outcomes. Specifically, this chapter examined early suicidal ideation (at age 8 years) as a mediator of the link between early adversities and adolescent psychosocial outcomes. Study group: 779 American children identified as maltreated or at risk for maltreatment. Methods: Data on exposure to maltreatment victimization (review of administrative records) and witnessed violence (self-report) were collected through age 8. Suicidal ideation (via self-report) was also assessed at age 8 years. Child outcomes (suicidal ideation, psychological distress, behavioral problems, social isolation, risk behaviors, and mental health services) were assessed at age 12 years. Results: Early maltreatment predicted age 12 suicidal ideation and use of mental health services; early

* Correspondence: Richard Thompson, PhD, Juvenile Protective Association, 1707 N Halsted, Chicago, IL 60614, United States. Email: rthompson@juvenile.org.

witnessed violence did not. Early witnessed violence predicted age 12 psychological distress; early maltreatment did not. Both adversities predicted age 12 behavioral problems and risk behaviors; neither predicted social isolation/popularity. Early suicidal ideation partially mediated the link between early adverse experiences and age 12 behavioral problems and between early maltreatment and mental health services between ages 8 and 12 years. Conclusions: Early suicidal ideation appears to partially explain the links between early adverse experiences and poor outcomes in early adolescence.

INTRODUCTION

Child maltreatment (physical and sexual abuse and neglect) and exposure to violence have been found to have proximal as well as distal impacts on children's well-being. Although individual studies have found effects of one or the other of these classes of adversity on child outcomes, the research suggests that they are both associated with a host of longer-term problems, in broadly similar ways. For example, suicidal ideation and suicide attempts (1,2), psychological distress and depression (3), behavioral problems (4), social isolation (5), and risky behaviors such as delinquency and early sexual behavior (3,6) have all been associated with both earlier maltreatment and exposure to violence. Additionally, because of the elevated risk of such problems, children with these experiences are at increased likelihood of using mental health services (7). Indeed, the use of mental health services may be seen as a potent indicator of the existence of serious psychosocial problems for children in general, and for those who have been exposed to violence more specifically (7).

Although the main effects of early adversities are clear, there is a need for a better understanding of how such experiences lead to long-term negative outcomes. One possible mediating factor may be a severe short-term response, taking the form of suicidal ideation. Suicidal ideation may represent an extreme pole on a dimension of acute psychological distress, particularly for children (8). As noted earlier, suicidal ideation is present even in very young children who have been maltreated or exposed to violence (9,10). Most models of the long-term outcomes of maltreatment or violence exposure have not examined this possibility, instead focusing only on the changes in world-view or personality produced by the experiences. A frequent focus is on the development of learned helplessness or other fundamental ways of viewing the world (11), which in turn influence longer-term outcomes. Such schemas are usually thought to directly increase the risk of later depression and thus suicidality, although these links have rarely been tested adequately (11). It is also possible, however, that it is the immediate psychological disturbances (particularly suicidal ideation) in response to these adverse experiences that put children at risk for later negative outcomes.

It has been proposed that suicidal ideation does not simply predict suicide attempts, but may be a potent marker of risk for a whole host of other negative outcomes later on (8). From a developmental psychopathology perspective (12), early suicidal ideation in response to maltreatment or violence exposure may interfere with the mastery of stage-salient skills. Indeed, early suicidal ideation may increase social isolation, interfere with mastery experiences, and thus lead to deficits in psychosocial functioning that become more pronounced as children progress further developmentally and fail to meet more age-appropriate developmental tasks. From this perspective, early suicidal ideation may be a mediator of the effects of early adversity in that it increases the impact of these experiences on development. Alternatively, early suicidal ideation may be a marker for the severity of depression, or of other problems. Children experiencing suicidal ideation may be demonstrating that they have inadequate coping resources to deal with the stressors they are experiencing, suggesting vulnerability to future stressors. There is limited evidence on this issue, however, because most research has examined suicidal ideation as an outcome, rather than as a predictor of other outcomes (1,9). The meaning of early suicidal ideation continues to be a source of controversy (8).

The few studies that have examined the predictive value of early suicidal ideation suggest that it marks children at particular risk for a variety of later psychosocial problems. For example, early suicidal ideation not only predicts later suicidal ideation and suicide attempts (2,13), but also depression and psychiatric illness more generally (13). In addition, it predicts behavioral problems and social isolation (2), as well as alcohol abuse (13). As well, some of this early expression of suicidal ideation may reflect an imitation of peers or the influence of portrayals of suicidality in the media (14). Any of these explanations, although not necessarily indicative of suicidal intent, would still be cause for concern in terms of risk of suicidal behavior.

Earlier work with a sample of children who were either maltreated or at risk for maltreatment demonstrated that exposure to both violence and maltreatment were particularly associated with suicidal ideation in young children (9). The analyses described here extended these findings by testing the overall hypothesis that early suicidal ideation mediates the link between negative early experiences (maltreatment victimization or witnessed violence) and later poor outcomes (suicidal ideation, psychological distress, behavioral problems, social isolation, and risk behaviors) in this same sample of at risk children.

OUR STUDY

The current analysis is based on pooled data from the LONGSCAN studies. LONGSCAN is a consortium of studies using common data collection instruments and protocols, located at five sites in different regions of the United States: the Southern, Eastern, Midwest, Northwest, and Southwest regions. At each study site, a sample of children who had been maltreated or were at risk of maltreatment was recruited when children were four years old or younger. Detailed information regarding the site-specific recruitment procedures, as well as more detailed information about LONGSCAN, is available elsewhere (15).

Each local site and the central coordinating center obtained institutional review board approval. Informed consent was obtained from caregivers and assent from child participants at each interview reported here. Children and caregivers participated separately in interviews administered by trained interviewers that included measures of many variables, including demographics, life events, behavioral problems and risk behaviors, emotional well-being, and several other psychosocial outcomes. Families were paid a fixed, nominal amount for their participation in this ongoing research, to compensate them for their time. Assessments of the same caregiver-child dyads are conducted periodically throughout the course of the study, which will continue until the child is 18 years. The analyses reported here focus on interview data collected at ages 8 through 12 years. Specifically, face to face interviews were conducted at ages 8 and 12 years and in intervening years, brief telephone interviews were conducted to track mental health service use.

Criteria for inclusion in these analyses included: having completed an age 8 years LONGSCAN interview (including non-missing data on suicidal ideation at age 8 years) and having completed an age 12 interview. There were 1136 child-caregiver dyads who completed an age 8 year LONGSCAN interview. Of these, 779 (68.6%) completed an age 12 years interview. There were no significant differences in available demographic or clinical variables assessed at age 8 between those who completed age 12 years interviews and those who had not.

Measures (Baseline (pre-age 8 years)

Following is a description of the baseline variables utilized based on data collected before age 8 (history of maltreatment and exposure to violence). This is a subset of the variables used in previous work examining correlates of suicidal ideation at age 8, which are described in greater detail elsewhere (9)

Maltreatment. Investigators at the five sites reviewed Child Protective Services records to determine the presence and nature of allegations of maltreatment among children in their samples. This review was done using the Modified Maltreatment Classification System (16). For the current analyses, maltreatment allegations were limited to those that occurred before the target child was 8 years old. Children were assigned a dichotomous code, based on whether maltreatment allegations occurring before age 8 were found in these record reviews.

Exposure to violence. A modified version of the "Things I Have Seen and Heard" scale (17) was administered to assess exposure to violence and feelings of safety at home, at school, and in the community. This measure has high test-retest reliability and good validity (17). The LONGSCAN version used in the present study added five items to include violence witnessed in the home, because the original version focused more on community and school violence. Children were asked to endorse the frequency of each item using a visual 4-point Likert-like scale. The sum of each rated item was used to indicate exposure to violence in the present study.

Mediator and control variables

Following is a description of the mediator and control variables collected at age 8 (suicidal ideation and demographic variables). This is a subset of the variables used in previous work examining correlates of suicidal ideation at age 8, which are described in greater detail elsewhere (9)

Suicidal ideation. Suicidal ideation was defined as endorsement of the self-report item "Wanting to kill yourself," from the Trauma Symptom Checklist for Children (18). This measure was completed by the child using a 4-point Likert-like scale. For the current analyses, this item was dichotomously scored as Absent ("never") or Present ("sometimes," "lots of the time" or "almost all the time").

Demographic variables. The caregiver interview included information on child gender and race.

Outcome (age 12 years)

At age 12 years, psychosocial outcomes included several behavioral and emotional outcomes (suicidal ideation, psychological distress, behavioral problems, popularity, and risk behaviors) as well as mental health service use between ages 8 and 12 years.

Suicidal ideation. As was the case at age 8, suicidal ideation was defined as endorsement of the self-report item "Wanting to kill yourself," from the Trauma Symptom Checklist for Children (18). This item was identical to the one used to define suicidal ideation at age 8.

Psychological distress. The remaining 45 items on the TSCC (18), excluding the item indicating suicidal ideation, were summed to produce a total psychological distress score. These items assess symptoms of depressed mood, anger, anxiety, dissociation, and post-traumatic stress.

Behavioral problems. The Youth Self-Report (19), a well-validated youth report of youth behavior problems, was administered. For these analyses the raw score on the Total Problems scale was used. The total problems scale is an overall indicator of behavioral problems and is the sum of the externalizing problems and internalizing problems scales as well as of three additional subscales: Social problems, thought problems, and attention problems.

Social isolation/popularity. LONGSCAN-developed questions related to youth peer relations were administered to the participating youth. Among these questions were two with responses on a 4-point scale, ranging from 1 ("almost none of the other kids at school") to 4 ("almost all of the other kids at school"). The two stem questions were "How many of the other kids at school are friendly to you?" and "How many of the other kids at school are unfriendly or mean to you?" The question about friendliness was subtracted from the question about unfriendliness to produce an index of youth self-rated social isolation.

Risk behaviors. LONGSCAN-developed questions related to child risk behaviors (e.g., having had sex, using alcohol or other substances, gang involvement, and history of arrest) were administered to the participating youth. To assess having had sex, participating youth were asked if they had "ever had sex". Using the sentence stem "In the past year, did you ...", youth were asked about their use of a range of substances (e.g., alcohol, marijuana, cocaine, methamphetamine, etc.). Based on these responses, youth were coded dichotomously on two separate questions: whether or not they had used alcohol and whether or not they had used other substances. Youth were also asked "In the past year did you ever take part in gang activities?" and "Have you ever been arrested?" These dichotomized items were summed to produce an index of youth risk behaviors that ranged from 0 to 5.

Mental health service use. Finally, data on mental health service use were gathered via caregiver report at child ages 9-12 years. At each annual interview, caregivers were asked, "In the last year, did [child] ever need any type of counseling or therapy, outside of school, for a psychological or behavioral problem?" If the answer to this was affirmative, a follow-up question was asked: "Did [child] get this kind of professional service, in the last year?" Affirmative responses to this follow-up question indicated that the child had received mental health services in the previous year. This variable was coded dichotomously; any indicator of service use in any of the four annual assessments (ages 9, 10, 11, or 12 years) was coded as service use during this four-year period.

Analysis

The primary goal of the current study was to examine whether early (age 8) suicidal ideation mediated the link between early negative experiences (maltreatment and exposure to violence) and later psychosocial outcomes. In order to test for mediation, it is necessary to meet three criteria for possible mediation (20): 1) a significant link between predictor (maltreatment history, exposure to violence) and mediator (suicidal ideation), 2) a significant link between mediator (suicidal ideation) and outcome, and 3) the link between predictor (maltreatment history, exposure to violence) and outcome is reduced in significance when the mediator (suicidal ideation) is controlled for. Aside from serving to test for possible mediation, examining criteria 2 and 3 also allowed testing secondary hypotheses.

The first criterion, a significant link between predictors (maltreatment and exposure to violence) and potential mediator (age 8 suicidal ideation) has been established with previous work using this sample (9). However, because the current analysis sample differed somewhat from the sample used in the earlier analyses (due to some participants having missing data at age 12), this relationship was re-evaluated in the analyses presented here. The remaining criteria were also tested, as a matter of course. Mediation effects of early suicidal ideation noted above were tested separately for the two predictor variables (maltreatment and exposure to violence).

FINDINGS

Table 1 presents descriptive data for the sample. The sample was almost equally split between males and females. A little more than half of the children were African American and about a quarter were white. The remainder of the children identified as Hispanic or "mixed race" with very small numbers of Asian and Native American children and children who claimed "other" as their ethnic background. Between ages 8 and 12 years, the rate of self-reported suicidal ideation decreased from 9.8% to 4.9%. Roughly a third of the children had received mental health services between age 8 and age 12 years. Nearly two thirds had been reported as maltreated by age 8 years.

The tests of mediation are presented in tables 2 and 3. Table 2 presents the analyses based on early maltreatment as the predictor variable. Table 3 presents the analyses based on early exposure to violence as the predictor variable. The summary of the results will be organized based on the criteria for mediation summarized above.

Criterion 1: Links between predictor variables (Early maltreatment and exposure to violence) and mediator (Early suicidal ideation)

The link between early maltreatment and early suicidal ideation is presented in the first column of table 2. The link between exposure to violence and early suicidal ideation is presented in the first column of table 3. Minor differences in the estimated coefficient are due to slight differences in the covariance structure of the models of the various outcomes, although the results are all very similar in each column. Consistent with earlier research findings (9) both of these links were found to be significant in the present study. Specifically, both early maltreatment and exposure to violence predicted early suicidal ideation.

Table 1. Description of sample (N = 779)

Variables	M (SD) or %
Demographics	
Gender: Female	51.5%
Race/Ethnicity: White	26.7%
African American	55.1%
Hispanic	5.8%
Native American	0.3%
Asian	0.4%
"Mixed Race"	11.5%
"Other"	0.2%
Baseline (Age 8)	
Suicidal Ideation (TSCC)	9.8%
Maltreatment through Age 8	63.9%
Violence Exposure WVA	14.33 (9.38)
Behavioral/Emotional Outcomes (Age 12)	
Suicidal Ideation (TSCC)	4.9%
Psychological Distress (TSCC)	17.29 (17.86)
Behavioral problems (YSR)	36.67 (21.31)
Social isolation	-1.83 (1.41)
Risk Behaviors Outcomes (Age 12)	
Sexual Experience	6.6%
Substance Involvement	3.0%
Alcohol Use	4.5%
Gang Involved	4.5%
Ever Arrested	4.0%
Total number of risk behaviors	0.22 (0.57)
Mental Health Services (Ages 9 through 12)	
Age 9	13.8%
Age 10	15.5%
Age 11	17.5%
Age 12	22.1%
Ages 9 to 12	33.8%

Criterion 2: Links between the mediator (Early suicidal ideation) and the outcome variables

The links between early suicidal ideation and the various outcome variables are presented in the second column of both table 2 and table 3. The estimated coefficients in the two cases are very similar, with only minor differences due to the covariance structures noted. Age 8 suicidal ideation was associated with age 12 behavioral problems, age 12 risk behaviors, and the use of mental health services between ages 9 and 12 years. It was not associated with age 12 suicidal ideation, age 12 psychological distress, or age 12 social isolation.

Table 2. Links between maltreatment and outcomes

Age 12 Outcome Variable	Maltx – SI Age 8			SI Age 8- Outcome			Maltx - Outcome			Maltx – Outcome w. SI Age 8			Estimated Mediation Effect
	Coef	SE	T	Coef	SE	T	Coef	SE	T	Coef	SE	T	
Suicidal Ideation	0.049	0.023	2.21*	0.028	0.027	1.02	0.049	0.017	2.89*	0.047	0.017	2.80*	0.001 (-0.001 – 0.007)
Psychological Distress	0.047	0.023	2.05*	2.272	2.240	1.01	2.201	1.392	1.58	2.096	1.396	1.50	0.106 (-0.063 – 0.467)
Behavioral Problems	0.052	0.023	2.25*	7.900	2.597	3.04*	4.116	1.663	2.48*	3.705	1.659	2.23*	0.411 (0.091 – 1.099)*
Social Isolation	0.056	0.023	2.42*	0.330	0.171	1.93	0.210	0.110	1.91	0.191	0.110	1.74	0.019 (0.000 – 0.058)
Risk Behaviors	0.057	0.023	2.47*	0.154	0.069	2.23*	0.103	0.044	2.35*	0.095	0.044	2.15*	0.009 (0.001 – 0.029)*
Age 9-12 MH services	0.057	0.023	2.47*	0.209	0.056	3.76*	0.160	0.036	4.47*	0.148	0.036	4.16*	0.012 (0.003 – 0.026)*

NOTE: Separate bootstrap mediation analyses were conducted for each outcome variable, with 3,000 bootstrap samples. All analyses were conducted controlling for child gender and race. Estimated indirect effect refers to the bias corrected estimate of the coefficient of the indirect (mediated) effect.

Maltx = early maltreatment; SI = suicidal ideation; MH = mental health. Asterisks and boldface denote coefficients significant at p < .05.

Table 3. Links between Violence exposure and outcomes

Age 12 Outcome Variable	Viol Exp – SI Age 8			SI Age 8- Outcome			Viol Exp - Outcome			Viol Exp – Outcome w. SI Age 8			Estimated Mediation Effect
	Coef	SE	T	Coef	SE	T	Coef	SE	T	Coef	SE	T	
Suicidal Ideation	0.004	0.001	3.56*	0.039	0.027	1.44	0.001	0.001	1.41	0.001	0.001	1.59	0.000 (0.000 – 0.001)
Psychological Distress	0.004	0.001	3.29*	1.661	2.237	0.74	0.232	0.069	3.34*	0.226	0.070	3.23*	0.006 (-0.008 – 0.031)
Behavioral Problems	0.004	0.001	3.13*	7.384	2.594	2.85*	0.306	0.082	3.72*	0.279	0.082	3.39*	0.026 (0.008 – 0.068)*
Social Isolation	0.004	0.001	3.61*	0.329	0.172	1.93	0.008	0.006	1.47	0.007	0.006	1.21	0.001 (0.000 – 0.004)
Risk Behaviors	0.004	0.001	3.57*	0.145	0.069	2.10*	0.006	0.002	2.74*	0.005	0.002	2.45*	0.001 (0.000 – 0.002)
Age 9-12 MH services	0.004	0.001	3.55*	0.228	0.056	4.04*	0.001	0.002	0.70	0.000	0.002	0.19	0.001 (0.000 – 0.002)

NOTE: Separate bootstrap mediation analyses were conducted for each outcome variable, with 3,000 bootstrap samples. All analyses were conducted controlling for child gender and race. Estimated indirect effect refers to the bias corrected estimate of the coefficient of the indirect (mediated) effect. Viol Exp = violence exposure; SI = suicidal ideation; MH = mental health. Asterisks and boldface denote coefficients significant at p < .05.

Criterion 3: Links between the predictor variables (Early maltreatment and exposure to violence) and outcome variables, which diminish after controlling for mediator (Early suicidal ideation)

Early maltreatment. As can be seen in the third column of table 2, early maltreatment was significantly associated with four of the age 12 outcomes examined: suicidal ideation, behavioral problems, risk behaviors, and use of mental health services. The final column in table 2 presents the estimated mediation effects for each link. Three of the links between maltreatment and specific outcomes (i.e., behavioral problems, risk behaviors, and use of mental health services) were partially mediated by early suicidal ideation. Though significant, these mediation effects were quite modest except for the relationship involving behavioral problems.

Violence exposure. The statistics shown in the third column of table 3 indicate that early violence exposure was significantly associated with three of the age 12 outcomes examined: psychological distress, behavioral problems, and risk behaviors. Only one of these links was partially mediated by early suicidal ideation: behavioral problems (see last column of table 3).

DISCUSSION

One focus of these analyses was to examine whether early suicidal ideation mediates the link between early adverse experiences and later poor outcomes in a sample of children with high rates of adverse experiences. Support for this hypothesis varied depending on the adverse experience and the outcome examined. In addition to examining the mediating effect of suicidal ideation, the analyses presented here also provided some interesting findings in terms of main effect relationships for both adverse experiences and early suicidal ideation. Each of these findings will be discussed in turn.

Regarding early suicidal ideation as a mediator of outcomes, the results were mixed. In particular, suicidal ideation at age 8 partially mediated the link between both types of adverse experience (maltreatment and witnessed violence) and behavioral problems at age 12, as reported by the youth. The mediating effect of SI on the link between maltreatment and behavioral problems was the strongest of the mediation relationships studied here. As well, the link between early suicidal ideation and behavioral problems was generally very strong, consistent with previous research on early suicidal ideation and later behavioral problems (2). Although maltreatment is a known risk factor for behavior problems, one possible path through which maltreatment may influence later behavioral outcomes could be through early suicidal ideation. Alternatively, early suicidal ideation may simply mark children who are particularly vulnerable to early adversity. In other words, suicidal ideation may not be involved in causally explaining how early adversities operate on problem behavior outcomes, but rather indicate children who are more vulnerable to such outcomes in the face of subsequent stressors.

Early suicidal ideation also partially mediated the link between early maltreatment history and risk behaviors. This finding suggests a link between previous findings of a relationship between early maltreatment and risk-taking behaviors in adolescence (6), and research that found that early suicidal ideation predicted the later emergence of some forms of risk-taking behavior (13). Further research should in more detail examine the links between early maltreatment, suicidal ideation, and risk-taking behaviors.

Finally, early suicidal ideation also partially mediated the link between early maltreatment history and later use of mental health services. This further supports the possibility that early suicidal ideation marks children at greatest need for services in response to trauma or adversity (8). Alternatively, children reported for maltreatment may be more likely to use mental health services because Child Protective Services (CPS) operates as a gatekeeper (i.e., facilitates referral to and ultimate receipt of services). This may also explain why there was no independent main effect of early witnessed violence on later services use. Specifically, those children who witness violence are only likely to receive mental health services when they are also reported to CPS, unless they happen to receive services for an unrelated reason. Given the absence of a main effect, there could be no mediation of the relationship between witnessed violence and service use. This issue will be further discussed below.

It is also important to note the mediation effects and main effects of suicidal ideation that were not found to be significant in this study. First and most strikingly, early suicidal ideation did not mediate the link between early adversities and later suicidal ideation. Indeed, there was no significant relationship at all between early and later suicidal ideation. There are several possible explanations for this finding. The validity of the assessment of suicidal ideation (particularly at age 8) has been frequently questioned (21), particularly as part of self-report batteries. On the other hand, it is also important to note that the rate of self-reported suicidal ideation declined dramatically from age 8 to age 12 in this sample. One possible explanation for this counterintuitive observation is that, because the sample was weighted heavily toward children with early maltreatment and exposure to violence, there was a "regression to the mean" of psychological distress generally, as the time gap between these early adversities and assessments grew. Alternatively, children at age 12 may have been more guarded in reporting their suicidal ideation. In any case, it is possible that the uncertain validity of the self-report measure of suicidal ideation (at either age 8 or age 12, or both) may have influenced the results. Alternatively, suicidal ideation, particularly by young children, may be a relatively transient experience. As suggested earlier, in pre-adolescent children, it may mark extremities of distress (8) or of a response to a very unsafe situation rather than a particular risk for suicidal behavior per se. As children age, they may develop other ways of expressing this distress or lack of safety. Thus, the construct that was measured at age 8 (nominally, suicidal ideation, but possibly extreme distress) may not have been the same as self-reported suicidal ideation at age 12; there may have been qualitative differences in the meaning to the respondents that the study was unable to capture.

In a related finding, suicidal ideation at age 8 failed to predict (and thus to mediate a link to) psychological distress at age 12, although it was strongly predictive of both risk behaviors and behavioral problems in general at age 12. These findings suggest that early suicidal ideation is more likely to mark children at risk for later acting-out and disruptive behavior than children who are prone to internalizing or distress related problems. Whether extreme distress at age 8 is a marker of such risk or whether it interferes with development of adaptive behavioral inhibition is a question worthy of further study.

Comparing the main effects of early adverse experiences, several findings were noteworthy. The fact that early maltreatment (assessed through case record review) predicted later suicidal ideation (self-report), while witnessed violence (self-report) did not, suggests that shared method variance is not an explanation for the prediction of age 12 suicidal ideation. Finally, because early suicidal ideation did not predict later suicidal ideation, it is hard to argue that the effect of early maltreatment on later suicidal ideation is an artifact of its link to earlier suicidal ideation. Instead, this finding adds to a growing literature of prospective evidence that early maltreatment increases risk of later suicidal ideation (1).

Early maltreatment also predicted subsequent mental health services use, while early witnessed violence did not. As noted earlier, a likely explanation is that an official report of maltreatment is often a "doorway" into services for children who might not otherwise have had these services available to them (22). However, given the many child problems associated with witnessing violence, increasing access to effective services for children exposed to witnessed violence should also be a priority (23). As well, treatment for maltreated children should integrate children's other experiences with violence, including comprehensive assessments of such histories of witnessing.

The importance of early witnessed violence is especially highlighted by the fact that it predicted later psychological distress, while reports of maltreatment did not. This may be influenced, again, by shared method variance, but it is also worth noting that both maltreatment and witnessed violence similarly predicted other self-reported outcomes. It is possible that witnessing violence in early childhood is more likely to affect such distress than is early maltreatment. The finding that both maltreatment and witnessed violence predicted self-reported behavioral problems and risk behaviors suggests that early adverse experiences may have long-lasting impacts on child risk-taking behaviors. Indeed, although the differences between the effects of witnessed violence and maltreatment have been highlighted here, it is important to underline the overarching similarity in their effects. The simplest conclusion is that both types of experience have important consequences for children, both immediately and in the longer term. In particular, the fact that both predict risk-taking behaviors, including drug use, early sexual behavior, and gang involvement, suggests an important public health implication of these early experiences. Early suicidal ideation very modestly mediated the link between maltreatment and risk-taking behaviors, consonant with some previous research highlighting the links between suicidal ideation and risk-taking behavior (13).

There are several limitations to keep in mind when considering these results. First, it is important to note that the children in the sample were selected because they had either been maltreated or were at significant risk for maltreatment. Thus, children with histories of early maltreatment and/or early exposure to violence were likely over-represented in the sample. If the sample had had lower base rates of these adversities, there would have been less variance with which to work in finding main effects. On the other hand, given a more representative sample, the reference group (children without a history of maltreatment or witnessed violence) would likely have fewer risk factors, and this may have added to, rather than attenuated, the variation in children's exposure to adverse experiences.

As well, the assessment of suicidal ideation relied on a single item from a standardized self-report measure ("Wanting to kill yourself") to indicate suicidal ideation. This assessment has face validity and, as past work has indicated, substantial construct validity (9). Single item assessments of suicidal ideation are very common in the literature. Ideally, future research will more frequently employ comprehensive and multidimensional measures of suicidal ideation, although such complex assessments may have limited utility with very young children (21).

It is also important to highlight that the behavioral/emotional outcomes at age 12 in this sample are consonant with normative data, rather than with the high-risk nature of this sample. The rate of self-reported suicidal ideation was low for this age group (and lower than this same sample had reported at age 8), and the means for psychological distress and behavioral problems were at or below normative samples of children at this age. As well, the rates of self-reported risk behaviors were relatively low. This suggests either that the sample was doing much better than might be expected given their earlier experiences, or that they were more guarded in reporting problems at age 12. In particular, it is possible that the reduction in reported suicidal ideation reflects such guardedness rather than a decline in actual suicidal ideation. Indeed, because the outcomes of interest are, for the most part, self-report, they rely on some assumptions that children are equally likely to disclose problems, should such problems be present. It is also important to note that there was no data on adverse experiences occurring between age 8 and 12. It is possible that the children in this study tended to have adverse experiences that were limited to their early lives and that the later lack of adversity may have contributed to their relatively normative rate of behavioral/emotional and risk behavior outcomes.

Overall, the effects on the outcomes of the predictors and mediator are relatively modest, as were the mediation effects. This may be due in part to the dichotomous nature of the mediator and predictor variables which failed to capture any dimension of severity or frequency. It is also important to keep in mind that the goal of this research was not to construct a comprehensive model of the various outcomes. Rather, the goal was to examine the links between early adverse experiences and later outcomes, and to examine the effects of one potential mediator of these links. To fully explain and predict child outcomes at age 12, it would be important to examine the frequency and severity of more proximal adverse experiences as well as a host of other potential predictors such as quality of parenting in homes where children experience maltreatment and/or witness violence.

Finally, several decisions were made in the measurement of the variables of interest that should inform their interpretation. Several of the assessments (most notably of popularity/social isolation, risk behaviors, and mental health service use) relied on measures that were designed for this study, rather than on existing measures. Although there is some evidence for their validity (9), including clear face-validity, caution should be used in interpreting them. It is also important to note that most of the measures (with the exception of official reports of maltreatment) relied on child self-report. Thus, the various measures are likely to have shared some method variance. Furthermore, at both age 8 and age 12, suicidal ideation was measured using a single item that was part of a larger measure of psychological distress. As noted earlier, the lack of significant relationship between age 8 and age 12 suicidal ideation may reflect a substantive lack of relationship, or some subtle difference in the construct validity of the measures at the different ages. As well, as suggested earlier, any self-report measure of suicidal ideation necessarily includes the willingness to disclose suicidal ideation. This problem of possible non-disclosure is endemic in the literature on suicidal ideation. (21)

CONCLUSION AND IMPLICATIONS FOR RESEARCH AND PRACTICE

Even after considering these limitations, the results highlight several important issues in understanding the impact of early adverse experiences on later outcomes. First, early adverse experiences in the form of both maltreatment and exposure to violence have an impact that extends into early adolescence. In particular, both forms of adversity predict self-reported behavioral problems and the use of mental health services. Early exposure to violence also predicted later psychological distress, while early maltreatment predicted later suicidal ideation. Most interventions for these experiences focus on the immediate, acute reactions children have to their experiences. These findings highlight the importance of addressing the longer-term implications of these early experiences. Longer-term interventions, or those guided by occasional follow-ups to "check in" with these children may be warranted. As well, future work should examine in more detail which aspects of maltreatment and of exposure to violence that represent particularly high risk. For example, is violence occurring in the home particularly salient for young children and predictive of latter outcomes?

As well, early suicidal ideation partially mediated the link between early adverse experiences and later behavioral problems. It also mediated the link between early maltreatment and both later service use and later risk behaviors. Along with adding to a large body of literature noting the negative long-term impact of early maltreatment and witnessed violence on later child outcomes (3, 6), these findings highlight the importance of early suicidal ideation, particularly among children exposed to adversity. It is unclear whether early suicidal ideation marks the children who are particularly at risk for the development of later psychosocial problems, or acts as a truly mediating mechanism, exacerbating the negative impacts of adversity. As well, the possibility that early suicidal ideation moderates these effects should be examined. Future research should also more actively integrate assessments of suicidal ideation in models devoted to the long-term outcomes of early adversity. In terms of clinical implications, it is important to highlight that children with early suicidal ideation are at risk for several negative outcomes. Effective screening for suicidal ideation would identify children at risk, not simply for risk of suicide, but for a host of psychosocial and behavioral problems. Early interventions with these children should have a similarly broad focus not only on ameliorating current problems, but on the possibility of also preventing the development of later problems.

ACKNOWLEDGMENTS

This research was supported by grants from the Office of Child Abuse and Neglect to the Consortium of Longitudinal Studies on Child Abuse and Neglect (LONGSCAN).

REFERENCES

[1] Dube SR, Anda RF, Felitti VJ, Chapman DP, Williamson DF, Giles WH. Childhood abuse, household dysfunction, and the risk of attempted suicide throughout the life span: Findings from the Adverse Childhood Experiences Study. JAMA 2001;286(24):3089-96.

[2] Reinherz HZ, Tanner JL, Berger SR, Beardslee WR, Fitzmaurice GM. Adolescent suicidal ideation as predictive of psychopathology, suicidal behavior, and compromised functioning at age 30. Am J Psychiatry 2006;163(7):1226-32.

[3] Hurt H, Malmud E, Brodsky NL, Giannetta J. Exposure to violence - Psychological and academic correlates in child witnesses. Arch Pediatr Adolesc Med 2001;155(12):1351-6.

[4] Lansford JE, Dodge KA, Pettit GS, Bates JE, Crozier J, Kaplow J. A 12-year prospective study of the long-term effects of early child physical maltreatment on psychological, behavioral, and academic problems in adolescence. Arch Pediatr Adolesc Med 2001;156(8):824-30.

[5]   Bolger KE, Patterson CJ. Developmental pathways from child maltreatment to peer rejection. Child Dev 2001;72(2):549-68.
[6]   Bank L, Burraston B. Abusive home environments as predictors of poor adjustment during adolescence and early adulthood. J Community Psychol 2001;29(3):195-217.
[7]   Thompson R, May MA. Caregivers' perceptions of child mental health needs and service utilization: An urban 8-year old sample. J Behav Health Serv Res 2006;33(4):474-82.
[8]   Jellinek M. Suicidal ideation in prepubertal children: what does it mean? What to do? J Dev Behav Pediatr 2006;27(1):40-1.
[9]   Thompson R, Briggs E, English DJ, Dubowitz H, Lee LC, Brody K, Everson MD, Hunter WM. Suicidal ideation among maltreated and at-risk 8-year-olds: Findings from the LONGSCAN studies. Child Maltreat 2005;10(1):26-36.
[10] O'Leary CC, Frank DA, Grant-Knight W, Beeghly M, Augustyn M, Rose-Jacobs R, Cabral HJ, Gannon K. Suicidal ideation among urban nine and ten year olds. J Dev Behav Pediatr 2006;27(1): 33-9.
[11] Lakdawalla Z, Hankin BL, Mermelstein R. Cognitive theories of depression in children and adolescents: A conceptual and quantitative review. Clin Child Fam Psychol Rev 2007;10(1):1-24.
[12] Raudenbush SW. Comparing personal trajectories and drawing causal inferences from longitudinal data. Annu Rev Psychol 2001;52:501–25.
[13] Fergusson DM, Horwood LJ, Ridder EM, Beautrais AL. Suicidal behaviour in adolescence and subsequent mental health outcomes in young adulthood. Psychol Med 2005;35(7):983-93.
[14] Gould MS. Suicide and the media. Ann N Y Acad Sci 2001;932:200–21.
[15] Runyan DK, Curtis P, Hunter WM, Black MM, Kotch JB, Bangdiwala S, Dubowitz H, English D, Everson MD, Landsverk J. LONGSCAN: A consortium for longitudinal studies of maltreatment and the life course of children. Aggression Violent Behav 1998;3(3):275-85.
[16] English DJ, LONGSCAN Investigators. Modified Maltreatment Classification System (MMCS) [Internet]. University of Chapel Hill North Carolina; 1997 [cited 2008 Nov 12]. Available from: http://www.iprc.unc.edu/longscan/.
[17] Richters JE, Martinez P. The NIMH Community Violence Project I: Children as victims and witnesses to violence. Psychiatry1993;56(1): 7-21.
[18] Briere J. Trauma Symptom Checklist for Children: Professional Manual. Odessa, FL: Psychol Assess Resources, 1996.
[19] Achenbach TM. Manual for Child Behavior Checklist/ 4-18 and 1991 Profile. Burlington, VT: Univ Vermont, 1991.
[20] Baron RM, Kenny DA. The moderator-mediator variable distinction in social psychological research: Conceptual, strategic, and statistical considerations. J Pers Soc Psychol 1986;51(6):1173-82.
[21] Silverman MM, Berman AL, Sanddal ND, O'Carroll PW, Joiner TE. Rebuilding the tower of Babel: A revised nomenclature for the study of suicide and suicidal behaviors. Part 1: Background, rationale, and methodology. Suicide Life Threat Behav 2007;37(3):248-63.
[22] Lyons JS, Rogers L. The U.S. child welfare system: A de facto public behavioral health care system. J Am Acad Child Adolesc Psychiatry 2004; 43(8):971-3.
[23] Harris WW, Lieberman AF, Marans S. In the best interests of society. J Child Psychol Psychiatry 2007;48(3-4):392-411.

In: Children, Violence and Bullying
Editors: J Merrick, I Kandel and H A Omar

ISBN: 978-1-62948-342-9
© 2014 Nova Science Publishers, Inc.

Chapter 15

A HOLISTIC VIEW OF SUICIDE

*Said Shahtahmasebi, PhD[*1] and Roxanne Shahtahmasebi[2]*

[1]The Good Life Research Centre Trust, Rangiora, New Zealand
[2]Division of Health Research, Lancaster University, Lancaster, United Kingdom
[3]University of Otago Medical School, Christchurch, New Zealand

ABSTRACT

In this chapter the focus is on social change, medical training and service development. Some researchers have suggested that there are already social models of suicide prevention implying that the models have been successful and that no further research in this area is necessary. The inspiration for this discussion paper was a medical student's project proposal that defied the conventional wisdom of offering a hypothesis test to research a complex human behaviour. One of the reasons that research to date has not provided much insight into suicide could well be due to a narrow research approach, which has made researchers, policy makers and the stakeholders part of the problem rather than the solution. In this paper we also discuss changes in suicide trends and the possible influences from macro- and micro-level change. The magnitude of the effect from these changes is unknown. It is not, therefore prudent to rely on the over stretched and ill-equipped health services to mop up the aftermath of a massive social change due to a policy change or failed policies. Policies that are designed to influence a social, political, economic or other change must have public protection strategies built-in as standard backed up with a unified database.

INTRODUCTION

Suicide has been studied widely and there is a large body of literature. The literature emphasises that suicide is a major public health issue (1,2), but then goes on to suggest that mental health professionals and physicians (GPs) should be on the lookout for symptoms of depression (e.g. see (3), http://www.nzma.org.nz/journal/117-1206/1200/). Although the

---

* Correspondence: Said Shahtahmasebi, The Good Life Research Centre Trust, 4 Orkney Street, Strowan, Christchurch 8052, New Zealand. E-mail: radisolevoo@gmail.com.

amount of literature on suicide is huge there has not been a *critical* assessment of the information that it purports to offer. It offers conflicting results. For example, in suicide research, Beautrais (4-6) claimed that depression and mental illness were the causes of suicide, Khan et al (7) claimed that antidepressants did not reduce suicide and may increase the risk of suicide, while Hall et al (8) claimed that antidepressants reduce suicide rates. A critical assessment may reveal that these studies have failed to address the methodological issues related to the design, data collection and analysis, thus resulting in misleading conclusions. Beautrais's psychological autopsy approach (4) is fundamentally flawed for several reasons, including: firstly, because of a high level of bias allowed in through an assessment of the suicide cases by friends and relatives, given that the public mindset is inclined to a causal relationship of depression/mental illness and suicide, particularly after the event; and secondly, for failing to account for bias in the data which leads to the confounding and compounding in data that will mask true systematic effects from random noise. Unfortunately, the Canterbury Suicide Project (4) has been a source of information both for the New Zealand Government policy makers which includes research funding of suicide and suicide prevention which is reflected in the suicide prevention strategy (3).

It is not surprising to note that there is a confused approach to public health policies on suicide with a heavy emphasis on a psychiatric service approach to suicide prevention. The NZ Medical Journal claims that depression is a common, serious and significant illness, that it is linked to suicide and recommends medication as treatment [http://www. nzma.org.nz/journal/117-1206/1200/]. The New Zealand Evidence-based Health Care Bulletin appears to adopt an authoritarian approach while at the same time alienating youth by stating that young people are at a high risk of mental disorders, recommends that every interaction with a young person should be used as an opportunity to check their psychosocial wellbeing regardless of the presenting complaint (http://www. nzgg.org.nz/ newsletter/dsp_article_template.cfm?articleID=454). It further recommends the use of a clinical assessment tool. It is horrifying to imagine that a visit to a clinician/practitioner may turn out to be something completely different. Moreover, this form of treatment could become part of the problem as the fear of seeking treatment may lead to the young person's refusal to take up treatment. This may be termed the *misinterpretation* of the *wrong* evidence obtained through *misapplication*. On the other hand the current uncritical acceptance of the depression-suicide relationship has paved the way for the unnecessary increase in prescribed anti-depressant medication across all age groups and an authoritarian approach to suicide prevention and treatment. While it is astonishing to hear that young people (including pre-school children) have been prescribed antidepressants, what is more alarming is the prescribing of antidepressants to children under a year old [http://www.nzherald. co.nz/section/1/story.cfm?c_id=1&objectid=10462684].

The New Zealand Government's suicide prevention strategy document (3) is testament to this confusion. The document attempts to demonstrate a move away from the medical model by including almost all other possible factors reported in the literature as potential contributors: from alcohol and drug abuse to bereavement, family break-ups, unemployment, educational and financial failure and so on. The strategy (3) is not clear as to how this wide range of contributory factors may relate to policy and therefore budget allocation. But, it may explain the rationale behind an education policy under which no one, in particular those in the lower socio-economic groups, fail their final year at school in some countries such as New Zealand. The following exert from a BBC comedy sketch best capture the fallacy of this type of policies "... since most accidents occur at home the Royal Society for the Prevention of Accidents advise you to move!"

The emphasis on mental illness and mental health services in the strategy is quite clear. In announcing a $6.4 million campaign to reduce the impact of depression, the New Zealand Government claimed "We know that up to 90% of suicides are *caused* by depression and that each year 500 New Zealanders are dying by suicide." The Government further claimed "The World Health Organisation has predicted that by the year 2020, depression will be second only to cardiovascular disease, in contributing to the global burden of disease. We must tackle this problem head on and the National Depression Initiative will go a long way to achieving this objective." [http://www.beehive.govt.nz/ViewDocument.aspx?DocumentID=27352]. This announcement is a reflection of the ineffectiveness of health and social policies in reducing cardiovascular disease. However, a more conservative estimate of depression in the population suggests that up to one in four women and one in ten men can expect to experience depression at some time in their lives [http://www.everybody.co.nz/page-75c9ff3f-7aa4-4b07-b63d-eaf5d92b88bb.aspx]. Applying these estimates to the New Zealand 2001 population estimates for males and females aged 15-85+ suggest that over one hundred and forty-five thousand males and over three hundred and eighty-eight thousand females may be suffering from depression. If depression is such a strong causal factor then should we not expect much larger suicide mortality than the 500 quoted by the government? On the other hand, it has been suggested that on average about two-thirds of suicide cases do not come into contact with psychiatric services and we know very little about them (9,10). Therefore the wisdom of uncritical statements which say that 90% of suicide cases are caused by depression emphasising a causal relationship has been challenged.

The major problem with suicide research is that the key informants are no longer available to provide an insight into the event. On the other hand, prospective designs require large samples over long periods of time, which are often ethically complex and financially prohibitive. For this reason, studies of suicide have mainly been retrospective, using psychiatric records and surveys of significant other (next of kin), or studying a sub-population e.g. those with a failed attempted suicide, or a history of self-harm.

These studies are limiting as they are subjective and exclude the dynamics of life processes. As such, they may lead to spurious relationships and give undue emphasis to some variables more than others. The view that suicide is not a result of mental illness is not new (11-13), but whatever the context (e.g. psychiatric, medical, social), suicide is a behavioural outcome. Therefore, compounded and confounded in suicide data will be high levels of measurement error and random noise due to subjectivity and unobserved/omitted characteristics associated with behavioural studies (14,15). Therefore the main issue is the availability of objective data to gain insight into the process of suicide in order to explore and examine its causal paths. On the other hand, objective data in the form of annual rates has been available and used in a limited way to explore change over time and conflicting trends (e.g. age and sex) (16). However, this type of data has been mainly used for monitoring purposes to inform policy making.

The above issues have been explored and discussed elsewhere (9,10,16,17). In this paper, we revisit the issue of seeking appropriate data to address suicide from a different slant; specifically, to debate the trivial issues of change and research.

UNDERSTANDING THE ISSUE

Unfortunately, some medical institutions still place a heavy emphasis on hypothesising and hypothesis testing to support evidence-based decision making. Students are encouraged to reduce a health issue into a single hypothesis, collect some data and perform a simple statistical test, on the basis of accepting or rejecting their hypothesis policy recommendations may be made. This could be interpreted as the preconditioning of students towards a RCT (randomised clinical trials) type research culture. The relationship between the research question, the hypothesis, the population, study design and analytical methodology is hardly explored. The irony is that the results from such an activity are then considered as evidence. This will have implications for research funding.

Many conventional techniques tend to use hypothesis testing. Within statistical modelling, hypothesis testing has a role to play in selecting a parsimonious model and, in this context, hypothesis testing is a logical part of the comprehensive analysis. This is in contrast to conventional statistical analysis in which hypothesis testing tends to be seen as an independent inferential statement often of meagre substantive value (18,19).

It is important that the researcher understands the nature of his or her subjects under investigation. For example, health or social issues are human activities and therefore they are by nature dynamic. There will be not only variations between individuals but also within. For example, individuals with similar characteristics may have different outcomes and the same individual's outcome may change over time.

Change does not happen on its own. Individuals do not wake up one morning finding themselves smokers or attempting suicide. In addition to individual decision processes, change is often brought about by collective activities such as government, social, health and economic policies. In the western democracy, these are often subject to change themselves due to changes in government or political pressure to appease voters. Therefore, change is almost inevitably continuous and continually interrupting routines. However, temporal dependencies will lead to different outcomes in individuals with similar characteristics. There may, for example, be inertial tendencies with individuals slow to react to changes in circumstances, perhaps as a result of exposure, changing social expectations and shifting social norms. Another example is the notion of 'cumulative inertia' in which the tendency to move in the next time period from the current state to another decreases with the length of duration in the current state (20,21).

This concept has been addressed in the context of human migration where a future move may not only depend on the current status but also the duration in the current status i.e. the length of time between moves (22). Factors underlying dependence include increasing social, economic and community ties with duration in a social state. The theory of cognitive dissonance is another example.

Under this theory individuals align their attitude to their current social state, upgrading the satisfaction with both positive and negative attributes of their current state and down grading those of possible alternatives. Thus, cross-sectionally, measures such as stress, trauma and self-esteem will appear as important parameters for developing a social/health policy. In the context of human behaviour, survey studies do not allow for the inclusion of the process of adjustment e.g. the notion of cognitive dissonance and cumulative inertia.

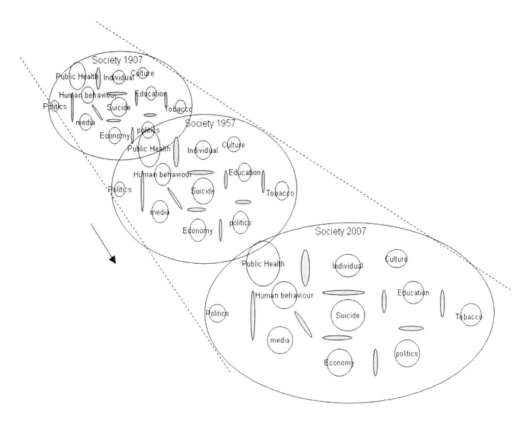

Figure 1. Holistic view of change in society operating on suicide.

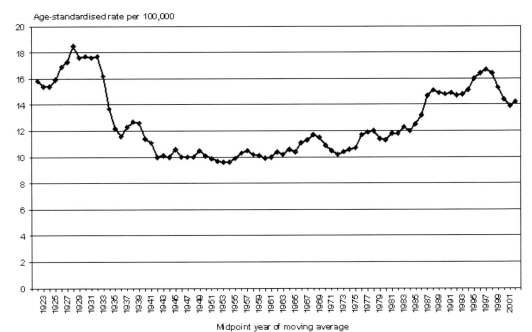

Source: New Zealand Health Information Service{Ministry of Health, 2006 #601}

Figure 2. Age-standardised suicide rates, three-year moving averages, New Zealand 1921–2003.

Temporal dependencies may be observed even when exploring suicide as an aggregate, rather than individual cases, such as the annual suicide rate over time. Thus suicide trends appear to have a memory, i.e. a pattern. Over a long period of time, the trends appear to suggest cyclic and seasonal variations (change), e.g. see figure 2. An interesting question may be what factors other than individual specific characteristics may be governing these cyclic effects. In addition, the changes in external factors that may cause the cycles appear to have a different effect or a lagged effect on competing trends. For example, in some countries the male suicide trend appears to behave differently to that for females e.g. a peak in the male suicide trend is coincided with a trough in the female trend (16). These external factors may be social, economical, political and environmental changes, such as the recent social and economical changes in China, the handover of Hong Kong to Chinese rule, or political and economical transformation in Russia or military conflict (23).

SUICIDE DATA

Regrettably, personal and individual information about intentions and reasons for suicide cannot be collected, because the case is no longer alive. Most suicide data are highly contentious and carry a high degree of bias, due possibly to the researcher, or the informants' relationship with the case, and the current mindset – which is helped by the management and dissemination of information by the media (see later), attempters (incomplete suicide cases), and so on. The only objective suicide data is the actual number of deaths due to suicide, which are collected annually, but are not released for several years due to the proceedings of the coroner's court. The World Health Organisation (WHO) provides a limited amount of aggregate suicide data for the countries that have supplied their data. A sample selection of the international suicide trends shown in figures 3-11 are based on a 5-yearly aggregate only, which hide the fluctuations and patterns – nevertheless it is possible to visualise pattern changes in the countries that have provided their suicide data to WHO [(http://www.who.int/mental_health/prevention/suicide/country_reports/en/)].

SUICIDE TRENDS

Although five year intervals for suicide trends (figures 3-11) do not provide a good view of the patterns, they do project some interesting associations. For example, Western countries that have followed similar political and economic changes in the late seventies, through to the eighties and early nineties appear to share similar suicide trends (e.g. see figures 3-7, UK, New Zealand, Australia, Italy and US). On the other hand, the massive economic, political and social change in Russia and the process of change of government in Hong Kong in the nineties appear to be accompanied with an upward suicide trend (figures 8-9). Although the suicide trends for China are from selected regions and only go up to 1999 (figures 10-11), the trends seem to suggest that unlike other countries the female suicide rate is higher in China. Furthermore, a much higher suicide rate can be observed in rural than in urban areas. If there are no issues with the data collection and coding, this should be a challenging issue for the Chinese public health authorities to grapple with; why do the Chinese age/sex trends show a different pattern of trends compared to other countries? The answer could lie in the method of suicide used.

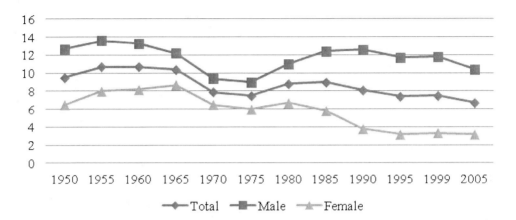

Figure 3. Suicide Rate per 100, 000: UK.

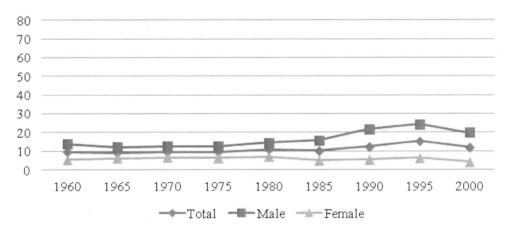

Figure 3. Suicide Rate per 100,000: New Zealand.

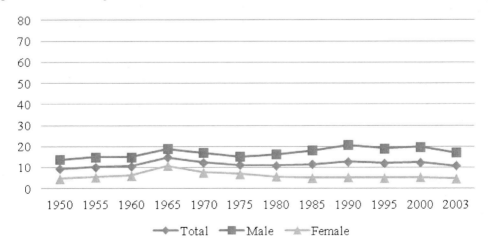

Figure 5. Suicide Rate per 100, 000: Australia.

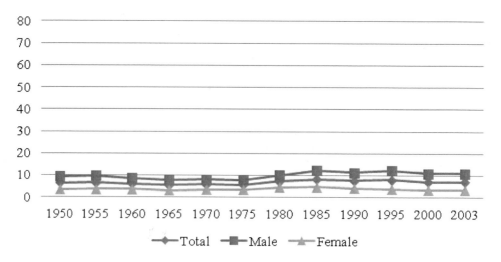

Figure 6. Suicide Rate per 100,000: Italy.

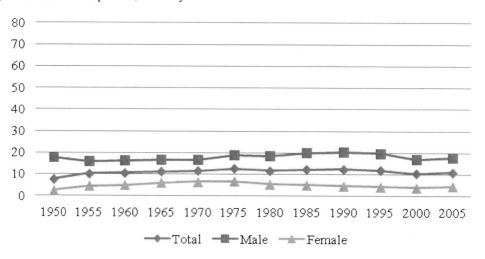

Figure 7. Suicide Rate per 100,000: USA.

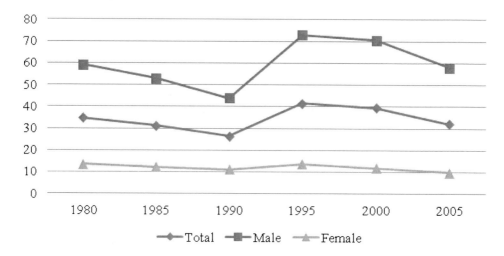

Figure 8. Suicide Rate per 100,000: Russia.

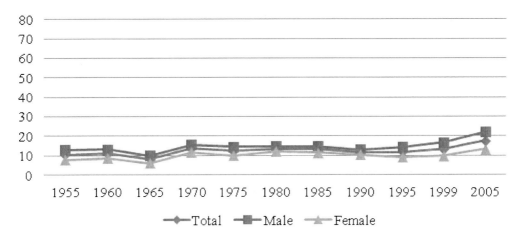

Figure 9. Suicide Rate per 100,000: China Hong Kong.

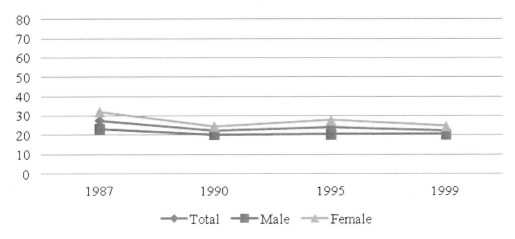

Figure 10. Suicide Rate per 100,000: China (Rural).

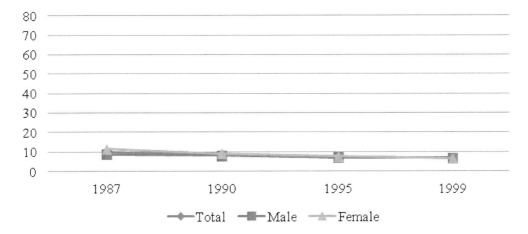

Figure 11. Suicide Rate per 100,000: China (Urban).

DISCUSSION

Perceptions and attitudes towards suicide may be influenced by establishing *precedence* i.e. that even though suicide is unacceptable it does occur. For example, in the UK, when reporting the case of a tetraplegic who travelled to another country for assisted suicide, the media had established precedence in the minds of the general public. Furthermore, the media named the European countries in which assisted suicide is legal. Moreover, they gave details of organisations that make the necessary arrangements for prospective candidates.

In its saturday edition (23/08/08), the front page of the family section of the Guardian (UK) had in big bold font the headline "I'm going to die on Monday at 6.15pm" followed by a large picture of a woman. In this report, the Guardian had decided to publish what they themselves termed a "shockingly" frank diary kept by the pictured person's son. In its subheading, the Guardian said that when Marc Weide's mother was diagnosed with terminal cancer, she *chose* euthanasia. Is the media attempting to influence public opinion of death by providing exposure of this kind, and trivialising death as an option? What possible purpose would the report serve where, on the one hand, details of assisted suicide are publicised, and on the other, suicide is portrayed as though it is an item on a shopping list to be taken off a supermarket's shelf. The impact on the public mindset is difficult to gauge but one thing is for sure; that there is more exposure to suicide and assisted suicide, to the delight of the supporters of euthanasia.

Earlier that same year, the BMJ published an article on suicide and the internet (24), supposedly to demonstrate the ease with which methods of suicide can be accessed. It appears that this publication has helped raise substantive as well as methodological and ethical issues (see Rapid Responses to Biddle et al. (24) http://www.bmj.com/cgi/eletters/336/7648/800). Needless to say that one of the consequences of this publication was publicising the internet as a source of information on suicide methods. The internet is a feature of daily life for most people and provides another medium for most media groups from news to entertainment. Therefore, public access and exposure to suicide methods, whether searching by design or accidentally by unsuspecting users, in particular younger users, is inevitable.

The role of the media in providing access to information about suicide methods is discussed elsewhere in relation to suicide and the internet (17). The retelling of suicide cases' stories helps establish precedence in the public mindset and is of concern because suicide becomes accepted as a solution. This is happening at a time when the society as a whole is trying to do the opposite, i.e. that suicide cannot be viewed as a way out, a solution to a problem and so on. In human behaviour, precedence is an important influence on an individual's decision processes (25-28). In other words, precedence facilitates the feedback effect; the knowledge that an outcome can not only be achieved but also has been achieved will *attenuate* the importance attached to the outcome[e.g. see (29). Thus the history or track record of an outcome – precedence - may change the perception of it which will in turn influence the process. For example, in the context of criminal justice, offending may lead to repeat offending (30) and suicide may lead to more suicide including copycat suicide or the acceptance of suicide as a real option.

The gravity of concern about the public discussion of suicide by the authorities and government departments is better demonstrated by the coverage of suicide by a broadsheet newspaper in New Zealand in 2005 (10). To generate debate and discussion, the newspaper published the names and a summary of a coroner's report for eleven suicide cases which had been before the coroner's court at that time. From the ensuing letters and reports from suicide survivors and practitioners, there were no clear conclusions about the role of the media, but the messages that were emphasised included depression and mental illness, and that men in particular should seek help. Interestingly, the guidelines from the New Zealand Suicide Prevention Strategy published in the same edition of the newspaper advised the public that if they are worried about someone to call a mental health care team or a psychiatric unit. This is all very well. However, the two main issues often ignored are: what do individuals look for in a treatment; and what do the practitioners offer as treatment if an individual were to seek help?

The newspaper omitted the methods of suicide from the case histories and coroner's report. One would assume the newspaper's action as courageous and noble, albeit a one off act. But, it is the media itself that, by playing politics and the rating game, fuel the creation of sub-cultures. In doing so, they publicise suicide and provide free airtime and a platform to pro-suicide groups e.g. see [http://www.scoop.co..nz/multimedia/tv/national/10243.html]. Over recent years, the concern appears to be of the utilisation of methods of suicide which is reported in the news media or portrayed fictionally, so much so that the policy makers and decision makers' emphasis is on blocking access to methods of suicide. For example, as reported earlier (17,31) health authorities limit access to medication, and as suggested above, media reports usually omit suicide methods when reporting on suicide cases. Furthermore, any public debate of suicide deliberately excludes methods. The evidence for such behaviour is not very clear. Quite apart from the fact that information on suicide methods is readily available, the problem is a lack of alignment between countries. For example, some countries may consider method of suicide a strong link with suicide rate and as a result attempt to control this link by omitting references to method of suicide. But other countries may take a different view and may continue to report method of suicide. Therefore, it is not very difficult to come across methods of suicide during an internet search. The concerted effort by authorities to omit methods of suicide from the public domain implicitly suggests that the reporting of the method of suicide is the cause of suicide!

We seem to make a lot of assumptions about what the suicide survivors need in order to deal with their loss, especially not knowing the reason why their loved one committed suicide. In response, researchers and practitioners assume cause, which is impossible to know as the only person who can provide the answers is deceased. Some may argue that various studies of specific populations such as psychological autopsy and studies of attempters has provided evidence of a cause and effect e.g. mental illness and suicide (6). However, as discussed elsewhere (9,10,16) these studies have often relied on the views of others (friends and family), who to all intents and purposes had no idea about the case's intentions until after the event. Furthermore, their views and perceptions are often attenuated and influenced by the general assumptions promoted by the medical model. That is, the immediate assumption is by association that suicide is caused by depression and mental illness. Critically viewed, the flaw is in the use of the information to infer conclusions about the population without due regard for the spurious relationships in the data.

So what is the problem with suicide research? Suicide is difficult to research for the central reason that the main informant cannot provide the necessary information to gain insight into suicide. On the whole we are ignorant of the processes involved in an individual's character and life to understand how decisions are made. The problem is further exacerbated by our education system which reinforces a narrow view of health issues; after all, health issues arise due to individuals'; whether they are patients, policy makers or medical they are all affected and shaped by human behaviour processes (see Fig. 1).

The problems for the policy makers are at least twofold: firstly, policy makers have no real evidence on which to base preventive or interventional policies. Secondly, policy makers have very little grasp of evidence based decision making. There is a lack of critical assessment of "evidence". It is the "tunnel vision" culture in which various groups are trained for their chosen profession. This is the feedback effect from education and training. Policy makers often have very little appreciation for a critical assessment of the literature and therefore are *selective* of their evidence. As mentioned above and elsewhere (9,10,16,17), studies of suicide are often biased either methodologically, analytically or both, e.g. the Canterbury project (4). The policy makers' uncritical use of this type of research is perhaps the biggest issue.

The continued challenge of the laws on assisted suicide by a portion of people - a wish to end life, not of their own, but someone else's; or a wish to die, but for someone else to do it for them – raises a number of issues. The first is that the law has never been instrumental in reducing or stopping suicide – so how will the law deter or hold the suicide case accountable? Secondly, once again it involves issues of human behaviour, and these are even more confused as they are concerned with not only the suicide case, but also their accomplices: e.g. a perceived ownership of life over and above our faith and beliefs that entitles us to take any decision about our own lives. In other words, in terms of suicide the law is powerless to prevent suicide nor can it bring action against a suicide case. Moreover, in this context suicide may be accepted as a solution to problems or a valid response to changes in life, or, if the case gives consent for their lives to be ended then it will not be a crime (regardless of the law on suicide). In fact the term *assisted* suicide is incorrect and misleading – because, *unless* the definition of suicide has changed recently, apart from an apparent "expressed" consent to die, the method is carried out by an accomplice i.e. the responsibility of taking own life is passed on to someone else. The question is that if no one was prepared to be an accomplice how many of the cases would actually complete suicide? Why would someone want to kill someone else under the guise of assisted suicide? It is plausible that people often confuse their own feelings and perceptions and project them as that of the case's – therefore, is it justified that they are no longer able to provide emotional and physical care for the person seeking assisted suicide? Whose intentions and actions does the guise of *relieving* the case from their pain and suffering, justify?

CONCLUSION

As mentioned in the abstract, a medical student's research proposal provided the inspiration for this paper. It was refreshing to see how one student challenge the conventional wisdom of hypothesis testing by discussing the issues raised here in this paper and propose a multi-method approach to address the multiplicity of suicide. Needless to say the student was penalised marks for an excellent piece of work which was difficult to mark as there was not a clear hypothesis! The point of the exercise was for the students to demonstrate an understanding of research and study design which must include the declaration of a hypothesis and the description of a statistical test.

Clearly, the feedback effect is not only inappropriate evidence from poor research carried out by poorly trained researchers but which affects society through the development of services and polices. Suicide affects many sections of society (e.g. youth, various mental and physical disorders, the elderly). The suicide population within each group appears heterogeneous and cannot be generalised to the group(s) and the general population. However, very little attention has been paid to the grouping of suicide (also see (17)). As discussed, economic, health and social policies will have an effect on society and interact with the individual's own processes such as employment, and lifestyle. Processes are dynamic by nature and the main consequence of a dynamic process is the feedback effect.

The processes listed in this paper all relate to human behaviour including politics (e.g. funding distribution, policy decisions, choice of evidence and selection of expert panels), media (e.g. editorial decisions, perception of public interest), lobby groups (euthanasia), health care profession, education and training, researchers, and the individuals themselves. Through politics these processes interact e.g. as mentioned earlier attempts by euthanasia groups to pressure the government to change the law on suicide received widespread publicity by media reporting which was then followed by public discussions of the ethics of suicide. Such reporting and discussions provided the unsuspecting public with a guide to the where and the how to arrange for euthanasia. Similarly, the publication in the BMJ (24) about suicide methods on the internet led to additional publicity for both suicide methods and the role of the internet. To some extent these processes are informed by evidence from research in particular the development of policies, treatment and primary care services. The ability to carry out quality research that is flexible and allows for the dynamics of human behaviour should be encouraged as part of education and training.

Therefore, in the context of suicide over and above individual characteristics there are many other processes such as health, social, economic and political that influence suicide and suicide rates. It cannot simply be claimed that one process on its own may be responsible for suicide. It is not just macro-level social change that may influence the suicide rate but also the right conditioning of other social, health and economic characteristics of individuals that prepares a society to respond positively or negatively to change. For example, Omar (32) describes a community based suicide prevention programme in the USA that appears to have made a positive effect on the community so far (after eight years): the suicide rate in the area covered by the programme has been stable or reducing and hospitalisation due to suicide attempts has fallen by 30%, whilst suicide and suicide attempts had increased in the rest of the state by 20% for the same period.

Most countries claim to have an economic safety-net to help the vulnerable, such as help with housing, means tested social benefits and so on. However, there is no such thinking for suicide prevention given the huge number of policy changes. It is not enough to class suicide as a mental illness and expect scarce and run down mental health services to provide a safety net. There are cases who have completed suicide whilst under psychiatric care, in mental health units and/or soon after being discharged from care (9).

Evidently, suicide is being considered a viable option or a solution to a problem. The research question, therefore, should not be why, but to encourage and condition a society that is supportive of life through inclusive social, health, economic and environmental, local and national polices. Death cannot be the answer and will not solve problems. Because of poor research and policies hastily based on an uncritical use of the literature, we (researchers, politicians, practitioners and the general public) are all part of the problem.

This paper has not been about macro-level social change and social models of suicide but about a *holistic* view of suicide i.e. as suggested by figure 2 and summarised in the conclusion.

REFERENCES

[1]   Mann JJ. Forword. In: Merrick J, G Zalsman. Suicidal behaviour in adolescence: An international perspective Tel Aviv: Freund, 2005:1-2.
[2]   Merrick J, Zalsman G. Suicide from an international perspective. ScientificWorldJournal 2005;5:888-90.
[3]   Associate Minister of Health. The New Zealand suicide prevention strategy 2006-2016. Wellington: Ministry Health, 2006. URL: http://www.moh.govt.nz/suicideprevention.
[4]   Beautrais AL, Joyce PR, Mulder RT. The Canterbury suicide project: Aims, overview and progress. Commun Ment Health NZ 1994;8(2):32-9.
[5]   Beautrais AL. Serious suicide attempts in young people: A case control study. Dissertation. Christchurch: Christchurch School Med, 1996.
[6]   Beautrais AL. Suicides and serious suicide attempts: Two populations or one? Psychol Med 2001;31:837-45.
[7]   Khan A, Warner HA, Brown WA. Symptom reduction and suicide risk in patients treated with placebo in antidepressant clinical trials: An analysis of the food and drug administration database. Arch Gen Psychiatry 2000;57:311-7.
[8]   Hall WD, Mant A, Mitchell PB, Rendle VA, Hickie IB, McManus P. Association between antidepressant prescribing and suicide in Australia, 1991-2000: Trend analysis. BMJ 2003;326(7397):1008.
[9]   Shahtahmasebi S. Suicides by mentally ill people. ScientificWorldJournal 2003;3:684-93.
[10]   Shahtahmasebi S. Suicides in New Zealand. ScientificWorldJournal 2005;5:527-34.
[11]   Maris R. Pathways to suicide: A survey of self- destructive behaviours Baltimore: Johns Hopkins Univ Press, 1981.
[12]   Maris R, Berman A, Silverman M. Comprehensive textbook of suicidology. New York: Guilford, 2000.
[13]   Wasserman D. Suicide: An unnecessary death. London: Martin Dunitz, 2001.
[14]   Shahtahmasebi S. Quality of life: A longitudinal analysis of correlates of morale in old age. ScientificWorldJournal 2004;4:100-10.
[15]   Shahtahmasebi S, Berridge D. Teenage smoking: A longitudinal analysis. Int J Adolesc Med Health 2005;17(2):137-55.
[16]   Shahtahmasebi S. Suicide research and adolescent suicide trends in new zealand. ScientificWorldJournal 2008;8:287-302.
[17]   Shahtahmasebi S. Can suicide be quantified and categorised? In: Sher L. Internet and suicide. New York: Nova Sci, 2008.
[18]   Shahtahmasebi S. Statistical modelling of dependency in old age. Dissertation. Bangor: Univ Wales, 1995.
[19]   Davies RB. The state of the art in survey analysis. In: Westlake A, et al. Survey and statistical computing. Amsterdam: Elsevier, 1992.
[20]   Ginsberg RB. Semi-markov processes and mobility. J Math Sociol 1971;1:233-62.
[21]   McGinnis R. A stochastic model of social mobility. Am Sociol Rev 1968;23:712-22.
[22]   Davies R, Flowerdew R. Modelling migration careers using data from a british survey. Geogr Anal 1992;24:35-57.
[23]   Shahtahmasebi S. War, massive personal and social change and suicide. In: Sher L. War and suicide. New York: Nova Sci, 2009.

[24] Biddle L, Donovan J, Hawton K, Kapur N, Gunnell D. Suicide and the internet. BMJ 2008;336(7648):800-2.

[25] Lagasse LL. Effects of good form and spatial frequency on global precedence. Percept Psychophys 1993;53(1):89-105.

[26] Litovsky RY, Colburn HS, Yost WA, Guzman SJ. The precedence effect. J Acoust Soc Am 1999;106:1633.

[27] Miller J, Navon D. Global precedence and response activation: Evidence from lrps. Q J Exp Psychol A 2002;55(1):289-310.

[28] Navon D. The forest revisited: More on global precedence. Psychol Res 1981;43(1):1-32.

[29] Tice DM, Bratslavsky E, Baumeister RF. Emotional distress regulation takes precedence over impulse control: If you feel bad, do it! J Pers Soc Psychol 2001;80(1):53-67.

[30] Jones CN, MacCulloch MJ, Bailey J, Shahtahmasebi S. Personal history factors associated with reconviction in personality disordered patients discharged from a special hospital. J Forensic Psychiatr 1994;5(2):249-61.

[31] Shahtahmasebi S. Researching health service information systems development. In: Dwivedi A, ed. Handbook of research on it management and clinical data administration in healthcare. Hershey, PA: IGI Global, 2009.

[32] Omar H. A model program for youth suicide prevention. Int J Adolesc Med Health 2005;17(3):275-8.

In: Children, Violence and Bullying
Editors: J Merrick, I Kandel and H A Omar

ISBN: 978-1-62948-342-9
© 2014 Nova Science Publishers, Inc.

Chapter 16

CHILDHOOD SUICIDE

Donald E Greydanus, MD, FIAP (HON), FAAP[*], *Swati Bhave, MD, DCH, FCPS and Roger W Apple, PhD*

Department of Pediatric and Adolescent Medicine,
Western Michigan University School of Medicine, Kalamazoo,
Michigan, US, Association of Adolescent and Child Care in India,
Indraprastha Apollo Hospital, New Delhi,
India and Psychological Evaluation and Consultation,
Kalamazoo Regional Educational Service Agency, Kalamazoo,
Michigan, US

ABSTRACT

Childhood suicide is often ignored because of societal horror at the thought of childhood self-murder, denial by parents and clinicians, underlying religious and ethnic factors, confusing classification systems, and focus of research on older age cohorts. Data collected by the World Health Organization from 104 countries reveal suicide rates per 100,000 at 0.5 in females and 1.5 males in the 5 to 14 year old cohort. Suicide is the 5th leading cause of death in 5 to 14 year old persons and the 4th leading cause of death in the 1 to 19 year old cohort. Four key components of understanding childhood suicide: universality, irreversibility, finality, and causality are discussed. Etiologic factors include depression, extreme family and/or environmental dysfunction, positive family history for suicidal behavior in first degree relatives, schizophrenia, disruptive behavior, and others. Suicide behavior as a child predicts suicidal behavior in later years when the child becomes an adolescent or young adult. Principles of primary and secondary prevention are considered.

[*] Correspondence: Donald E Greydanus, MD, Dr. HC (ATHENS), Professor and Chair, Department of Pediatric and Adolescent Medicine, Western Michigan University School of Medicine, 1000 Oakland Drive, D48G, Kalamazoo, MI 49008-1284, United States. E-mail: Donald.greydanus@med.wmich.edu.

INTRODUCTION

Society has been concerned about suicide by its children and adolescents probably since Homo sapiens emerged as a species over 60,000 years ago. Advances in health care usually were beneficial to adults and gradually over the past 1,000 years, became inclusive of children. The preeminent physician of ancient Persia, Rhazes (Muhammad ibn Zakariya Razi, 865-925 AD), initiated the birth of pediatric knowledge with his book on children's disorders (1).

Western medicine belatedly tried to catch up with textbooks by Trotula Platearius of Salerno, Italy (De Mylierum Passionibus) in 1050 AD and by Thomas Phaer in 1544 AD (The Boke of Chyldren) (1). Thomas Phaer was a pediatrician, lawyer, and author in England whose landmark treatise was the first book on pediatrics written in the English language and was the first to provide a distinction between the critical stages of childhood and adulthood. Though the term, adolescence (Latin: adolescere) was first used in 15th Century Europe, attention to health care issues of youth was considered a bêta noire until the middle to late 20th century.

As interest in problems of adolescents gradually developed, the subject of suicide in Pediatrics came under closer scrutiny. For example, the Vienna Psychoanalytic Society sponsored a conference in 1910 to deal with what was perceived to be a growing epidemic of youth suicide. This conference mentioned the powerful influence of Goethe's "The Sorrows of Young Werner" from the 19th century in which an adolescent took his own life after losing his girl friend. Loss of one's love interest and intense academic pressure are often common underlying themes when seeking explanations for teen suicide. The conclusion of the 1910 Vienna conference and that of a US Surgeon General's report on suicide published several decades later was the same—a call to acknowledge pediatric suicide and for more research on this perplexing phenomenon (2).

Acknowledging the possibility of suicide in children has been a taboo subject for many millennia. Various over-riding complexities have arisen from religious and ethnic origins that have prevented the study of children taking their own lives in response to the stresses in their lives. This publication focuses on current research analyzing perhaps an even more troublesome, and much less recognized concern, than adolescent suicide—the phenomenon of childhood suicide.

OUR REVIEW

Internet searches were conducted using the Cochrane Database of Systematic Reviews, the Evidenced-Based Mental Health Treatment for Children and Adolescents group, Evidenced-based Therapy site, PsychInfo, EbcoHost, and Medline/PubMed. Keywords included suicide, childhood, children's perception of death, children's concept of death, adolescence, etiology, methods, and prevention. The search yielded many articles and a succinct summary is presented in this article. Specific issues now reviewed include suicide epidemiology, childhood concepts of death, etiologic factors behind childhood suicide, methods of suicide, cultural aspects, and prevention of childhood suicide.

SUICIDE EPIDEMIOLOGY

Suicide is a tragic phenomenon that affects nearly all age cohorts and all nations (3-17). Suicide rates continue to rise from childhood until 49 years of age, is reduced until age 74 years and once again rises at age 75 years (12). The World Health Organization (WHO) estimates that about 2 million persons die each year, because of homicide or suicide and in 2002, globally there were about 877,000 persons from all age cohorts, who committed suicide (3,4).

Death is not recorded as suicide in US national statistics in the 1 to 4 year age group though suicide has been documented in children as young as 3 years of age (17). In 2003, the number one cause of death in 1 to 4 years of age was unintentional injury, though some of this may have been intentional injury or overt suicide. In older children death may be blamed on accidental injury and not suicide as parents, police, clinicians, religious officials, and other authorities are reluctant to use the word suicide. This reluctance is likely exacerbated due to the difficulties of objectively measuring suicidal thoughts and behaviors in young children. In this regard, the problem of accurately identifying suicidal behavior in young children is very similar to the problem of accurately diagnosing mental illness in young children. As a result, suicidal behavior and mental illness often remain un-diagnosed or under-diagnosed in young children.

Information on childhood suicide is often hidden in data dealing with adolescent suicide that involves the 10 to 14 year old cohort or the 5 to 14 year old cohort, leading some researchers to conclude that childhood suicide per se does not exist (13,14). It may be theorized that puberty is a precursor that is needed to increase the cognitive ability to consider suicide as well as succumb to the needed pressure to commit or carry out overt plans of suicide (15,16). Since the onset of puberty varies, the prevalence of suicide may vary as well in those under the standard age of puberty, making it difficult to separate out childhood from adolescent suicide.

Table 1 lists different data on suicide in children based on various studies, though they all agree that childhood suicide rates are low in comparison to adolescents and older persons. Research also agrees that suicide rates in both the 5 to 14 year old cohort and the 10 to 14 year old cohort has increased over the latter part of the 20th century in the United States (12-14,17,19). For example, a US Surgeon General noted a 100% increase in suicide among 10 to 14 year olds in the US between 1980 and 1996 (19). There were approximately 324 reported suicides in those under 14 years of age in the United States in 1998 and 292 reported suicides in 2004 (17). Suicide is the 5th leading cause of death in 5 to 14 year old persons and the 4th leading cause of death in the 1 to 19 year age group (17). At least 90,000 adolescents (19 years of age or younger) commit suicide annually in the world at a rate of one every 5 minutes and out of a context of 4 million suicide annual attempts in addition to 100,000 to 200,000 annual suicides in persons 15 to 24 years of age (3,5-11). The male to female ratio is 3:1 for 5 to 14 year olds and 6:1 for 15 to 24 year olds (13,14). Reported suicide rates vary around the world with the lowest reported adolescent suicide rates (under 6.5 per 100,000) in Middle East Arabic countries and Latin America while the highest rates (over 30 per 100,000) being reported in Slovenia, the Russian Federation, Lithuania, Finland, and New Zealand (4) (see table 2). Increasing rates of suicide in all ages in the last part of the 20th century have been reported in China, Spain, Asia, and other areas of the world (17).

Table 1. Suicide rates in 5 to 14 year old cohort

5 to 14 years in US [13,14]	0.4/100,000 in 1979	0.8 in 1990s
5 to 14 years old in 104 countries (WHO) in 2000 [18]	0.5/100,000 in females	1.5 in males
10-14 yrs in US [12]	1.2/100,000 combined males and females	0.5 (females); 1.7 (males)
5 to 14 ys old from 1974-1999 [61]	Canada	15 per Million
5 to 14 ys old from 1974-1999 [61]	USA	12 per Million
5 to 14 ys old from 1974-1999 [61]	Netherlands	8 per Million
5 to 14 ys old from 1974-1999 [61]	Spain	3 per Million
5 to 14 ys old from 1974-1999 [61]	Italy	8 per Million
5 to 14 ys old from 1974-1999 [61]	England and Wales	1 per Million

Table 2. 1996 global suicide rates (per 100,000) 15 to 24 year olds*

Country	Males	Females
Greece	3.8	0.8
Portugal	4.3	2.0
Italy	5.7	1.6
Spain	7.1	2.2
Netherlands	9.1	3.8
Sweden	10.0	6.7
Japan	10.1	4.4
Israel	11.7	2.5
United Kingdom	12.2	2.3
Germany	12.7	3.4
Denmark	13.4	2.3
France	14.0	4.3
Bulgaria	15.4	5.6
Czech Republic	16.4	4.3
Poland	16.6	2.5
Ukraine	17.2	5.3
Hungary	19.1	5.5
Austria	21.1	6.5
Ireland	21.5	2.0
United States	21.9	3.8
Belarus	24.2	5.2
Canada	24.7	6.0
Switzerland	25.0	4.8
Australia	27.3	5.6
Norway	28.2	5.2
Estonia	29.7	10.6
Finland	33.0	3.2
Latvia	35.0	9.3
Slovenia	37.0	8.4
New Zealand	39.9	6.2
Russian Federation	41.7	7.9
Lithuania	44.9	6.7

*World Health Organization: http://www.unicef.org/pon96/insuicid.htm

CHILDHOOD CONCEPTS OF DEATH

The concept of "death" is an emotional and complex conundrum and very gradual process that is appreciated by children as they mature toward an adult cognitive perspective (20). Thus, it is difficult for clinicians and researchers to image a child committing suicide until this person cognitively understands what "death" is or is not and is able to cognitively plan suicide. Young children typically link the word "death" with "sleeping" though most children 6 to 7 years of age will note, when asked, that everyone "dies." The concept of death becomes more real as children see relatives "pass away" or observe animals being killed or dying. Gradually the concept of death "solidifies" in maturing children though even those in early puberty often do not understand that death is an issue for every living person—that is, everyone eventually will die.

At the end of the Piagetian sensorimotor stage (birth to age 2 years), children acquire object permanence in which objects continue to exist for them even if not touched, seen, or heard. Death is more complicated and remains an abstract concept for children in the Piagetian Preoperational Stage (ages 2 to 7) and even the Concrete Operational Stage (ages 7 to early adolescence). The understanding of death as a concept begins by late childhood (ages 9 to 10) and solidifies in early to middle adolescence as Piagetian cognitive skills change from pre-operational to concrete to formal operational (21). Children may not grasp the concept of permanence regarding death until early adolescence at 13-15 years of age in which they understand that people do not return from death.

The four key components of universality (death is something that happens to everyone), irreversibility (death is permanent), finality (bodily functions stop) and causality (understanding factors that cause death) are cited throughout the literature as relative to understanding children's concept of death (22-28). As children gradually acquire more sophisticated cognitive abilities, as described by Piaget's stages of development, their accuracy in conceptualizing death increases (23). Thus an accurate concept of death occurs when there is sufficient cognitive ability to create a synthesis of the four key components. In general, most children develop an accurate concept of death by age 10 years; however, because children's development is continuous, some children may have developed an accurate concept of death by age 6 while others may not have until well into adolescence. Some research has found that children can begin to understand the biological concept of death as young as 4 years of age (27); however, as stated above, most children are unable to develop an accurate concept of death until the age of 6 years.

Parent's perception is that children's concept of death begins to develop between the ages of 5-7 years (24) which is consistent with cognitive and developmental research. Many people believe that if children experience death at young ages they will more quickly develop an accurate concept of death; however, this is not always true possibly due to variance in cognitive development. One study of 1,528 parents acknowledged that 4% of their children had attempted suicide (17). However, most parents do not consider nor accept the concept that their children may actually consider suicide and are typically very hesitant to discuss death and suicide with their children. Parents and others in society may teach death as a positive state from a religious viewpoint in which the child learns that the dead person is "with God" or is in "heaven" or "paradise" and is "better off" than when in life. This glorification of death can be very confusing to children.

Other places children can learn about death include school, though school officials also do not typically teach children about death. Often the group that first approaches this subject is the media (movies, cable, internet) who "teach" that suicide is what cartoon or video characters or even humans in movies do after loss of a romantic love or when one becomes very frustrated and/or angry over something. Though relief of depression may be a motive in adolescents contemplating suicide, it is not a typical reason for suicide as portrayed in the media. The media also teaches children that suicide is invoked by media or video characters who do not get their own way or have a need for revenge after being seriously insulted or wronged by another media or video character.

Table 3. Risk factors for suicide and suicide attempts in children

Depression (including anhedonia)
Severe irritability or agitation
Schizophrenia
Violent behavior (including aggressive conduct disorder) (especially males)
Schizophrenia
Previous attempt(s)
Family history of completed suicide
History of abuse (sexual or physical)
Precocious puberty (with precocious cognitive development)
Family and environmental dysfunction (including family history of suicide)
Substance abuse disorder (patient or parental) (males)
Widespread availability of firearms and suffocation methods
Loss of parent (s)
Being bullied
Substance use (males)
Community chaos or dysfunction
Personality disorder (borderline, antisocial)
School failure (including absence from school)
Non-compliance with mental health treatment
Frequent moving from one residence to another
Life on the street (throw-away or runaway adolescents)
Involvement in war

Table 4. Children and suicidal behavior risks

STUDY	AGES	RISK FACTOR
Pfeffer (33)	Pre-pubertal	Previous suicide attempt
Nock & Kazkin (34)	6-13 year olds	Depression and previous suicide attempt associated with suicidal behavior
Gould (35)	9 to 12 year olds	Mood and Anxiety disorders increased risk of suicidal ideation
Workman (36)	Pre-pubertal children	Depression
Kovacs (37)	Pre-pubertal children	Depression
O'Leary (38)	Pre-pubertal chidlren	Depression
Jackson & Nuttall (39)	5-12 year olds	42% with suicidal behaviors and most frequent diagnosis was depression
Agergo (44)	Adolescents	Family History of suicidal behavior

CHILDHOOD SUICIDE: ETIOLOGIC FACTORS

Tables 3 and 4 list risk factors for children attempting and/or completing suicide. In one review of 466 adolescents treated for depression, 24% had attempted suicide (29). Studies consistently noted that a history of severe depression is a major risk factor for suicide attempt and suicide completion in pediatric and adolescent males and females (30,31). As noted in youth or older persons, severe depression in a child may also lead to contemplation and increase risks for overt acts of suicide behavior (32-41) (see table 4).

Childhood psychopathology other than severe depression can increase risks for childhood suicide as well, including attention deficit hyperactivity disorder (especially with impulsivity), anxiety disorders, conduct disorder, oppositional defiant disorder, and schizophrenia (17,42,43) (see table 3).

A prior suicidal attempt by a child increases the risk for further suicide attempts and completion as a child or later as an adolescent or young adult (34). When assessing previous suicide attempts it is important to discuss previous "accidents" for the possibility of suicidal behavior that was not identified (25). Suicide attempts and completions in parents, twins, and other first degree relatives increase attempts in the child, especially during adolescence (44-46). Precocious puberty along with advanced cognitive development may be a risk factor for suicide in children (47). Chronic illness may also increase risks for suicide attempts in adolescents or young adults by precipitating depression or inducing central nervous system injury due to complications of trauma, epilepsy, chemotherapy, or infection (48). Further research is needed to understand if this impacts on childhood suicide as well.

Children who are in extreme family or environmental dysfunction, sexual or physical abuse, bullying in school, frequent moving without a stable family or residency, substance use, or damage from war are at risk of suicidal behavior (17,46,49-54). As many as 140 million children and adolescents are affected by war in the world whether as solders, civilians, or refugees (5). Countless numbers of children are either raped by solders or forced to become solders since children make fearless fighters. WHO notes that 170 million children and adolescents live on the streets of the world because of family poverty and societal chaos, including 30 million in Asia, 10 million in Africa, and 40 million in Latin America (55-58). Untold numbers of children are sold as sex objects around the world and few are rescued by an impartial and otherwise pre-occupied world.

When children find themselves in the middle of a major life crisis without caring adults to steer these cognitively-immature persons out of their problems, suicide may become an option. When pain from life becomes unbearable, suicide becomes an option for those who no longer can tolerate their mental or physical pain (59).

Sometimes they learn from other family members, peers, or the media that suicide may be a "solution" to what seems to be overwhelming and unsurpassable problems. If they contact their internet "friends" and ask for advice, the answer may be encouragement of suicide. Children who are violent or involved in substance abuse are also at increased risk for suicide, especially if they are males. As noted, adolescents or adults who exhibited suicidal behavior as prepubertal children are at increased risk for further suicidal behavior (41).

Table 5. Methods of suicide in 10-19 year olds (73)

Firearms	49%
Suffocation (mainly hanging)	38%
Poisoning	7%
Miscellaneous*	6%

*Running into traffic, motor vehicle accidents, burning, others.

METHODS OF SUICIDE

Table 5 lists methods of suicide by children. Access to firearms along with a crisis situation is a deadly combination as noted in the United States where relatively easy access to guns is part of the American culture. As noted in table 5, firearms were the methods of suicide in 49% of 10-19 year olds in the United States (60). From 1988 to 1997, 1,588 firearm suicides were reported in the 5 to 14 year old cohort (61). Eliminating gun access would lower completed suicides among children and adolescents by 32% (62). Suffocation became more common than firearms in those 10-14 years of age beginning in 1997 in the US (63). Hanging is the most common method of suicide in the world and in agrarian societies, death by use of pesticides is the most common cause of suicide (64). Other means of suicide in the 6 to 12 year old cohort include burning, head banging (and severe self-hitting), jumping from heights, running into traffic, and stabbing (21,65).

CULTURAL ASPECTS OF CHILDHOOD SUICIDE

Cultural aspects of childhood suicide are complex and not well-understood. Factors that influence rates of suicide include local customs, mores, taboos, religious dogma, level of industrialization, poverty, and others (66). Many societies and religions are reluctant to consider suicide as a cause of death for a child. In some religions, suicide is a serious negative reflection on the child's parents that brings great shame and condemnation to parents and even their society. Though low, childhood suicide rates in ages 1 to 14 years of age in the US are twice that of 26 other industrialized countries in a study looking at these statistics between 1990 and 1995: 0.55 per 100,000 for the US versus 0.27 for the other nations (67). This increase may reflect the widespread availability of firearms in the US, as noted earlier. Another study looked at World Health Organization data of suicide rates in 5 to 14 year olds from 1974 to 1999, as summarized in table 1 (68). Cultural factors may also include such issues as reduced social status of some persons (as reported in Chinese women versus men) (69) or social issues (alcohol consumption, attitude toward suicide) found in high suicide rates in young men in Finland, Baltic countries, Russian Federation, and New Zealand (16,70).

Children under the age of 3 years have almost no understanding of death (89); however, it is very important to remember that these children will react to grief they see adults experiencing. Because of this it is extremely important to provide very young children with concrete information about death to avoid confusion as they mature. Contrary to popular belief, talking to very young children about death and allowing them to attend funerals is not harmful. Unfortunately, American culture tends to avoid death; however, over 100 years ago death was much more a part of life in the United States for both children and adults. This avoidance of death in United States culture likely hastens children's development of an accurate concept of death.

PREVENTION AND ASSESSMENT OF CHILDHOOD SUICIDE

One major problem is that children rarely receive preventative treatment (26). However, by increasing understanding that prevention of childhood suicide involve primary and secondary issues, an increase in preventative treatment may occur. Primary prevention relates to preventing children from becoming suicidal by reducing or eliminating underlying risk factors; these factors include family dysfunction, poverty, depression, firearm availability, and abuse (see tables 3 and 4). Various governmental and public health programs can be developed in each country and local districts that teach awareness of this problem and encourage school-prevention programs, crisis intervention, telephone hotline services, school support for troubled or depressed students, and programs educating parents on raising their children based on parenting principles that minimize suicide potential in their children (2,17,20,54,71).

A multi-method approach is recommending in assessing for suicide risk among children (25). Such an assessment should include a thorough clinical interview, general and play observations, screening instruments, and psychological testing. Clinicians caring for children should screen them frequently for their state of mental health and seek to prevent these young patients from reaching a point of desperation where ending one's life seems the only way out of their problems. Clinicians should ask their pediatric patients and the parents or guardians about depression, school conflicts, bullying in school, abuse in the home or other places, availability of guns, and thoughts of suicide (72-74). Training in this area should be provided to clinicians caring for children since research suggests physicians on the front line of care feel inadequate to effectively provide such screening in their pediatric patients (75). Teachers can be encouraged to identify children in their classrooms with evidence of depression and refer for a comprehensive psychological evaluation. Teachers can also teach their students that some sadness is part of normal living and that help is available for those with depression and other mental health problems. The collaboration of medical, mental health, and school systems can be a useful tool in prevention and assessment.

Clinicians and counselors can emphasize the acquisition of coping skills by children while also seeking to raise the awareness of parents and one's community about childhood suicide and eliminating the means or methods of suicide (48). Clinicians can use handouts and posters in their offices that encourage discussion with children and their parents regarding the handling of emotions and sadness. Primary care settings are important places for such primary prevention since there is often a paucity of mental health counselors (as child psychiatrists) in many parts of the world along with a variety of barriers toward pediatric patients receiving mental health care. Early detection and treatment of depression and other psychiatric disorders reduces the risk of suicide (76). Guidelines for adolescent depression management can also be applied to children and these guidelines have been developed by researchers from the United Kingdom, Canada, and the United States with application now occurring in many primary pediatric care offices (77).

Secondary prevention involves early detection and management of children and adolescents with suicidal behavior. It is critical that medical students, pediatric residents, and clinicians in primary care who deal with children and adolescents learn how to effectively communicate with children so that sufficient interview skills are learned to identify children and adolescent at high risk for suicidal ideation and suicidal action. Direct interview of these children is important since relying on parental reports of their child's suicidal ideation is not reliable (78).

Most suicidal pediatric patients are relieved to know that a trusted clinician is asking about such issues and willing to help prevent them from killing themselves. Identifying such children and youth and helping them learn about the positive options of life are important steps to reducing and even eliminating childhood suicide in the world. Children who are contemplating suicide need protection from their cognitive immaturity, limited judgment skills, aged-related-impulsivity, and easy availability of suicide methods (46). The role of the primary care clinician is greatly emphasized by research that notes approximately 50% of persons under age 25 who committed suicide had contacted their clinician in the 3 months prior to committing suicide (79).

Prevention of childhood suicide is a collaborative approach between the family, school officials, primary care clinicians, and mental health professionals. It must be recognized that simply providing access to only one of these professional groups does not result in a significant decrease in suicide outcomes (80). Access to primary care is important as it is often the first place suicidal children come in contact with professionals who could provide help. It is also important to note that asking a child or adolescent about potential suicidal thoughts does not cause but can actually prevent suicidal action (81).

Medication (as anti-depressants) does not have a role to play in suicide prevention of children unless anti-psychotics are necessary to manage psychosis (82). Childhood and adolescent suicidal behavior can be influenced from a positive or negative perspective by greater social contexts, such as community role models, media coverage, and societal or ethnic taboos (83). Careful and persistent follow-up of suicidal behavior in children and adolescents is critical though tragically, research notes such follow-up is often not done (84-88). Caring for the family members and other affected individuals when a child does complete suicide is also important to reduce the tragic consequences in those left behind after the child dies (89).

CONCLUSION

Childhood suicide is a topic often ignored by society because of societal horror at the thought of childhood self-murder, denial by parents and clinicians, underlying religious and ethnic factors, confusing classification systems, and focus of research on older age cohorts. Worldwide data collected by the World Health Organization from 104 countries reveal suicide rates per 100,000 in the 5 to 14 year old cohort at 0.5 in females and 1.5 males. Suicide is the 5th leading cause of death in 5 to 14 year old persons and the 4th leading cause of death in the 1 to 19 year old cohort. A 100% increase in suicide in 10 to 14 years was reported in the United States from 1980 to 1996.

Etiologic factors behind childhood suicide include depression, extreme family and/or environmental dysfunction, positive family history for suicidal behavior in first degree relatives, schizophrenia, disruptive behavior, substance use, and others (see tables 3 and 4) (90,91). Suicide behavior as a child predicts suicidal behavior in later years when the child becomes an adolescent or young adult. Methods of childhood suicide include hanging, firearms (if available), poisoning, burning, running into traffic, motor vehicle accidents, and others (see table 5).

Primary prevention and identification of childhood suicidal ideation includes acknowledging that this phenomenon is real and seeking to reducing factors leading to the suicide (see tables 3 and 4). Secondary prevention includes early detection and management of children with suicidal behavior. Medication has no role in suicide prevention unless anti-psychotics are needed to manage schizophrenia. Clinicians and school officials must learn to screen children for potential suicide ideation as well as suicide action while working with other elements of society to reduce this preventable threat to our children.

REFERENCES

[1]   Merrick J. Foreword. In: Greydanus DE, Patel DR, Pratt HD, Calles JL, eds. Behavior pediatrics, 3rd ed. New York : Nova Sci, 2009:ix-xi.

[2]   Satcher W. National strategy for suicide prevention: Goals and objectives for action. Washington, DC: SAMHSA, CDC, NIH, HRSA, 2001.

[3]   United Nations Childrens Fund (UNICEF). The progress of nations, 1996. URL: www.unicef.org/pon96/insuicid.htm.

[4]   Mann JJ, Apter A, Bertolote J, et al. Suicide prevention strategies: A systemic review. JAMA 2005;294(16):2064-74.

[5]   World Health Organizataion. The second decade: Improving adolescent health and Development. Geneva: WHO, 2001.

[6]   Barker G. What about boys: A literature review in the health and development of adolescent boys. Geneva: WHO, Dept Child Adolesc Health, 2000.

[7]   Brown P. Choosing to die. A growing epidemic among the young. Bull World Health Org 2001;79(12):1175-7.

[8]   Diekstra R. Suicide and the attempted suicide: An international perspective. Acta Psychiatr Scand 1989;80(Suppl 354):1-24.

[9]   Keith CR. Adolescent suicide: Perspective on a clinical quandary. JAMA 2001;286:3126-7.

[10]   Centers for Disease Control and Prevention. Suicide and attempted suicide. MMWR 2004;53:471.

[11]   Pfeffer CR. Suicide in mood disordered children and adolescents. Child Adolesc Psychiatr Clin North Am 2002;11:639-48.

[12]   National Center for Injury Prevention and Control (NCIPC). Leading causes of death and fatal injuries: Mortality reports (online database). Atlanta, GA: CDC. URL: http://www.cdc.gov/ncipc/wisqars/

[13]   Pfeffer CR. The suicidal child. New York: Guilford, 1986.

[14]   Pfeffer CR. Suicide. In: Wiener JM, ed. Textbook of child and adolescent psychiatry, 2nd ed. Washington, DC: Am Psychiatr Press, 1997:727-38.

[15]   Shaffer D, Fisher P. The epidemiology of suicide in children and adolescents. J Am Acad Child Adolesc Psychiatry 1981;20:545-65.

[16]   Pelkonen M, Marttunen M: Child and adolescent suicide: Epidemiology, risk factors, and approaches to prevention. Pediatr Drugs 2003;5(4):243-65.

[17]   McClanahan KK, Omar HA. Suicidal behavior in children and adolescents. In: Greydanus DE, Patel DR, Pratt HD, Calles JL, eds. Behavior pediatrics, 3rd ed. New York : Nova Sci, 2009:300-25.

[18]   WHO Statistics. URL: http://www.who.int/mental_health/prevention/suicide/suicide_rates_chart/en/index.html

[19]   Service United States Public Health. The Surgeon General's call to action to prevent suicide. Washington, DC: US Public Health Serv, 1999.

[20]   Mishara BL. How the media influences children's conceptions of suicide. Crisis 2003;24(3):128-30.

[21]   Shaffer D, Pfeffer CR, Bernet W, et al. Practice parameters for the assessment and treatment of children and adolescents with suicidal behavior. J Am Acad Child Adolesc Psychiatry 2001;40:24S-51S.

[22]   Childer P, Wimmer M. The concept of death in early childhood. Child Dev 1971;42(4):1299-1301.

[23]   Mahon MM. Concept of death in a sample of Israeli kibbutz children. Death Stud 1999;23(1):43-59.

[24]   Ellis JB, Stump JE. Parents' perception of their children's death concept. Death Stud 2000;24(1):65-70.

[25]   Wise AJ, Spengler PM. Suicide in children younger than age fourteen: Clinical judgment and assessment issues. J Ment Health Couns 1997;19(4):318-35.

[26]   Pompili M, et al., Childhood suicide: A major issue in pediatric health care. Issues Compr Pediatr Nurs 2005;28:63-8.

[27]   Nguyen SP, Gelman SA. Four and 6-year olds' biological concept of death: The case of plants. Br J Dev Psychol 2002;20:495-513.

[28]   Willis CA. The grieving process in children: Strategies for understanding, educating, and reconciling children's perceptions of death. Early Childhood Educ J 2002;29(4):221-6.

[29]   Andrews JA, Lewinsohn PM. Suicidal attempts among older adolescents: Prevalence and co-occurrence with psychiatric disorders. J Am Acad Child Adolesc Psychiatry 1992;31(4):655-62.

[30]   Shaffer D. The epidemiology of teen suicide: an examination of risk factors. J Clin Psychiatry 1988;49:36-41.

[31]   Shaffer D, Garland A, Gould M, et al. Preventing teenage suicide: A critical review. J Am Acad Child Adolesc Psychiatry 1988;27(6): 675-87.

[32]   Greydanus DE, Calles J Jr. Suicide in children and adolescents. Prim Care Clin Off Pract 2007;34:259-73.

[33]   Pfeffer CR. Suicidal behavior in prepubertal children: from the 1980s to the new millennium. In: Maris RW, Canetto SS, McIntosh JL, Silverman MM, eds: Review of suicidology. New York: Guilford, 2000:159-69.

[34]   Nock MK, Kazdin AE: Examination of affective, cognitive, and behavioral factors and suicide-related outcomes in children and young adolescents. J Clin Child Adolesc Psychol 2002;31:48-58.

[35]   Gould MS, King R, Greenwalk S, et al. Psychopathology associated with suicidal ideation and attempts among children and adolescents. J Am Acad Child Adolesc Psychiatry 1998;37:915-23.

[36]   Workman CG, Prior M: Depression and suicide in young children. Issues Compr Pediatr Nurs 1997;20:125-32.

[37]   Kovacs M, Goldston D, Gatsonis C. Suicidal behaviors and childhood-onset depressive disorders: A longitudinal investigation. J Amer Acad Child Adolesc Psychiatry 1993;32:8-20.

[38]   O'Leary CC, Frank DA, Grant-Knight W, et al. Suicidal ideation among urban nine and ten year olds. Dev Behav Pediatr 2006; 27:33-9.

[39]   Jackson H, Nuttall RL. Risk for preadolescent suicidal behavior: An ecological model. Child Adolesc Soc Work J 2001;18:189-203.

[40]   Pfeffer CR. Childhood suicidal behavior: A developmental perspective. Psychiatr Clin North Am 1997;20:552-62.

[41]   Greening L, Stoppelbein L, Fite P, et al. Pathways to suicidal behaviors in children. Suicide Life Threat Behav 2008;38(1):35-45.

[42]   Livingston RL, Bracha HS. Psychotic symptoms and suicidal behavior in hospitalized children. Am J Psychiatyr 1992;149:1585-6.

[43]   Resch F, Parzer P, Brunner R. Self-mutilation and suicidal behaviour in children and adolescents: prevalence and psychosocial correlates: results of the BELLA study. Eur Child Adolesc Psychiatry 2008;17 (Suppl 1):92-8.

[44]   Agerbo E, Nordentoft M, Mortensen PB. Familial, psychiatric, and socioeconomic risk factors for suicide in young people: Nested case control Study. BMJ 2002;325:74-8.

[45] McGuffi jP, Marusic A, Farmer A. What can psychiatric genetics offer Suicidology? Crisis 2001;22:61-5.

[46] Dervic K, Brent DA, Oquendo MA. Completed suicide in childhood. Psychiatr Clin North Am 2008;31(2):271-91.

[47] Shaffer D. Suicide in childhood and adolescence. J Child Psychol Psychiatry 1974;15:275-91.

[48] Greydanus DE, Bacopoulou F, Tsalamanios E. Suicide in adolescents: A worldwide preventable tragedy. Keio J Med 2009;58(2):95-102.

[49] Pfeffer CR, Normandin L, Tatsuyuki K. Suicidal children grow up: Suicidal behavior and psychiatric disorder among relatives. J Am Acad of Child Adolesc Psychiatry 1994;33:1087-97.

[50] Pfeffer CR, Normandin L, Tatsuyuki K. Suicidal children grow up: Relations between family psychopathology and adolescents' lifetime suicidal behavior. J Nerv Ment Dis 1998;136:269-75.

[51] Brown J, Cohen P, Johnson JG, et al. Childhood abuse and neglect: Specificity of effects on adolescent and young adult depression and suicidal behavior. J Am Acad Child Psychiatry 1999;38:1490-6.

[52] Qin P, Mortensen PB, Pedersen CB. Frequent change of residence and risk of attempted and completed suicide among children and adolescents. Arch Gen Psychiatry 2009;66(6):628-32.

[53] Brezo J, Paris J, Vitaro F, et al. Predicting suicide attempts in young adults with histories of childhood abuse. Br J Psychiatry 2008; 193(2):134-9.

[54] Dunn MS, Goodrow B, Givens C, Austin S. Substance use behavior and suicide indicators among rural middle school students. J School Health 2008;78(1):26-31.

[55] Patel DR, Greydanus D. Homeless adolescents in the United States. Int Pediatrics 2002;17:71-5.

[56] US General Accounting Office. Children and youths: About 68,000 homeless and 186,000 in shared housing at any given time. Report to congressional committees. PEMD-89-14). Washington, DC: US General Accounting Office, 1989.

[57] Finkelhor D, Hotaling G, Sedlak A. Missing, abducted, runaway, and throwaway children in America: First report: Numbers and characteristics, National incidence studies. Executive summary. Washington, DC: US Dept Justice, 1990.

[58] Le Roux J. Street children in South Africa: Findings from interviews on the background of street children in Pretoria, South Africa. Adolescence 1996;31:423-31.

[59] Maris RW. Suicide. Lancet 2002;360:319-26.

[60] Anderson RN, Minino AM, Fingerhut LA, et al. Deaths: injuries 2001. Natl Vit Stat Rep 2004;52(21):1-86.

[61] Miller M, Azrael D, Hemenway D. Firearm availability and unintentional firearm deaths, suicides, and homicides among 5-15 year olds J Trauma 2002;52:267-75.

[62] Shenassa ED, Catlin SN, Buka SL. Lethality of firearms relative to other suicide methods: A population based study. J Epidemiol Comm Health 2003;57:120-24.

[63] Methods of suicide among persons 10-19 years-United States, 1992-2001. MMWR 2004;53:471-74.

[64] Berman Al, Jobes DA, Silverman MM. Adolescent suicide: Assessment and intervention. Washington, DC: Am Psychol Assoc, 2006.

[65] Pfeffer CR, Plutchik R, Mizruchi MS, et al. Suicidal behavior in child

[66] psychiatric inpatients, outpatients, and in non-patients. Am J Psychiatry 1986;143:733-8.

[67] Maharajh HD, Abdool PS. Culture and suicide. In: Merrick J, Zalsman G, eds. Suicidal behavior in adolescence: An international perspective. London: Freund, 2005:201-17.

[68] Johnson GR, Krug E, Potter LB: Suicide among adolescents and young adults: A cross-national comparison of 34 countries. Suicide Life Threat Behav 2000;30:74-82.

[69] Pritchard C, Hansen L. Child, adolescent and youth suicide or undetermined deaths in England and Wales compared with Australia, Canada, France, Germany, Italy, Japan, and the USA. In: Merrick J, Zalsman G, eds. Suicidal behavior in adolescence: An international perspective. London: Freund, 2005:19-32.

[70] Pritchard C. Suicide in the People's Republic of China categorized by age and gender: evidence of the influence of culture on suicide. Acta Psychiatr Scand 1996;93:362-7.

[71] Värnik A, Wasserman D. Suicides in the former Soviet republics. Acta Psychiatr Scand 1992;86:76-8.

[72] Riesch SK, Jacobson G, Sawdey L, et al. Suicide ideation among later

[73]   elementary school-aged youth. J Psychiatr Ment Health Nurs 2008; 15:263-77.

[74]   Greydanus DE, ed. Caring for your adolescent: Ages 12-21. Elk Grove, IL: Am Acad Pediatr, Bantam Books, 2003.

[75]   World Health Organization: Preventing suicide: A resource for counselors. Geneva: WHO, Dept Ment Health Subst Abuse, 2006.

[76]   Greydanus DE, Patel DR, Feinberg AN, Reddy V, Omar HA, eds. Handbook of clinical pediatrics. Singapore: World Imperial Press, 2010.

[77]   Jellinek J. Suicidal ideation in prepubertal childen: What does it mean? What to do? Dev Behav Pediatr 2006;27:40-1.

[78]   Goldney RD. Suicide prevention: A pragmatic review of recent studies. Crisis 2005;26:128-40.

[79]   Cheung AH, Zuckerbrot RA, Jensen PS, et al. The GLAD-PC Steering Group: Guidelines for adolescent depression in primary care (GLAD-PC): II. Treatment and ongoing management. Pediatrics 2007;129(5):e1313-26.

[80]   Kerr DCR, Owen LD, Pears KC, Capaldi DM. Prevalence of suicidal ideation among boys and men assessed annually from ages 9 to 29 years. Suicide Life Threat Behav 2008;38(4):390-402.

[81]   Hawton K, Houston K, Shepperd R. Suicide in young people. Study of 174 cases, aged under 25 years, based on coroners and medical records. Br J Psychiatr 1999;175:271-6.

[82]   Cotgrove S, Zirinski L, Black D, Weston D. Secondary prevention of attempted suicide in adolescence. J Adolescence 1995;18:569-77.

[83]   Elliott GR, Smiga SM. Mood disorders in children and adolescents. In: Greydanus DE, Patel DR, Pratt HD, eds. Behavioral pediatrics, 2nd ed. Lincoln, NA: iUniverse Publishers, 2006:589-617.

[84]   Calles J, Nazeer A. Psychosis. Int J Child Adolesc Dev, in press.

[85]   Harrington R. Depression, suicide, and deliberate self-harm in adolescence. Br Med Bull 2001;57:47-60.

[86]   Lewis G, Hawton K, Jones P. Strategies for preventing suicide. Br J Psychiatry 1997;171:351-4.

[87]   Greenhill LL, Waslick B. Management of suicidal behavior in children and adolescents. Psychiatr Clin North Am 1997;20: 641-66.

[88]   Knox KL, Caine ED. Establishing priorities for reducing suicides and its antecedents in the United States. Am J Publ Health 2005;95: 1898-1903.

[89]   Fergusson DM, Horwood LJ, Riddere EM, Beuatrais AL. Suicidal behavior in adolescence and subsequent mental health outcomes in young adulthood. Psychol Med 2005;35:983-93.

[90]   Gould MS, Greenberg T, Velting DM, Shaffer D. Youth suicide risk and preventive interventions: a review of the past 10 years. J Am Acad Child Adolesc Psychiatry 2003;42:386-405.

[91]   Berman AL, Jobes DA, Silverman MM. Survivors of suicide and postvention. Adolescent suicide: Assessment and intervention. Washington, DC: Am Psychol Assoc, 2006:335-64.

[92]   Greydanus DE, Shek D. Deliberate self-harm and suicide in adolescents. Keio J Med 2009;58:144-53.

[93]   Merrick J, Zalsman G, eds. Suicidal behavior in adolescence: An international perspective. London: Freund, 2005.

In: Children, Violence and Bullying
Editors: J Merrick, I Kandel and H A Omar

ISBN: 978-1-62948-342-9
© 2014 Nova Science Publishers, Inc.

Chapter 17

SUICIDE RISK FACTORS: VITAMIN D LEVELS

Tzvetelina Dimitrova[1,2], Elizabeth Streeten[3],
Muhammad M Tariq, MD[1,2] and Teodor T Postolache, MD[*1,2]*

[1]Mood and Anxiety Program, Department of Psychiatry, University of Maryland
School of Medicine, Baltimore, Maryland
[2]St Elizabeth's Hospital Residency Training Program, Washington DC
[3]Division of Endocrinology, Diabetes and Nutrition, University of Maryland
School of Medicine, Baltimore, Maryland, US

ABSTRACT

There is a growing evidence that established risk factors (worsening depression, anxiety, psychosis, and certain medical conditions) for suicidal self-directed violence are associated with low 25(OH)vitamin D (25(OH)D) levels. Very low 25(OH)D levels were very recently found to be associated with suicide. Moreover, suicidal behavior follows a seasonal pattern peaking in late spring. 25(OH)D levels are lower at the end of winter as a result of the lower production in the skin due to decreased surface exposure and duration of sun exposure, as well as low heat index and solar radiation. We hereby present a brief summary of the recently published peer-reviewed literature on the effects of vitamin D deficiency and its potential association with risk factors for suicide.

INTRODUCTION

Suicide is the second leading cause of death among the 15-35 year olds and the 10th leading cause of death worldwide (1-3). Suicide attempts are 2 to 3 times more likely than death by suicide (4). Most of the individuals (approximately 90%) who complete suicide are likely suffering and could be diagnosed with a psychiatric illness. About 9.5% of the population of the United States suffers from a mood disorder with 6.7% being diagnosed with major

* Correspondence: Teodor T Postolache, MD, Mood and Anxiety Program (MAP), Department of Psychiatry, University of Maryland School of Medicine, 685 West Baltimore Street, MSTF Building Room 930, Baltimore, MD 21201 United States. E-mail: tpostolache@psych.umaryland.edu.

depressive disorder. 18.1% are diagnosed with an anxiety disorder and 1.1% with a psychotic disorder, most commonly schizophrenia (1-3,5). The risk of suicidality increases in individuals with comorbid psychiatric disorders. In a study of adolescents and young adults with suicide attempts, 79% had co-morbid psychiatric disorders, with those diagnosed with three or more coexsiting disorders significantly more likely to attempt suicide as compared to healthy controls (4,6).

Vitamin D is essential for proper bone and mineral metabolism, growth, neurodevelopment and immune maturation. The organism replenishes its needs by synthesizing Vit. D in the skin under the influence of ultraviolet B light from the sun or through consuming Vit. D rich food such as fatty fish or supplemented dairy products. Residents at high latitudes, high altitudes or cold climate or limited skin exposure due to certain clothing choices could have insufficient amounts of the circulating 25-hydroxyvitamin D (25(OH)D, the metabolite that reflects vitamin D stores. If not adequately corrected with vitamin supplements, vitamin D deficiency will persist.

In this chapter we will discuss Vitamin D physiology and will summarize the recently published literature on the association between the serum 25(OH)D levels and suicide risk factors, such as 1) Psychiatric disorders, including anxiety, mood and psychotic disorders, 2) family history of suicide, including genetic and early developmental factors and 3) chronic medical illnesses. We will also assess the potential use of Vit. D in suicide prevention.

VITAMIN D

Table 1. Natural, enriched and supplemental sources of vitamin D

NATURAL, ENRICHED AND SUPPLEMENTAL SOURCES OF VITAMIN D	
Nutritional Sources	Vitamin D Content
NATURAL	
Salmon	
Fresh (3.5 oz)	600-1000 IU
Farmed (3.5 oz)	100-250 IU
Canned Tuna (3.6 oz)	250 IU
Shiitake Mushrooms	
Fresh (3.5 oz)	100 IU
Sun-Dried (3.5 oz)	1,600 IU
Yolk of an egg	20 IU
ENRICHED	
Milk (8 oz)	100 IU
Orange Juice (8 oz)	100 IU
Cereals (1 serving portion)	100 IU
SUPPLEMENTS	
Infant formula (8 oz)	100 IU
Ergocalciferol	50,000 IU/Capsule
Dristol liquid supplement	8000 IU/Ml
Over-Counter Multivitamin	400 IU
UV-B Radiation (5-10 min in sunlight)	3,000 IU

Vitamin D is a fat-soluble prohormone. It exists in two forms: vitamin D_3 (cholecalciferol) and vitamin D_2 (ergocalciferol). They differ in their side chain. Table 1 presents natural, enriched and supplemental sources of vitamin D.

7-dehydrocholesterol (7-DHC) is the cholesterol substrate normally present in skin keratinocytes. Upon exposure to natural or artificial ultraviolet (UVB) light, 7-DHC is converted to pre-vitamin D_3. The highest concentrations of 7-dehydrocholesterol are found in the epidermal layers of the skin. Pre-vit D_3 is then spontaneously isomerized to vitamin D_3 in the skin. The so formed Vit.D_3 can go down two pathways: it can be converted into active vitamin D_3 ($1,25(OH)_2D_3$) (calcitriol) within the skin or it can bind to proteins in the blood and be transported to the liver. Vitamin D_2 is obtained by irradiation of plant materials or foods. Both vitamin D_2 and D_3 undergo the same activation process involving first, 25-hydroxylation in the liver, followed by 1 alpha-hydroxylation in the kidney to make the biologically active compounds $1,25(OH)_2D_2$ and $1,25(OH)_2D_3$, respectively. Vit. D_3 can also be directly obtained from dietary sources (eg. fatty fish). Most studies focus on Vit. D_3 since the synthesis and action of $1,25(OH)_2D_3$ is well known. However there is little evidence to suggest that these two active forms differ in their mode of action. They bind to the same receptor, Vitamin D Receptor (VDR).

The cytochrome P-450 liver enzyme system is responsible for the first step in metabolic activation of vitamin D, creating 25(OH) D_3 (calcidiol) by the action of 25-hydroxylase. Then $25(OH)D_3$ is metabolized to $1,25(OH)_2D$ by the action of 1alpha-hydroxylase located in the inner mitochondria in the kidney cells. The synthesis of $1,25(OH)_2D$ by the renal 1alpha-hydroxylase is tightly regulated by parathyroid hormone (PTH). Although the kidneys are the primary source for serum $1,25(OH)_2D$, most other tissues can produce $1,25(OH)_2D$ locally, serving as a differentiating factor for these tissues.

Excretion

Both synthesis and degradation of vitamin D are tightly regulated. The catabolism of 25(OH)D to $24,25(OH)_2D$ is facilitated by 24-hydroxylase, a mitochondrial cytochrome P-450 enzyme. It also catalyzes $1,25(OH)_2D$ to $1,24,25(OH)_3D$. Both $24,25(OH)_2D$ and $1,24,25(OH)_3D$ are water soluble and are excreted after formation. 24-Hydroxylase is strongly induced in target cells by both 25(OH)D and $1,25(OH)_2D$ but it prefers $1,25(OH)_2D_3$ as a substrate. It is now known that this hydroxylation by 24-hydroxylase occurs in all vitamin D target tissues that also have 1-alpha hydroxylase function, including enterocytes, osteoblasts, keratinocytes and parathyroid cells.

UVB induced synthesis of active vitamin D ($1,25 (OH)_2D_3$) in the skin and its significance

Vit.D has a broad effect in the prevention of a variety of diseases including some malignancies. The synthesis of calcitriol in the epidermis under the influence of UV-B regulates important cellular functions in the keratinocytes and immunocompetent cells. Calcitriol and other vitamin D analogues have antiproliferative and prodifferentiating effects which are utilized in the treatment of psoriasis vulgaris. The antipsoriatic effect of the sunlight could in part be mediated by the UV-B induced synthesis of calcitriol. 1 alpha-hydroxylase is also present in brain tissue which suggests that the central nervous system (CNS) can synthesize the active form of vitamin D (7). Therefore serum 25(OH)D levels may also influence paracrine production of 1, 25 (OH)$_2$D directly in the CNS (8-10).

Mechanisms of action of vitamin D

Vitamin D metabolites circulate in the blood bound to vitamin D binding proteins. They bind to vitamin D receptors (VDRs) which are located in the nuclei of the target cells. This complex then forms a heterodimer with a retinoid receptor and acts as a transcription factor that modulates the gene expression of certain proteins like calcium binding protein or osteocalcin. This is a slow process that can take up to several days. In another pathway 1, 25(OH)$_2$D may influence calcium channels by binding to a plasma membrane receptor triggering a second messenger cascade mediated by Mitogen-Activated Protein (MAP) Kinase or Cyclic Adenosine Monophosphate (cAMP) (11). The effect of 1,25(OH)$_2$D on pancreatic beta cells, vascular smooth muscle, the intestines and monocytes is exerted through the rapid response of a second messenger.

Functions of vitamin D

One of the key functions of 1,25(OH)$_2$D is to increase calcium absorption from the intestine which is essential for longitudinal bone growth, osteoblast and osteoclast activity. This function is facilitated by both 1,25(OH)$_2$D and VDR (12). 1, 25 (OH)$_2$D is also responsible for up-regulatinggenes such as osteocalcin, osteopontin, calbindin, 24-hydroxylase and others (13). 1,25(OH)$_2$D has an antiproliferative effect and can down-regulate the expression of inflammatory markers such as IL-1 and IL-12 and decrease the levels of parathyroid hormone (PTH) and parathyroid hormone-related protein (PTHrP) through a negative vitamin D responsive element (13). There is a strong positive relationship between serum 25(OH)D and physiological performance (14) as the active metabolite of 1,25(OH)$_2$D is responsible for many biological functions. It stimulates calcium absorption, osteoclastic bone resorption and osteoblasts; it stimulates cell differentiation and the immune system and influences insulin secretion and muscular function. It decreases PTH secretion and the production of collagen type I.

Measuring vitamin D nutritional status

The blood levels of 1,25(OH)$_2$D are tightly regulated and depend on the body calcium requirements. An increased need leads to 1 alpha-hydroxylation, whereas an abundance of calcium results in 24-hydroxylation. 25(OH)D has a strong affinity for the vitamin D binding protein (DBP) which stabilizes the circulating form (15). Vitamin D nutritional status is measured by the serum calcidiol (25(OH)D) levels. At present there is no expert consensus on the optimal 25(OH)D level due to different interpretations and insufficient studies on the effect of Vit. D status on non-bone tissues.The most recent guidelines from the US Endocrine

Society define vitamin D deficiency as 25(OH)D less than 20 ng/ml (50nmol/l), vitamin D insufficiency as 25(OH)D between 21 and 29 ng/ml, and the safety margin to minimize the risk of hypercalcemia as 25(OH)D less than 100 ng/ml (250 nmol/l)(16).

Risk factors for vitamin D deficiency

Risk factors that lead to vitamin D deficiency include but are not limited to premature birth, highly melanized skin, low sunshine exposure, low dietary intake, obesity and malabsorbtion. Elderly individuals are prone to Vit. D deficiency due to less skin production. There is high prevalence of vitamin D deficiency among nursing home residents (up to 75%) and institutionalized patients (17). Prevalence is high in African Americans due to the effect of melatonin on skin permeability to ultraviolet light (17).

Consequences of vitamin D deficiency

The manifestations of deficiency may vary from hypocalcemic seizures, tetany in infancy and adolescence, when severe, to mineralization deficit creating florid rickets in toddlers or osteomalacia in adults. Vitamin D deficiency increases PTH secretion, causing bone resorption, contributing to the pathogenesis of osteoporosis and increasing the risk of hip fractures (18).

Vitamin D deficiency can be implicated in the pathogenesis of autoimmune disease. Inan animal model of multiple sclerosis the active metabolite $1,25(OH)_2D$ had a protective effect against autoimmune encephalomyelitis. By down-regulating the dendritic and Th-2 lymphocytes, Vitamin D metabolites could prevent the development of diabetes mellitus type I (19). Serum 25(OH)D was positively related to insulin sensitivity and negatively related to first and second phase insulin response (20). Vitamin D also influences pancreatic beta cell function.

Vitamin D has an effect on cancer development. Genes in prostate, colon, and breast cancer cells are positively or negatively regulated through the vitamin D receptor (13). $1,25(OH)_2D$ suppresses proliferation and stimulates differentiation of cancer cells. Several Ecological studies have demonstrated higher cancer prevalence or cancer mortality for colon and breast cancer in geographical areas of lower sunshine exposure.

Genetic and environmental triggers related to vitamin D and suicide

The manifestation of psychiatric disorders and many chronic diseases is the result of genetic predisposition and environmental factors. A genetic component has been implicated to the development of cancer (21-24), multiple sclerosis (25,26), fibromyalgia (27-29), depression (30,31), anxiety disorder (312 and schizophrenia (33-37), and all other risk factors for suicide. All this evidence suggests that there might be a genetic predisposition to suicidal ideation and suicidal behavior. Knowledge of genetic risk factors for suicidality could lead to early detection and prevention.

The effect on genes and environment on vitamin D status was demonstrated in a cross-sectional study of 1762 men and women. A multivariable-adjusted analyses of the results determined heritability of 25(OH)D serum levels to be 28.8%. 24% of the variability between individuals was explained by nongenetic components such as seasonality, supplements, cholesterol, waist circumference, and the use of hormonal replacement therapy in women.

A compounding body of evidence demostrates the role of vitamin D in brain proliferation, differentiation, neurotrophism, neuroprotection, neurotransmission, and neuroplasticity. In a recent review of the literature, the role of Vitamin D in various psychiatric disorders could be explained with its effect on fetal programming epigenetics and gene regulation (38). It also upregulates genes involved in DNA repair and raises the seizure threshold (39), an important implication since epilepsy is associated with high level of suicidality (40).

CHRONIC MEDICAL ILLNESS

As we already pointed out the role of chronic medical illnesses to the predisposition, precipitation and perpetuation of suicidal behavior (1). Vitamin D potentially plays a vital link between health impairments and suicide.

Autoimmune diseases

There is an increased risk of suicidality in patients suffering from autoimmune diseases (1) but until recently role of Vitamin D in it has not been well researched (25,26). Vitamin D plays the role of an immune regulator of both the innate and adaptive immune system (41,42). Among other effects, it inhibits the proliferation of T-cells through decreasing the secretion Th1 cytokine and suppresses the proliferation of B-cells. As a result, symptoms of autoimmune diseases such as encephalomyelitis, rheumatoid arthritis, systemic lupus erythematosus, and multiple sclerosis could be suppressed with a calcium-rich diet and Vit. D supplements as reported by Deluca et al and Royal III et al (25,26). VDR cites congregate near lymphocytes. They are also found in the parathyroid gland, in the pituitary cells and hypothalamus. All those areas are implicated in mood regulation, therefore it may be extrapolated that if vitamin D hormone levels are affected in autoimmune disease, then a likely increased risk for suicidal behavior may be evident.

Walter Royal III et al (2009) reported that individuals with lower 25(OH)D levels were at a high risk of developing multiple sclerosis (MS). Vitamin D deficiency is associated with higher prevalence, relapse rate and progression of multiple sclerosis. The relationship between limited sunlight and MS is well known. Those findings suggest that biological and environmental exposure to vitamin D is necessary to maintain adequate T-cell modulation. However in a recently published study of an animal model of MS, the authors concluded that the ability of vitamin D to ameliorate neuroinflammation is dependent on the stage of development. The authors concluded that childhood and adolescence are the best target for the most effective preventive treatment of MS (43).

Based on the above data the regulation of vitamin D levels in autoimmune diseases with high risk of suicidality is warranted. Although studies in humans of those effects are still limited, a proper Vit. D status through exposure to sunlight, dietary and nutritional supplements should be encouraged.

Fibromyalgia

Fibromyalgia is a rheumatologic disorder (33) characterized by widespread pain at multiple trigger-points throughout the body as a result of hypersensitivity of the central nervous system (CNS) (27,28). Although 10-12% of the world population complains of chronic pain, only 2% of those meet the criteria for Fibromyalgia. 30-60% of fibromyalgia patients have co-occurring depression. Both disorders frequently coexist and are also strong predictors of one another (28). Pain is a negative predicting factor for relapse in depression and decreases the chance of remission by about 38% (44). Patients diagnosed with fibromyalgia were 4.3 times more likely to develop major depressive disorder and 4.7 times more likely to develop anxiety disorders. Recent evidence suggests that neuropathic pain, mood and anxiety disorders share common pathways and triggers (28). They tend to disrupt the circuits' neuroendocrine and neuroimmune regulatory systems which can lead to inflammatory responses by T-cells, further interfering with the feedback autoregulation of the hypothalamic-pituitary-adrenal axis and immune system.

As VDRs may be localized on pituitary, hypothalamus and hippocampus target cells, (25) Vit. D may play a role in functions pertaining to the neuroendocrine and neuroimmune systems involved in behavioral, mood and anxiety regulation. Future studies are needed to further investigate the proposed connection between vitamin D and neurological pathways associated with certain conditions predisposing or triggering suicide. If such relationship does exist, then there will be neurophysiologic support for an overall connection between suicide and vitamin D levels.

Cancer

There is an increased risk of suicide in cancer patients (1). There is a much higher risk for cancers such as colorectal cancer (35), prostate cancer (22), breast cancer (22,23) and squamous cell carcinoma of the head and neck cancer (24) in people with Vit. D deficiency. Death rates from breast cancer were also found to be associated with vitamin D exposure (23). In a meta-analysis of 31 studies the Fok1 VDR polymorphism was associated with breast cancer risk both in the general population and in Caucasians. The ApaI polymorphism might be associated with breast cancer risk in Asian populations (45).

A limited number of studies have investigated the Vit. D status in children with cancer. In a recent study (46) the prevalence of hypovitaminosis was found to be 72% with 43% considered deficient and 8% severely deficient. After adjusting for other characteristics (AOR=3.23; 95% CI, 1.11-9.40) hypovitaminosis was found to play a significant role in the outcome in children 6 year old and above.

PSYCHIATRIC DISORDERS

Mood and anxiety disorders

Patients with anxiety and panic disorders are at increased risk for suicide (47,48). Animal models of anxiety establish a negative correlation between 25(OH)D levels and anxiety (22). There are no sufficient studies in humans but since the vitamin D-VDR system in mice is similar to that of humans (31) it may be extrapolated that these results will be replicated in the human model as well.

Mortality risk for suicide in patients with depression is many times the risk of the general population (49). More than half of all people who die by suicide meet the criteria for depressive disorder at the time of the attempt (50). A number of studies explore the implication of vitamin D deficiency as a cause of or a risk factor for developing depression and its pontial use in the treatment of depression (51).

Consistently, a recent study of 65 adolescents ages 12-18 found that boys with MDD have lower bone mineral density (BMD), especially in the hip in comparison to healthy controls after adjusting for body mass and maturity. This association was not observed in girls (52).

Further studies controlling for calcium and vitamin D intake, separately and in tandem, while also broadening the sample size, using a more diverse population and controlling for other confounding factor are need to provide more definitive results on the effects of vitamin D supplementation on symptoms of depression.

Lansdowe and Provost hypothesized that Vitamin D3 supplementation will improve positive affect in subjects (30). They compared the effects of three batches of vitamin combinations. The first group took ten capsules of 10,000 IU of vitamin A a day with no vitamin D3; the second group was administered five capsules of 9,000 IU of vitamin A a day with five capsules of 400 IU of vitamin D3 a day; and the third group was given ten capsules of 8,000 IU of vitamin A a day and ten capsules of 800IU of vitamin D3 a day. The Positive and Negative Affect Schedule (PANAS), self-reported scores based upon positive adjectives (e.g. enthusiasm, interest and determined) and negative adjectives (e.g. scared, afraid and upset,) was used to measure changes in affect. Results demonstrated improvement in positive affect in both groups receiving Vit. D supplements. However the study was conducted in healthy volunteers, not in patients with depression. There might have been a different outcome if the samples were more representative of those in need of vitamin D supplementation.

Future studies of vitamin D deficient depressed patients are needed to better assess the effects of vitamin D supplementation on mood. Moreover, the use of more objective scales would likely provide more robust results since many individuals tend to either inflate or deflate the report of their current emotional state and therefore skewing the results.

In a study of 89 patients suffering from depression, schizophrenia or alcoholism (25, 34, and 30 subjects respectively), Schneider et al (48) measured both 25(OH)D and 1,25(OH)$_2$D-hydroxyvitamin D3 . The results demonstrated significantly lower levels of both metabolites in both schizophrenic and depressed patients than healthy controls (p<0.01, both, Mann-Whitney U-Test.) (53). The diminished levels of 25(OH)Dand 1,25(OH)$_2$Ds in depressed patients supports the hypotheses that vitamin D has an implication on the neurological pathways associated with mood regulation.

Altered levels of Vitamin D metabolites and parathyroid hormone (PTH) have been reported in depression. In a large population-based cohort study of elderly individuals, Hoogendijk et al (34), found that the 14% lower levels of 25(OH)D in persons with minor and major depressive disorder were statistically significant (P < .001) compared to the levels in the control individuals. Levels of PTH were 5% and 33% higher (P = .003).

Further studies are needed to illuminate more specifically which interactions between vitamin D and PTH levels have an effect on the expression of depressed symptoms. Since PTH regulates levels of $1,25(OH)_2D$, correcting vitamin D deficiency may reduce the risk of depression by better inhibiting the production of PTH.

Bipolar patients have increased suicide risk (1). About 10-15% of patients with bipolar disorder die by suicide shortly after being diagnosed (54). Bipolar patients frequently have other comorbid conditions such as substance abuse (55) and anxiety disorder 56) associated with risk of suicide. Bipolar patients with Generalized Anxiety Disorder (GAD) and other anxiety disorders are at high risk for current and lifetime suicide ideation (57). Considering the fact that 62.5% of patients with bipolar disorder were found to have a co-morbid anxiety disorder (58), there is a probability that both disorders may share psychoneurophysiological pathways inducing this common co-morbidity (59). The implications of vitamin D on mood dysregulation or anxiety may be related to either a trait (genetic, developmental factors) or state (by exacerbation of these conditions due to low levels).

The effect of the FOKI polymorphism of Vitamin D receptor (VDR) on the relative expressions of the dopamine D1 receptor gene and its significance for the development of bipolar disorder was studied in a case-control study of 196 patient with schizophrenia, 119 patients with bipolar disorder and 192 healthy individuals. The frequency of "ff" genotype was more common in patients with bipolar disorders compared to the healthy control group (Odds ratio=1.84, 95% CI; 0.81 to 4.17) with increased relative risk (Relative risk=1.31, CI 95%; 0.86 to 1.99). In addition, the "ff" genotype was associated with lower expression of dopamine D1 receptor gene (60).

Seasonal affective disorder (SAD) is a group of mood disordersthat presents with recurring depressive symptoms occurring during a particular season, most commonly winter, and remitting spontaneously at the end of the season. One of the best studied treatment modalities for the condition is visible bright light (with no UV). Some of the recent research supports the hypothesis that Vit. D deficiency may play a role in the exacerbation of SAD.

Basile et al (61) studied a cohort of 100 infants born at latitude 32°72'. They determined that the levels of 25(OH)D of the cohort born between April 1 and October 31 were 7.2 ng/mL higher than the levels of the cohort born between November 1 and March 31.

In a randomized clinical trial (N=15) by Gloth et al (1999) the eight subjects who received 100,000IU of vitamin D expressed significant improvement in all outcome scales (r^2=0.26; *p*=0.05) compared to the seven subjects treated with phototherapy who showed no significant change in depression scale measures (62). However due to the limited number of participants, the reported positive relationship between 25(OH)D levels and improved depression scale scores could not be generalized to the population of patients with SAD.

A study by Oren et al (1994) compared the levels of $1,25 (OH)_2D$ in winter in 15 subjects with SAD (six men and nine women) and 15 controls who were matched for age and gender while "on" and "off" light treatment. There was no statistical difference between groups.

However the small sample and the inadequate attention to dietary and other vitamin D supplements may have confounded the results.

Similarly to SAD, epidemiological studies in many countries show a seasonal pattern of suicide with increased rates towards the end of winter and spring when 25(OH)D levels are lowest. Further research is needed to determine the effect of vitamin D deficiency on the predisposition to SAD or the development of symptoms during fall and winter.

Schizophrenia

Schizophrenia is one of the most common causes of suicide (1). The life-time risk of suicide is approximately 4.9%in patients with schizophrenia with a majority of patients committing suicide usually soon after being diagnosed (63). The risks of suicide is greatly increased by the presence of substance abuse or other co-morbid mental disorders (50). In this section we will discuss the role of Vit. D in the pathogenesis of schizophrenia. Symptoms of depression are common in schizophrenia and we already had a chance to present the association of Vit. D with depression.

A number of studies have shown that individuals born in winter and spring as well as at high latitudes are at an increased risk for developing schizophrenia (32-34) providing a potential relationship between developmental vitamin D deficiency and schizophrenia. Furthermore, the children of immigrants with high pigmented skin who moved to colder climates had a higher incidence of developing schizophrenia compared to the lightly melanized native born children (64). This correlation is preserved in the second generation of immigrants with highly pigmented skin as well (65,66). As we pointed out, similar environmental factors play a role in the development of Vit. D deficiency: It is more common in winter and spring, at high altitudes, in individuals with high melanin in the skin and in those born in urban versus rural locations (67,68). Vit. D deficiency is common among African American women of childbearing age (approximately 40%) (70) and could reach 80% in some female populations (64,71). Highly concentrated melanin in the skin, compounded with living in cold climates, tends to increase the development of Vit. D deficiency (69)

Some reports show a link between a reduced risk of schizophrenia in male offsprings of mothers who took Vit. D supplements during pregnancy. Feron et al (72) studied this hypothesis by measuring the 25(OH)D levels taken during the third trimester of pregnancy of banked maternal sera as part of the National Collaborative Perinatal Project (72,73). This study included 15,721 surviving offspring of a sample of 11,971 women. Of those, 119 offsprings were diagnosed with an adult psychotic disorder (0.76%). 39 offsprings met the DSM criteria for schizophrenia or schizoaffective disorder depressed type (0.25%). 27 of these 39 were randomly selected. Each case subject was matched by two healthy controls by gender, ethnicity, and date of birth. 25(OH)D levels, the most appropriate indicator of vitamin D status, were significantly lower in winter and spring than during summer and autumn (mean ng/ml SD= 8.18 and 25.59ng/mL, SD= 10.02 respectively; t=-4.50, p<0.001) (73). Although the study found no significant differences in third semester maternal 25(OH)D levels between cases and matched controls (OR=0.98, 95% CI 0.92-1.05), the African American mothers of patients with schizophrenia, had on average significantly lower levels of 25(OH)D compared to Caucasian mothers (11.76 ng/mL, SD= 6.48 and 22.06ng/mL, SD=

9.80 respectively, t (75)=4.46, p<0.001). In addition, the study demonstrated a trend level difference when African Americans were examined separately (Case Mean= 8.44 (SD=3.25); Control Mean= 13.42 (SD=7.13); OR=0.78, 95% CI 0.55-1.08) which opens the possibility that factors associated with skin melanization may influence the putative association between vitamin D and schizophrenia. There was no significant difference (OR=1.01, 95% CI 0.94-1.10) within the Caucasian subjects. In a post hoc analysis of maternal 25(OH)D levels less than 15ng/mL (vitamin D deficiency) of cases versus controls (70), 12 of 26 mothers of cases and 15 of 51 mothers of controls had levels below 15 ng/ml (OR= 2.06, 95% CI 0.77-5.47). Although not a statistically significant difference, it represented a two fold-increase in the risk of schizophrenia in these offspring.

In a recently published article, (74) the authors tested whether maternal prenatal 25(OH)D levels are associated with risk of psychotic experiences. They took a community sample of 2047 participants. Maternal prenatal 25(OH)D concentrations were assessed with tandem mass spectroscopy. Psychotic experiences of the offsprings were assessed at age 18 years using a semi-structured clinical interview. 177 cohort members reported suspected or definite psychotic experiences with 29 of those meeting the criteria for a psychotic disorder at age 18. The association between psychotic experiences and maternal 25(OH)D concentrations as quartiles (p=0.85 hypothesis test of general association versus no association across the quartiles) or as a continuous variable (p=0.89) were not statistically significant.

In a study of 50 patients with schizophrenia, 33 patients with major depression and 50 controls with no major psychopathology Itzhaky et al. (75) reported that the lowest serum 25(OH)D concentrations were found in patients with schizophrenia (15.0 +/- 7.3 ng/ml) followed by patients with depression (19.6 +/- 8.3 ng/ml) and then controls (20.2 +/- 7.8 ng/ml, P < 0.05). However, there was no correlation between disease activity, as measured by the PANSS score, and 25(OH)D levels.

Schneider et al (71) assessed the levels of 25(OH)D, 1,25(OH)$_2$D- calcium, phosphate and PTH levels in patients with schizophrenia, major depression disorder, and alcoholism versus healthy controls. The levels of 25(OH)D and 1,25(OH)$_2$D were significantly lower (p<0.02) in all groups of psychiatric patients compared to normal controls. Patients with schizophrenia and patients with depression had significantly lower 1,25(OH)$_2$D levels than controls (p<0.01) and as compared to patients with alcoholism (p<0.02 and p<0.05 respectively). However, there were no significant differences of vitamin D metabolite levels between the groups of psychiatric patients. There were no differences in the levels of phosphate, calcium and PTH.

In addition to a possible epidemiological link between vitamin D deficiency and risk for schizophrenia, there is also evidence of structural and molecular brain abnormalities suggesting an association between schizophrenia and developmental vitamin D deficiency.

Enlargement of lateral ventricles and low levels of plasma nerve growth factor are both associated with vitamin D deficiency and schizophrenia (58). There were many similarities between the abnormalities found in the genomic and proteomic work in adult rats born to vitamin D-deficient dams and patients with schizophrenia (61,62). Synapsin II mRNA that codes for a protein involved in the synaptogenesis and neurotransmitter regulation as well as protein levels were reduced in the brains of adult rats that were deprived of vitamin D during development (7). Microarray analyses of the prefrontal cortex of patients with schizophrenia alsoshowed consistent robust decrease in Synapsin II mRNA (73).

There is sufficient evidence to suggest that vitamin D deficiency is implicated in the pathogenesis of schizophrenia. Taking in consideration the fact that schizophrenia is one of the leading psychiatric diseases associated with suicide worldwide, the potential role vitamin D deficiency plays in its development may prove an indirect causative factor of suicidality. Further studies are needed to determine if vitamin D supplementation can lead to a reduction of suicide rate.

SUICIDE

To assess the association between 25(OH)D levels and suicide, NIH investigators studied active duty personnel in a prospective, nested, case-control study measuring serum levels of 25(OH) D drawn within 24 months of the suicide using samples stored in the Department of Defense Serum Repository from the 2002-2008 period. All verified suicide cases (n = 495) were matched to the same number of controls by rank, age and sex. The results showed that low 25(OH)D levels were common in active duty service members with more than 30% of all subjects having 25(OH)D values below 20 ng/mL. And although the average serum concentration of 25(OH)D showed no difference between suicide cases and controls, the risk estimates indicated that subjects in the lowest octile of season-adjusted 25(OH)D (<15.5 ng/mL) had the highest risk of suicide (76). This is an important conceptual finding, as it strongly suggests that the relationship between 25(OH) D levels and suicide is nonlinear, with a threshold effect that is localized in the "deficiency", rather than "insuficiency" domain or normal domain. In other words, higher levels beyond deficiency are not adding additional protection.

ADEQUATE INTAKE OF VITAMIN D

The dietary needs for vitamin D are not well studied and still remain the subject of controversy among experts (73-79). According to current guidelines by the Institute of Medicine, adequate intake of vitamin D for adults up to 70 years of age is600 IU/day, and 800 IU/day for adults over 70 years. Daily vitamin D intake should not exceed 10,000 IU/day (80). All individuals with Vit. D deficiency whether symptomatic or not should be treated with vitamin D supplements as Stoss therapy or daily or weekly oral regimens, combined with calcium supplements, if dietary calcium is inadequate. There is an increased consensus that routine supplementation should start even from the newborn period with prevention by sensible sunlight exposure, food fortification and routine supplementation.

CONCLUSION

There is a need for further exploration of the association between Vitamin D deficiency and suicidal self directed violence as Vitamin D deficiency contributes to multiple diseases identified as risk factors for suicide. More specifically, seasonal fluctuations of 25(OH)D levels with troughs in late winter and early spring might be studied in relationship to exacerbation of mood disorders in spring and well replicated seasonal peaks in suicide in spring. The reported association between suicide and Vitamine D deficiency requires replication. Finally, considering the high rates of suicide and Vit. D deficiency in the elderly, normalizing 25(OH)D levels in the elderly, especially of those residing in nursing homes, may not only improve mood and wellbeing, but also reduce mortality.

ACKNOWLEDGMENTS

Supported by a grant from the American Foundation for Sucidide Prevention (PI Postolache).

APPENDIX

The vitamin D content found in naturally rich, dietary enriched or fortified foods and supplements as measured in international units (IU). From: Holick 2007. (64)

REFERENCES

[1] Hawton K, van Heeringen K. Suicide. Lancet 2009;373: 1372-81.
[2] Beautrais A. Suicidality in pre-adolescence and early adulthood is associated with psychosocial and psychiatric problems in young adulthood. Evid Based Ment Health 2005;8:48.
[3] Mann JJ. Neurobiology of suicidal behaviors. Neuroscience 2003;4: 819-28.
[4] Wunderlich U, Bronisch T, Wittchen HU. Comorbidity patterns in adolescents and young adults with suicide attempts. Eur Arch Psychiatry Clin Neurosci 1997;248:87-95.
[5] National Institute of Mental Health (NIHM). The Numbers Count: Mental Disorders in America. URL: http://www.nimh.nih.gov/health/publications/the-numbers-count-mental-disorders-in-america/index.shtml.
[6] Boden JM, Furgusson DM, Horwood LJ. Anxiety disorders and suicidal behaviors in adolescence and young adulthood: findings from a longitudinal study. Psychol Med 2006;37:431-40.
[7] Eyles DW, Feron F, Cui X, Kesby JP, Harms LH, Ko P, McGrath JJ, Burne TH. Developmental vitamin D deficiency causes abnormal brain development. Psychoneuroendocrinology. 2009 Dec;34 Suppl 1:S247-57.
[8] Hosseinpour F, Wikvall K. Porcine microsomal vitamin D(3) 25-hydroxylase (CYP2D25). Catalytic properties, tissue distribution, and comparison with human CYP2D6. J Biol Chem 2000;275(44):34650-5.
[9] Sutherland MK, Somerville MJ, Yoong LK, Bergeron C, Haussler MR, McLachlan DR. Reduction of vitamin D hormone receptor mRNA levels in Alzheimer as compared to huntington hippocampus: Correlation with calbindin-28k mRNA levels. Brain Res Mol Brain Res 1992;13(3):239-50.
[10] Zehnder D, Williams MC, McNinch RW, Howie AJ, Stewart PM, Hewison M. Extrarenal expression of 25-hydroxyvitamin d(3)-1 alpha-hydroxylase. J Clin Endocrinol Metab 2001;86(2):888-94.
[11] Feldman D, Pike JW, Glorieux FH,eds. Vitamin D, second ed. London: Elsevier, Academic Press, 2005.
[12] Panda DK, Miao D, Bolivar I, Li J, Huo R, Hendy GN, Goltzman D. Inactivation of 25-hydroxyvitamin D 1a-hydroxylase and vitamin D receptor demonstrates independent and interdependent effects of calcium and vitamin D on skeletal and mineral homeostasis. J Biol Chem 2004;279:16754-66.

[13]   Nagpal S, Na S, Rathanchalan R. Noncalcemic actions of vitamin D receptor ligands. Endocrine Rev 2005;26:662-87.

[14]   Wicherts IS, van Schoor NM, Boeke AJP, Lips P.Vitamin D deficiency and neuromuscular performance in the Longitudinal Aging Study Amsterdam (LASA). J Bone Miner Res 2005;20(Suppl 1):S35.

[15]   Cooke NC, Haddad JG. Vitamin D binding protein. In: Feldman D, Glorieux FH, Pike JW, eds. Vitamin D. San Diego, CA: Academic , 1997:87-101.

[16]   Holick MF, Binkley NC, Bischoff-Ferrari HA, et al. Evaluation, treatment, and prevention of vitamin D deficiency: an Endocrine Society clinical practice guideline. J Clin Endocrinol Metab 2011; 96:1911–1930.

[17]   Holick MF. McCollum award lecture. Vitamin D: New horizons for the 21st century. Am J Clin Nutr 1994;60:619-30.

[18]   Lips P, Duong T, Oleksik AM, Black D, Cummings S, Cox D, et al. A global study of vitamin D status and parathyroid function in postmenopausal women with osteoporosis: baseline data from the multiple outcomes of raloxifene evaluation clinical trial. J Clin Endocrinol Metab 2001;86:1212-21.

[19]   Mathieu C, Gysemans C, Guilietti A, Bouillon R. Vitamin D and diabetes. Diabetologica 2005;48:1247-57.

[20]   Chiu KC, Chu A, Go VL, Saad MF. Hypovitaminosis D is   associated with insulin resistance and beta cell dysfunction. Am J Clin Nutr 2004;79:820-5.

[21]   Grant WB, Mohr SB. Ecological studies of ultraviolet B, vitamin D and cancer since 2000. Ann Epidemiol 2009;19:446-54.

[22]   Garland CF, Garland FC, Gorham ED, Lipkin M, Newmark H, Mohr SB. The role of vitamin D in cancer prevention. Am J Public Health 2006;96(2):252-61.

[23]   Garland CF, Gorham ED, Mohr SB, Grant WB, Giovannucci EL, Lipkin M, et al. Vitamin D and prevention of breast cancer: pooled analysis. J Steroid BiochemMolecular Biol 2007;103:708-11.

[24]   Lui Z, Caldeeron JI, Zhang Z, Sturgis EM, Spitz MR, Wei Q, Polymorphisms of vitamin D receptor gene protect again the risk of head and neck cancer. Pharmacogenetics Geonomics 2005;15:159-65.

[25]   Deluca H, Cantorna M. Vitamin D: its role and uses in immunology. FASEB J 2001;15:2579-85.

[26]   Royal W 3rd, Mia Y, Li H, Naunton K.Peripheral blood regulatory T cell measurements correlate with serum vitamin D levels in patients with multiple sclerosis.J Neuroimmunol. 2009 Aug 18;213(1-2):135-41.

[27]   Mazza M, Mazza O, Pomponi M, DiNicola M, Padua L, Vicini M, et al.What is the effect of selective serotonin reuptake inhibitors on temperament and character in patients with fibromyalgia? Comprehensive Psychiatry 2009;30:240-4.

[28]   Maletic V, Raison CL. Neurobiology of depression, fibromyalgia and neuropathic pain. Frontiers Biosci 2009;14:5291-5338.

[29]   Assumpcao A, Cavalcante AB, Capela CE, Sauner JF, Chalot SD, Periera CAB, et al. Prevalence of fibromyalgia in low socioeconomic status population. BMC Musculoskeletal Disord 2009;10:1-20.

[30]   Lansdowne ATG, Provost ST. Vitamin D3 enhances mood in healthy subjects during winter. Psychopharmachology 1998;135:819-23.

[31]   Lipska B, Weinberger D.To model a psychiatric disorder in animals: schizophrenia as a reality test. Neuropsychopharmacology 2000;23(3):223-39.

[32]   Torrey EF, Miller J, Rawlings R, Yolken RH. Seasonality of births in schizophrenia and bipolar disorder: a review of the literature. Schizophr Res 1997;28:1-38.

[33]   Saha S, Chant DC, Welham JL, McGrath JJ. The incidence and prevalence of schizophrenia varies with latitude. Acta Psychiatr Scand 2006;114:36-9.

[34]   Hoogendijk WJG, Lips P, Dik MG, Deeg DJ, Beekman ATF, Penninx BWJH. Depression is associated with decreased 25-hydroxyvitamin D and increased parathyroid hormone levels in older adults. Arch Gen Psychiatry 2008;65(5):508-12.

[35]   Sachan A, Gupta R, Das V, Agarwal A, Awasthi PK, Bhatia V. High prevalence of vitamin D deficiency among pregnant women and their newborns in northern India. Am J Clin Nutr 2005;81:1060-4.

[36]   Mc Grath J, Eyles D, Mowry B, Yolken R, Buka S. Low maternal vitamin D as a risk factor for schizophrenia: a pilot study using banked sera. Schizophrenia Res 2003;63:73-8.

[37]   Geerlings SW, Beekman AT, Deeg DJ, Twisk JW, Van Tilburg W. Duration and severity of depression predict mortality in older adults in the community. Psychol Med 2002;32(4):609-18.

[38]   Hossein-Nezhad A, Holick MF. Vitamin d for health: a global perspective. Mayo Clin Proc. 2013 Jul;88(7):720-55. doi: 10.1016/j.mayocp.2013.05.011. Epub 2013 Jun 18.

[39]   Cannell JJ. Autism, will vitamin D treat core symptoms? Med Hypotheses. 2013 Aug;81(2):195-8.

[40]   Andres M Kanner, MD. Suicidality and Epilepsy: A Complex Relationship That Remains Misunderstood and Underestimated. Epilepsy Curr. 2009 May; 9(3): 63–66.

[41]   Bikle DD. What is new in vitamin D: 2006-2007. Curr Opin Rheumatol 2007;19:383–388.

[42]   Van Etten E, Mathieu C. Immunoregulation by 1,25-dihydroxyvitamin D3: basic concepts. J Steroid Biochem Mol Biol 2005;97:93–101.

[43]   Adzemovic MZ, Zeitelhofer M, Hochmeister S, Gustafsson SA, Jagodic M. Efficacy of vitamin D in treating multiple sclerosis-like neuroinflammation depends on developmental stage. Exp Neurol. 2013 Aug 13. pii: S0014-4886(13)00242-2. doi: 10.1016/j.expneurol.2013.08.002. [Epub ahead of print]

[44]   Goodwin FK, Jamison KR. Manic-depressive illness: bipolar disorders and recurrent depression, 2nd ed. New York: Oxford Univ Press, 2007.

[45]   Wang J, He Q, Shao YG, Ji M, Bao W. Associations between vitamin D receptor polymorphisms and breast cancer risk. Tumour Biol. 2013 Jul 31. [Epub ahead of print]

[46]   Helou M, Ning Y, Yang S, Irvine P, Bachmann LM, Godder K, Massey G. Vitamin D Deficiency in Children With Cancer. J Pediatr Hematol Oncol. 2013 Jul 3. [Epub ahead of print]

[47]   Harris EC, Barraclough B. Excess mortality of mental disorder. Br J Psychiatry 1998;173:11-53.

[48]   Schneider B, Weber B, Frensch A, Stein J, Fritze J. Vitamin D in schizophrenia, major depression and alcoholism. J Neural Transm 2000;107:839-42.

[49]   Cavanagh JTO, Carson AJ, Sharpe M, Lawrie SM. Psychological autopsy studies of suicide: a systematic review. Psychol Med 2003;33:395-405.

[50]   Hollis BW, Wagner CL, Kratz A, Sluss PM, Lewandrowski KB. Normal serum vitamin D levels. New Engl J Med 2005;352:515-6.

[51]   Howland RH. Vitamin D and depression. J Psychosoc Nurs Ment Health Serv. 2011 Feb;49(2):15-8.

[52]   Fazeli PK, Mendes N, Russell M, Herzog DB, Klibanski A, Misra M. Bone density characteristics and major depressive disorder in adolescents. Psychosom Med. 2013 Feb;75(2):117-23.

[53]   Harris EC, Barraclough B. Excess mortality of mental disorder. Br J Psychiatry 1998;173:11-53.

[54]   Khan A, Leventhal RM, Khan S, Brown WA. Suicide risk in patients with anxiety disorders: a meta-analysis of the FDA database. J Aff ect Disord 2002;68:183-90.

[55]   Cassidy F, Ahearn EP, Carroll BJ. Substance abuse in bipolar disorder. Bipolar Disor 2002:3(4): 181-8.

[56]   Mirnics K, Middleton FA, Marquez A, Lewis DA, Levitt P. Molecular characterization of schizophrenia viewed by microarray analysis of gene expression in prefrontal cortex. Neuron2000;8:53–67.

[57]   Murphy P, Wagner CL. Vitamin D and mood disorders among women: an integrative review. Am Coll Nurse-Midwives 2008;53(5): 440-6.

[58]   Simon NS, Zalta AK, Otto MW, Ostacher MJ, Fischmann D, Chow CW, et al. The association of comorbid anxiety disorders with suicide attempts and suicidal ideation in outpatients with bipolar disorder. J Psychiatr Res 2007;41:255-64.

[59]   Lehmann B, Querings K, Reichrath J. Vitamin D and skin: new aspects for dermatology. Exp Dermatol 2004;13(4):11-5.

[60]   Ahmadi S, Mirzaei K, Hossein-Nezhad A, Shariati G Vitamin D receptor FokI genotype may modify the susceptibility to schizophrenia and bipolar mood disorder by regulation of dopamine D1 receptor gene expression. Minerva Med. 2012 Oct;103(5):383-91.

[61]   Basile LA, Taylor SN, Wagner CL, Quinones L, Hollis BW. Neonatal vitamin D status at birth at latitude 32°72': evidence of deficiency. J Perinatol 2007;27:568-71.

[62]   Gloth FM3rd, Alam W, Hollis B. Vitamin D vs. broad spectrum phototherapy in the treatment of seasonal affective disorder. J Nutr Health Aging 1999;3(1):5-7.

[63]   Cantor-Graae E, Selten JP, Schizophrenia and migration: a meta-analysis and review. Am J Psychiatry 2005;162:12-24.

[64]   Harrison G.Searching for the causes of schizophrenia: the role of migrant studies. Schizophr. Bull 1990;16:663–71.

[65]   Selten JP, Veen N, Feller W, Blom JD, Schols D, Camoenie W, et al. (2001) Incidence of psychotic disorders in immigrant groups to the Netherlands. Br. J. Psychiatry 2001;178: 367–72.

[66]   Mortensen PB, Pedersen CB, Westergaard T, Wohlfahrt J, Ewald H, Mors O, et al..Familial and non-familial risk factors for schizophrenia: a population- based study. Schizophr Res 1998;29:13.

[67]   Holick MF. Environmental factors that influence the cutaneous production of vitamin D. Am J Clin Nutr 1995;61:638S-45.

[68]   Nesby-O'Dell S, Scanlon KS, Cogswell ME, et al. Hypovitaminosis D prevalence and determinants among African American and white women of reproductive age: third National Health and Nutrition Examination Survey, 1988-1994. Am J Clin Nutr 2004;76:187–92.

[69]   Grover SR, Morley R. Vitamin D deficiency in veiled or dark-skinned pregnant women. Med J Aust 2001;175:251-2.

[70]   Vieth R.Vitamin D supplementation, 25-hydroxyvitamin D concentrations, and safety. Am J Clin Nutr 1999;69:842-56.

[71]   Schneider B, Weber B, Frensch, Stein J, Fritze J. Vitamin D in schizophrenia, major depression and alcoholism. J Neural Transm 2000;107:839-42.

[72]   Feron F, Burne TH, BrownJ, Smith E, McGrath JJ, Mackay- Sim, et al. Developmental vitamin D3 deficiency alters the adult rat brain. Brain Res Bull 2005;65:141-8.

[73]   Almeras L, Eyles D, Benech P, Laffite D, Villard C, Patatian, et al., Developmental vitamin D deficiency alters brain protein expression in the adult rat: implications for neuropsychiatric disorders. Proteomics 2007;7:769-80.

[74]   Sullivan S, Wills A, Lawlor D, McGrath J, Zammit S. Prenatal vitamin D status and risk of psychotic experiences at age 18years-a longitudinal birth cohort. Schizophr Res. 2013 Aug;148(1-3):87-92.

[75]   Itzhaky D, Amital D, Gorden K, Bogomolni A, Arnson Y, Amital H. Low serum vitamin D concentrations in patients with schizophrenia. Isr Med Assoc J. 2012 Feb;14(2):88-92.

[76]   Umhau JC, George DT, Heaney RP, Lewis MD, Ursano RJ, Heilig M, Hibbeln JR, Schwandt ML. Low vitamin D status and suicide: a case-control study of active duty military service members. PLoS One. 2013;8(1):e51543.

[77]   Hollis BW. Circulating 25-hydroxyvitamin D levels indicative of vitamin sufficiency: Implications for establishing a new effective DRI for vitamin D. J Nutr 2005;135:317-22.

[78]   Hathcock JN, Shao A, Vieth R, Heaney R.Risk assessment for vitamin D. Am J Clin Nutr 2007;85:6-18.

[79]   Holick MF. Vitamin D deficiency. N Engl JMed 2007;357:266-81.

[80]   Ross AC, Taylor CL, Yaktine AL, Del Valle HB, eds. Committee to Review Dietary Reference Intakes for Vitamin D and Calcium. Washington, DC: National Academies Press, 2011.

In: Children, Violence and Bullying   ISBN: 978-1-62948-342-9
Editors: J Merrick, I Kandel and H A Omar   © 2014 Nova Science Publishers, Inc.

Chapter 18

SUICIDE IN THE GENERAL HOSPITAL

Pranayjit Adsule[1,2], Janaki Nimmagadda[2], MD Farooq Mohyuddin[2], MD and Teodor T Postolache[1,], MD*

[1]Mood and Anxiety Program, Psychiatry Department,
University of Maryland School of Medicine, Baltimore, Maryland
[2]St Elizabeths Hospital, Washington DC, US

ABSTRACT

In the medico-surgical wards of general hospitals, patients can potentially be led to a prosuicidal state due to the various elements they encounter. It is commonly understood that most people find the experience of being in a hospital stressful and uncomfortable. Medical illnesses directly affect suicide risk, and are often associated with pain and sleep impairment, which are independent risk factors themselves. In addition, stress related to poor prognosis, terminal illness, or failure of treatment of last resort may all contribute to suicidal risk. In such cases, the stress along with hopelessness and helplessness can be a trigger with contribution from a marked diminution of abilities, functioning and self worth. Suicidality has also been associated with certain medications; these and other medications may induce depression and anxiety.

In majority of non-psychiatric hospitalizations, there is diminished access to social support; which acts as a protective factor against suicide in the outpatient setting. Hospitalization may provide access to lethal means of committing suicide, such as jumping from heights, hanging, sharp objects and medications. In cases of open access on the other hand, there might be a risk of patient completing suicide by leaving the hospital. Certain specific risk factors like alcohol intoxication on admission or alcohol abuse, severe medical illness, past suicide attempts, older age and male gender may complicate the presentation in addition to depression. An abbreviated review of the literature and recommendations at multiple levels- administrative, clinical and educational will be presented in the following chapter. We believe that in the long run developing and testing a suicide related vital sign (e.g. a psychological pain scale administered simultaneously with the physical pain scale) will contribute to early detection and better monitoring of

---

* Correspondence: Teodor T Postolache, MD, Mood and Anxiety Program (MAP), Department of Psychiatry, University of Maryland School of Medicine, 685 West Baltimore Street, MSTF Building Room 930, Baltimore, MD 21201 United States. E-mail: tpostolache@psych.umaryland.edu.

suicide risk considering that many suicide attempts in the non-psychiatric milieu are impulsive, difficult to predict, and serious. A team approach with a psychiatrist, somatic physician, nursing staff, social worker, and often a pastoral counselor or chaplain, in close contact with a close relative or significant other, along with administrative efforts for suicide education and reducing access to lethal means is recommended.

INTRODUCTION

A suicide is committed every 40 seconds, leading to one million suicide deaths worldwide, and an overall rate of 14.5 death/ 100,000 [1]. An often overlooked but significant proportion of these happen in general hospital settings. One study found that inpatients had an 8.25 times higher risk of suicide than the general population [2]. The Joint commission (JC) published a Sentinel Event Alert on preventing inpatient suicides on medical and surgical units in 2010. Suicide in a hospital setting was considered a 'never' event i.e. adverse events that are usually, preventable, unambigious (clearly identifiable and measurable), and serious (resulting in serious disability or death). From 2000-2010, suicides were one of the commonest reported sentinel events [3]. Suicide completion and attempts are related to poor physical health.We found it important to review the implications for suicide in the non psychiatric hospital environment considering that while most psychiatric inpatient units are equipped to be safe for suicidal individuals and have staff with specialized training, typically, medical/surgical units and emergency departments are not designed or assessed for suicide risk and do not have staff with specialized training to deal with suicidal individuals. Moreover, they can also generally be the first points of contact with a suicidal attempter. Patients in general hospitals can be at increased risk due to the presence of severe medical and surgical conditions, the pain related to surgical procedures, the sense of inadequacy associated with functional impairment, relative isolation from social support and in certain cases, poor prognosis along with more readily available means in comparison to psychiatric wards.

Suicide in a hospital (psychiatric or non-psychiatric) is a particularly distressing event to the staff, physicians and remaining patients along with the relatives of the person committing suicide. There may be questions about responsibility besides feelings of guilt and reproach that rise [4, 5]. For the medical facilities, legal complications are also frequently a concern when a hospitalized patient has committed suicide [6]. Although there is a breadth of literature available about suicide risk in psychiatric hospitals, the literature on suicide in the medical setting is limited. More data about general hospital suicides would be important as they appear to have distinct characteristics [6]. This chapter reviews the psychiatric literature in an attempt to help the clinicians identify and reduce risk, and save lives.

PREDICTION OF SUICIDE IN PATIENTS ADMITTED TO NON-PSYCHIATRIC DEPARTMENTS

Reason for admission

The most common medical conditions associated with completed suicides as reported by Ballard et al [8] in their review article, were as follows: 25.2% of patients who completed suicide in the medical setting had neoplasms, followed by cardiovascular diseases (16.1%), pulmonary diseases (15.4%) and neurological conditions (13.3).

According to a Hong Kong study by Ho and Tay [9], 26% of suicidal patients in general ward had neoplastic disease although not all of them were at the terminal stage.

A study conducted at a general hospital in New York [10] from the pool of psychiatric consult requests for suicidality showed that 60% of the suicide consults were on the medical service, 20% were on surgery and 10% were on neurology. This was similar in pattern to all psychiatric consultations in general.

Medical disorders associated with suicide

The most common diagnosis among suicides in a medical setting is cancer [11]. Medical conditions such as cancer (head and neck cancers in particular), multiple sclerosis, epilepsy, Huntington's disease, HIV/AIDS, Respiratory diseases, spinal-cord injury, peptic ulcer, renal disease and systemic lupus erythematosus are associated with suicide completion as is pain which is an independent factor by itself [1, 12]. In a recent study, higher rates of suicidal ideation were seen in Infectious diseases, Oncology and Hematology units [12].

In United States, the incidence of suicide in patients with cancer is nearly twice that of the general population. Cancers of different anatomic sites are associated with different rates of suicide. Male sex, white race, and older age at diagnosis of cancer were associated with higher suicide rates according to a study done by Misono S. et al (2008) [13]. Cancers of the lung and bronchus were observed to have highest suicide risk (standardized mortality ratio [SMR] = 5.74; 95% CI, 5.30 to 6.22), followed by stomach (SMR = 4.68; 95% CI, 3.81 to 5.70), oral cavity and pharynx (SMR = 3.66; 95% CI, 3.16 to 4.22), and larynx (SMR = 2.83; 95% CI, 2.31 to 3.44). The first 5 years after diagnosis with cancer were found to have the highest Standardized Mortality Ratios.

Table 1. Medical diagnoses of 286 completed suicides in the medical setting per ballard (2008)

Medical diagnosis	Frequency among completed suicides
Neoplasms	72 (25.2%)
Cardiovascular diseases	46 (16.1%)
Pulmonary diseases	44 (15.4%)
Neurological conditions	38 (13.3%)
Gastrointestinal	16 (5.6%)
Injuries	15 (5.2%)
Allergies and infectious disease	14 (4.9%)
Orthopedic and rheumatological	12 (4.2%)
Genito-urinary	12 (4.2%)
Other	17 (5.9%)

* Cases where the principle medical diagnosis was missing or ambiguous(n = 3) or reported as suicide attempt (n = 11) were excluded from analysis.

Patients on chronic renal dialysis had a higher incidence of suicidal behavior than among the general population as was emphasized by a study by Abram et al [14]. There is evidence suggesting that suicide rate is increased in patients with a diagnosis of cancer [13, 15, 16], head injury [15] and peptic ulcer [11]. Huntington's chorea, multiple sclerosis and spinal cord injury are also found to be associated with an increased risk of suicide (15). Pregnancy and puerperium was reported to have a decreased risk of suicide [17].

Previous suicide attempt

Prior suicidal attempts have been found to be the strongest predictor of future attempts and death by suicide is most likely in the following year after the index event in hospitalized patients [18]. It was found that about 35% of hospitalized non-psychiatric patients attempting suicide had made prior suicide attempts in a seven-year study by Reich and Kelly [19].

Friedman and Cancellieri [20] reviewed charts of all patients admitted to a Fordham hospital in New York from 1954 to 1957 for attempted suicide. There were 272 patients who were admitted for suicidal attempt, among them 22 died and the remaining patients did not make another attempt while in the hospital.

Chronicity of medical/surgical illness

Medical condition was acute in 55.6% of subjects evaluated for suicide potential and chronic in 25.9% according to a study by Berger [10]. Terminal medical condition was adjudged to be present in eighteen percent of them and none with impending death.

The association between existence of a medical condition and suicidality was studied in a survey of 7589 individuals between the ages of 17 and 39 years conducted by Druss and Pincus [21]. People with general medical illness were found to be much more likely to have suicidal ideation and have attempted suicide than people without medical illness. Two or more medical illnesses increased the risk of suicidal ideation and attempt. Patients with asthma and bronchitis were seen to have a two thirds increase in odds of life time suicidal ideation in this study. Cancer and asthma were each associated with a 4 fold increase in the likelihood of a suicide attempt. The authors speculated that both asthma and bronchitis have a chronic course characterized by acute exacerbations, which has a significant effect on the quality of life. Cancer may cause chronic pain and disability depending upon the site and type of cancer. Factors like chronicity of medical/physical disability, chronic pain and their social consequences may thus cause the patient to consider his/her life not worth living.

Level of physical discomfort

About 50% of evaluations requested for suicide were for patients rated as either in physical pain or distress in the study by Berger (1993) [10]. In a study by Bahk et al. in 2010, it was found that pain is associated with suicidal ideation, as well as, worsening of depression and a decreased quality of life [22]. Pollack [23] found that, three out of eleven male patients in the study, who committed suicide while under medical treatment, had severe dyspnea. Most of the suicides committed by general ward patients in their study were classified as "rational" suicides by Brown and Piestsky [24] as they seemed to be a better alternative to the patient from long-term dependency, pain and hopelessness. However, many times the hopelessness, helplessness and narrowing of the existential repertoire of the patient is the result of depression which if effectively treated can potentially lower the risk.

History of alcohol/substance abuse

It is difficult to find a direct cause and effect relationship because most alcohol/substance abuse/dependence co-occurs with other psychiatric diagnoses and variables associated with suicidal behavior despite there being an unquestionable association between self-harming behavior and history of alcohol and other substance abuse. Acute alcohol consumption in suicidal attempters brought to the emergency room was emphasized by many of the studies reviewed for this article. Substance abuse in particular has been associated with greater mortality and suicidal attempts in literature. 7% of suicides in non-psychiatric units showed acute substance/alcohol intoxication or withdrawal as a precipitant of suicidality [10]. It is important to note that acute alcohol intoxication is an equally important risk factor for suicidal behavior among both chronic alcohol abusers and non-alcoholics [25] increasing the potential risk during the early admission.

Soukas and Lonnqvist [26], in a study conducted in a Finnish University hospital found that 62% of the patients with suicide attempts brought to emergency room reported that they had recently ingested alcohol. They were more likely to be young or lonely men with past suicidal behavior. A five-year follow-up of these patients revealed high rates of completed suicide and mortality. Thirty percent of patients who eventually killed themselves were habitual alcohol consumers and 67% used it acutely before the suicidal act. Recent acute alcohol consumption was reported to be a more important risk factor for suicide attempt than chronic alcohol consumption [27] in a Mexican study, conducted at eight hospital emergency rooms. This highlights the importance of a detailed substance abuse history as part of a good suicide risk assessment.

Current smoking has also been consistently associated with suicidality [28, 29]. Smoking cessation [28], especially in those with a history of depression [30, 31, 32] is thought to increase suicidality. Smoking cessation medications such as bupropion, rimonabant (not available in US) and varenicline have been found to be associated with increased suicidality [28, 33].

Demographic factors

There have been a few pertinent demographic trends observed in hospitalized suicidal patients. In a recent study by Botega et al., an association between suicide ideation and younger age was found. Among individuals below 36 years of age, the odds were 2.5-fold that of individuals who were 63 years old or more [12]. In 1993, in a study conducted in a general hospital in the Bronx, New York, the demographic data for all psychiatric consultations among 27 medical patients with suicidality was compared by Berger [10] and found a predominance of male patients in the group consulted for suicidality (65% males in the suicidal group vs. 44% as a whole). Among the suicidal patients, 80% percent were unmarried (single, separated, divorced or widowed), 82.4% were not working and 75% were reported to have a high Axis IV (psychosocial and environmental problems) stress level. The male-to- female ratio for completed suicides was 4:1(67%-81% males) and for attempted suicides it was nearly 1:1(58%-68% males) in a study by Ho & TP (2004) in general hospitals in Hong Kong [9]. Older patients with physical disability posed a greater suicide risk [23], according to Pollack (1957). It is found among people aged 80 or more that those hospitalized with medical illness have a significantly higher suicide risk those with no hospitalization [34].

Severity of medical illness

The chronicity and severity of physical illness was found to be more important than specific medical diagnoses when it comes to suicidality. Suicidal acts are more directly associated with the level of suffering experienced by the patients. Depression and other mental disorders can be a consequence of chronic medical illnesses and are strongly associated with suicide attempts [9]. In a study done by Kasai et al [29], it was seen that there were five deaths by suicide among 14,987 patients with spinal disease as compared with no deaths by suicide among 54,874 patients with orthopedic disease other than spinal disease. Brown and Pisetsky [36] found similar results in a study conducted on the general ward, in the VA Hospital in Bronx, New York from 1947 to 1948. In that study, severe chronic illnesses and multiple medical problems affecting the quality of life [36] were seen in all medical patients who committed suicide. Additionally, in cancer patients, the risk of suicide increases with increased severity and poorer prognosis [15].

Underlying psychiatric illness/symptoms

Underlying mental illness/ symptoms can be a major risk factor for suicidal attempts as was shown by Reich and Kelly [19]. It has been reported to be the strongest risk factor for suicidal attempts [18]. Among the patients attempting suicide in non-psychiatric units of the hospital, close to 90% had mental illness as shown by history, behavior or mental status. Specifically, 70% had personality disorders, 25% had primary psychosis and 20% had secondary psychosis due to organic brain syndrome. The possibility of undiagnosed underlying psychiatric illness in hospitalized patients has been brought up by other studies as well.

Precipitants of suicidality

Berger [10] reported that although the precipitants varied for different subjects, acute change in medical condition was seen in about 55% of the cases. It could either be an onset of new symptoms or patient's newly acquired knowledge or perception of a diagnosis or prognosis. In the study, about 44% had suffered a loss of physical function, 40% faced a loss of role function and 33% showed a maladaptive reaction to their illness. Thirty-three percent among them had major depression, 22% were showing reaction to pain, 22% had interpersonal conflict, 18% had conflict with staff, 15% had family conflict and 15% were going through bereavement. Organic disorder (delirium/dementia), reaction to acute loss of emotional support and real or imaginary loss of face was considered to be the precipitant in an equal percentage of subjects i.e. 11% each. Drug/alcohol intoxication or withdrawal and an attempt to influence the patient's social situation were both seen to be the precipitating factor for suicidality in about 7% of patient. In this study, a pertinent negative noted was that conflict with other patients or psychosis was not found as the precipitating factor in any of the cases.

Reich and Kelly [19] found that most of the patients with suicide attempts in non-psychiatric units had prior psychiatric illness. Recent changes in mental status of the patients prior to the suicidal attempt varied according to their psychiatric diagnosis. Severe anxiety or agitation have been found to be acute predictors of inpatient suicide and thus should be appropriately managed [37]. All patients with personality disorders who attempted suicide were found to do so, when the veracity of their physical symptoms was questioned. Most of them had been admitted for vague complaints and were close to being discharged upon negative evaluation results. Pain management was the second most common reason for admission of the patients with personality disorders and they attempted suicide when their need for pain medication was challenged. Anger about real or perceived abandonment and interpersonal conflict is considered to be the reason behind these suicidal attempts. None of the patients gave any indication of suicidal thoughts and all the suicide attempts in the study were thought to be impulsive in nature. Among the terminal cancer patients who attempted suicide and did not suffer from a concomitant psychiatric diagnosis, the attempts were seen to be when they found that their treatment was not working. Prior to the suicidal attempt, a sudden change in their mood and affect towards dysphoria was noted.

Brown and Pisetsky emphasized the role of the sense of helplessness and dependence on the caregiver seen in victims of suicide with medical illness [36].

Psychiatric patients in partial hospitalization

Due to the policies and pressures of managed care, patients can now be denied insurance coverage if the insurers think they could be treated in an outpatient setting. Some insurance companies may also limit the number of psychiatric admissions as well as length of stay in hospital.

Partial hospitalization is a treatment option under such circumstances. Since the early 90s, many patients who express death wishes and suicidal ideation are being treated as outpatients and by partial hospitalization. Admissions include a brief course of antidepressant drugs or electro-convulsive therapy, to be followed up in the outpatient clinic.

Literature review by Freed and Rudolph [38] showed outcome studies about the quality and cost-effectiveness of such strategies remained inconclusive. Moreover, there are legal implications in case of a suicidal patient that make careful evaluation of these patients by mental-healthcare providers extremely important. In a study by Asnis et al [39], a range of thoughts extending from death wish to plan of suicide were found in all psychiatric patients in an outpatient clinic. While patients with major depression and borderline personality disorder are most likely to have suicidal thoughts [40], it is also important to monitor patients with substance abuse [41]. There are several symptoms that are described to be of predictive value for suicide among mentally ill by Fawcett, Clark and Busch [42]. These behaviors include panic attacks, severe psychic anxiety, impaired concentration, psychomotor agitation, global insomnia, moderate alcohol abuse and severe anhedonia. Thus, presence of any of these behaviors indicates the need for further exploration of possible self-harm. Factors that should be evaluated carefully in these patients include thought content and process, seriousness of intent, emotional states, any sudden change in mood (better or worse) or behavior, lethality of plan, family history, past attempts, recent hospital discharge, alcohol or drug abuse and support systems. If a decision was made to admit the patient to the hospital, voluntary stay had a better outcome as compared to involuntary commitment [43, 44]. Considering the presence of suicidal thoughts from time to time in patients with psychiatric diagnosis, they should be evaluated at every appointment during outpatient treatment for risk of suicidality [45].

Medications associated with depression and suicide

Patients predisposed to depression seem to be more likely to be affected by medication induced depression. Various classes of drugs have been associated with depression. Isotretinoin, rimonabant, and alphainterferons have the highest risk of drug induced depression [46], although the findings might be provisional. Also, drugs such as Corticosteroids, Varenicline, Progesterone inserts and Finasteride have a moderately high risk of medication induced depression [46]. Thus, risks and benefits need to be carefully evaluated on a case by case basis, especially since these medications are used in various medical conditions.

A drug as widely used as Propranolol has also been frequently linked to medication induced depression [46]. Interestingly, the beta blocker Pindolol on the other hand, has been studied as an augmenting agent in the treatment of depression, signifying that all beta blockers may not be related to medication induced depression [46]. The data about calcium channel blockers, ACE inhibitors, angiotensin receptor blockers, betainterferons, and leukotriene antagonists (Montelukast) [47] and their association with depression [46] is inconsistent as well.

There is an FDA warning about an increased risk of suicidality for patients taking medication like Antidepressants, Antiepileptics, Interferons (Alfa2a, 2b, Beta1a, 1b and Alfacon1), Isotretenoin, Montelukast, Rimonabant (not available in USA), and Varenicline [33].

In a review from 2013 however, it was reported that available data is not yet methodologically strong enough to support or reject the claimed increased risk of suicidality with Antiepileptic drugs [48].As previously mentioned though, the risks should be balanced with the benefits when choosing these medications. In many cases, the risks of not treating the patients might be greater.

Some drugs such as sedatives and hypnotics are associated with an increased risk of suicide particularly in late life. Hence, as these medications are commonly used in elderly populations, an evaluation of suicide risk prior to starting these in an elderly individual is warranted [49]. The findings on antidepressant induced suicidality in adults are contradictory and are seen rarely. Close monitoring and follow up care after starting a new antidepressant is thus generally indicated [50]. This makes the treatment of a depressed patient with suicidal thoughts challenging. In a study on Bipolar disorder patients on the other hand, Gibbons' et al reported that antiepileptics do not increase the risk of suicide attempts in patients with bipolar disorder compared to those who are not treated with anti-epileptics or lithium [51]. Infact, the suicide attempt rates were reduced by anti-epileptic treatment as compared to patients not taking any psychotropic medication and also compared to their pretreatment levels [51]. The American Society of Health-System Pharmacists (ASHP) maintains a list of medications that can induce suicidality [52].

WHEN DOES IT HAPPEN?

Time of the day

According to a study in general hospitals in Hong Kong (9), no specific peak hours were found for the 132 suicides attempted in general wards (20% took place between midnight - 6:00 am, 26% [6:00 am − noon], 29% [noon-6.00pm] and 25% [6:00 pm - midnight]) but completed suicides were found to occur mostly after midnight (41% between midnight and 6:00 am, 22% [6:00 am − noon], 9% [noon - 6:00 pm] and 28% [6:00 pm − midnight]). However, Reich and Kelly in 1976 found that most of the suicide attempts took place during busy times of the day [19]. During their seven years of study, seventeen suicide attempts occurred and sixteen among them happened between 8 a.m. and 10 p.m. Ten of these sixteen occurred between 3:40 p.m. and 10 p.m.

Day of hospitalization

In a study in Hong Kong by Ho and Tay [9], 34 out of 132 suicides took place at a mean of 8 days after admission whereas attempted suicides occurred after 17 days [9]. They also studied this data with respect to the reason for admission and it was observed that among patients admitted for pain and breathing problems, suicidal acts occurred at a mean of 12.9 days after admission.

Among patients with altered mental status, the mean was 8.1 days and for patients admitted to general ward for a suicidal attempt it was 1.2 days; signifying the highest risk of suicide for these patients just after admission. In a review of literature by Ballard et al., mean duration of medical hospitalization prior to suicide varied widely, from 2 days to several months, with an average length of stay of 31.1 days (n= 60) [11].These findings are quite different from data collected during psychiatric hospitalizations in which there were two peaks of suicide, first being one week after admission and second, one week after discharge from a psychiatric hospital [53].

The possible reasons for these findings could be that the first week represents the period of maximum instability that brought the patients to the hospital, as well as maximum self esteem impact by stigma.While on medico-surgical wards,cases where a diagnosis that carries a more reserved prognosis takes more than 1 week to reach through laboratory work, and pain inflicting invasive procedures have a greater risk right after the operative treatment takes place (usually not occurring immediately after admission), or have an exacerbated risk during the immediate rehabilitation process.

LOCATION

Ho and Tay [9] observed that majority of attempted suicides took place in patient's beds or inside the ward. A smaller number of suicidal attempts took place in places like the garden, outpatient department, lift lobby, rear exit of the ward and roof of hospital building. In terms of completed suicides, majority occurred in the ward toilet or outside the hospital [9]. Those patients who took their lives outside the hospital had left the hospital without notifying the staff and majority of them committed suicide within 1 hour of leaving the ward [9].

MEANS/METHODS

Jumping from heights is the commonest way of completing suicide, with a close second suicide method being hanging [9, 15, 20]. Hanging meanwhile was the predominant method in the psychiatric hospital. 20% of patients who attempted were successful in their suicidal attempt (34 out of 166 total) in the Hong Kong study of suicide in general hospitals [9]. The rate of completed suicide was 1.93 per 100,000 admissions. Majority of attempted suicides involved some sharp object like knife, scissors, cutter, shaving blade, broken window glass etc [9]. 40% of attempters used the same methods used by the completers i.e. jumping from heights or hanging and strangulation in the study by Ho and Tay [9]. In a few cases, there were attempts at self-harm by poisoning that included chemicals like shampoo, hypnotic, deodorant, aspirin etc. This data seems to indicate that it would be virtually impossible to completely eliminate the risk of suicide by restricting the means considering the varied and common nature of objects used by patients for suicidal acts in this study.

Jumping from a window or open ramp to the ground was the method of suicide in all patients except one in a study by Pollack [23]; the only one patient who did not jump killed himself by cutting his throat and was hospitalized on the first floor.

CHILDREN AND ADOLESCENTS

The pediatric population provides its own difficulties and challenges when it comes to suicidal behavior. According to a surveillance report by the CDC, Suicide is the second most common cause of death among children aged 12-17yrs in 2010 in the United States [54, 55]. It has been observed that the number of suicidal attempts among adolescents is increasing over the past few decades. Various studies report that girls have a higher rate of suicidal ideation and attempts while boys have a higher rate of completed suicide [54, 56]. The risk was also seen to be higher in older children (aged 15–19 years) than younger children (aged 10–14 years) [54]. The most common risk factors for suicidal attempts and suicide among adolescents include previous suicidal ideation and behavior, depressive disorders, Borderline personality disorder, substance abuse, conduct disorder and a history of adverse childhood experiences [57, 58, 59]. Adverse childhood experiences including physical or sexual abuse has been associated with a higher risk of suicidal attempts in various studies [60, 61, 62]. A Chinese study showed a 2.7 fold increase in suicidal attempts in adolescents who had been exposed to sexual abuse as children [60]. Substance abuse is a common problem among adolescents as well as a major risk factor for suicidal ideation. Findings suggest that alcohol use may hasten the transition from suicidal ideation to suicide attempt in adolescents with low levels of depressed mood, In a 10 year review, Heroin was found to have the strongest association with suicidal ideation followed by Methamphetamine and Steroids [63].

It has been shown that somatic symptoms are commonly associated with depression, severity, poor prognosis and suicidal thoughts in adolescence. The somatic presentations (headache being the commonest) also lead to a high number of adolescents with depressive symptoms seeking help in a general health care setting [64]. This makes it imperative for general medical professionals to be able to assess suicidal risks factors whether or not adolescents present with a psychiatric history or not. While a psychiatric disorder is very common in adolescent suicides as a whole, Bridge et al noted that 40% of suicide completers under the age of 16 do not appear to have a diagnosable psychiatric disorder, while having a lower intent and a greater role for the availability of lethal means [65]. This has resulted in a need and recommendations for a screening tool to assess risk in a short time in a non psychiatric setting. Tools such as the HEADS-ED, CANS-MH 3.0 or combined versions of PHQ-9 and Columbia Suicide Severity Rating Scale have shown some benefit in this respect [66, 67].

With respect to hospitalization, it has long been advocated that adolescents be admitted in specialized adolescent units for better care provision [68]. Moreover, with respect to youth with mental health problems, 87% of nurses in a study highlighted that young people with mental health problems should be nursed by mental health nurses in separate adolescent units [69]. Given the importance young people give to privacy and confidentiality, it has been recommended that there be a dedicated room where interviews can be conducted. This is especially important because young people are reluctant to discuss sensitive health concerns unless asked directly and with some assurance of confidentiality [70]. In many cases, social and family interventions can go a long way in assessing and preventing suicidal behaviors as psychological and social factors are major determinants of suicidal attempts in adolescents. As far as treatment is concerned, having a psychiatric team on board is essential. Anti depressants, which are the mainstays of pharmacological treatment of depressive symptoms come with a FDA black box warning of increasing suicidal ideation among adolescents and this risk is highest immediately after initiation. This calls for increased monitoring of patients in such situations. A combination of Fluoxetine and CBT has been shown to have the best improvement in depressive symptoms [71] in adolescents. However, it has been found that there is an 85% risk reduction in hospital readmission in patients when they are started on anti depressants [72].

CLINICAL, ADMINISTRATIVE AND LEGAL IMPLICATIONS FOR CARE

It is important for physicians in medical and surgical practice to be aware of the possibility of suicide in a patient who does not have prior psychiatric history or diagnosis so as to carry out evaluation of suicide risk and for a practical approach towards prevention. All patients with delirium should be considered as suicide risks by non psychiatric physicians and at least minimal precautions should be taken [73]. It is important to have an increased awareness and a heightened sensitivity to the suicidal risk in particular among the withdrawn and quiet patients who may silently suffer from depression. In major disabling conditions such as cancer or spinal cord injury, the oncologists and spinal surgeons respectively, should take efforts to monitor the psychological status of a patient carefully [29].

Suicide contracts though widely used, do not prevent death [74]. As far as possible, family members and significant others should be involved and informed about treatment plans, HIPAA guidelines and suicidal risk [74]. Documentation of the rationale for all decisions is paramount.

JC recommends the following steps to screen for suicidal risk [3]:

1. Watch for behaviors, mental status, or conditions that may indicate a risk of imminent suicide:
   a) acute signs of depression, anxiety, agitation, delirium and dementia
   b) medical or psychological problems that significantly impact judgment, including intoxication with alcohol or drugs
   c) chronic pain or other debilitating problems, including chronic illness and terminal cancer
2. Screen patients who demonstrate these behaviors, mental status characteristics or conditions increasing risk of suicide risk.
3. Provide for suicide screening in the emergency department.
4. As part of the hospital inpatient admission process, screen all patients for depression.
5. Use suicide screening and assessment tools that are appropriate for the person's age and characteristics.
6. Provide a psychological consultation to assess immediate risk of individuals admitted for medical treatment following a suicide attempt.

It is considered a duty of the clinicians to reasonably prevent the suicide of a patient [74]. Litigation is thus a common possibility in the aftermath of a suicide. Although concerns regarding safety rather than litigation should be the primary factor for health professionals, it is important to have a legal counsel involved as soon as possible after a suicide [75]. In suicide related negligence cases, there are 4 'D's that are essential to prove to find the clinician culpable: a) A **D**ereliction of b) **D**uty c) that **D**irectly (proximately) d) causes **D**amages [74]. There is a considerable variation in the laws based on the jurisdiction. Although in most cases, liability would be determined based on the fulfillment of two elements- i) Foreseeability (a reasonable evaluation of the potential of suicide attempt based on the assessment of risk and anticipation of potential risk of no action or negligence [to be done on every patient and every occasion]) and ii) Causation. Physicians are not legally responsible for the outcome or inaccuracy of prognosis after they have adequately examined the patient, established the diagnosis, assessed the risk, and provided competent care [42]. They might however be expected to maintain a 'standard of care' i.e the watchfulness, attention, caution and prudence that a reasonable person in the circumstances would exercise.

Seminars or workshops on suicide risk factors and its prevention can be organized for all clinical staff. An effort should be made to provide more opportunities to improve skills to care for suicidal patients and understand the complicated pattern of suicidal ideation and its prevention in hospitals [76]. Educational and training activities about suicide in the hospital are very important for suicide prevention. A new initiative called the Mental Health First Aid (www.MentalHealthFirstAid.org) has been developed with the intention of providing non mental health staff with valuable skills. The importance of organizing a periodic suicide-review conference, a periodic retraining in suicide risk assessment specifically targeted to the audience (ER physicians, primary care physicians, nursing staff, social workers, medical residents, psychiatric residents) as well as morbidity- mortality conferences cannot be over emphasized.

Finally, religion has been seen to have multilevel suicide protective effect [77] which exists across denominations. Both religious beliefs and practices have been reported to have suicide preventive effects [46]. A significant degree of suicide protection is present even in patients who are not practicing their religion, or have spiritual beliefs that are independent of any doctrine, moral and religious objections to suicide [78]. In addition, an important suicide protective factor is the social support associated with organized religion.

In fact, suicide risk during hospitalizations might be increased by the abrupt deprivation of certain religious routines and religion related social supports. Thus, pastoral care, pastoral counseling or chaplain services are powerful allies in the battle to reduce suicide risk in religious patients.

These should be available, and offered rather than imposed. If services are used, then the chaplain or the pastoral counselor should be included in the treatment team.

Environmentally, the access to any physical opportunity for a lethal jump should be restricted- including windows and ramps. Care would be taken that wall and ceiling fixtures should not be able to support a full body weight, and access to medications and surgical instruments should be monitored and restricted. The units should also be monitored to prevent patients from leaving without the knowledge of the staff.

It is important that the responsible consultant offer to see the relatives of the victim of suicide. As mentioned previously, this is a difficult time for everyone associated with the patient and thus this is a potentially critical meeting, as relatives are often puzzled, guilty, angry or openly litigious. The meeting offers an opportunity for the treating team not only to explain and discuss the various events leading up to death but also provide comfort with an empathetic presence for the family. Adequate understanding, explanation, sympathy and bereavement counseling can prevent the development of a pathological grief reaction which could have serious impacts for relatives and staff alike [79].

It is important to understand that suicide is a taxing situation and the treating team needs emotional and professional support from their colleagues, including senior nurses, physicians and managers to cope better after a patient has committed suicide while in the hospital [80]. Suicide in a hospital can many a times create a sense of failure or guilt among the members of treating team and they need the most support during the time when shock gives way to flow of intense feelings.

The hospital administrators should provide several means of expression, by arranging team meetings and also by informal staff discussions over a period of time. A debriefing meeting among the staff involved in the care of the patient and anyone in particular in need for psychological counseling can go a long way in preventing long term sequelae of the tragedy although the data for the same is not definitive. It should be recognized that the steps taken as a result of the incident are not an 'over reaction' and any changes should be carefully thought through and implemented [75].

CONCLUSION

It is important to note that even patients in a non-psychiatric unit might contemplate and be serious in their intention and resort to lethal means available to them. Not all patients with a risk of suicide will show either a suicidal attempt or prior psychiatric diagnosis history. However, patients can commonly have history of both suicidal attempts and prior psychiatric symptoms.

Patients exhibiting psychiatric symptoms should thus be evaluated psychiatrically for suicidal risk. Among patients with psychiatric co-morbidity, severe depression, anhedonia, insomnia, psychomotor agitation or retardation, panic attacks, severe anxiety, moderate alcohol abuse and borderline personality disorder increase the risk of suicidal behavior. Acute alcohol intoxication increases the risk of suicidal act especially early in the hospitalization, in both chronic alcohol abusers and non-alcohol users. The risk for completed suicide is high in elderly males with chronic physical illness. It is important to pay attention to factors like acute agitation, psychosis or altered mental status. There is a trend of acute change in medical condition, loss of physical or role function and depression in the suicidal patients. It is important to note that although it is imperative to be aware of a patient's mental status, a history or symptoms of mental illness may or may not be recognized in these patients before the suicidal act. Multiple chronic illnesses with physical pain, disability and breathing problems have an increased association with completed suicides. Most of these suicides are impulsive in nature and so, can occur without warning. Patients who are found more isolated emotionally or having conflicts with staff need more close observation to prevent such incidents. It is important for the night staff to be more vigilant as completed suicides take place mostly after midnight. Attempted suicides tend to happen more frequently during the busy day hours. These suicidal attempts can be a call for attention, acting out behavior or need to be engaged and the staff should be aware of patients requiring more attention. Patients should be sought and found as soon as possible, if missing because the highest suicides risk is present in the first few hours.

Because patients use all means available to them, it is essential that staff be vigilant to patients' access to potentially lethal objects e.g. sharps (knives, blades or glass), chemicals and things like ropes, neckties or belts which could be used for hanging. Windows in higher floors of hospital buildings should be locked as jumping off is one of the most common forms of completing suicide, if not the commonest. Patients should be transferred to a psychiatric unit if possible, or be under continuous observation on the medico-surgical floor under any suspicion of suicidal ideation. Stairways should not be accessible freely and bathrooms should be regularly inspected for self- harm potential. To prevent the risk of hanging, fixtures in the ceilings, walls or doors in the hospital should not be able to carry the weight of a person. A crucial factor in suicide prevention is staff and physician rapport with the patient. Training and awareness of hospital staff and medical/ surgical doctors, primary and ER physicians regarding suicide and emotional wellbeing can improve detection, evaluation, and treatment planning. It goes without saying that gentle and tactful questioning may bring out suicidal ideations in suspected patients as talking about suicide, however discomforting, is essential to decrease the risk of suicide. Knowledge of depressogenic or prosuicidal potential of certain somatic medications in individual patients is important. A dialogue between the medico-surgical team, the psychiatrist, the nursing staff, social workers and family, a review of previous medical records and collateral information are paramount. Finally, if mood ratings are used, the suicide item needs to be checked immediately rather than filing the mood rating in a chart of folder. From a research standpoint, developing and testing a scale analogous to the Likert pain scale, "psychological pain scale" (from 0 -no psychological pain to 10 - "it hurts so much I feel like ending it all") administered by nurse together with the pain scale and allowing a written expression of suicidal ideation or intent may prove important especially in the medico- surgical environment. Finally, we strongly recommend that mental health providers in a hospital environment pay close attention to acute changes in medical conditions and somatic medication that may increase risk for suicide. Rather than limiting ourselves to eliciting suicide ideation, inquiring and gently educating individuals about the reasons for living and tactfully challenging the often constricted existential and behavioral repertoire of suicidal patients is a worthy pursuit.

REFERENCES

[1]   Hawton K, Heeringen KV. Suicide. *Lancet* 2009; 373:1372-81.

[2]   Tseng MC, Cheng IC, Hu FC. Standardized mortality ratio of inpatient suicide in a general hospital. *J. Formos. Med. Assoc.* 2011 Apr; 110(4):267-9.

[3]   A follow-up report on preventing suicide: focus on medical/surgical units and the emergency department. *Sentinel. Event Alert.* 2010 Nov 17;(46):1

[4]   Cotton PG, Drake RE Jr, Whitaker A, Potter J. Dealing with suicide on a psychiatric inpatient unit. *Hosp. Comm. Psychiatry* 1983; 34(1):55-9.

[5]   Crammer JL. The special characteristics of suicide in hospital in-patients. *Br. J. Psychiatry* 1984; 145:460-3.

[6]   Bongar B, Greaney SA. Essential clinical and legal issues when working with the suicidal patient. *Death Studies* 1994; 18:529-548.

[7]   Bostwick JM, Rackley SJ. Completed suicide in medical/surgical patients: who is at risk? *Curr. Psychiatry Rep.* 2007; 9(3):242-6.

[8]   Ballard ED., Pao M., Henderson D., Lee L., B.S.N; Bostwick J, Rosenstein D. Suicide in the medical setting. *Jt. Comm. J. Qual. Patient Saf.* 2008; 34(8):474–481.

[9]   Ho TP, Tay MSM. Suicides in general hospitals in Hong Kong: retrospective study. *Hong Kong Med. J.* 2004; 10(5):319-24.

[10]   Berger D. Suicidal Evaluation in medical patients. *Gen. Hosp. Psychiatry* 1993; 15(2):75-81.

[11]   Ballard ED, Pao M., Henderson D., Lee L., B.S.N; Bostwick J, Rosenstein D. Suicide in the Medical Setting. *The Joint Commission Journal on Quality and Patient Safety.* August 2008 Volume 34 Number 8.

[12]   Botega NJ, Azevedo RC, Mauro ML, Mitsuushi G, Fanger P, Lima D, Gaspar KC, L.C.P., Da Silva V. Factors associated with suicidal ideation among medically and surgically hospitalized patients. *General Hospital Psychiatry* 32 (2010) 396–400.

[13]   Misono S. Incidence of suicide in persons with cancer. *J. Clin. Oncol.* 2008; 26(29):4731-8.

[14]   Abram HS, Moore GL, Westervelt FB Jr. Suicidal behavior in chronic dialysis patients. *Am. J. Psychiat.* 1971; 127(9):1199-1204.

[15]   Mackenzie, TB, Popkin, MK. Suicide in the medical patient. *Int. J. Psychiatr. Med.* 1987; 17(1):3-22.

[16]   Allebeck P, Bolund C, Ringback G. Increased suicide rate in cancer patients. A cohort study based on Swedish Cancer- environment register. *J. Clin. Epidemiol.* 1989; 42(7):611-616.

[17]   Harris EC, Barraclough BM. Suicide as an outcome for medical disorders. *Medicine (Baltimore)* 1994; 73(6):281-96.

[18]   Alberdi-Sudupe J, Pita-Fernández S., Gómez-Pardiñas S., Iglesias-Gil-de-Bernabé F, García-Fernández J, Martínez-Sande G, Lantes-Louzao and Pértega-Díaz S. Suicide attempts and related factors in

patients admitted to a general hospital: a ten-year cross sectional study (1997-2007) *BMC Psychiatry* 2011, 11:51.

[19]   Reich P, Kelly MJ. Suicide attempts by hospitalized medical and surgical patients. *N. Engl. J. Med.* 1976; 294:298-301.

[20]   Friedman JH, Cancellieri R. Suicide risk in a municipal general hospital. *Dis. Nerv. Syst.* 1958;19:556-60.

[21]   Druss B, Pincus H. Suicidal ideation and suicidal attempts in general medical illness. *Arch. Intern. Med.* 2000; 160:1522-26.

[22]   Bahk WM, Park S, Jon D, Yoon BH, Min KJ, Hong JP. Relationship between painful physical symptoms and severity of depressive symptomatology and suicidality. *Psychiatry Research* 189 (2011) 357–361.

[23]   Pollack S. Suicide in a general hospital. In: Shneidman E, Farberow NL, eds. *Clues to suicide.* New York: McGraw-Hill 1957:152-63.

[24]   Brown W, Pisetsky JE. Suicidal behavior in a general hospital. Am J Med 1960;19:307-15.

[25]   Hufford MR: Alcohol and suicidal behavior. *Clin. Psychol. Rev.* 2001; 21(5):797-811.

[26]   Suokas J, Lonnqvist J. Suicide attempts in which alcohol is involved: a special group in general hospital emergency rooms. *Acta Psychiatr. Scand.* 1995; 91(1):36-40.

[27]   Borges G, Rosovsky H. Suicide attempts and alcohol consumption in an emergency room sample. *J. Stud. Alcohol* 1996; 57(5):543-8.

[28]   Hughes JR. Smoking and suicide: A brief overview. *Drug Alcohol Depend.* 2008; 98(3):169-78.

[29]   Breslau N, Schultz L, Johnson E, Peterson E, Davis G. Smoking and the risk of suicidal behavior. *Arch. Gen. Psychiatr.* 2005; 62:328–33.

[30]   Hughes JR. Depression during tobacco abstinence. *Nicotine & Tobacco Reasearch* 2007:; 9(4):443-6.

[31]   Tsoh JY, Humfleet GL, Munoz RF, Reus VI, Hartz DT, Hall SM. Development of major depression after treatment for smoking cessation. *Am. J. Psychiatr.* 2000; 157:368–74.

[32]   Bock BC, Goldstein MG, Marcus BH. Depression following smoking cessation in women. *J. Substance Abuse* 1996; 8:137-44.

[33]   Website: www.fda.gov.

[34]   Erlangsen A, Vach W, Jeune B. The effect of hospitalization with medical illnesses on the suicide risk in the oldest old: a population- based register study. *J. Am. Geriatr. Soc.* 2005; 53(5):771-6.

[35]   Kasai Y, Kawakita E, Uchida A. Suicide during hospitalization in patients with spinal disease. *Spine* 2006; 31(17):1981-82.

[36]   Brown W, Pisetsky JE. Suicidal behavior in a general hospital. *Am. J. Med.* 1960; 19:307-15.

[37]   Busch KA, Fawcett J, Jacobs DG. Clinical correlates of inpatient suicide. *J. Clin. Psychiatry* 2003; 64:14–19.

[38]   Freed PE, Rudolph S. Protecting partial-hospitalization patients from suicide. *Perspect. Psychiatr. Care* 1998; 34(2):14-23.

[39]   Asnis GM, Friedman TA, Sanderson WC, Kaplan ML, Pragg HMV, Harkavy-Friedman JM. Suicidal behaviors in adult psychiatric outpatients, I: Description and prevalence. *Am. J. Psychiatry* 1993; 150:108-12.

[40]   Zisook S, Goff A, Sledge P, Shuchter SR. Reported suicidal behavior and current suicidal ideation in a psychiatric outpatient clinic. *Ann. Clin. Psychiatry* 1994; 6(1).

[41]   Moscicki EK. Epidemiology of suicidal behavior. *Suicide and Life Threatening Behavior* 1995; 25(1):22-35.

[42]   Fawcett J, Clark DC, Busch KA. Assessing and treating the patient at risk for suicide. *Psychiatric Annals* 1993; 23:244-55.

[43]   Maltsberger JT. Calculated risk taking in the treatment of suicidal patients: Ethical and legal problems. *Death Studies* 1994; 18(5):439-452.

[44]   Monahan J, Hoge SK, Lidz C, Roth LH, Bennett N, Gardner W, Mulvey E. Coercion and commitment: understanding involuntary mental hospital admission. *Int. J. Law Psych.* 1995; 18(3):249-63.

[45]   Schuckit MA. Suicide: a preventable catastrophe. *Drug Abuse Alcohol Newsletter* 1997; 26(1):1-3.

[46] Rogers, D, Pies, R. General medical drugs associated with depression. *Psychiatry* (Edgemont) 2008; 5(12):28–41.5(12):28–41

[47] Manalai P, Woo JM, Postolache TT. Suicidality and Montelukast. *Expert. Opin. Drug Saf.* 2009; 8(3):273-82.

[48] Marco Mula and Josemir W Sander. Suicide risk in people with epilepsy taking antiepileptic drugs. *Bipolar Disorders* 2013: 15: 622–627.

[49] Carlsten A, Waern M. Are sedatives and hypnotics associated with increased suicide risk of suicide in the elderly? *BMC Geriatrics* 2009; 9:20.

[50] Reeves RR, Ladner ME. Antidepressant-induced suicidality: implications for clinical practice. *South Med. J.* 2009; 107(7):713-8.

[51] Gibbons RD, Hur K, Brown H, Mann JJ. Relationship between antiepileptic drugs and suicide attempts in patients with bipolar disorder. *Arch. Gen. psychiatry* 2009; 66(12): 1354-60.

[52] Website: http://www.ashp.org/suicidality.

[53] Qin P, Nordentoft M. Suicide risk in relation to psychiatric hospitalization. Evidence based on longitudinal registers. *Arch. Gen. Psychiatry* 2005; 62:427-32.

[54] Perou R, Blumberg SJ, Pastor P, Ghandour RM, Gfroerer JC, Hedden SL, Crosby AE, Visser SN, Schieve LA, Parks SE, Hall JE, Brody D, Simile CM,Thompson WW, Baio J, Avenevoli S, Kogan MD, Huang LN *MMWR Surveill Summ.* 2013 May 17; 62 Suppl 2:1-35. *Mental health surveillance among children*--United States, 2005-2011.

[55] Centers for Disease Control and Prevention. Web based Injury Statistics Query and Reporting System (WISQARS). Available at: http://www.cdc.gov/injury/wisqars/ index.html. Accessed Jun 2, 2009.

[56] Eaton DK, Kann L, Kinchen S, et al. Youth risk behavior surveillance–United States, 2005. *MMWR Surveill Summ.* 2006; 55(SS-5):1–112.

[57] Fergusson DM, Woodward LJ, Horwood LJ. Risk factors and life processes associated with the onset of suicidal behaviour during adolescence and early adulthood. *Psychol. Med.* 2000; 30:23–39.

[58] Sharp C, Green KL, Yaroslavsky I, Venta A, Zanarini MC, Pettit J. (2012) The incremental validity of borderline personality disorder relative to major depressive disorderfor suicidal ideation and deliberate self-harm in adolescents. *J. Pers. Disord.* 2012 Dec;26(6):927-38.

[59] Glenn CR, Bagge C, Osman A. Unique associations between Borderline Personality Disorder features and suicide ideation and attempts in adolescents. *Journal of Personality Disorders,* 27, 2013, 102.

[60] Lin D, Li X, Fan X, Fang X (2011) Child sexual abuse and its relationship with health risk behaviors among rural children and adolescents in Hunan. *China. Child Abuse Negl.* 35(9).

[61] Ystgaard M, Hestetun I, Loeb M, Mehlum L (2004) Is there a specific relationship between childhood sexual and physical abuse and repeated suicidal behavior? *Child Abuse Negl.* 2004 Aug; 28(8):863-75.

[62] Isohookana R, Riala K, Hakko H, Ra¨sa¨nen P. (2013) Adverse childhood experiences and suicidal behavior of adolescent psychiatric inpatients. *Eur. Child Adolesc. Psychiatry* (2013) 22:13–22.

[63] Wong SS, Zhou B, Goebert D, Hishinuma ES. The risk of adolescent suicide across patterns of drug use: a nationally representative study of high school students in the United States from 1999 to 2009. *Soc. Psychiatry Psychiatr. Epidemiol.* 2013 Jun 7.

[64] Bohman H, Jonsson U, Von Knorring AL, Von Knorring L, Päären A, Olsson G. Somatic symptoms as a marker for severity in adolescent depression. *Acta Paediatr.* 2010 Nov; 99(11):1724-30.

[65] Bridge JA, Goldstein TR, Brent DA.. Adolescent suicide and suicidal behavior. *Journal of Child Psychology and Psychiatry* 47:3/4 (2006), pp 372–394.

[66] Cappelli M, Gray C, Zemek R, Cloutier P, Kennedy A, Glennie E, Doucet G, Lyons JS. The HEADS-ED: a rapid mental health screening tool for pediatric patients in the emergency department. *Pediatrics.* 2012; 130: e321-e327.

[67] Anderson RL, Lyons JS, Giles DM, Examining the reliabilityof the Child and Adolescent Needs and Strengths-Mental Health (CANS-MH) scale from two perspectives: a comparison of clinician and research ratings. *J. Child Fam. Stud.* 2002; 12:279Y289.

[68] Payne D, Kennedy A, Kretzer V, Turner E, Shannon P, Viner R. Developing and running an adolescent inpatient ward. *Arch. Dis. Child Educ. Pract.* Ed 2012; 97:42-47.

[69] Buckley S, Caring for those with mental health conditions on a children's ward. *British Journal of Nursing*, Vol. 19, Iss. 19, 28 Oct 2010, pp 1226 – 1230.

[70]   Brown JD, Wissow LS. Discussion of sensitive health topics with youth during primary care visits: relationship to youth perceptions of care. *J. Adolesc. Health* 2009; 44:48–54.

[71]   Tracy K. Richmond and David S. Rosen The treatment of adolescent depression in the era of the black box warning. *Current Opinion in Pediatrics* 2005, 17:466—472.

[72]   Fontanella CA, Bridge JA, Campo JV.Psychotropic medication changes, polypharmacy, and the risk of early readmission in suicidal adolescent inpatients. *Ann. Pharmacother.* 2009; 43:1939-47. Epun 24 Nov 2009.

[73]   Pollack S. Suicide problems in medical practice. *Calif. Med.* 1958; 89(5): 343-4.

[74]   Berman AL. Risk management with suicidal patients. *J. Clin. Psychol.* 2006; 62(2)171-184.

[75]   Ballard ED, Pao M, Horowitz L, Lee LM, Henderson DK, Rosenstein DL. Aftermath of Suicide in the Hospital: Institutional Response. *Psychosomatics,* 2008-11-01, Volume 49, Issue 6, Pages 461-469.

[76]   Reid W, A. The role of the nurse providing therapeutic care for the suicidal patient. *J. Adv. Nurs.* 1993; 18(9):1369-76.

[77]   Gearing RE, Lizardi D. Religion and suicide. *J. Religion Health* 2009; 48(3):332-41.

[78]   Lizardi D. The role of moral objections to suicide in the assessment of suicidal patients. *J. Psych. Res.* 2008; 42:815-21.

[79]   Lloyd, G.G. Suicide in hospital: guidelines for prevention. *J. R. Soc. Med.* 1995; 88:344-346.

[80]   Midence K, Gregory S, Stanley R. The effects of patient suicide on nursing staff. *J. Clin. Nurs.* 1996; 5(2):115-120.

SECTION THREE: PREVENTION

In: Children, Violence and Bullying
Editors: J Merrick, I Kandel and H A Omar

ISBN: 978-1-62948-342-9
© 2014 Nova Science Publishers, Inc.

Chapter 19

ADOLESCENT VIOLENCE PREVENTION

*Hatim A Omar, MD, FAAP**

Division of Adolescent Medicine and Young Parents Program,
Kentucky Children's Hospital, UK Healthcare, Department of Pediatrics,
University of Kentucky College of Medicine, Lexington, Kentucky, US

ABSTRACT

Violence in adolescence has seen an increase since the 1990s with dramatic statistics on violent death and risk behaviors. School violence has been focused upon by a huge media coverage of especially violent cases that could have had some endemic consequences worldwide. We present a case of a 14 year old white male with change in school behavior, strategies for the case investigation, its results and long term prevention. Other research has shown that preventive measures during pregnancy, infancy and childhood can prevent adolescent and adult delinquency.

INTRODUCTION

Homicide rates in the United States are the highest of any developed country and adolescents are at the highest risk of violent death (1). The prevailing rates of lethal and non-lethal violence among adolescents are at an all time high (2). School-associated violence became widely recognized as a common and increasing problem in the mid-1990s (3-5). Adolescent violence represents a public health concern, because of its potential to adversely affect the emotional and social development of the perpetrators, victims and witnesses (6). It is generally accepted that antisocial behavior that begins in early childhood continues to adolescence and adulthood (7).

---

* Correspondence: Hatim A Omar, MD, FAAP, Professor of Pediatrics and Obstetrics/Gynecology, Children's Miracle Network Chair, Chief, Division of Adolescent Medicine and Young Parents Program (J422), Kentucky Children's Hospital, UK Healthcare, Department of Pediatrics,University of Kentucky College of Medicine, Lexington, KY 40536, United States. E-mail: haomar2@uky.edu.

AN EXAMPLE

CD was a 14 year-old white male in 6th grade referred to the adolescent clinic for evaluation by his school, because of deteriorating grades and suspensions for non-compliance with class rules of conduct. This is a special arrangement with the school authorities, where our clinic provides risk assessment, counseling and intervention for the students within a school-based health promotion center.

During the initial interview the patient was hostile, uncooperative and insisting that he was well and did not need help. However, explained that based on the school evaluation he would be suspended again or transferred to a specialized school for problem teens, if unwilling to cooperate, he agreed to go along with the interview. In response to our specific questioning, he admitted that he has been acting inappropriately in class. He explained that by the "bad teachers" who "do not know anything".

On questioning about his home situation, he claimed that his father and stepmother were drug addicts and child abusers. He went on to say that he did not need his parents or anybody else, since he already ran his own "business" and had enough money. The business consisted of selling drugs to peers at the school and on the street. He admitted to smoking, drinking alcohol and drug use (marihuana, inhalants and crack cocaine) on a daily basis. He denied being depressed or any thoughts about suicide.

When asked why he did not report being abused at home, he said that this was when he "was a kid" and now he can "beat his father up". He denied access to firearms, but admitted using a pocket knife he carried taped to his ankle and proceeded to show it in clinic. At this time we interviewed the father and stepmother, who appeared to be genuinely concerned about CD. They disclosed that CD has changed in the last four months and they could barley recognize him anymore. They did not know what caused the change.

The only new thing in his life appeared to be his new group of friends, who were older with school problems. The parents denied ever abusing CD in any form and were very cooperative with child protective services. Interviews with relatives and neighbors as well as home inspections collaborated the story and their two other children (ages 10 and 12 years) denied any abuse and expressed concern about CD. He was allowed to go to school the next day and to come back to our clinic after school.

One day later CD was suspended again from school for possession of marihuana on school premises. During our second interview with CD we felt he was cooperative but extremely hostile toward the school, especially the teachers and two of his classmates that reported him to the teachers for drug use. He repeatedly said "they will be sorry", but refused to specify how. At this point we felt that this patient presented a possible threat for himself and others. We contacted the parents, who denied having any firearms in the house. We contacted the police to check if they had any information about any illegal weapon purchase or theft in his neighborhood and were told that CD's next door neighbor has reported that someone had broken the widows of his car last night and his gun was missing from the car. The police requested permission from CD's parents to search the house, which was granted and the stolen gun was found in CD's room together with a note listing the names of three teachers and seven of his classmates with the phrase "will die" at the bottom of the list.

After this CD admitted to the police that he was planning to take the gun and "punish" those people, who "hated him". He also supplied the names of three older teens, who supplied him with drugs for his own use and for sale. A juvenile court ordered CD admitted to a psychiatric hospital for further evaluation and assessment, He was diagnosed with bipolar disorder and substance abuse and is now under treatment. The drug distributors were arrested and under investigation.

DISCUSSION

This case illustrates the complexity of adolescent development and the multiple factors leading to violence or potential violence. Drug use, lack of communication with adults (parents, teachers), mental health problems, exposure to violence in the media or in real life with negative peer influence can lead to violence. This can happen specifically in young adolescents that have not yet developed abstract thinking.

Children immersed in communities that expose them to violence have been shown to be at high risk for victimization and perpetration of violence (8). Viewing violence on television has been linked with imitative violence, aggressive behavior, acceptance of hostility, and willingness to deliver painful stimuli to others (9). Additional adverse effects on the mental and physical health of children exposed to violence include the emergence of Posttraumatic Stress Disorder (PTSD), internalizing states such as anxiety and depression, and externalizing behaviors such as aggression and risking-taking (6).

Important risk factors for delinquency and violence include poor parenting, untreated conduct disorder, social stress, poverty and school failure (7). Valois et al (10) detailed six major categories (individual, family, school/academic, peer-related, community and neighborhood and situational) as they relate to the risk factors and behaviors associated with adolescent aggression and violence.

Many of the secondary and tertiary prevention programs that focus on incarceration and rehabilitation have not significantly decreased the rate of recidivism. It has been suggested that the most successful prevention programs are likely to be those concentrated in childhood as primary prevention (2). It is thought that through early, supportive involvement with significant adults, adolescents will develop greater self-determination and improved behavior (11).

CONCLUSION

The complex and interactive components of adolescent violence require a preventive plan comprised of a comprehensive community partnership. In the case presented here, the cooperation between multiple agencies was a key in preventing potential violence. As in confronting other risky behaviors, the development of a close working relationship between committed agencies and individuals (parents, police, social services, community health workers, schools and voluntary agencies) was of critical importance (12).

REFERENCES

[1]   Sege RD. Adolescent violence. Adoles Health Update 1999;12(1).

[2]   Rachuba, L, Stanton B, Howard D. Violent crime in the United States: an epidemiologic profile. Arch Pediatr Adolesc Med 1995;149:953-60.

[3]   Sheley JF, McGee ZT, Wright JD.Gun-related violence in and around inner-city schools. Am J Dis Child 1992;146:677-82.

[4]   National School Board Association. Violence in the schools: How America's school Boards are safeguarding our children. Alexandria, VA: National School Boards Association, 1993.

[5]   National League of Cities. School Violence in America's Cities: NLC Survey Overview. Washington, DC: National League of Cities,1993.

[6]   Howard DE, Feigelman S, Li X, et al. The relationship among violence victimization, witnessing violence, and youth distress. J Adolesc Health 2002;31:455-62.

[7]   Rivara FP, Farrington DP. Prevention of violence. Arch Pediatr Adolesc Med 1995;149:421-9.

[8]   Bell CC, Jenkins EJ. Community violence and children on Chicago's southside. Psychiatry 1993;56:446-54.

[9]   Sargent JD, Heatherton TF, Ahrens B, et al. Adolescent exposure to extremely violent movies. J Adolesc Health 2002;31:449-54.

[10]   Valois RF, MacDonald JM, Fischer BL, et al. Risk factors and behaviors associated with adolescent violence and aggression. Am J Health Behav 2002;26:454-64.

[11]   DiNapoli, PP. Adolescent violent behavior and ego development. J Adolesc Health 2002;31:449-54.

[12]   Christian J, Gilvarry E. Specialist services: the need for multi-agency partnership. Drug Alcohol Depend 1999; 55:265-74.

In: Children, Violence and Bullying
Editors: J Merrick, I Kandel and H A Omar

ISBN: 978-1-62948-342-9
© 2014 Nova Science Publishers, Inc.

Chapter 20

PREVENTION: SEXUAL VIOLENCE AGAINST ADOLESCENT AND YOUNG ADULT WOMEN

Kimberly K McClanahan, PhD[1], Marlene B Huff, PhD[2],
*Hatim A Omar, MD, FAAP[*2]*
and Joav Merrick, MD, MMedSci, DMSc[2,3,4,5]

[1]Pathways, Inc, Ashland, Kenticky
[2]Division of Adolescent Medicine and Young Parents Program,
Kentucky Children's Hospital, UK Healthcare, Department of Pediatrics,
University of Kentucky College of Medicine, Lexington, Kentucky, US
[3]National Institute of Child Health and Human Development, Jerusalem, Israel
[4]Office of the Medical Director, Health Services, Division for Intellectual and
Developmental Disabilities, Ministry of Social Affairs and Social Services,
Jerusalem, Israel
[5]Division of Pediatrics, Hadassah Hebrew University Medical Center,
Mt Scopus Campus, Jerusalem, Israel

INTRODUCTION

Sexual violence is a "profound social and public health problem in the United States," according to the Centers for Disease Control and Prevention, and it has been found that adolescent females aged 16-24 years are four times more likely to be victims of sexual violence than women in all other age groups, with a lifetime prevalence of rape or attempted rape as high as 42% (1). Sexual assault has historically been viewed as a stranger in the bushes phenomenon, where an unknown perpetrator attacks the victim after which the victim reports the assault to the police and evidence is collected immediately (1,2). However, evidence-based research shows that sexual assault by a known perpetrator is much more

---

[*] Correspondence: Hatim A Omar, MD, FAAP, Professor of Pediatrics and Obstetrics/Gynecology, Children's Miracle Network Chair, Chief, Division of Adolescent Medicine and Young Parents Program (J422), Kentucky Children's Hospital, UK Healthcare, Department of Pediatrics,University of Kentucky College of Medicine, Lexington, KY 40536, United States. E-mail: haomar2@uky.edu.

prevalent than sexual assault by a stranger (3) and is often either an acquaintance or dating partner (1). Rates of sexual assault by known perpetrators range between 50 to 88% of total identified assaults (3).

Rape is the most common violent crime on American college campuses today, and ninety percent of college women who are victims of rape know the perpetrator (2). Studies of college-aged populations suggest that a significant portion of young adult victims do not report acquaintance rape, specifically because of the relationship (4). In fact, fewer than five percent of college women who are victims of rape report it to the police (2). It has been postulated that adolescent victims may be even more reluctant to report acquaintance rape due to past sexual intimacy with the perpetrator or due to date-specific behaviors such as the use of alcohol or drugs (4). Table 1 shows a list of the most frequent reasons female college students choose not to report sexual assault experiences to the authorities.

Table 1. Reasons for not reporting acquaintance rape (2)

Embarrassment and shame
Fear of publicity
Fear of reprisal from perpetrator
Fear of social isolation from the perpetrator's friends
Fear that the police will not believe victim
Fear that the prosecutor will not believe victim or will not bring charges

RISK FACTORS FOR SEXUAL ASSAULT AGAINST ADOLESCENT AND YOUNG ADULT FEMALES

Many factors have been associated with increased risk for sexual assault against adolescent and young adult females. One risk consistently cited is that of a history of sexual victimization as either a child younger than 12 years or an adolescent younger than 18 years (1). Some research has shown that young adult females with sexual abuse histories may have difficulty in accurately perceiving risk in potentially harmful sexual situations and may, therefore, be more vulnerable to repeated victimizations (5). Other identified risk factors include number of dating and sexual partners, earlier age at menarche and/or first date, history of dating violence, and a sexually active peer group (1). The context in which the date occurs may also impact the probability of sexual assault. If the male initiates the date, pays for the date, and drives, the possibility of sexual assault increases. Additionally, the use of alcohol and/or drugs by the victim, perpetrator, or both also increases the likelihood of a sexual assault (1).

SEQUELAE OF SEXUAL ASSAULT

Females who experience sexual assault also often experience a dramatic negative impact on their functioning. As many of 50% of rape victims will develop Posttraumatic Stress Disorder and many will develop other psychological disorders (6). Victims also often have more somatic complaints and more chronic pain than nonvictims. Rape victims have been shown to utilize health care services twice as often and report engaging in twice as many negative health behaviors, such as smoking or drinking excessively, when compared to nonvictims (6). Regardless of the ill effects, many victims of sexual assault do not inform their healthcare providers nor do they seek mental health treatment, even though disclosure has been identified as an important step in recovery and improved health (4).

SCREENING AND REFERRAL FOR SEXUAL ASSAULT IN ADOLESCENT AND YOUNG ADULT FEMALES

The American Academy of Pediatrics, the American College of Obstetricians and Gynecologists and the American Medical Association all endorse universal screening for intimate partner violence (IPV), one form of which is sexual assault (4) and it has been recommended that all female patients over age 14 years be screened regardless of symptoms or signs of abuse, and regardless of whether the provider suspects abuse has occurred (7). Further, a number of practice organizations have practice guidelines that recommend screening for IPV (8). Nonetheless, actual screening rates remain low (9).

In recent research asking whether young women between the ages of 15 and 24 years supported universal screening for IPV in a healthcare setting, the majority surveyed indicated overwhelming support. However, underage females (15-18 years), were 2.9 times more likely to voice many concerns regarding violence screening by a provider than those young women aged 19-21 years (10). It was speculated that females under the age of majority may have greater concerns of confidentiality, since there might be a greater likelihood that adults would be given information that the younger teens might not want revealed. A study (6) with regard to violence screening specific to sexual violence, showed that 52% of women reported that they had never been screened for sexual violence nor provided any type of information about sexual violence by their healthcare professional. Table 2 includes some tips for physicians when they see a victim of acquaintance rape.

Table 2. Tips for physicians

1	Listen to the victim without expressing shock or judgment
2	Determine the nature of the relationship with the perpetrator and whether or not the sexual victimization occurred in the past, present, and/or is ongoing
3	Explain the rights and options the victim has with regard to reporting, prosecution, and treatment
4	Involve the victim's parents when possible and appropriate
5	Provide resources and referrals for support and treatment
6	Perform a physical examination, if appropriate, including tests for sexually transmitted infections and pregnancy
7	Explain the necessity for reporting the assault to the authorities, i.e., the law determines what is reportable, and make the report in a timely manner
8	Schedule a follow-up appointment for the discussion of test results, information obtained regarding the legal report, and assessment of victim's emotional status and progress toward obtaining support and treatment
9	Continue medical treatment for the victim as determined by need and desire on the part of the victim

Healthcare providers have been questioned regarding their reasons for not screening their patients for sexual and other types of violence. In one review of 12 studies identifying barriers to IPV screening, respondents reported several concerns, including the lack of effective interventions for IPV once identified, fear of offending patients, lack of provider education about IPV, and limited time. Additionally, providers reported that they were concerned about patient nondisclosure, patient fear of repercussions, and patient noncompliance (9,10).

PREVENTION

A publication by the World Health Organization (WHO) together with the London School of Hygiene and Tropical Medicine on preventing intimate partner and sexual violence against women outlined several key strategies (11):

During infancy, childhood and early adolescence

- Implement home-visitation and parent-education programmes to prevent child maltreatment
- improve maternal mental health programs
- identify and treat conduct and emotional disorders in children
- improve interventions for children and adolescents subjected to child maltreatment and/or exposed to intimate partner violence
- improve school-based social and emotional skills development
- implement school-based training to help children to recognize and avoid potentially sexually abusive situations
- implement bullying prevention programmes

During adolescence and early adulthood

- implement school-based programmes to prevent dating violence
- school-based multi-component violence prevention programmes
- sexual violence prevention programmes for school and college populations

During adulthood

- execute empowerment and participatory approaches to reduce gender inequality
- apply home visitation programs to prevent intimate partner violence
- execute multi-component programs (like the program to prevent suicide by the US Air force, which with is multi-purpose program managed to reduce the rate of suicide by 33% and the rates of severe and moderate family violence by 54% and 30% respectively)

All life stages

- reduce access to and harmful use of alcohol

- change social and cultural norms related to gender that support intimate partner and sexual violence

The WHO report (11) found it important to achieve change at the population level and target societal-level factors in the primary prevention of intimate partner and sexual violence. This can be achieved by various startegies, like enactment of legislation and the development of supporting policies that protect women; addressing discrimination against women and helping to move the culture away from violence – thereby acting as a foundation for further prevention work.

CONCLUSION

Sexual assault against adolescent and young adult females is a public health problem of great prevalence. Most sexual assault is committed by a person known to the victim, and the majority of victims do not report the assault even though it has been shown that disclosure is often an important part of the healing process. Universal screening for sexual and other types of violence in personal relationships is recommended by a number of healthcare practice organizations, but many healthcare practitioners do not practice universal screening for a variety of reasons, including lack of knowledge regarding referral or intervention after a disclosure and lack of provider education about IPV. Healthcare providers would benefit from formal education and training regarding sexual and other forms of violence against women. They should also be provided with referral and treatment resources for females who are victims of violence.

REFERENCES

[1]   Rickert VI, Wiemann CM, Vaughan RD, White JW. Rates and risk factors for sexual violence among an ethnically diverse sample of adolescents. Arch Pediatr Adolesc Med 2004;158(12):1132-9.

[2]   Sampson R. Acquaintance rape of college students. Washington, DC: US Department Justice, Office Community Oriented Policing Services, 2002:5.

[3]   Jones JS, Wynn BN, Kroeze B, Dunnuck C, Rossman L. Comparison of sexual assaults by strangers versus known assailants in a community-based population. Am J Emerg Med 2004;22(6):454-9.

[4]   Rickert VI, Wiemann CM, Vaughan RD. Disclosure of date/acquaintance rape: Who reports and when. J Pediatr Adolesc Gynecol 2005;18(1):17-24.

[5]   Messman-Moore TL, Brown AL. Risk perception, rape, and sexual revictimization: A prospective study of college women. Psychol Women Quart 2006;30(2):159-72.

[6]   Littleton HL, Berenson AB, Breitkopf CR. An evaluation of health care providers' sexual violence screening practices. Am J Obstet Gynecol 2007;196:564-7.

[7]   Saltzman LE, Green YT, Marks JS, Thacker SB. Violence against women as a public health issue: Comments from the CDC. Am J Prev Med 2000;19(4):325-9.

[8]   Trabold N. Screening for intimate partner violence within a health care setting:a systematic review of the literature. Soc Work Health Care. 2007;45(1):1-18.

[9]   Waalen J, Goodwin MM, Spitz AM, Petersen R, Saltzman LE. Screening for intimate partner violence by health care providers: Barriers and interventions. Am J Prev Med 2000;19(4):230-7.

[10]   Zeitler MS, Paine AD, Breitbart V, et al. Attitudes about intimate partner violence screening among an ethnically diverse sample of young women. J Adolesc Health 2006;39(1):119.

[11]   World Health Organization/London School of Hygiene and Tropical Medicine. Preventing intimate partner and sexual violence against women: taking action and generating evidence. Geneva: World Health Organization, 2010.

In: Children, Violence and Bullying
Editors: J Merrick, I Kandel and H A Omar

ISBN: 978-1-62948-342-9
© 2014 Nova Science Publishers, Inc.

Chapter 21

YOUTH SUICIDE PREVENTION

*Said Shahtahmasebi, PhD**

Centre for Health and Social Practice, Wintec, New Zealand,
The Good Life Research Centre Trust,
New Zealand and Division of Adolescent Medicine,
Department of Pediatrics, Kentucky Children's Hospital, University of Kentucky,
Lexington, Kentucky, US

ABSTRACT

The suicide literature suggests that mental illness and in particular depression are the main causes of suicide. Worldwide government policies of addressing mental illness have been the main focus for suicide prevention, which coupled with a moratorium on reporting and public debate of suicide appears to deliver ineffective services. A prevention scheme that is based on intervention will be ineffective because intervention mainly occurs at or after an outcome such as incidence of an illness. Not everyone suffers from mental illness, and not everyone who suffers from mental illness will commit suicide. However, there is a growing body of literature that challenges the mental illness-suicide link. This paper argues that suicide is the result of a complex decision making process by individuals who live in communities and contribute to society. Therefore any interventions must be holistic and at grassroots level. The application of Kentucky University's 'stop youth suicide' campaign to a New Zealand community is briefly discussed.

INTRODUCTION

In spite of the large volume of literature on suicide the public health strategy on suicide prevention is still reliant on a medical model that treats suicide as a mental illness. There is however, confusion within the literature which is often due to poor study design and

---

* Correspondence: Said Shahtahmasebi, The Good Life Research Centre Trust, 4 Orkney Street, Strowan, Christchurch 8052, New Zealand. E-mail: radisolevoo@gmail.com.

methodological flaws associated with human behaviour. Suicide data, in particular those based on psychological autopsy type investigations such as Beautrais (1-3), are often plagued with a high degree of bias. Given the current public mindset, helped by the medical model and the media, that depression causes suicide, the collection of data on suicide cases from friends and relatives after the event of suicide will be highly biased towards mental illness, as is the case with the Canterbury Suicide Project (1-3). Studies that fail to address the methodological issues related to design, data collection and analysis will lead to misleading and conflicting conclusions. For example, Beautrais (1-3) used a psychological autopsy method and collected information about suicide cases from family and friends to conclude that mental illness causes suicide. Khan et al (4) claimed that antidepressants do not reduce suicide and may increase the risk of suicide, while, Hall et al (5) claimed that antidepressants reduces suicide rates.

The suicide literature also suggests a link between other health, social and environmental factors with suicide. For example, some studies suggest bereavement, e.g. (6-8), early childhood trauma, e.g. (9), socio-economic group and employment issues, e.g. (6), financial strain and negative life events, e.g. (10, 11) and so on as risk factors for suicide. Although, suicide prevention is very slowly and gradually taking notice of alternative medical models, nevertheless, in terms of policy development suicide prevention is still listed under mental health policy. Despite a move by WHO to increase awareness on mental illness which was taken up by some governments (e.g. UK's no health without mental health policy document (12)), more of the same appears to be the main policy for suicide prevention. In other words, the policy documents recommend more mental health services to be made available to the public (13). In the meantime the suicide rates appear to maintain an overall upward trend with cycles where suicide rate trends may reverse for a short period of time. The response from the authorities has often been to praise mental health services during the cycle(s) when trends appear to be downwards, but when the trends reverse it is claimed that suicide is a very complex public health issue and depends on many social, economic and environmental variables which require further research. The lack of progress in suicide prevention appears to be related to budgeting, developing and carrying out "further research" as policy documents appear to suggest "further research" and further investment is often translated into more of the same, i.e. more investment into mental health services (13).

Furthermore, the problems with suicide prevention are exacerbated with the restrictions in the reporting of suicide in the media and public places such as schools and youth clubs which matter most. One main implication of banning discussions of suicide is for the suicide survivors (e.g. see (14)). The ban on an open discussion of suicide has effectively been to shut survivors out and restrict discussion of suicide with their counsellor, if they had one. It is obvious that there will be further complications such as the availability of skilled and culturally sensitive counsellors. This is an important issue when the suicide case is a young adolescent person survived by parents, siblings and friends.

In this paper we discuss the rationale for adopting a holistic approach to suicide prevention and in order to have an impact on future suicide rates emphasis should be placed on educating the young. The issues of interest will be illustrated through a real life application of a grassroots approach to youth suicide prevention.

RATIONALE

Over the years there has been more discussion in the literature about other non-medical risk factors for suicide (15-24) suggesting that a medical model alone will not be an effective form of treatment and prevention. Over the last decade or so, researchers and governments' strategy policies appear to acknowledge the complexities of suicide, however, their action plans seem to divert from these complexities towards a medical model for both prevention and intervention (e.g. see (25, 26)), in other words governments' action policy only offer more of the same (13).

In New Zealand, like other countries, there has been a long established view of the direction of causality from mental illness (specifically depression) to suicide. This has been achieved by the hasty reporting of so called research and in particular the media's slant and uncritical reporting. In announcing a $6.4 million campaign to reduce the impact of depression, the New Zealand Government claimed "We know that up to 90% of suicides are *caused* by depression and that each year 500 New Zealanders are dying by suicide." The Government further claimed "The World Health Organisation has predicted that by the year 2020, depression will be second only to cardiovascular disease, in contributing to the global burden of disease. We must tackle this problem head on and the National Depression Initiative will go a long way to achieving this objective." [http://www.beehive.govt.nz/ViewDocument.aspx?DocumentID=27352]. This announcement is a reflection of the ineffectiveness of health and social policies in reducing cardiovascular disease.

The New Zealand Government's suicide prevention strategy document (25) is testament to this confusion. The document attempts to demonstrate a move away from the medical model by including almost all other possible factors reported in the literature as potential contributors: from alcohol and drug abuse to bereavement, family break-ups, unemployment, educational and financial failure and so on. The strategy (25) is not clear as to how this wide range of contributory factors may relate to policy and therefore budget allocation. It is imperative that policy makers do not fall in the trap of attempting to achieve a perceived desired effect by symbolic manipulation of an outcome process, e.g. removing the 'fail' as an outcome in school exam. In other words, such a policy unwisely assumes that removing 'fail' from an education outcome will lead to positive adolescents. This is analogous to a policy that encourages people to move from their homes because most accidents happen at home.

The main point of concern that all of us (not just practitioners and researchers) must remember, is that at the centre of this decision making process there is a person. In the case of young adolescents, the individual has already gone through their own process of decision making by which time it is too late for any external influence/intervention. Time is a particularly important factor in preventing adolescent suicide due to the fact that the process of decision making takes place much more rapidly than in adults. In adolescents the risk of a complete suicide is heightened when there is immediate access to quick methods of killing (e.g. guns) following a 'trigger' event/factor. Conversely, this risk can be reduced as quickly when the access to means is denied or made difficult thus providing time for the young individuals to reflect on the trigger event whilst attempting suicide. This is not to say that some teenagers do not take time and plan to end their own lives. Although, these suicides may appear as sudden decisions, this does suggest a wish by the individual to be in the driving seat and is in control.

As reported earlier, most of the suicide cases had no psychiatric records suggesting that for these people the decision making process had been completed and executed before any "intervention" could be actioned. Clearly, in these cases not even a holistic treatment would have been effective because of the choice they made. However, such an approach may be modified and extended to understand individuals through an understanding of the society they live in, in order to influence the individual's process of decision making. In medical treatments a "holistic" approach is often referred to as treating the person and not just the physical or emotional symptoms. Ventegodt and Merrick (27) suggest that we must, as holistic physicians and health practitioners, support and guide our patients through the *dynamics* of suicide. To understand the dynamics of human behaviour in the current age of an advanced information culture, the "holistic" notion must go beyond the individual and accept that decision making processes are influenced by many other processes such as social, economic, environment, media (28). Physicians on their own have little or no control over these dynamic processes.

The Good Life Approach (28) may be adopted to develop social and health policy actions incorporating possible influences from these processes. As shown in Fig. 1, the Good Life model assumes the individual as well as society are the central processes that are subject to influence from other processes. Some of these processes we know about and are related to human behaviour; politics, economy, education, public health and medicine, whilst others such as the environment are inter-related with human behaviour but we do not have complete control over them. The problem is that the dynamics of human behaviour may influence these processes in a conflicting and diverging direction to contradict and lead to adverse interactions between the processes. Erroneous results and mis-conclusions from a biased and subjective assessment of suicide will have further ramifications for policy and treatment. For example, anti-smoking or anti-violence policies may be ineffective in the light of how politicians behave, and the media's portrayal of a hero as a violent smoker who dabbles in risky behaviour.

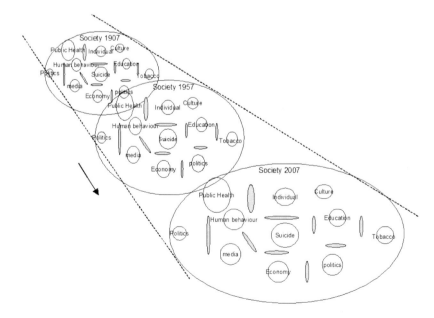

Figure 1. An example of a conceptual holistic model of suicide.

The main points being presented here are:

- the current list of risk factors for suicide and suicidal behaviour (e.g. see (25, 26)) suggests that suicide is a complex health and social issue that can affect anyone. In other words the whole population is at risk of suicide.
- There are overlaps and conflicts in human behaviour leading to conflicting consequences in behaviour outcomes such as the interaction between entertainment media, social and health policies, and behaviour outcomes such eradicating family and sexual violence, reducing smoking rates, and preventing a suicide.

CONCEPTUALISATION

It can be visualised from figure 1 that prevention actions based on a single model may not have an impact on suicide but will affect the parameters of other processes and can itself be affected by them. Such dynamic interactions may in fact produce outcomes in the opposite direction not just in the process of interest, e.g. suicide prevention, but also other health and social behaviour outcomes, e.g. social attitudes and perceptions of mental illness as the main cause of suicide and a lack of service uptake, e.g. see (17, 29). The main impact of a medical model on suicide outcomes has been the establishment of a causal relationship between mental illness and suicide in the public mindset. Furthermore, the generally upward trends since World War II in Fig. 2 can be interpreted that such an approach of relying on a sustained application of a single model has not worked.

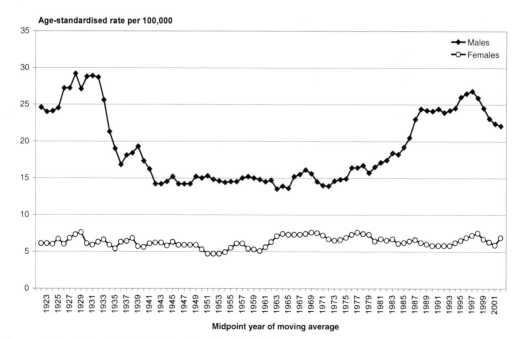

Source: New Zealand Health Information Service (30)

Figure 2. Death from suicide by sex, New Zealand, 1921-2003.

Surely, after so many decades of 'more of the same' it must be time to follow a different direction and adopt a more collaborative approach. However, bearing in mind the conceptual model in figure 1, we must first try and understand not just suicide but human behaviour. Second, any new direction and approach must take account of the residual effects of health and social policies on behaviour. For example, it will not be easy to reverse the effects on policy development of the well-established view in the public mind set that mental illness causes suicide.

As suggested above, risk factors for suicide are many and cover many aspects of society. The literature on suicide (25,26) suggests a large number of variables from depression to trauma, bereavement, unemployment, marriage break up, poor health, drug and alcohol abuse, poor nutrition, childhood events and so on may cause suicide. A pragmatic translation of the literature is that the general population is at risk of suicide. This interpretation actually makes sense and reinforces that suicide cannot be explained by one discipline or a model. Suicide is a process of decision making.

Suicide prevention policy development should allow a multidisciplinary approach to include input from members of the public. However, in most countries the policy development for suicide prevention and intervention has been a top-down approach where governments develop mental health strategy documents with respective policy action documents in order to allocate and distribute resources. As discussed elsewhere (13), strategy documents and policy actions are often translated into mental services which the public are told they need. In other words there is no input from the public about what they really need and what they really want.

It is evident that suicide prevention and intervention must start with a willingness from the public to take part in (31). In order to achieve this the direction of policy development must be reversed. That is, prevention and interventional policies must be holistic, and to be holistic they must be developed at the grassroots.

Community-based actions are not new phenomena. The University of Kentucky's "stop youth suicide" Campaign (http://stopyouthsuicide.com) started in 2001 because the coroner was concerned to see so many young suicide cases. His approach was without presumption and simple. He approached the adolescent medicine department at the University of Kentucky and asked the question 'what can we do to reduce youth suicide? The "stop youth suicide" campaign began with the knowledge and understanding of adolescents and therefore their communities. That is, we must understand or gain insight into the young persons who engage in suicide or suicidal behaviour before assuming mental illness. Through such an approach we can then gain insight into the society and communities of these young people. Within a year the "stop youth suicide" Campaign had enlisted community workers, politicians, schools, teenagers themselves (32).

The Campaign has been successful in reducing youth suicide rates from around 19 to under 12 per 100,000 and attributes this success to the involvement at grassroots. The Campaign has brought about law changes including gun-safety, public discussion of suicide, and suicide education programmes at schools. Most of these programmes are longitudinal and are an integral part of the curriculum to maintain continuity.

THE NEW ZEALAND EXPERIENCE

As mentioned in the background, New Zealand aligns itself with Western democracies on suicide. Despite acknowledging the multidimensional risk for suicide, the prevention and interventional strategies are top-down and based on a medical model. Internationally, New Zealand's suicide rate is high. In 2008, 497 people died as a result of suicide. The national suicide rate is 11.2 per 100,000 people (http://www.health.govt.nz/publication/suicide-facts-deaths-and-intentional-self-harm-hospitalisations-2008). Youth suicide is of particular concern in New Zealand. Suicide rates for young people are high, with deaths between the ages of 15 and 24 making up 23% of all suicides in the Waikato region. Suicide is the second most common cause of death for young people. Between 2002 and 2006, over a quarter of deaths in the Waikato region for people aged 15-19 were due to suicide.

In New Zealand, the author experienced a lack of interest in a holistic approach in gaining insight into suicide from the authorities, academic colleagues, government agencies and funders. In 2009, the author joined the School of Health at Waikato Institute of Technology (Wintec) which is a tertiary education provider with a strong commitment to the community it serves. In 2010, a proposal was made to Wintec to host the creator of "stop youth suicide" Campaign, Professor Hatim Omar, for a discussion with the School of Health. The proposal was funded with the condition that Professor Omar facilitate a couple of lectures to staff and public. A programme of four workshops targeting communities that had been identified with high rates of youth suicide and a public lecture was hastily put together.

It was during these workshops that the extent of community despair and frustration caused by suicide and its politics became evident. Despite the high level of frustration with the politics of suicide most front line service providers and those affected by suicide demonstrated a strong passion about suicide prevention and wanted to talk about it. In New Zealand, like most Western countries, there is a moratorium on a public discussion of 'method' of suicide in particular within the media. Unfortunately, the moratorium has been abused and misinterpreted by many including some employers to shut staff down. Some attendees reported that their employer had threatened them with legal action and termination of contract for attempting to discuss with other staff how best they could contribute to suicide prevention in the workplace. It is not comforting to know that the majority of these organisations were educational establishments. Despite limited publicity for the workshops, the workshops were well attended. We received email messages from disappointed members of the public who had heard about the workshop too late. It must also be reported that we received messages from other communities wanting workshops but of note is the heart rending message we received from a community outside of the Waikato Region. This community had suffered many suicides in a spate of several months averaging one suicide a month. They had no resources or funding to travel to the workshops. We organised a special workshop on a Saturday before Professor Omar's return to Kentucky.

Workshop evaluations were 100% positive and demonstrated a very strong demand for a community-based strategy. The workshop evaluations also suggested a strong demand for more details of workshops providing skills training. At least one community set up a support group made up of volunteers. The media showed interest, too, but the workshops did not get much air time due to an unfortunate major mine disaster with many fatalities in New Zealand around the same time as the workshops. However, one of the key messages was that we cannot keep suicide a secret and must talk about it otherwise our youth could make *un-informed* decisions about their understanding of suicide based on secretive rumours.

Due to the feedback and demand for training and in discussion with the communities, the author developed, submitted and was granted a Fulbright Specialist Grant to invite Professor Omar to facilitate advanced youth suicide prevention workshops. Wintec's community alliance consisted of many frontline health and social services groups including Waahi Whanui, Huntly Community Advice, Raukura Waikato Social Services, mental health awareness forum or the Maori Women's Welfare League, South Waikato District Council, Raukawa Iwi and Te Puna Oranga (Māori Health Service) Waikato District Health Board (DHB), Population Health Service of the Waikato DHB, Safe Kawerau Kids Injury Prevention Project (SKKIPP) and Rangatahi group for Kawerau. The Fulbright grant was supplemented with local communities' financial support and a major grant from Trust Waikato to cover expenses. These workshops were run during the later part of November 2011. There were more communities who had joined the first group of communities which stretched from Thames (North Waikato), central and South Waikato, and an interest group in Christchurch (in the south Island). Needless to say it was a punishing schedule but a rewarding one. Quite unexpectedly, a number of interventions occurred during these workshops. Although, the workshops were designed for the health professionals (including social workers, counsellors, health promoters, GPs, psychiatrist and mental health workers), attendance was open to the public with an interest in youth suicide prevention. Some had attended the workshop as a last resort so that perhaps they could find the help they were looking for which was not forthcoming from the services in their own community. Multi-agency help as per their expressed needs of the persons was organised immediately following the workshops through the suicide prevention liaison agents who were available at every workshop. Those who simply were happy to discuss their issues and to vent off frustration with lack of services or a failure of the authorities to listen, help was offered and coordinated by counsellors and social workers who happened to be in the same room attending the workshops. A lack of communication between the various service providers themselves, and the communities they serve is an artefact of the top-down model.

The communities that were involved with the workshops have now joined forces and have regular contact with each other to share information and action plans, and to support each other and share scarce resources where there are overlaps. Most of the communities have now set up support groups made up of mostly volunteer parents, concerned individuals, suicide survivors (parents who have lost to suicide). These groups do not see themselves as frontline suicide prevention workers but as a buffering force, to be a 'non-threatening' and approachable resource for young people or anyone to feel comfortable to contact and talk about their issues. The groups have collated a list of resources including emergency phone numbers to crisis, national suicide prevention, mental health services and other local services that may be appropriate.

The groups have no funds nor have they any resources to operate effectively. However, armed with a knowledge of their community and a passion to prevent suicide have adopted a strategy of simple actions that could have a major impact on the outcome. For example, talking about the evils of suicide, providing a cell phone help-number for people to contact, taking a chance and start a conversation with people at any opportunity e.g. at the bus stop or in the park. Simple steps like talking to people have already helped some people in the community who had otherwise been contemplating suicide. The irony is that, social contact and community involvement is an integral human behaviour that appears to have been eroded to such an extent that it is being taught as though it is a new discovery. As explained earlier, this may be the result of residual health, social and economic policies (see Fid. 1). However, without any resources even the simple steps can become a major problem and could take months if not years to organise. As an example, one group recognised a community need for youth to contact the group but found organising a cell phone very difficult. Although, it was relatively easy to get hold of a handset which was donated by a local resident, getting mobile service providers on-board to donate air time has not come to fruition despite its success and local relevance and the cost is being borne by the group. The group has already received calls from local youths seeking help.

Amongst other success it appears that suicide is beginning to lose its taboo stature and is being discussed and debated at a community level. Lifeline Aotearoa (www.lifeline.org.nz) is launching a three month television campaign on Maori TV called 'start the conversation today- Me timata te korero i tenei ra!'

CONCLUSION

A top-down approach coupled with a lack of communication between support service agencies is often ineffective and has very little effect on the outcomes for which the services are designed in the first place (13, 33). Within a top-down policy formation, the authorities become less receptive to community input. For example, it is reported that the Associate Health Minister was to chair a meeting of media, mental health professionals and researchers early this year to update the guidelines (http://www.stuff.co.nz/the-press/news/4550480/Anger-over-missing-voice). There is no mention of communities or victims/survivors of suicide in this statement of intent. Such groups were mentioned in a non-specific way by a spokesman for the Associate Health Minister that family and friends would be able to participate in the meetings this year, after an uproar by suicide survivors.

Relevant and effective policy actions can be developed through the *depoliticisation* of research and science so that collaboration can occur more fluidly within and between the various agencies in conjunction with the communities at grassroots level. By engaging the community and the public at the beginning of the process of decision making will help make policy actions more relevant and effective. At the time of writing, the author received a report from one of the communities that through engaging the public a young teenager intervened and prevented a potential suicide of another adolescent by turning up at their doorstep.

In the context of a grassroots approach, the role of the experts would be to critique the available research collaboratively and not in competition. It must be remembered that every policy action will have a multi-dimensional reaction on behavioural outcomes (Figure 1). We must avoid a situation where society and communities are defined by individualism, thus, eroding the most intrinsic of human behaviour, which is keeping in contact and looking out for friends and neighbours and other members of the community.

REFERENCES

[1]   Beautrais AL. Serious suicide attempts in young people: A case control study. Dissertation. Christchurch: Christchurch School Medicine, 1996.

[2]   Beautrais AL. Suicides and serious suicide attempts: Two populations or one? Psychol Med 2001;31:837-45.

[3]   Beautrais AL, Joyce PR, Mulder RT. The canterbury suicide project: Aims, overview and progress. Commun Ment Health NZ 1994;8(2):32-9.

[4]   Khan A, Warner HA, Brown WA. Symptom reduction and suicide risk in patients treated with placebo in antidepressant clinical trials: An analysis of the food and drug administration database. Arch Gen Psychiatry 2000;57:311-7.

[5]   Hall WD, Mant A, Mitchell PB, Rendle VA, Hickie IB, McManus P. Association between antidepressant prescribing and suicide in Australia, 1991-2000: Trend analysis. BMJ 2003;326:1008.

[6]   Agerbo E, Nordentoft M, Mortensen PB. Familial, psychiatric, and socioeconomic risk factors for suicide in young peopl: Nested case-control study. BMJ 2002;325(7355):74-7.

[7]   Murphy SA, Tapper VJ, Johnson LC, Lohan J. Suicide ideation among parents bereaved by the violent deaths of their children. Issues Ment Health Nurs 2003;24(1):5-25.

[8]   Rozenzweig A, Prigerson H, Miller MD, Reynolds CFr. Bereavement and late-life depression: Grief and its complications in the elderly. Annu Rev Med 1997;48:421-8.

[9]   van der Kolk BA, Hostetler A, Herron N, Fisler RE. Trauma and the development of borderline personality disorder. Psychiatr Clin North Am 1994;17(4):715-30.

[10]   Baumeister RF. Suicide as escape from self. Psychol Rev 1990;97(1):90.

[11]   Duberstein PR, Conwell Y, Conner KR, Eberly S, Caine ED. Suicide at 50 years of age and older: Perceived physical illness, family discord and financial strain. Psychol Med 2004;34(1):137-46.

[12]   Department of Health. No health without mental health: A cross-government mental health outcomes strategy for people of all ages. HM Government, 2011.

[13]   Shahtahmasebi S. A review and critique of mental health policy development. Int J Child Health Hum Dev 2012;5(3):forthcoming.

[14]   Shahtahmasebi S, Aupouri-Mclean C. Bereaved by suicide. Primary health care: Open access, 2011. URL: http://wwwomicsgrouporg/journals/ArchivePHCOA/currentissuePHCOAphp

[15]   Abbar M, Caer Y, Schenk L, Castelnau D. [psychosocial stress factors and suicidal acts]. Encephale 1993;19(Spec No 1):179-85.

[16]   Conwell Y, Duberstein PR. Prevention of late life suicide: When, where, why and how. Psychiatr Clin Neurosci 1995;49(Suppl 1):S79-83.

[17]   Hamdi E, Price S, Qassem T, Amin Y, Jones D. Suicides not in contact with mental health services: Risk indicators and determinants of referral. J Ment Health 2008;17(4):398-409.

[18]   Heikkinen M, Aro H, Lonnqvist J. Life events and social support in suicide. Suicide Life Threat Behav 1993;23(4):343-58.

[19]   Heikkinen M, Aro H, Lonnqvist J. Recent life events, social support and suicide. Acta Psychiatr Scand Suppl 1994;377:65-72.

[20]   Murphy BM, Puffett A. Pathways to suicide prevention. Br J Hosp Med 1995;54(1):11-4.

[21]   Neeleman J. Beyond risk theory: Suicidal behavior in its social and epidemiological context. Crisis 2002;23(3):114-20.

[22]   Shahtahmasebi S, Shahtahmasebi R. A holistic view of suicide: Social change and education and training. J Altern Med Res 2010;2(1):115-28.

[23]   Ventegodt S, Clausen B, Merrick J. Clinical holistic medicine: The case story of anna. Iii. Rehabilitation of philosophy of life during holistic existential therapy for childhood sexual abuse. ScientificWorldJournal 2006;6:2080-91.

[24]   Webb D. Bridging the spiritual gap. Aust e-Journal Adv Ment Health (AeJAMH) 2005;4(1). URL: http://wwwauseinetcom/journal/vol4iss1/webbpdf

[25]   Associate Minister of Health. The new zealand suicide prevention strategy 2006-2016. Wellington: Ministry of Health 2006. URL: http://www.moh.govt.nz/moh.nsf/pagesmh/4904/$File/suicide-prevention-strategy-2006-2016.pdf.

[26]   Lorant V, Kunst AE, Huisman M, Costa G, Mackenbach J. Socio-economic inequalities in suicide: A european comparative study. Br J Psychiatry 2005;187(1):49.

[27]   Ventegodt S, Merrick J. Philosophy of life and suicide: To be or not to be is still the question. In: Merrcik J, Zalsman G, eds. Suicidal behaviour in adolescence: An international perspective. Tel Aviv: Freund, 2005:9-17.

[28]   Shahtahmasebi S. The good life: A holistic approach to the health of the population. ScientificWorldJournal 2006;6:2117-32.

[29]   Shahtahmasebi S. Suicides by mentally ill people. ScientificWorldJournal 2003;3:684-93.

[30]   Ministry of Health. New zealand suicide trends: Mortality 1921-2003, hospitalisations for intentional self-harm 1978-2004. Wellington, NZ: Ministry of Health, 2006.

[31]   Shahtahmasebi S. Suicide research and adolescent suicide trends in New Zealand. ScientificWorldJournal 2008;8:287-302.

[32]   Omar H. A model program for youth suicide prevention. Int J Adolesc Med Health 2005;17(3):275-8.

[33]   Shahtahmasebi S, van den Berg L, Hermann F. What do you do when no health and social agency wants to care for you? Int J Child Health Hum Dev, in press.

SECTION FOUR: ACKNOWLEDGMENTS

In: Children, Violence and Bullying
Editors: J Merrick, I Kandel and H A Omar

ISBN: 978-1-62948-342-9
© 2014 Nova Science Publishers, Inc.

Chapter 22

ABOUT THE EDITORS

Joav Merrick, MD, MMedSci, DMSc, born in Copenhagen, is professor of pediatrics, child health and human development affiliated with Kentucky Children's Hospital, University of Kentucky, Lexington, Kentucky, United States and the Division of Pediatrics, Hadassah Hebrew University Medical Center, Mt Scopus Campus, Jerusalem, Israel, the medical director of the Health Services, Division for Intellectual and Developmental Disabilities, Ministry of Social Affairs and Social Services, Jerusalem, the founder and director of the National Institute of Child Health and Human Development in Israel. Numerous publications in the field of pediatrics, child health and human development, rehabilitation, intellectual disability, disability, health, welfare, abuse, advocacy, quality of life and prevention. Received the Peter Sabroe Child Award for outstanding work on behalf of Danish Children in 1985 and the International LEGO-Prize ("The Children's Nobel Prize") for an extraordinary contribution towards improvement in child welfare and well-being in 1987. E-mail: jmerrick@zahav.net.il

Isack Kandel, MA, PhD, is a former senior lecturer at the Faculty of Social Sciences, Department of Behavioral Sciences, Ariel University, Ariel. During the period 1985-93 he served as the director of the Division for Intellectual and Developmental Disabilities, Ministry of Social Affairs and Social Services, Jerusalem, Israel. Several books and numerous other publications in the areas of rehabilitation, disability, health, public health and intellectual disability. E-mail: kandel.isack@gmail.com

Hatim A Omar, MD, FAAP, Professor of Pediatrics and Obstetrics and Gynecology; Professor of Family Studies; and Chief of the Division of Adolescent Medicine, Department of Pediatrics, University of Kentucky, Lexington. He is the holder of the Children's Miracle Network Endowed Chair in Pediatrics. Dr. Omar has completed residency training in obstetrics and gynecology as well as pediatrics. He has also completed fellowships in vascular physiology and adolescent medicine. He is the recipient of the Commonwealth of Kentucky Governor's Award for community service and volunteerism in 2000, Kentucky Teen Pregnancy Coalition Award for outstanding service 2002, Awards for suicide prevention from the Ohio Valley Society for Adolescent Medicine and Kentucky Pediatric Society in 2005 and 2007, Sexual Abuse Awareness Month Award for his work with sexual abuse victims from the Kentucky Association of Sexual Assault Professionals in 2007, Special Achievement Award from the American Academy of Pediatrics 2007 and the Founders of Adolescent

Medicine Award from the AAP in 2007. He is well known internationally with numerous publications in child health, public health, pediatrics, adolescent medicine, pediatric and adolescent gynecology. E-mail: haomar2@uky.edu

In: Children, Violence and Bullying   ISBN: 978-1-62948-342-9
Editors: J Merrick, I Kandel and H A Omar   © 2014 Nova Science Publishers, Inc.

Chapter 23

ABOUT THE NATIONAL INSTITUTE OF CHILD HEALTH AND HUMAN DEVELOPMENT IN ISRAEL

The National Institute of Child Health and Human Development (NICHD) in Israel was established in 1998 as a virtual institute under the auspicies of the Medical Director, Ministry of Social Affairs and Social Services in order to function as the research arm for the Office of the Medical Director. In 1998 the National Council for Child Health and Pediatrics, Ministry of Health and in 1999 the Director General and Deputy Director General of the Ministry of Health endorsed the establishment of the NICHD.

MISSION

The mission of a National Institute for Child Health and Human Development in Israel is to provide an academic focal point for the scholarly interdisciplinary study of child life, health, public health, welfare, disability, rehabilitation, intellectual disability and related aspects of human development. This mission includes research, teaching, clinical work, information and public service activities in the field of child health and human development.

SERVICE AND ACADEMIC ACTIVITIES

Over the years many activities became focused in the south of Israel due to collaboration with various professionals at the Faculty of Health Sciences (FOHS) at the Ben Gurion University of the Negev (BGU). Since 2000 an affiliation with the Zusman Child Development Center at the Pediatric Division of Soroka University Medical Center has resulted in collaboration around the establishment of the Down Syndrome Clinic at that center. In 2002 a full course on "Disability" was established at the Recanati School for Allied Professions in the Community, FOHS, BGU and in 2005 collaboration was started with the Primary Care Unit of the faculty and disability became part of the master of public health course on "Children and society". In the academic year 2005-2006 a one semester course on "Aging with disability" was started as part of the master of science program in gerontology in our collaboration with the Center for Multidisciplinary Research in Aging. In 2010 collaborations with the Division of Pediatrics, Hadassah Hebrew University Medical Center, Jerusalem,

Israel around the National Down Syndrome Center and teaching students and residents about intellectual and developmental disabilities as part of their training at this campus.

RESEARCH ACTIVITIES

The affiliated staff have over the years published work from projects and research activities in this national and international collaboration. In the year 2000 the International Journal of Adolescent Medicine and Health and in 2005 the International Journal on Disability and Human Development of De Gruyter Publishing House (Berlin and New York) were affiliated with the National Institute of Child Health and Human Development. From 2008 also the International Journal of Child Health and Human Development (Nova Science, New York), the International Journal of Child and Adolescent Health (Nova Science) and the Journal of Pain Management (Nova Science) affiliated and from 2009 the International Public Health Journal (Nova Science) and Journal of Alternative Medicine Research (Nova Science). All peer-reviewed international journals.

NATIONAL COLLABORATIONS

Nationally the NICHD works in collaboration with the Faculty of Health Sciences, Ben Gurion University of the Negev; Department of Physical Therapy, Sackler School of Medicine, Tel Aviv University; Autism Center, Assaf HaRofeh Medical Center; National Rett and PKU Centers at Chaim Sheba Medical Center, Tel HaShomer; Department of Physiotherapy, Haifa University; Department of Education, Bar Ilan University, Ramat Gan, Faculty of Social Sciences and Health Sciences; College of Judea and Samaria in Ariel and in 2011 affiliation with Center for Pediatric Chronic Diseases and National Center for Down Syndrome, Department of Pediatrics, Hadassah Hebrew University Medical Center, Mount Scopus Campus, Jerusalem.

INTERNATIONAL COLLABORATIONS

Internationally with the Department of Disability and Human Development, College of Applied Health Sciences, University of Illinois at Chicago; Strong Center for Developmental Disabilities, Golisano Children's Hospital at Strong, University of Rochester School of Medicine and Dentistry, New York; Centre on Intellectual Disabilities, University of Albany, New York; Centre for Chronic Disease Prevention and Control, Health Canada, Ottawa; Chandler Medical Center and Children's Hospital, Kentucky Children's Hospital, Section of Adolescent Medicine, University of Kentucky, Lexington; Chronic Disease Prevention and Control Research Center, Baylor College of Medicine, Houston, Texas; Division of Neuroscience, Department of Psychiatry, Columbia University, New York; Institute for the Study of Disadvantage and Disability, Atlanta; Center for Autism and Related Disorders, Department Psychiatry, Children's Hospital Boston, Boston; Department of Paediatrics, Child Health and Adolescent Medicine, Children's Hospital at Westmead, Westmead,

Australia; International Centre for the Study of Occupational and Mental Health, Düsseldorf, Germany; Centre for Advanced Studies in Nursing, Department of General Practice and Primary Care, University of Aberdeen, Aberdeen, United Kingdom; Quality of Life Research Center, Copenhagen, Denmark; Nordic School of Public Health, Gottenburg, Sweden, Scandinavian Institute of Quality of Working Life, Oslo, Norway; The Department of Applied Social Sciences (APSS) of The Hong Kong Polytechnic University Hong Kong.

TARGETS

Our focus is on research, international collaborations, clinical work, teaching and policy in health, disability and human development and to establish the NICHD as a permanent institute at one of the residential care centers for persons with intellectual disability in Israel in order to conduct model research and together with the four university schools of public health/medicine in Israel establish a national master and doctoral program in disability and human development at the institute to secure the next generation of professionals working in this often non-prestigious/low-status field of work.

Contact

Joav Merrick, MD, MMedSci, DMSc
Professor of Pediatrics, Child Health and Human Development
Medical Director, Health Services,
Division for Intellectual and Developmental Disabilities,
Ministry of Social Affairs and Social Services, POB 1260, IL-91012 Jerusalem, Israel.
E-mail: jmerrick@zahav.net.il

In: Children, Violence and Bullying
Editors: J Merrick, I Kandel and H A Omar

ISBN: 978-1-62948-342-9
© 2014 Nova Science Publishers, Inc.

Chapter 24

ABOUT THE DIVISION OF ADOLESCENT MEDICINE, KENTUCKY CHILDREN'S HOSPITAL AT THE UNIVERSITY OF KENTUCKY, LEXINGTON, KENTUCKY, UNITED STATES

The Kentucky Children's Hospital is the only facility in central and eastern Kentucky dedicated to the expert medical and surgical care of infants, children and adolescents. The University of Kentucky (UK) has a proud and distinguished history of providing comprehensive programs and innovative care to the children of the region. Although patients are referred from every county of the Commonwealth of Kentucky and from every adjacent state, the majority of patients are from the Bluegrass region around Lexington and from Appalachian counties in the eastern part of Kentucky. The Department of Pediatrics has provided service and education from the opening of UK College of Medicine in 1961.

The passion for teaching is palpable at the Kentucky Children's Hospital. Most years about 15% of our graduates or more choose to train in pediatrics. The University of Kentucky had one of the earliest combined Internal Medicine-Pediatrics residency program with "med-peds" graduates very well represented throughout the faculty. This, in addition to a strong adolescent medicine program, is among factors which have led to a focus upon adolescent and adult graduates of pediatric care from Kentucky Children's Hospital.

The approach at the Kentucky Children's Hospital (KCH) is focused on family-centered care. Full-time child life coverage, facilities for families to stay with children overnight, age-appropriate playrooms, children's library facilities, in-hospital school services, a dedicated television channel, a computer laboratory and many other features provide the special environment to provide the best of care for children. The Kentucky Children's Hospital includes a 12-bed Pediatric Intensive Care Unit, a 66 bed Level 3 Neonatal Intensive Care Unit, 44 acute care pediatric beds, a 26 bed normal newborn nursery, and an 8 bed short stay admissions/observation unit. KCH has grown from about 3,750 discharges per year in 2004 to about 5,400 in 2009.

Pediatric medical and surgical outpatient facilities are primarily located in the Kentucky Clinic, which is attached to the hospital. Each year, the pediatric clinic has over 46,000 patient visits. Of these, over 15,300 patient visits are in the general pediatric and continuity clinics, over 17,400 occur in the various subspecialty clinics. Kentucky Children's Twilight

Clinic is open all but two days of the year in addition to the state-of –the-art pediatric emergency center.

Specialty care includes medical and surgical cardiac care, endocrinology, pediatric kidney disease, developmental pediatrics, pediatric allergy and immunology, solid organ transplantation, behavioral pediatrics, pediatric emergency medicine, intensive care pediatrics, neonatology, gastroenterology and hepatology, dysmorphology, biochemical genetics, pediatric rheumatology, oncology, hematology, infectious diseases, hospitalist care, adolescent medicine, adolescent gynecology, child neurology, pediatric surgery, pediatric orthopedics, pediatric imaging, child psychiatry, pediatric anesthesiology, pediatric otorhinolaryngology, speech disorders, pediatric pathology, pediatric physical medicine, pediatric neurosurgery and many other fields. The Young Parents Program is an innovative service of the Adolescent Medicine Division, which has been very successful. Many of these specialties cover outreach clinics throughout underserved Appalachian counties of Kentucky as well as in Lexington. New facilities are in preparation, because of the remarkable growth in clinical programs for children.

The growth of clinical programs and service capability has been matched by considerable growth in pediatric research at UK. Substantial programs in vascular biology and diabetes, pediatric inflammatory biology, molecular pediatrics, developmental biology, pediatric health policy research, epidemiology, prevention, cancer research and pediatric pharmacology are growing rapidly. The Kentucky Children's Hospital is located on the UK campus. Access to faculty in the other colleges including social sciences and humanities enhances the Kentucky Children's Hospital scholarly environment and provides unique opportunities for collaborative work.

As we approach our 50th year anniversary, we remain committed to improving the lives and health of young people of the Commonwealth and improving the future for their families.

DIVISION OF ADOLESCENT MEDICINE

The Division of Adolescent Medicine was founded in 1998 to provide state of the art care for adolescent patients from all areas of the commonwealth of Kentucky, to serve as a state wide resource for education and training for local providers on adolescent issues, to study specisifc factors on the local level affecting youth in the state, to help teach medical students and residents and to provide community service to help improve teen future in the commonwealth.

The division provides comprehensive, holistic team approach to adolescents, where teens receive all aspects of care from mental health to routine care from a team of professionals including physicians, mental health providers, social workers, psychologists, nutritionists and nursing staff. One unique program within the division is the Young Parent Program, where pregnant teens are cared for throughout pregnancy then they and their babies are cared for together in the program. The division is active in research with many peer reviewed articles published each year as well as several books and special journal editions.

In the community, the program has founded several grass route programs to help prevent youth suicide, teen pregnancy, accidental death and substance abuse among adolescents in Kentucky.

The division has provided more than 300 lectures, worshops, media events and teaching for community providers, parents, teachers and school counselors. It also provides adovocacy work on behalf of teens with active work at the state legislative and executive government as well as local governments to help improve the lives of teens.

COLLABORATIONS

The Division of Adolescent Medicine collaborates locally with school boards, youth service centers, state and local goverments, other universities and child advocacy centers as well as with regional adolescent medicine programs.

Internationally with the Institute for Child Health and Human Development in Israel, the Division of Adolescent Medicine at Santa Casa University, Brazil, Quality of Life Research Center and Nordic School of Holistic Health, Copenhagen, Denmark, Department of Applied Social Sciences, The Hong Kong Polytechnic University, Hong Kong.

THE VISION

The vision of the Division of Adolescent Medicine is to improve the health and long term wellbeing of Kentucky Youth to grow into productive adults. We also invision global work to help positive youth development world wide.

TARGET AREAS OF INTERESTS

The interest areas of the division are all aspects of youth development and adolescent health with focus on prevention and community involvement in colloboration on the local, national and global level with programs having the same goal.

Contact

Hatim Omar, MD, FAAP
Professor of Pediatrics and Obstetrics/Gynecology
Director of Adolescent Medicine & Young Parent programs
J422, Kentucky Clinic
Department of Pediatrics, Kentucky Children's Hospital
University of Kentucky College of Medicine
Lexington, KY 40536
E-mail: haomar2@uky.edu
Website://www.mc.uky.edu/

In: Children, Violence and Bullying
Editors: J Merrick, I Kandel and H A Omar

ISBN: 978-1-62948-342-9
© 2014 Nova Science Publishers, Inc.

Chapter 25

ABOUT THE BOOK SERIES
"PEDIATRICS, CHILD AND ADOLESCENT HEALTH"

Pediatrics, child and adolescent health is a book series with publications from a multidisciplinary group of researchers, practitioners and clinicians for an international professional forum interested in the broad spectrum of pediatric medicine, child health, adolescent health and human development.

- Merrick J, ed. Child and adolescent health yearbook 2011. New York: Nova Science, 2012.
- Merrick J, ed. Child and adolescent health yearbook 2012. New York: Nova Science, 2012.
- Roach RR, Greydanus DE, Patel DR, Homnick DN, Merrick J, eds. Tropical pediatrics: A public health concern of international proportions. New York: Nova Science, 2012.
- Merrick J, ed. Child health and human development yearbook 2011. New York: Nova Science, 2012.
- Merrick J, ed. Child health and human development yearbook 2012. New York: Nova Science, 2012.
- Shek DTL, Sun RCF, Merrick J, eds. Developmental issues in Chinese adolescents. New York: Nova Science, 2012.
- Shek DTL, Sun RCF, Merrick J, eds. Positive youth development: Theory, research and application. New York: Nova Science, 2012.
- Zachor DA, Merrick J, eds. Understanding autism spectrum disorder: Current research aspects. New York: Nova Science, 2012.
- Ma HK, Shek DTL, Merrick J, eds. Positive youth development: A new school curriculum to tackle adolescent developmental issues. New York: Nova Science, 2012.
- Wood D, Reiss JG, Ferris ME, Edwards LR, Merrick J, eds. Transition from pediatric to adult medical care. New York: Nova Science, 2012.
- Isenberg Y. Guidelines for the healthy integration of the ill child in the educational system: Experience from Israel. New York: Nova Science, 2013.

- Shek DTL, Sun RCF, Merrick J, eds. Chinese adolescent development: Economic disadvantages, parents and intrapersonal development. New York: Nova Science, 2013.
- Shek DTL, Sun RCF, Merrick J, eds. University and college students: Health and development issues for the leaders of tomorrow. New York: Nova Science, 2013.
- Shek DTL, Sun RCF, Merrick J, eds. Adolescence and behavior issues in a Chinese context. New York: Nova Science, 2013.
- Sun J, Buys N, Merrick J. Advances in preterm infant research. New York: Nova Science, 2013.
- Tsitsika A, Janikian M, Greydanus DE, Omar HA, Merrick J, eds. Internet addiction: A public health concern in adolescence. New York: Nova Science, 2013.
- Shek, DTL, Lee TY, Merrick J, eds. Promotion of holistic development of young people in Hong Kong. New York: Nova Science, 2013.
- Shek DTL, Ma C, Lu Y, Merrick J, eds. Human developmental research: Experience from research in Hong Kong. New York: Nova Science, 2013.
- Merrick J, ed. Chronic disease and disability in childhood. New York: Nova Science, 2013.
- Rubin IL, Merrick J, eds. Break the cycle of environmental health disparities: Maternal and child health aspects. New York: Nova Science, 2013.
- Rubin IL, Merrick J, eds. Environmental health disparities in children: Asthma, obesity and food. New York: Nova Science, 2013.
- Rubin IL, Merrick J, eds. Environmental health: Home, school and community. New York: Nova Science, 2013.
- Rubin IL, Merrick J, eds. Child health and human development: Social, economic and environmental factors. New York: Nova Science, 2013.

Contact

Professor Joav Merrick, MD, MMedSci, DMSc
Medical Director, Medical Services
Division for Intellectual and Developmental Disabilities
Ministry of Social Affairs and Social Services
POBox 1260, IL-91012 Jerusalem, Israel
E-mail: jmerrick@zahav.net.il

SECTION FIVE: INDEX

INDEX

anxiety, 11, 39, 48, 50, 143, 156, 177, 185, 217, 225, 226, 229, 231, 232, 233, 239, 241, 247, 252, 254, 263
anxiety disorder, 217, 226, 229, 231, 232, 233, 239
appointments, 64, 69, 132, 174
Argentina, 123
arousal, 35, 157, 162
arrest, 113, 146, 185
Asia, 122, 213, 217
Asian Americans, 114
assault, 106, 141, 142, 143, 151, 265, 266, 267, 269
assertiveness, 157, 172, 176, 177
assessment, 35, 45, 53, 60, 63, 64, 71, 74, 76, 77, 78, 80, 83, 134, 135, 139, 146, 154, 158, 167, 190, 191, 196, 206, 219, 222, 240, 252, 258, 263, 267, 274
assessment tools, 135, 139, 252
asthma, 244
asymptomatic, 37
ATF, 238
attachment, 122, 138, 157, 163, 164, 167
attachment theory, 157, 167
attitudes, 58, 65, 67, 69, 80, 81, 87, 88, 102, 103, 143, 151, 152, 153, 157, 158, 159, 204
attribution, 114, 151
audit, 56, 57, 58, 83
Austria, 75, 214
authorities, 22, 69, 117, 118, 121, 140, 172, 200, 204, 205, 213, 262, 266, 267, 272, 277, 278, 279
authority, 25, 73, 87, 149, 156
autism, 134, 295
autoimmune disease(s), 229, 230, 231
autonomy, 137
autopsy, 196, 205, 239, 272
avoidance, 70, 165, 166, 219
awareness, 29, 30, 31, 32, 67, 68, 111, 135, 136, 137, 144, 147, 150, 219, 251, 254, 272, 278

B

background information, 21, 22
ban, 272
barriers, 26, 36, 56, 144, 219, 268
base, 76, 148, 161, 168, 191, 206
base rate(s), 191
basic needs, 116
battered women, 49
batteries, 190
behavior modification, 166
behavior therapy, 157
behavioral change, 125, 159, 162
behavioral problems, 18, 181, 182, 183, 185, 187, 189, 190, 191, 193

behavioral theory, 163
behaviors, 25, 28, 78, 84, 86, 87, 88, 90, 91, 96, 99, 102, 103, 105, 126, 127, 128, 129, 130, 131, 132, 133, 138, 142, 144, 151, 152, 157, 181, 182, 183, 185, 187, 189, 190, 191, 192, 193, 213, 222, 247, 252, 256, 257, 261, 263, 264, 266, 267
Beijing, 16
Belarus, 214
benefits, 57, 137, 147, 248
beta blocker, 248
bias, 163, 188, 196, 200, 272
biologically active compounds, 227
bipolar disorder, 233, 238, 239, 249, 257, 263
births, 67, 68, 238
blame, 6, 45, 58, 119, 121, 141, 145, 162
bleeding, 108
blood, 174, 227, 228, 238
body dissatisfaction, 99, 113
body image, 143
body mass index, 25
body size, 114
body weight, 90, 94, 95, 99, 105, 109, 253
bonds, 164
bone, 30, 59, 77, 83, 108, 142, 226, 228, 229, 232
bone growth, 228
bone resorption, 228, 229
borderline personality disorder, 164, 168, 247, 254, 257, 280
boredom, 161
Botswana, vii, 11, 12, 14, 15
brain, 59, 60, 228, 230, 235, 237, 240, 246
brain abnormalities, 235
brainstorming, 132
Brazil, 293
breakdown, 67, 68, 84
breast cancer, 229, 231, 238, 239
breathing, 249, 254
bronchitis, 244
bronchus, 243
brothers, 38
budget allocation, 196, 273
buffering children, 34
Bulgaria, 117, 123, 214
bullying, vii, viii, 1, 3, 11, 12, 13, 15, 16, 28, 112, 118, 121, 122, 168, 171, 172, 173, 175, 176, 177, 217, 219, 268
Bureau of Justice Statistics, 101
burn, 78

C

cable television, 99, 114
calcium, 228, 230, 232, 235, 236, 237, 248

D

E

N

O

P

T

DATE